DAILY DOSE
_of_
KNOWLEDGE™

HISTORY

Publications International, Ltd.

Cover: (from left to right) the Parthenon, King Henry VIII, Germans atop the Berlin Wall

Daily Dose of Knowledge is a trademark of Publications International, Ltd.

Louis Weber, CEO
Publications International, Ltd.
7373 North Cicero Avenue
Lincolnwood, Illinois 60712

Permission is never granted for commercial purposes.

ISBN: 978-1-4127-1518-8

Manufactured in China.

8 7 6 5 4 3 2 1

Library of Congress Control Number: 2008923003

Introduction: History as a Part of Daily Life 7

Ancient History

Medieval History

Early Modern History

Modern History

Contemporary History

History as a Part of Daily Life

THE STUDY OF HISTORY gives so much back to the reader. It is one of the most inspiring fields of learning because it brings people into contact with the high points of human existence. There are great acts of moral leadership, such as the young students in Munich who bravely formed an organization called the "White Rose" to resist Hitler's racist policies. There are also impressive efforts in science and philosophy, such as medieval Arab thinker Al-Farabi's contributions to logic, cosmology, and music theory; and Austrian psychoanalyst Sigmund Freud's quest to understand the subconscious human mind.

It is exhilarating to be reminded on a regular basis of humankind's outstanding achievements, but there is more to history than great people doing great things. History does not just inspire us by its examples; it also pains us with its misfortunes. The Black Death, the African slave trade, the Nazi genocide—these are not things we celebrate, yet we should remember them. To reflect on the disasters of our past is part of being a well-informed and thoughtful person.

Some dimensions of history are neither good nor evil. These historical paradoxes show how opposites—above all, idealism and violence—are sometimes intertwined. The French Revolution of 1789 began with the intention of creating democracy, yet it led to mass executions, terror, and a new monarchy under Napoleon Bonaparte. The bombing of Hiroshima helped end World War II, but it also caused the deaths of many innocent people and opened up a new era where the threat of mass destruction hangs over our planet.

Daily Dose of Knowledge™: *History* aims to reveal the spirit of history in these diverse modes. To interact regularly with the highs, the lows, and the ironies of history can be refreshing and enlightening. The following pages provide a daily excursion for the general reader who wishes to wander through the immense mansion of history.

Many of us are simply too busy to settle down with a heavy tome, and *Daily Dose* strives to make learning about world history that much more palatable. In order to keep the book educational as well as lively, we've made the format of the book simple: Just read one page per day. Each page addresses a significant topic, whether it be a great discovery, a momentous battle, or the formation of an empire. It will be factually informative, and we hope it will contain at least one striking thought, one unexpected insight or interpretation, for every reader. One page of reading boosts the intellect every day, bringing readers outside themselves and enriching their lives with new understandings of the world.

It was a challenge to distill what is meaningful from the chosen topics and present them in a concise fashion. There may be some who argue that one cannot reduce a significant subject, such as the Spanish Inquisition or the signing of the American Constitution, to a single page. But we strongly believe that one only understands something important when one can sketch it out in a few words that make sense to nonexperts.

The content of *Daily Dose* ranges from antiquity to the present, with an emphasis placed on Western history (though non-Western matters do appear in the mix). The topics, however, are not arranged in chronological order: By juxtaposing different kinds of events from different eras and places, *Daily Dose* aims to keep the reader in a state of surprise.

However, to maintain some sense of historical overview, and to help readers maintain a sense of chronological order, a header referring to basic eras accompanies each topic:

- **Ancient**—from earliest times to the fall of Rome, about A.D. 500

- **Medieval**—from the fall of Rome to the Renaissance, beginning around A.D. 1400

- **Early Modern**—from the Renaissance to the American and French revolutions, dating respectively to 1776 and 1789

- **Modern**—from the late 18th century to the end of World War II in the 1940s

- **Contemporary**—from the end of World War II to the present

The use of these headers, as well as the inclusion of background information in each article, will keep readers grounded in fact and chronology. Today, when core curriculum that used to be "common knowledge" is often no longer being taught in schools, a review of simple points of information is always in order. "Postscripts," added to the end of some articles, serve to highlight a little-known fact about the topic.

Increasing one's knowledge doesn't have to be an overly intrusive and strenuous task. We hope that readers will sit back and enjoy the combination of facts and reflections—the daily doses of history—that this book has to offer.

The Signing of the American Constitution

THE U.S. CONSTITUTION is the oldest written constitution in the world that still has the force of law. Because it has been the law of the land for more than two centuries, many Americans see it as a sacred text.

However, the framers who drafted the Constitution in Philadelphia in 1787 did not see it the same way. They saw the Constitution as an imperfect text based on compromises. One of the major issues was slavery. Gouverneur Morris was highly critical of slavery, yet he also realized that the Southern states would never accept a constitution that banned it. A compromise emerged. The word *slavery* was deliberately left out because James Madison thought this ugly term would dishonor the document. However, by omitting the word, the Constitution's indirect language acknowledged that slavery would continue on American soil.

The Constitutional Convention

Another fundamental issue that divided the founders was the question of how democratic the government should be. Elbridge Gerry refused to sign the Constitution because he felt it was too democratic. George Mason, in contrast, feared that the Constitution was not democratic enough—that it gave too much power to a central government that could oppress the people.

It was decided that a good constitution is partly democratic. Madison argued that it was essential for the House of Representatives to be based on popular vote. He also emphasized that the Constitution itself must be ratified through a popular vote after the framers signed it.

On September 17, 1787, Benjamin Franklin admitted that the Constitution had many faults, but he noted that it was "the best" among all known constitutions. Morris said he would "take it with all its faults" and signed. Mason, however, said he would rather "chop off his right hand than put it to the Constitution as it now stands." In the end, 39 of the 55 delegates signed, and Americans have debated this great compromise ever since.

The English Peasants' Revolt

THE ENGLISH PEASANTS' REVOLT OF 1381 started when tax collectors attempted to squeeze a poll tax from villagers in Essex. It didn't go well, and the tax collectors were run out of the village. When troops arrived to enforce order, a peasant mob ran them off as well and beheaded six clerks who had come along to do the math. By now, the counties of Essex and Kent were in full revolt.

While the widely despised poll tax—the third in four years—had sparked the uprising, popular grievances extended beyond taxes. Less than 20 years before, the Black Death had killed millions. The resulting shortage of labor altered the relationship between serf and landowner—now that their labor was more valuable, the serfs wanted more rights. Church ownership of vast tracts of land, as well as the belief that corrupt advisors were profiting from the weakness of 14-year-old King Richard II, added to the popular discontent.

Among the leaders of the disgruntled peasants was Walter "Wat" Tyler. Under his direction, an "army" marched on London to present their grievances directly to the king. This was no peaceful band of petitioners —mobs of armed peasants attacked manors and religious institutions. They burned Savoy Palace, freed prisoners, and destroyed legal records. They even entered the Tower of London and executed Simon Sudbury, Lord Chancellor and Archbishop of Canterbury.

King Richard met with Tyler's army in mid-June. The peasants asked for a variety of reforms, including the abolition of serfdom, division of church lands, and implementation of fair rents. Richard agreed, but Tyler did not live to savor his apparent victory. There is no consensus on what happened next—in some accounts William Walworth, the Mayor of London, was reportedly offended by Tyler's insolence. A melee ensued, and one of the king's squires stabbed Tyler.

For a moment it appeared Tyler's army would attack, but Richard quickly addressed the mob, reassured them, and regained control. The threat ended soon afterward when a large force loyal to the king surrounded the rebels. Though some leaders were executed, the king largely pardoned the peasants, and they drifted back to their homes.

Richard subsequently retracted his promises, but the revolt had shocked large landowners. Many of them recognized the new reality and proceeded to implement reform voluntarily. It was an important first step toward the end of medieval serfdom in England.

Birth of the Ottoman Empire

THE BYZANTINE EMPIRE ran from 330 to 1453 and covered what was considered the Eastern Roman Empire. When it began to disintegrate in the 1200s along with the Seljuk Sultanate in Anatolia, armed camps of the nomadic Turkish horsemen called *ghazis* began to emerge. The Ottoman Empire began as one of these semi-independent Turkish principalities.

The first ruler of the principality, Ertuğrul, held the title as a vassal of the Seljuk sultan, but his son, Osman I, from whom the name *Ottoman* is derived, decided to take advantage of the fading Byzantine Empire. In 1299, Osman declared himself independent of the dying sultanate and began to lead his army on raids into Byzantine territory. Nomadic warriors eager for battle and prize money flocked to Osman's banner, giving him an armed force considerably disproportionate to his available resources. In 1308, his troops reached the Bosporus Strait, and by 1326 his son Orkhan had seized the Byzantine town of Bursa, making it the first Ottoman capital.

The Ottoman state continued to grow under a number of successful leaders. By 1354, the Ottomans had reached the Dardanelles Strait, which connects the Black Sea to the Mediterranean Sea. Led by Orkhan, they crossed to Gallipoli in 1354, and, having established a foothold in Europe, they rapidly occupied northern Greece, Macedonia, and Bulgaria. Nearly 20 years later, the Ottomans had seized the greater part of Byzantine territory in the Balkans.

The Ottomans still faced a challenge from the Serbian kingdoms, which had become the most important power in the Balkan Peninsula as Byzantine power declined. The Ottoman victory over the Serbs at the Battle of Kosovo on June 28, 1389, effectively ended Serbian power and left the Ottomans the masters of the Balkans.

Under Bayezid I, known as "The Thunderbolt," the Ottomans began to annex rival Turkish principalities in western Anatolia. In response, the deposed emirs turned to Timur, the Turco-Mongol conqueror of Samarqand, for help.

In 1402, Timur defeated the Ottomans and captured Sultan Bayezid at the Battle of Ankara. Deposed rulers reclaimed their lands, and amid the subsequent scouring of Anatolia, it looked like the end of the Ottoman Empire. The vicious succession struggle between the remaining Ottoman princes lasted for ten years until 1413, when Mehmed I defeated his rivals and began to restore the empire his father had nearly lost.

The Origins of the British East India Company

At the 1494 Treaty of Tordesillas, Pope Alexander VI divided Atlantic maritime rights between Portugal and Spain, giving Portugal a virtual monopoly over the ocean-borne spice trade with Asia.

When Philip II of Spain seized the Portuguese crown in 1580, Spain's enemies became Portugal's enemies. Protestant England and Holland found themselves cut off from Portuguese spice markets, and free trade became both a political issue and a religious matter. Portugal's claim to a monopoly on trade east of the Cape of Good Hope depended on the Roman Catholic Church, and Protestant England rejected the pope's standing as the arbiter of diplomatic disputes. English merchants began to reconsider a direct approach to the markets of Asia.

Breaking the Portuguese monopoly was not easy. Portugal protected its trade routes with a series of armed forts from the west coast of Africa to the South China Sea. Foreign ships caught entering "Portuguese" waters were seized, and their crews sentenced to the galleys. Those suspected as spies were arrested and sent to Lisbon for trial.

In 1589, establishing direct trade with the Indies became possible when a Dutchman named Hugo van Linschoten smuggled information about the Portuguese trade routes out of Goa. By 1595, Dutch merchants were successfully trading in Indonesia, right under the nose of the Portuguese.

Inspired by the Dutch, a group of London merchants petitioned Queen Elizabeth I in 1599 for a charter to trade in the East Indies. The queen put the petition aside, unsigned. Peace negotiations with Spain were at a critical stage, and Elizabeth was not willing to jeopardize them. Eventually, peace seemed impossible; on December 31, 1600, Elizabeth signed the charter for "The Company of Merchants of London trading in the East Indies."

The East India Company began operations a year later. Unable to sell British woolens in the East, the company's merchants learned to manipulate the established internal trade of Asia: using silver to buy fine cottons in India, which could then be traded for spices in Indonesia. Piracy remained a standard method of operation, and British merchants had to defend themselves against both their Portuguese and Dutch counterparts. Reluctantly, the company turned its attention from the spice islands of Indonesia toward the Arabian Sea and Mughal India, hoping to find an undisputed point of entry to the Asian luxury trade.

"I Have a Dream"

O<small>N</small> A<small>UGUST</small> 28, 1963, on the steps of the Lincoln Memorial, Martin Luther King, Jr., delivered his famous "I Have a Dream" speech as part of the March on Washington for Jobs and Freedom. His words created one of the defining moments in American history.

Over 200,000 people came to lend their support. In his speech, King outlined his vision for social justice in a land where all races would live in harmony and peace. "I have a dream that one day this nation will rise up and live out the true meaning of its creed: 'We hold these truths to be self-evident, that all men are created equal,'" he said.

Though he had a prepared speech, King veered from it and incorporated sections of a speech he had given a few months earlier in Detroit, Michigan. His delivery was that of an old-fashioned black Baptist preacher with a rich use of anaphora, a rhetorical device where the speaker repeats a phrase at the beginning of each sentence for emphasis. Each time King repeated "I have a dream," expectations rose. The masterful intertwining of biblical allusions, Lincoln's Gettysburg Address, the Declaration of Independence, and the Constitution make it one of the most quoted speeches in American history.

In the afterglow of a string of legislative victories that expanded legal rights and undermined de jure racial segregation, and in the shadow of King's own tragic assassination, it is often forgotten how insistent his speech really was. King's vision was a challenge and a resolve. "When the architects of our republic wrote the magnificent words of the Constitution and the Declaration of Independence, they were signing a promissory note to which every American was to fall heir," he said. "The note was a promise that all men, yes, black men as well as white men, would be guaranteed the unalienable rights of life, liberty and the pursuit of happiness. It is obvious today that America has defaulted on this promissory note.... America has given the Negro people a bad check, which has come back marked 'insufficient funds.'"

On that day, with a voice strong and clear, King announced that Americans of good conscience had come to collect.

St. Augustine of Hippo (A.D. 354–430)

IT'S FUNNY WHERE life takes you. In the case of Augustine of Hippo, he began life as self-indulgent hedonist and ended up a saint.

Considered one of the most important figures in the development of Christianity, Aurelius Augustinus was born in what is now Algeria. His mother was a devout Catholic, but young Augustine fell into a far less pious lifestyle. To his mother's despair, he kept a concubine and sired a son out of wedlock.

Still, Augustine was well educated, and he became familiar with Latin literature and Cicero, which sparked his interest in philosophy. He conducted a school of rhetoric in Carthage, and in late 383 he became professor of rhetoric for the imperial court at Milan.

In the meantime, Augustine had been struggling with an ongoing crisis of faith. Disillusioned with his immoral lifestyle, he still hesitated to fully embrace Catholicism. He was a man with a sense of humor, however, and he recognized his own ambiguity with his famous prayer, "Grant me chastity and continence, but not yet."

In the summer of 386, Augustine heard an unseen child in his garden tell him to take up and read the Bible. Opening the book at random, he read, "Let us walk honestly, as in the day; not in rioting and drunkenness, not in chambering and wantonness, not in strife and envying." Inspired, he decided to live a celibate life, devoting himself entirely to serving God. Augustine returned to North Africa, where he gave his inheritance to the poor and began a monastic foundation. He was later named Bishop of Hippo, a position he would hold until his death.

A philosopher and theologian, Augustine wrote prolifically and formulated numerous views that became central to the Christian Church, including the concepts of original sin, predestination, free will, and the idea of "just war."

He detailed his own struggle of choice and battle against lust, which he viewed as a major obstacle to a virtuous life, in his autobiography, *Confessions,* widely viewed as the first Western autobiography. Augustine also argued against a literal interpretation of the Bible, recognizing that such a reading often defied common sense.

The contributions of the one-time libertine to Christianity were recognized by his canonization centuries later. His feast day is August 28, the day on which he died.

Loyalists Flee to Canada

THE AMERICAN REVOLUTION is popularly, though incorrectly, viewed as a unanimous uprising against British rule. A substantial number of colonists—known as Loyalists or Tories—opposed the Revolution and sided with King George III. The exact number of Loyalists is impossible to determine; some estimates range as high as 500,000, or 20 percent of the white population. As many as 19,000 Loyalists actually fought with the British army.

Loyalist sentiment spanned all classes. Wealthy businessmen and members of the upper classes often tended to be Loyalists, perhaps because they had more to lose in a revolution. However, there were also Loyalists among newly arrived colonists and among certain ethnic groups, such as the Scottish farmers in the Carolinas. It is estimated that as much as half the population of New York was Loyalist.

Many paid a price for their stance. Their property was frequently confiscated, and they were routinely harassed. In late 1775, Congress called for the arrest of all Loyalists who presented a danger to "the liberties of America."

As the war turned against the British, large numbers of Loyalists left the colonies; many relocated to the British colonies in modern-day Canada. When the war finally ended in 1783, Loyalists were given the option to leave the colonies. Most declined. It is estimated that 300,000 to 400,000 former Loyalists chose to remain in the newly formed nation.

Approximately 70,000 to 100,000, however, did opt to leave. Among them was Benjamin Franklin's son William. Of the total that left during and after the war, about 46,000 went to Canada; 7,000 to Great Britain; and 17,000 to British colonies in the Caribbean. Of those heading north, about 32,000 went to Nova Scotia (an early destination was Shelburne). The newcomers did not receive a particularly warm welcome, so the colony of New Brunswick was created for them. Others went to Quebec and Upper Canada in what is modern-day Ontario.

The transplants had a major influence on Canada, possibly even helping to ensure that it would not be absorbed by the United States. Their numbers and deep antipathy to the colonies' tumultuous republicanism helped steer Canada on a different course toward independence.

Today it is estimated that one in ten Canadians can claim a Loyalist ancestor. There is even an organization, The United Empire Loyalists' Association of Canada, which perpetuates their history.

The Nuremberg Trials

IN MAY 1945, the German army surrendered to the Allied forces of France, Britain, the Soviet Union, and the United States. World War II in Europe was over. Hitler was dead, but other important Nazi leaders were still alive. The victorious Allies faced a serious problem: what to do with the Nazis who had perpetrated horrible acts?

While English Prime Minister Winston Churchill wanted to execute the Nazis without a trial, U.S. Supreme Court Justice Robert H. Jackson was asked to write a report on how the Nazis should be dealt with. In his report, dated June 6, 1945, Jackson stated that killing the Nazis without

a trial "would not set easily on the American conscience or be remembered by our children with pride."

Jackson recommended that a new international court be established in the German city of Nuremberg. Prosecutors would present evidence against the Nazis, who would have a chance to defend themselves. The Nuremberg Trials established a new kind of international law under which leaders were to be punished for destroying world peace and for committing crimes against humanity. Jackson himself became the chief prosecutor.

In his famous opening speech in November 1945, Jackson declared, "The wrongs which we seek to condemn and punish have been so calculated, so malignant, and so devastating, that civilization cannot tolerate their being ignored, because it cannot survive their being repeated.... We will show them [the Nazi prisoners] to be living symbols of racial hatreds, of terrorism and violence, and of the arrogance and cruelty of power."

There were 22 defendants at Nuremberg, including Hermann Göring, who had been Hitler's second in command. Twelve prisoners were found guilty and sentenced to death. Göring, who was found guilty, committed suicide the night before his scheduled execution. Others received lighter sentences. Three prisoners were found to be innocent and were set free. Jackson did not consider this a failure, saying, "The world yields no respect to courts that are organized merely to convict." He proved that it was possible to treat even one's wartime enemies with fairness.

The Elizabethan Age

ELIZABETH I RULED as queen of England from 1558 to 1603. She ascended the throne at a time of great turbulence. Her father King Henry VIII had turned England from the Catholic Church to a moderate form of Protestantism, while his daughter Mary I ruled for five years (1553–1558) afterward and returned England to the Catholic Church. About 300 people were executed during the ensuing religious tumult.

Even Elizabeth was in danger of execution during Mary's reign. Once on the throne, Elizabeth announced her choice of Protestantism for her country. In 1563, the Anglican Church was officially established as the national church. But there were protesters who believed Elizabeth had not gone far enough to purify the church; these people were called Separatists, or Puritans.

Elizabeth was unmarried when she came to the throne and would remain so throughout her lifetime. She also had to worry about her cousin, Mary Stuart, Queen of Scots, who was at the center of rumors of plots to depose Elizabeth. Mary's desire to impose Catholicism on her adopted country of Scotland had backfired and forced her to flee to England. There she conspired with other nobles to place herself on the throne in place of Elizabeth, but she ultimately failed. Mary was charged with treason and beheaded in 1587.

Mary Stuart's death coincided with Spain's decision to attack England. The Spanish gathered a large fleet, the infamous "Spanish Armada," which was sent into the English Channel in 1588 to clear the way for an invasion. Stormy Atlantic weather delayed the armada's invasion, and although outnumbered, Elizabeth's fleet defeated the armada and kept England safe.

Elizabeth put the country's growing resources behind the voyages of explorers such as Sir Francis Drake, Sir Martin Frobisher, and Sir Walter Raleigh. In spite of failed colonies in the New World and the failure to find the fabled Northwest Passage to Asia, English seafarers paved the way for the permanent colonies of the 17th century. In 1600, the queen helped establish the East India Company, which would become one of England's most important commercial ventures.

Elizabeth also ruled during the revival of English literature, best represented by William Shakespeare. Her reign featured a rising upper middle class but also was accented by a rising poverty rate, which the queen tried to remedy with various new laws. When she died in 1603, Elizabeth was beloved by most of her country.

Ireland's Fight for Independence

For centuries, Ireland struggled against England for its independence. The radical Irish Republican Brotherhood thought that with England distracted by World War I, it could achieve independence by violence, leading to the bloody and unsuccessful 1916 Easter Rising.

In 1919, members of the Sinn Féin ("We Ourselves") political party in the British Parliament proclaimed themselves the Republic of Ireland—in effect, a breakaway government. This action led to two years of savage fighting between British forces and the guerrilla army of the Irish Republic (IRA) in the Irish War of Independence. Using their famous "flying columns" of citizen-soldiers, the IRA fought Britain to a standstill. In December 1920, the British broke off the six largely pro-English northern Irish counties to form the new national province of Northern Ireland.

IRA women with stockings over their faces

The next year, Britain and Ireland signed a treaty establishing the Irish Free State. The treaty—which contained an oath of allegiance to the British king—split the IRA, plunging the country into the Irish Civil War. By the spring of 1923, the war was over, enabling the Irish Free State to begin operation. The IRA focused on reuniting Northern Ireland with the Irish Free State, and they soon began activities there. However, their terrorist tactics only strengthened the resolve of Northern Ireland's majority Protestants to never rejoin their Catholic neighbors to the south.

In 1927, Eamon De Valera and his followers in the Fianna Fáil political party came to power in the Irish Parliament, and together they began dismantling the parts of the treaty tying Ireland to England. In 1937, they enacted a new constitution that abolished the Irish Free State and renamed the country Eire. In April 1949, Ireland left the British Commonwealth and became an independent nation.

In 1969, the Provisional IRA or Provos split from the IRA and launched a new wave of terrorist attacks designed to persuade Northern Ireland to reunite with Ireland. Throughout the next three decades, the violence in Northern Ireland continued unabated. On Good Friday 1998, a historic peace agreement brokered by the United States was reached between the warring factions. In the autumn of 2001, the IRA began disarming; finally, Ireland could enjoy real peace.

Japan's Annexation of Korea

IN 1910, Korea became a victim of imperialist aggressions—not by greedy Western powers, but by its own neighbor, Japan.

Japanese interests in Korea extended back to at least 1876 when the Meiji government forced Korea to sign the Treaty of Kanghwa. The treaty—which, ironically, was very similar to one forced on Japan by the United States in 1854—granted extraterritorial and trade rights to Japan. It represented an early effort to bring Korea under Japanese influence and subvert China's traditional dominance on the peninsula.

That effort took a bloody turn in 1895 when Japanese agents assassinated Korean Queen Min (also known as Empress Myeongseong), who had tried to resist Japan's interference in her nation's affairs. Victory over China that year in the First Sino–Japanese War further consolidated Japan's grip on Korea.

Korean overtures to Russia ended abruptly with Japan's stunning 1905 victory in the Russo–Japanese War. Under the terms of the peace treaty, Russia acknowledged Japan's "paramount political, military and economic interest" in Korea. Korea was subsequently forced to become a Japanese protectorate.

King Gojong secretly sent representatives to the Second Peace Conference at The Hague in 1907 in hopes of bringing his nation's plight to the world's attention. The Japanese government was greatly displeased by the Korean complaints, and King Gojong was forced to step down. Three years later, on August 22, Japan annexed Korea through the Japan–Korea Annexation Treaty. Under the terms of the treaty, signed under duress by Korean Prime Minister Lee Wan-Young, Korea was conceded to the Emperor of Japan.

Korea remained a Japanese colony until the end of World War II. Some resistance groups were formed but had little effect. Military rule tightened in the 1930s. Dissidence was suppressed with simple brutality. Reports told of entire village populations herded into public buildings and burned alive on suspicion of aiding rebels. Korea's suffering continued through World War II with citizens impressed into forced labor, prostitution, and Japanese military service.

Japanese dominance over Korea ended with Japan's defeat in World War II. Twenty years later, the 1965 Basic Treaty between Korea and Japan voided the former protectorate and the 1910 annexation treaty. However, Korean resentment toward Japan continues to linger into this century.

Eleanor Roosevelt (1884–1962)

ELEANOR ROOSEVELT ONCE WROTE, "No one can make you feel infe-rior without your consent." And throughout her remarkable life, she never gave her consent.

She was born on October 11, 1884, in New York City. Her mother, Anna Hall, often discussed the fact that bucktoothed Eleanor was not pretty while her daughter was in the room. Eleanor felt closer to her alcoholic father, Elliott, who was Teddy Roosevelt's younger brother. In 1899, Eleanor was sent to England to attend Allenswood, a finishing school run by Frenchwoman Marie Souvestre, an outspoken advocate of social justice.

In 1902, Eleanor returned to New York and began doing volunteer work in the city's slums. She met her future husband (and distant cousin) Franklin Delano Roosevelt, and three years later, the two were married. The couple had six children in ten years (one died in infancy).

Eleanor realized that being solely a wife and mother was not enough for her. After helping her husband battle polio and keep his political ambi-tions alive, Eleanor began making political speeches. By 1928, she headed the Women's Division of the Democratic National Committee. After her husband was elected governor of New York, she went on inspections of hospitals, schools, and government institutions in his place.

After FDR won the presidency in 1932, she initially dreaded her role as First Lady, but she learned to use her accessibility to her husband to promote causes and push issues. She wrote a daily newspaper column called "My Day" that promoted her passions and offered a glimpse into the White House. She also fought vehemently for civil rights for African Americans. In 1939, when the Daughters of the American Revolution denied black singer Marion Anderson permission to sing in Washington's Constitution Hall, Eleanor resigned from her DAR membership and helped arrange a concert for Anderson at the Lincoln Memorial.

Eleanor was named a delegate to the first United Nations general assem-bly in London in December 1945. She helped draft a Universal Decla-ration of Human Rights, which passed three years later. A ceaselessly crusading reformer, she consistently topped a Gallup Poll of the world's most admired women until her death.

The Reign of King Tut

NEBKHEPERURE TUTANKHAMUN, or King Tut, stands as one of the most well-known Egyptian pharaohs in history—not only because of the 1922 discovery of his tomb, but also because of the mysterious circumstances surrounding his death.

Although dates vary, it is estimated that Tutankhamun succeeded Smenkhkare and assumed the throne when he was about ten years old, sometime between 1361 and 1332 B.C. The identity of his parents is a mystery, though historians speculate whether another pharaoh, Akhenaten, was his father. As a small child, he was exposed to the Aten, the religious cult that Akhenaten worshipped to the exclusion of all else, and to the detriment of Egypt. His given name, Tutankhaten, clearly showed his Aten roots with the suffix -aten. However, during the second year of his reign, the suffix was changed to -amun, and thus Tutankhamun, indicating a swift downfall for the Aten sect after Akhenaten's death.

Tut married the royal princess Ankhesenpaaten, but this decision, like the return to traditional gods instead of the Aten, was likely the work of Ay, the Pharaoh's chief adviser. It is probable that Ay ran the country for the boy. Horemheb, another adviser, ran the military. The slightly built Tut apparently liked to hunt, as there are depictions of him hunting lions and gazelles. But if he was growing into the job of pharaoh, everything came to a halt during the ninth year of his reign, when Tut died at age 19.

Generations of archaeologists and historians have wondered how the young pharaoh died. A wound found on Tut's skull next to his left ear and X-rays showing a piece of broken bone at the base of the skull gave rise to murder and conspiracy theories, with Ay and Horemheb the likely suspects. But in 2005, CT scans of Tut's mummy by archaeologist and Egyptologist Dr. Zahi Hawass revealed that he was likely not murdered violently. Hawass could not rule out poison or some other insidious type of death.

Tut's youth and short reign would have left him a minor pharaoh had not British archaeologist Howard Carter discovered his tomb and intact burial chamber in November 1922. But along with the riches and fame associated with finding the tomb came a supposed "mummy's curse" rumored to kill everyone involved with the tomb's opening. The curse has been more of a bonanza for the entertainment industry and has helped keep King Tut's name alive.

Gettysburg

THE THREE-DAY FIGHT that occurred in and around the small Pennsylvania town of Gettysburg in July 1863 is considered by many historians to be the climactic battle of the American Civil War—and yet it was a battle that came about by accident.

In mid-June, General Robert E. Lee, commanding the Confederate Army of Northern Virginia, launched an invasion of the North. When he learned that the Union Army of the Potomac, led by Major General George G. Meade, was in Maryland and marching north, he recalled his scattered units and began to concentrate his army just west of Gettysburg.

It was there, on the morning of July 1, that elements of both armies clashed. Union troops repelled the first Confederate attacks, but by mid-afternoon, Lee had more troops arriving on the field. His relentless attacks pushed the Yankees through Gettysburg to Cemetery Hill. Meade had already decided to fight at Gettysburg, and his army concentrated on the high ground of Culp's and Cemetery Hills, Cemetery Ridge, and Little Round Top overnight. On July 2, Lee launched a series of attacks that almost seized Little Round Top. Repulsed on both flanks, Lee decided to send 15,000 troops in a frontal assault on Meade's center the next day. The resulting "Pickett's Charge" was a disaster for the Confederates.

By the end of the day, more than 51,000 men had been killed, wounded, or captured. Of the 95,000 men in his army, Meade had suffered a loss of 23,000. Lee, with 75,000 soldiers, counted his loss at more than 28,000. Lee finally retreated on July 4, and the Civil War continued for another year and a half.

The Union dead, who had been quickly interred in shallow graves, were eventually dug up and reburied in the newly rededicated Gettysburg National Cemetery. President Lincoln was invited to say a few appropriate remarks. On the afternoon of November 19, 1863, Lincoln rose from his seat and delivered a remarkable two-minute speech known as "The Gettysburg Address," in which he promised Americans "a new birth of freedom" that would bring equality to all citizens and create a unified nation.

POSTSCRIPT

After hearing Lincoln's speech, noted orator Edward Everett (who also spoke that day) wrote to the president that he had said in two minutes what Everett himself had taken two hours to say.

Decolonization of Africa

IN THE LATE 19TH CENTURY, France, England, Portugal, and Germany had divided Africa among themselves with little regard for tribal or regional boundaries during the aptly named "Scramble for Africa."

But World War II exhausted these European countries, leaving them with little energy for maintaining colonial empires. In addition, African soldiers who recently had fought to end fascist tyranny saw little reason why their countries should continue being ruled by others. Independence movements arose in African countries as nationalism swept the continent.

In 1954, a war for independence broke out in Algeria between French and guerilla forces. Egypt's triumph in the 1956 battle for control of the Suez Canal sent notice to the region that colonialism in Africa was coming to an end. In 1958, Guinea became independent. Two years later, the other tropical French African colonies became independent, with continuing links to France. Algeria finally won its own battle for independence in 1962.

A Shilluk tribal king (left) talks with a British district commissioner

Fearing another Algerian situation, Belgium withdrew from the Congo in 1960. That decade also saw the end of Great Britain's colonial empire as former territories became independent: Nigeria in 1960, Tanzania and Sierra Leone in 1961, Uganda in 1962, and Kenya in 1963. By 1968, even smaller British colonies such as Botswana had gained their freedom.

Portugal tried to hang on to its colonial empire but realized by the early 1970s that fighting African wars of liberation was bleeding the country dry. The former British colony of Rhodesia, now surrounded by independent African states, instituted majority rule in 1979 and became the independent state of Zimbabwe a year later. Namibia gained its freedom in 1990, leaving the ruling white minority in South Africa virtually alone in its fight against majority rule.

Nelson Mandela's 1994 inauguration as president of South Africa swept away the last vestiges of colonial rule from Africa. But, as the continent has since learned, freedom from colonialism has not meant total freedom, as struggles against oppressive regimes continue to this day.

John Locke and
Two Treatises of Government

JOHN LOCKE WAS BORN IN 1632, the son of a middle-class county solicitor and landowner. Locke occupied various government posts during his life, including serving as secretary to Lord Chancellor Shaftesbury from 1672 to 1675. After Shaftesbury was thrown out of office, Locke left for Holland in voluntary exile; once there, he was charged with treason. He returned to England in 1689 and later served as Commissioner of Trade and Plantations.

Locke was especially famous for his philosophical and political writings, the most important of which were published shortly after his return from exile. He rejected the notion that humans are born with innate ideas; in *An Essay Concerning Human Understanding,* he asserted that at birth the mind was a tabula rasa on which experience acted.

Locke's next major work, *Two Treatises of Government,* is arguably one of the most crucial documents in the history of political philosophy. The first *Treatise* specifically attacked the views of Sir Robert Filmer, who had defended the idea of an absolute monarch's divine right to rule. Filmer claimed that human beings were not naturally free and needed to have their destructive instincts controlled by an absolute monarch. He even asserted that monarchs were in fact descended from Adam, the first man, who had dominion over nature. Locke contended that both empirical and scriptural evidence failed to support these contentions.

In the second *Treatise,* Locke developed his alternative positive theory of government, arguing that all humans are born with certain natural rights: both the right to survive and the right to have the means to survive, specifically life, liberty, and property. Citizens establish governments in order to protect these rights. In other words, governments exist by the consent of the governed and not through the divine right of monarchs. Moreover, Locke argued that if a civil government failed in its duty to protect the natural rights of the citizens who consented to that government, the citizenry had an inalienable right to rebel and form a new government.

His philosophy deeply influenced the founders of the United States, as well as the French Revolution. His argument for the consent of the governed and the right to revolution lay at the heart of the American Declaration of Independence.

The Rise of the Printing Press

Most people think of Johannes Gutenberg as the inventor of the printing press. However, that is only partially right.

The desire for printed material existed long before the ability to create it. Ancient Babylonians used stamps in clay and stones with figures scratched on the surface. Egyptians, Greeks, and Romans copied written material by hand with ink and brush.

Reproduction was pricey. Typically, free-hand work was done by monks in monasteries or literate slaves. The average Bible took a single monk 20 years to complete. Parchment, made from animal skin, was often used as paper, but it took 170 calves or 300 sheep to make one copy of the Bible. Many historians point toward an unlikely catalyst: the Black Plague. People died by the thousands as the epidemic spread across medieval Western Europe, including many of the same literate clerics whose talents were desperately needed. As the number of people who could make reproductions dwindled, an impetus for the invention of a way to reproduce images and words rose.

Another factor was sheer demand. After the dark medieval age, the importance of education increased. During the Renaissance, literacy was on the rise; the Bible was important, but people wanted to explore secular ideas as well. Scientists also demanded reliable and accurate information to share and expand upon.

The solution came together rather piecemeal. The idea for using metal type for letters instead of wood was an indirect result of a mining boom. Painters created an oil-based paint that would stick to the metal. In the early 1450s, German Johannes Gutenberg figured out how to replace the wood-block style of printing with movable metal, creating typography— it was the last step toward the first printing press. Gutenberg soon created a beautiful and intricate Bible that became known as the Gutenberg Bible.

By 1500, about 20 million books had been printed in Europe. The printing press had an enormous impact on the world. It spread information that, for the first time, did not originate with the Catholic Church. This contributed to the Scientific Revolution later in the 16th century, which altered the way people viewed the world and even the universe.

Fidel Castro (1926–present)

B EARDED, CIGAR-SMOKING FIDEL CASTRO is one of the most recognizable men of our time. Adored as a liberator and reviled as a dictator,
he ruled Cuba for more than 45 years, outlasting nine U.S. presidents.

Castro was born August 13, 1926, in the Oriente province of eastern
Cuba. His father was a well-to-do landowner, and Castro was educated in
private Catholic schools. He was an outstanding athlete and, in 1943, was
named the best secondary school athlete in the country.

Castro attended the University of Havana, where he earned a law degree.
It was during his time at the university that he developed his socialist,
anti-imperialist political activism. In 1952, he ran for Congress as a
member of a populist movement called the Ortodoxos. The Ortodoxos
promised social, economic, and political reform, but in 1952, military
strongman Fulgencio Batista overthrew the constitutional government.

Castro attempted an insurrection, leading an attack against a military
barracks on July 26, 1953. He was seized and imprisoned for two years.
Granted amnesty in 1955, he went to Mexico and trained a small revolutionary force to return to Cuba. In late 1956, he and 81 comrades
returned to Cuba and started a guerilla war against the Batista dictatorship. That spark ignited a popular uprising in 1959 that drove Batista
from the country and brought Castro to power as the undisputed leader
of the revolution.

Charismatic, passionate, and backed by the support of the people, Castro
embarked upon the reconstruction of Cuba under the socialist model.
The nationalization of American firms in Cuba brought early conflict
with the United States and led Castro into a relationship with the Soviet
Union. That same struggle led to the Bay of Pigs fiasco in 1961 and
brought the Soviet Union and the United States to the brink of nuclear
war over the Cuban Missile Crisis a year later.

Castro ruled over a society that emphasized the importance of revolutionary consciousness; where unity and the collective whole were
emphasized over the individual; where central control took precedence
over pluralism or local autonomy. He resigned from office on February,
12, 2008. Since his own power stemmed from his direct relationship with
the Cuban people rather than any particular governmental mechanism,
just how Cuba will continue after Castro remains to be seen.

The 1936 Olympic Games

THE IDEA OF BERLIN hosting the Olympic Games did not appeal to Adolf Hitler, and Propaganda Minister Joseph Goebbels had to convince him that the games were one of the best possible ways to spread Nazi ideology—as well as bring in much-needed revenue from tourists.

The Olympic Games had been assigned to Berlin several years before Hitler took control. After his rise to power, there was a great deal of debate over whether or not the games should be boycotted. The United States was ambivalent about participating but finally accepted Germany's invitation.

To prepare for the games, Germany built four huge stadiums, along with several swimming pools, an outdoor theater, and a polo field. Everything was covered in Nazi banners; however, all of the "Jews Not Welcome" signs were temporarily removed.

The Nazis wanted to convey the ideal of the white Master Race to the rest of the world. German filmmaker Leni Riefenstahl recorded everything and made a movie. The games were also televised for the first time; picture quality was poor but still managed to capture the events.

German athlete Lutz Lang was poised to prove the Master Race theory correct. He excelled at the long jump and was the poster boy of Hitler's idea of Aryan perfection. Hitler could not wait to show Lang off, especially to the 18 African American athletes who arrived with the U.S. team.

Hitler's plan to prove the superiority of the Aryan race ended with the appearance of U.S. track star Jesse Owens. This young black man, nicknamed the "Tan Cyclone," won four gold medals, broke 11 Olympic records, and defeated Lang in the long jump. Whenever Owens entered the stadium, the German crowd chanted his name. Whenever he left, autograph hounds mobbed him.

Hitler was furious, and when it came time for the gold medalists to receive their ribbons, he refused to place one around Owens's neck. Interestingly, Owens did make one good friend during the competition—his blue-eyed competitor Lutz Lang.

The Chivalric Code

THE MIDDLE AGES were a time of great violence, rampant disease, and limited life spans. Yet, this same era inspires romantic visions of Camelot, damsels in distress, and chivalrous knights on selfless quests.

Beginning in the 12th century, the chivalric code was part of the culture of the Middle Ages. The code was reflected in long poems and ballads performed by minstrels and in written tales of knightly deeds. It was echoed and perpetuated in the Arthurian legends of Camelot and the Knights of the Round Table, with their dedication to honor and chivalry.

It is ironic today to consider a knight riding out to a bloody battle with a lady's scarf fluttering from his lance, but the two realities are not mutually exclusive. Knights were expected to be strong and dauntless in battle, but they were also expected to temper the aggressiveness of the warrior with a knightly code of conduct, displaying qualities such as bravery, courtesy, and honor toward women.

Many works were written about chivalry, including *The Art of Courtly Love* by Andreas Capellanus and *The Romance of the Rose* by Guillaume de Lorris and Jean de Meun. A famous Code of Chivalry appears in *The Song of Roland,* a French work written around 1100. Sometimes referred to as Charlemagne's Code of Chivalry, it required many things of a knight, including to maintain the church; serve his lord; protect the weak and defenseless; assist widows and orphans; live for honor and glory; despise monetary reward; fight for the welfare of all; guard the honor of fellow knights; speak the truth; respect the honor of women; never refuse the challenge of an equal; and never turn his back on a foe.

Chivalry as a social institution waned with the diminishing importance of knights as a weapon of war. More powerful archery and the advent of firearms empowered the common foot soldier and diminished the role of heavy cavalry. It also brought about a change of attitude on the battle-field. At the Battle of Agincourt in 1415, King Henry V's forces killed thousands of captured French knights—quite unchivalrously—to remove them as a future threat.

The concept of chivalry was resurrected and romanticized by Victorian writers such as Lord Alfred Tennyson, with his idyllic accounts of the Arthurian legends. As late as World War I, aviators often viewed themselves as "Knights of the Sky" as they spared a vanquished enemy. Today's modern armies often regard such behavior as an antiquated, and dangerous, sentimentality.

The French–Algerian War

THE END OF WORLD WAR II saw increased unrest in the French colony of Algeria. Open warfare erupted on November 1, 1954, when members of the Front de Liberation National (FLN) attacked military installations, police, communications centers, and public utilities. An FLN radio broadcast urged Algerian Muslims to rise up for the "restoration of the Algerian state" in an Islamic framework. But the French government was not about to let Algeria go easily. The French minister of the interior was blunt, stating, "the only possible negotiation is war."

The FLN guerrilla campaign spread, driving many of the European settlers, called *colons,* to find refuge in Algiers. In August 1955, the FLN, which had previously confined its attacks to government targets, massacred 123 European civilians near Philippeville. French troops, police, and colons retaliated by killing an estimated 12,000 Algerians.

By 1956, France had more than 400,000 troops in Algeria. Outgunned, the FLN turned to raids and ambushes, then blended back into the civilian population. Captured soldiers, colons of any age or gender, and Muslim civilians who refused to support the guerillas were routinely murdered. Guerrillas planted bombs in cafés and public places, killing French civilians in what became known as the Battle of Algiers. The French responded with torture and murder, and, by the summer of 1957, Algiers was brought under control.

In the countryside, villages suspected of aiding the guerrillas were bombed. As many as two million people were relocated into camps in an effort to deprive the FLN of its civilian base. French military forces were successful, but defeat was looming on the political home front. Opposition to the war was growing, as was international pressure to grant Algeria independence. In reaction to indications that Premier Charles de Gaulle was prepared to end the war, the colons, backed by military elements, staged uprisings in January 1960 and April 1961.

Undeterred, the French government arranged a cease-fire with the FLN on March 19, 1962, and peace accords were approved in June. On July 1, some six million Algerians voted overwhelmingly for independence. De Gaulle proclaimed Algeria independent two days later.

The war had cost the French 25,000 dead. More than 50,000 died on the Algerian side. Unfortunately, independence did not bring stability. Perhaps because of its violent beginnings, terrorism, coups, and civil conflict have continued to plague Algeria.

The Harnessing of Electricity

I t's commonly believed that Benjamin Franklin discovered electricity. He didn't. Franklin was just one of many who contributed to the harnessing of electricity.

He and other early inventors experimented with electricity using Leyden jars. Invented by Pieter van Musschenbroek in 1745, the Leyden jar was the first capacitor. Using the jars, Franklin drew a parallel between the static electric sparks he created in his laboratory and the natural phenomenon of lighting. He also deduced that electricity had qualities similar to fluids and that its flow could be directed.

Still, Franklin is probably most famous for his highly dangerous 1752 kite-flying experiment. The experiment led Franklin to develop the lightning rod/electrode system still used to protect buildings against lightning strikes.

In 1781, Luigi Galvani used an electrical current, generated with the help of two metal plates, to make a dead frog's legs twitch. Though he didn't realize it, he had discovered the basic elements of a chemical battery. Galvani's discovery that muscles respond to electrical currents also inspired the classic tale of reanimation: Mary Shelley's *Frankenstein.* The effect of electrical current on the body also led to a variety of devices touting electricity as a medical cure-all for various ailments.

Alessandro Volta, a professor of physics at Italy's University of Pavia, built upon Galvani's findings. In 1800, he developed an electric cell, using zinc and copper plates and paper soaked in salt water. By stringing these cells together, he created an early chemical battery. The term *ampere,* a unit of measurement of electrical current, recognizes the work of French physicist André-Marie Ampère. He was the first to measure the flow of electrical current and is regarded as one of the discoverers of electromagnetism in 1825.

Another major contributor was English chemist Michael Faraday. Despite his lack of formal education, Faraday became one of the important scientists of his day. In the 1830s, he was first to realize that an electric current could be produced magnetically. This breakthrough marked the beginning of the modern age of electricity and made the use of large-scale electrical systems practical.

The Barnette Case:
Flag Salute Not Mandatory

IN 1940, the West Virginia state legislature enacted laws that required all public schools to conduct courses in history and civics. They also required classes on the Constitution "for the purpose of teaching, fostering, and perpetuating the ideals, principles and spirit of Americanism and for increasing the knowledge of the organization and machinery of the government."

On January 9, 1942, the State Board of Education adopted a resolution making the salute to the American flag a regular part of the program. Any student who refused to salute the flag and recite the Pledge of Allegiance was considered insubordinate and was dealt with accordingly. That typically meant expulsion from school.

Subsequently, members of the Jehovah's Witness religion filed a lawsuit in federal district court for an injunction restraining the enforcement of the required flag salute. Their religion forbade them from pledging to any symbol, be it religious, political, or otherwise. According to the pleadings filed by the Jehovah's Witnesses, some of their children had been expelled from school, while others had been threatened with expulsion for no apparent reason.

The outcome of the lawsuit was that the district court prevented the state school board from enforcing its policy of saluting the flag in relation to the parties involved in the lawsuit. The U.S. Supreme Court was asked to review the district court's decision.

In the majority opinion written by Justice Robert Jackson, the court held that the action of requiring a flag salute violated the purpose of the First Amendment because a compelled flag salute and pledge transcended constitutional limitations. By ruling as it did, the Court overturned its decision in an earlier case, *Minersville School District v. Gobitis,* which had upheld a required salute of allegiance to the flag.

Justice Felix Frankfurter had authored the Court's opinion in *Gobitis.* In *Barnette,* he wrote the dissenting opinion, stating it was the duty of the legislature, not the courts, to make needed changes in legislation. The dissent advocated judicial restraint in such cases, since legislatures were the ultimate guardians of people's liberties and welfare.

The Birth of Islam

According to tradition, in A.D. 610, the Prophet Muhammad, then a merchant in the wealthy commercial city of Mecca, received a command from the angel Gabriel to "recite" the message of God. As a result of this vision, Muhammad became a messenger of God, sent to confirm and correct the Scriptures previously given to the Jews and Christians. He described his task as bringing people back to the religion revealed to Abraham, which he called *Islam,* which means "submission."

Muhammad's attempts to bring the message of Islam to the people of Mecca met with little success and a good deal of danger. The real turning point for Islam began in 622 with the flight of Muhammad and his followers to Medina. It was there that Islam became a community of believers with its own system of government, laws, and institutions.

For the next ten years, Muhammad concentrated on expanding the Islamic community throughout the Arabian Peninsula via a combination of force and diplomacy. He began his efforts with Mecca, which welcomed the prophet home in 630 after a number of years of armed conflict. By the time of Muhammad's death in 632, Islam was the dominant religious and political system among Arabian tribes.

The spread of Islam in the years following Muhammad's death was swift, brought about by conversion as often as by conquest. The religious community of Medina grew into an empire under Muhammad's immediate successors, the four "Rightly-Guided" caliphs, chosen from among the Companions of the Prophet. Within ten years, the Army of the Faithful defeated the Byzantine and Persian armies and introduced the rule of Islam into Iraq, Syria, Palestine, Persia, and Egypt.

Expansion continued under the Umayyad dynasty, which came to power following the assassination of the fourth caliph. Within a century of Muhammad's flight to Medina, Islam ruled from Sind in northern India to Spain.

By the time the second hereditary dynasty of caliphs, the Abbasids, came to power in 749, the first age of external conquest was over, and the golden age of Islamic civilization had begun.

POSTSCRIPT

■ The year of the *hejira,* Muhammad's flight to Medina, was taken as the first year of the new Muslim calendar.

The Rise of the Slave Trade

LACKING AGRICULTURAL WORKERS, Portugal was the first modern European nation to meet its labor demands by importing slaves. Portuguese ships in the 1440s were primarily interested in the Guinea coast for its gold and pepper. But when Captain Antam Goncalvez enslaved an African, he unintentionally set in motion a process that would see the extensive use of African labor in the New World.

Shortly after Christopher Columbus's arrival in the New World in 1492, enslaved Africans were transported across the Atlantic Ocean. They were brought in great numbers; in fact, by the end of the 16th century, more Africans than Europeans had been transplanted to the New World.

African slaves were used on profitable Brazilian and Caribbean sugar plantations as well as in British North America. The Spanish put some blacks to work in Mexico as soldiers and guides. Most blacks, however, labored in the gold and silver mines or worked to produce the export crops that came to be a major source of European wealth.

Slaves in the American South

Contrary to popular misconception, there were people of African descent living in the Chesapeake before a Dutch warship arrived carrying blacks to the colony of Jamestown. Records indicate that there were 32 people of African descent living there.

The African men and women who arrived on the warship were part of a group of more than 300 blacks. Initially there was some confusion over their status. The black people who were already in Jamestown and the new Angolan arrivals were regarded as unfree, but they were not considered slaves. This was in part because the English had not yet devised a slave code and because the Portuguese had already converted the Angolans to Christianity—it would be unconscionable to enslave coreligionists.

But that philosophy did not last long. Racial and cultural differences, the fact that other British colonies in the West Indies were profitably enslaving Africans, and growing British participation in the Atlantic slave trade would eventually lead to codified bondage. Within a generation, Africans would be reduced to the level of livestock and personal property.

The Battle of Britain

To HITLER, the Battle of Britain looked good on paper: attack by air and simply bomb the English people to the point of surrender. To his frustration and disappointment, however, it did not work out like he had hoped.

As Hitler's war machine rumbled and rolled across Europe during World War II, France was one of its casualties. Once it had fallen, Hitler turned his eyes to the next enemy: Great Britain. His first step in destroying the British was to attempt to annihilate their Royal Air Force (RAF) with the Luftwaffe, or German air force. This effort would eventually come to be known as the Battle of Britain, the very first battle to be fought entirely in the air.

In July 1940, the skies over the English Channel and England's east and south coasts were filled with the roar of planes and the whistle of bombs. German planes blew up British airfields and ports. The RAF immediately retaliated with their 700 Spitfire and Hurricane fighters, but they were vastly outnumbered—the Luftwaffe had more than 2,600 bombers and fighters on their side. However, Britain had a distinct advantage: It had radar. This gave them one of the most advanced warning systems in the world. In addition, the Spitfire was a superb fighter plane, and the Hurricane could take an immense amount of damage and still keep going.

The bombings continued with the Luftwaffe sending out more than 1,000 aircraft a day. The Germans were determined to win, but Great Britain was just as determined to survive. They were not about to give in to Hitler's power and be added to his list of conquered countries. When the RAF dared to attack Berlin and some of Germany's industrial areas, Hitler was so incensed that he ordered his planes to bomb English cities nonstop, day and night, in what became known as "The Blitz." The bombing was devastating to the people of Britain, but they did not give up. Germany lost 1,700 planes—far more than was planned, as they were going down faster than new ones could be built. Because the Germans' attention was focused on the Blitz, British air bases were able to quickly recover.

The Battle of Britain ended in October when Hitler finally withdrew the Luftwaffe. Britain was safe from invasion, but 500 airmen had been lost, and tens of thousands of civilians died during the bombings. Later, Prime Minister Winston Churchill said of the RAF, "Never in the field of human conflict was so much owed by so many to so few."

The Klondike Gold Rush

O N JULY 17, 1897, the headlines of the *Seattle Post-Intelligencer* screamed, "Gold! Gold! Gold!" News that the steamship *Portland* had landed with two tons of gold caught the imagination of a country that had been struggling with an economic recession since 1883.

On August 16, 1896, George Carmack, Skookum Jim Mason, and Tagish Charlie found gold in Rabbit Creek, a tributary of the Klondike River that was soon renamed Bonanza Creek. Since the Yukon River froze in September and cut off all communication with the outside world, it took a year for news of the discovery to reach Seattle.

More than 100,000 prospectors, mostly from the United States, rushed to Dawson City and the Klondike gold fields of the Yukon in 1897 and 1898. Most of the men were physically unprepared and poorly equipped for the severe climate and terrain. The most direct route to the gold fields was by boat to the Lynn Creek in Alaska, over the 33-mile-long Chilkoot Trail into Canada, and down the Yukon River. Conditions on the Chilkoot were so hazardous that novelist Jack London renamed it "Dead Horse Trail." Only 30,000 of those who set out actually completed the trip. When they arrived, they found that local miners had staked out the good claims the previous year. Fewer than 4,000 prospectors found gold; fewer still made a fortune from their claims. Many went home; others found jobs in Dawson City, working at the hotels, saloons, and other businesses that supported the miners.

The rush lasted for five years and produced an estimated $50 million worth of gold, but the real fortunes were made by the suppliers who outfitted the "Stampeders." The Canadian government, fearing mass starvation among the would-be gold miners, required everyone traveling to the sparsely inhabited Yukon to bring enough food and equipment to last a year. Seattle, the American city closest to the gold fields, successfully promoted itself as the best place to buy the required "ton of provisions." The Alaskan ports of Skagway and Dyea boomed with mine-related business. Shipping lines and railway companies advertised good rates to hopefuls headed for the gold fields, and publishers rapidly produced guidebooks to the unknown region of the Klondike.

Tupac Amaru II (1742–1781)

Tupac Amaru II was a Peruvian "Braveheart," a champion of the Incan people. Tragically, like his Scottish counterpart William Wallace, he was destined to die a miserable death at the hands of his oppressors.

Tupac Amaru II was born José Gabriel Condorcanqui Noguera in Tinta, just south of Cuzco, Peru. The great-grandson of the Incan leader Tupac Amaru, he was wealthy, well-educated, and a member of a native aristocracy the ruling Spanish had established to help govern Peru.

Upon the death of his oldest brother, Condorcanqui became the *cacique* (hereditary chief) of Tungasuca and Pampamarca, governing on behalf of the Spanish regime.

Despite his outwardly Spanish ways, Condorcanqui retained great respect for his Incan heritage and for his people. Though in a position of power, he sympathized with the native people who lived in poverty and suffered great hardships in the mines, textile mills, and plantations. He petitioned the Spanish government to rectify these wrongs but was ignored.

As he became more alienated from the Spanish, Condorcanqui adopted his great-grandfather's Incan name and a more native style of dress. Finally, in late 1780 he decided to address the situation more directly. First he ordered the seizure and execution of Governor Antonio de Arriaga of Tinta, whose actions against the populace had become intolerable.

Responding to Amaru's calls to end abuse, the native population revolted. With the help of some Creoles (American-born Spaniards), the revolt spread through Peru, Bolivia, and northern Argentina—an indication of the widespread popular discontent with Spanish rule.

Despite early success, the revolt was eventually brought under control by Spanish military forces with their superior weapons. Amaru was taken prisoner, and on May 18, 1781, he was forced to watch the execution of his wife, sons, and some supporters in the plaza at Cuzco. He was then tortured and drawn and quartered; his head was displayed on a stake.

Despite the loss of their leader, Amaru's revolt dragged on for two more years but was finally extinguished by the Spanish. For years afterward, Amaru's legend continued to inspire others in the search for Peruvian independence.

Geronimo (1829–1909)

Geronimo was born in 1829 in what is now New Mexico. He was originally named Goyathlay ("One Who Yawns"). On March 5, 1858, Mexican soldiers killed his mother, wife, and three children in an attack on the Chiricahua Apache encampment. He spent years exacting revenge, terrorizing Mexican settlements and white people in general. Dubbed "Geronimo" by Mexican soldiers, his name became a watchword for cruelty. "I have killed many Mexicans," he remarked. "I do not know how many, for frequently I did not count them."

Though Geronimo was never a chief in the formal sense, his people regarded him as a seer, medicine man, spiritual guide, and leader in battle. The U.S. government saw him as a dangerous menace. In 1876, the government forced the relocation of some 4,000 Apache to the San Carlos Reservation. Geronimo fled but was soon arrested and sent to the reservation.

In 1881, Geronimo escaped from the reservation. Raids on settlers intensified. He and his band of warriors were surprised by soldiers the following year and brought back to San Carlos. In 1885, Geronimo escaped yet again. Pursued by 5,000 soldiers, 500 scouts, and 4,000 Mexicans, his band finally surrendered on September 3, 1886, the last of the Indian fighting forces to formally surrender to the United States. This time the government removed Geronimo to Florida, then to Alabama. Finally, in 1894, he was sent to Fort Sill, Oklahoma.

Once a feared warrior, Geronimo became something of a curiosity. He appeared at fairs, including the 1904 World's Fair in St. Louis. In 1905, he rode in President Theodore Roosevelt's inaugural parade. Geronimo reportedly pleaded with Roosevelt to allow the Apache to return to their homeland. "I pray you to cut the ropes and make me free," he said. "Let me die in my own country as an old man who has been punished enough and is free."

Despite his advancing years, Geronimo was not permitted to return to his homeland. In February 1909, after a night of drinking, Geronimo passed out and lay outside for hours in the cold. He subsequently contracted pneumonia and died on February 17.

The Battle of Hattin

In 1099, the Crusaders captured Jerusalem, and the Four Crusader states were established in the Middle East. Despite hardships, the states were able to maintain themselves against a Muslim world torn apart by many political rivalries.

In the late 1160s, a new Muslim leader rose to confront the Crusaders. His name was Salah al-Din Yusuf ibn Ayyub, known in English as Saladin. In 1169, Saladin succeeded his uncle as vizier of Egypt's Fatimid dynasty. He bided his time, and two years later, after the Shiite caliph died, he announced Egypt's return to Sunnite Islam. He effectively became Egypt's ruler, though as a representative of Syrian leader Nur al-Din.

When Nur al-Din died in 1174, Saladin assumed the title of sultan and led his troops into Syria, adding it to his growing empire. Thus began the Ayyubid dynasty. Saladin attacked the Crusaders three years later but was badly defeated. A truce followed, but the knight Raynald of Châtillon, whose small fleet of ships preyed upon Muslim shipping, continually broke it.

Angered over Raynald's actions, Saladin declared war and entered Crusader territory, besieging Tiberias, on the western shore of the Sea of Galilee. Led by King Guy of Jerusalem, Raynald, and Raymond III of Tripoli, the Crusaders were divided as to strategy. Raymond and those who were familiar with the area favored waiting, while others advocated an immediate attack on the Muslims.

King Guy was persuaded to order an advance, and so on the morning of July 3, 1187, the Crusaders left the town of Saffuriya, 15 miles from Tiberias. Their route led across an arid, waterless desert; by evening, the troops were tired and thirsty. At dawn the next day, Saladin's men set fire to the dry grass near the Crusader camp. Wind blew smoke into the faces of the Crusaders. Saladin then ordered an attack, and his mounted archers and heavy cavalry destroyed the Crusader infantry. A number of the Crusader cavalry managed to escape and reform on the Horns of Hattin, so named for an ancient extinct volcano overlooking the Jordan River valley, but they could not hold off the Muslims. By nightfall, the Crusader army had been eradicated, and a number of their leaders captured. Saladin ordered the members of the army to be executed, ransomed, or enslaved—he took the responsibility of executing Raynald himself.

Captain James Cook Explores the South Seas

Talk about aiming high: Explorer James Cook once said his goal was "not only to go farther than anyone had gone before but as far as possible for man to go."

In 1768, the British navy appointed 40-year-old Cook to lead an expedition into the Pacific Ocean, known at the time as the Spanish Lake. His main goal was to record the transit of Venus across the face of the sun, which could be seen from Tahiti. He also had secret orders to find the unknown southern continent that geographers had long speculated kept the world in balance. Although he did not find this southern continent, Cook's ship, the *Endeavour,* reached Tahiti in April 1769. In October, he became the first European to visit New Zealand. In April 1770, he sailed into Botany Bay and claimed the east coast of Australia for Great Britain.

Cook led two more voyages of exploration. In July 1772, he sailed back to the Pacific with two ships, the *Resolution* and the *Adventure,* in a second attempt to find the rumored southern continent. Cook sailed further south than any European had ever gone and yet circled Antarctica without ever seeing it.

Four years later, he went in search of the Northwest Passage, the long-sought northern sea route between Europe and Asia. He began by sailing to New Zealand and other Pacific Islands, becoming the first known European to see Hawaii, which he named the Sandwich Islands after Britain's chief naval minister, the Earl of Sandwich. In 1778, he sailed up the northwest coast of North America, through the Bering Strait and into the Arctic Ocean. Walls of ice blocked the progress of the *Resolution* and the *Discovery.*

Cook headed back to the Sandwich Islands in August of that year. On February 14, 1779, his crew became involved in a fight with islanders regarding the theft of a boat from the *Discovery,* and Cook was stabbed to death.

POSTSCRIPT

■ Cook pioneered the prevention of scurvy on his long voyages by feeding his crew a diet high in vitamin C, including limes, sauerkraut, and cress. The experiment became standard practice on British ships, leading to the nickname *limeys* for British sailors.

The "Apology" of Socrates

GIVEN A CHOICE between apologizing and staying true to himself, the ancient Greek philosopher Socrates chose his principles and died as a result.

Athens in 400 B.C. was not the mighty city it had once been. The decades-long Peloponnesian War against Sparta had ended disastrously for the Athenians. The Spartans had installed their own cruel government to run the once-proud birthplace of democracy. Even though revolution had eventually restored democracy, Athens was a shell of its former self. Many of its young men had died fighting, while approximately one-third of the population had died from plague. A scapegoat was needed for the city's fall from grace, and it fell on Athens's most famous philosopher, Socrates.

Socrates (seated) *is given poison hemlock*

Born around 469 B.C., Socrates was a well-known figure in Athens. He spent his whole life questioning, debating, and encouraging people to probe beyond the obvious. Critical of Athenian democracy and leaders, he could make anyone look foolish and often did. Young men loved him for the way he deflated pomposity, but he also made many powerful enemies.

Socrates was charged with disbelieving in the ancestral gods and corrupting young men. The death penalty was demanded. One of his students, a philosopher named Plato, wrote about Socrates's trial in the *Apology*. Socrates chose to defend himself, and as he faced a jury of 500 Athenian men, he told the jury of his mission, given by the god Apollo, to find a man wiser than himself. Unimpressed, the jury voted to convict Socrates 280–220. Despite the conviction, Socrates asked not for punishment but reward for his service to Athens. He even suggested that he receive free meals, an honor usually given to great generals or Olympic heroes. Angered, the jury voted for the death penalty by an even greater majority: 360–140. On the day he was to die, Socrates was cheerful while his friends wept and proclaimed his innocence.

But Socrates's philosophy continued to live on. His Socratic method, a form of teaching by asking questions, contains the bedrock principles on which modern ethics and critical philosophy are based.

Nat Turner's Rebellion

Few African Americans have been the subject of more controversy than Nat Turner. Born in Southampton County, Virginia, on October 2, 1800—five days before Gabriel Prosser was hanged for his role in his own abortive slave revolt—Nat Turner was the leader of a rebellion that resulted in the deaths of dozens of whites.

Turner was a "privileged" slave who had been encouraged by his first owner to study the Bible. He also knew of the successful Haitian slave revolt led by Toussaint L'Ouverture. Although his father had abandoned his family and escaped to freedom, Turner felt that it was his destiny to lead his people against their bondage.

Turner also was a mystic who was impelled to action by a series of "signs." He saw what he believed was the final sign on August 13, 1831, when the sun appeared bluish green. A week later, Turner and six other men met in the woods and made their plan. At 2:00 A.M., they set out for the closest neighboring household, where they killed the entire sleeping family. Ultimately, Turner's band numbered between 60 and 70 people. In just 48 hours, about 60 white men, women, and children were slaughtered—the largest number killed by any American slave revolt.

On August 22, they made it to the closest town, which was ironically named Jerusalem. By then the word of their rebellion had spread. Confronted by a group of Virginia militia, the rebels scattered. Turner managed to avoid capture for nearly two months, but eventually he was discovered near the homestead where it had all began. His "confessions" were dictated while he was imprisoned in the county jail.

The state of Virginia ultimately executed 55 people, banished many more, and for a brief moment flirted with abolishing slavery. Close to 200 blacks, most of whom had nothing to do with the revolt, were murdered by mobs bent on revenge. As for Turner, he was hanged and then skinned on November 11, 1831.

A year later, in 1832, the Virginia legislature engaged in a heated debate spurred by the Turner revolt. Nonslaveholding Virginians, especially from the western part of the state, urged the gradual emancipation and ultimate deportation of slaves from the state. A motion before the Virginia House of Delegates was defeated 73–58. The "peculiar institution" of slavery endured for another generation.

The Leakeys' Skull Discovery

L OUIS AND MARY LEAKEY were a British husband-and-wife team who dedicated their lives to exploring the planet in order to get a glimpse at what life was like millions of years ago. With seemingly endless passion and enthusiasm, they searched for clues to humanity's past.

In 1959, Mary unearthed a skull while on a dig in Tanzania's Olduvai Gorge in the eastern region of the Serengeti Plain. As Mary examined the skull's nearly complete cranium, she suspected it was a clue to the origins of mankind.

The skull was of a human-like Australopithecine that the Leakeys named in genus *zinjanthropus* (meaning "East Africa" in Arabic), or zinj for short. The hominid's large teeth indicated a diet of coarse vegetables and dated the creature to an estimated 1.75 million years ago. Later, Louis showed the skull to the researchers at the Third Pan African Congress of Prehistory and Paleontology. The find resulted in continuous funding for the Leakeys through the National Geographic Society and earned Africa credit as being "the cradle of mankind."

After Louis's death in 1972, Mary continued to explore and dig. From 1976 to 1981, she worked to uncover the oldest evidence of human origins to date, a trail of footprints preserved in volcanic ash. Once again, the find was in Tanzania, in a region known as Laetoli. These "Laetoli footprints" were determined to be 3.6 million years old. "I think it's the most important find in view of human evolution. . . . They look startlingly like our own," she said. This evidence rocked the scientific world, showing that humans walked upright far earlier than had been thought previously.

In December 1996, Mary Leakey died at age 83. Not long before she died, she returned to Laetoli to visit her historical find one more time. In describing the footprints—and their creator—Mary said, "She stops, pauses, turns to the left to glance at some possible threat or irregularity, and then continues to the north. This motion, so intensely human, transcends time."

The Smallpox Vaccine

EDWARD JENNER was an English country doctor who accomplished a feat that had defied the medical profession for centuries: He found a way to prevent smallpox.

Smallpox was a fearsome affliction. Around 20 percent of victims died from the disease, mostly infants and young children. The survivors were often badly disfigured by pockmarks. Traditional treatment was to inoculate healthy people with liquid from the pustules of those suffering a mild case of disease. Unfortunately, this often killed the patient.

Jenner was born on May 17, 1749, in Berkeley, Gloucestershire. He had been a keen observer of nature since his youth. During a smallpox outbreak in the region, Jenner noticed an interesting phenomenon: Milkmaids who had been exposed to a disease called cowpox seemed to be immune to the more deadly smallpox.

In 1796, a milkmaid named Sarah Nelmes came to see Jenner. She had blisterlike sores on her hands from cowpox, contracted from a cow named Blossom. Jenner extracted liquid from the blisters. He then found a test subject when the father of a local boy, James Phipps, agreed to let Jenner try an experiment on his son. Jenner made two small cuts on the boy's left arm and inserted liquid from Nelmes's cowpox sores. Phipps caught the cowpox but was not terribly sick. Six weeks later, when the boy had recovered, Jenner vaccinated him again, this time with liquid taken from the sores of a patient with a mild case of smallpox. The experiment worked—Phipps did not come down with smallpox.

In 1797, Jenner submitted a paper to the Royal Society detailing his breakthrough. The Society asked for more proof, and so Jenner proceeded to carry out the experiment on several other patients to verify his results. His findings were published, and a new term entered the language: *vaccine*, derived from *vacca*, the Latin word for *cow*.

Jenner's findings were widely ridiculed at first. Cartoons showing people sprouting cow heads appeared in the press, and some clergy called it ungodly to inoculate people with material from diseased animals. But the results spoke for themselves; by 1800, doctors were widely using the procedure, and the incidence of smallpox began a dramatic decline.

Jenner received government funding to continue his studies on vaccination, and in 1821 was appointed physician extraordinary to King George IV. In 1980, the World Health Assembly declared the world free from endemic smallpox.

The Spanish Civil War

IN 1936, Spain was a country wracked by political upheaval. The monarchy had collapsed, and the move toward a constitutional government was hampered by disputes among anarchists, Socialists, Communists, and right-wing groups. These groups divided into the Popular Front on the left and the National Front on the right.

The February 1936 election saw a narrow victory for the Popular Front, which immediately released all leftist prisoners and introduced agrarian reforms at the expense of major landowners. Conservative Spanish army officers, including General Francisco Franco, soon began plotting to overthrow the new government.

Female snipers during the Spanish Civil War

Civil war broke out on July 17, 1937, with roughly half the Spanish army siding with the ruling Republican government and half with Franco and the Nationalists. Virtually all of the officers sided with the Nationalists.

Large numbers of foreign volunteers poured into Spain to support the Republican cause, including Socialists, Communists, and starry-eyed idealists who fought in a variety of "International Brigades." The Soviet Union also provided assistance, tanks, and planes. The Nationalist cause was aided by Hitler's Germany and Mussolini's Italy. The Germans sent an air force unit called the "Condor Legion" to aid Franco. By the end of the war, more than 19,000 Germans had participated in the conflict, while Mussolini sent nearly 80,000 Italians to bolster the Nationalists.

In a portent of the world war to come, bombing raids on cities made no distinction between soldiers and civilians. One of these air raids, conducted by the Condor Legion on Guernica in 1937, inspired Pablo Picasso to paint one of the most famous works of art in the 20th century.

On March 27, 1939, the Nationalist army entered Madrid almost entirely unopposed. Four days later, the war was declared over, and Franco took power as dictator of Spain. It is estimated that 500,000 people perished during the Spanish Civil War—a mere taste of the horrors to come in World War II.

The *Amistad* Case

Though it was little known outside academia until Steven Spielberg's 1997 movie *Amistad,* the events surrounding a group of kidnapped Africans helped galvanize the abolition movement in pre–Civil War America.

In early 1839, a group of Africans was kidnapped in Sierra Leone, shipped across the Atlantic to Spanish-run Cuba, and sold as slaves. Placed on board the coastal trader *Amistad,* the slaves were sent from Havana to another Cuban port. On June 30, led by Sengbe Pieh, the slaves revolted and commandeered the vessel. They tried to return to Africa, but the Spanish navigator steered the ship northward, where it was captured by a U.S. naval vessel off the coast of Long Island. The ship was taken to New London, Connecticut, where the Africans were placed in jail.

After investigating the matter, the local district judge recommended that the Africans should be charged with piracy and murder at a future date. The Spanish claimed that the Africans were legitimate slaves, and even renamed Pieh "José Cinque" to keep up the charade. Since the Africans did not speak English, they could not defend themselves.

Abolitionists rallied to their defense, found an interpreter, and hired lawyers; pictures of Cinque were sold for a dollar each to raise money for their defense. The local circuit court judge passed the case along to the U.S. district court. Meanwhile, the Spanish government protested and wanted the slaves—who were regarded as property—returned to them. The situation had become very sticky politically.

On January 13, 1840, the judge issued his ruling: The slaves had been kidnapped and sold into slavery in violation of Spanish law (Spain was a signatory to the 1820 law that ended the Atlantic slave trade), and thus they should be freed and returned to their homeland.

The United States appealed, and the case went to the Supreme Court. Former President John Quincy Adams came on board to help the Africans. On March 9, 1841, the Supreme Court issued its ruling agreeing with the district attorney's appraisal of the case; the Africans were free. But their battle wasn't over yet. President Van Buren refused to provide a vessel, and so abolitionists still had to raise money to purchase a ship for the trip.

POSTSCRIPT

▒ Ironically, *amistad* means "friendship" in Spanish.

Italian Renaissance Cities

The Renaissance was a cultural movement that began in what is now Italy in the mid-14th century and lasted until about 1600. The quest for Greek and Roman culture led to a rebirth of European civilization as it emerged from the medieval era. Some historians attribute the rise of the Renaissance to the great migration of Byzantine scholars from their collapsing empire to the Italian peninsula, where they introduced many learned men to ancient civilization.

The Renaissance was centered in the dozens of city-states throughout the Italian peninsula. Cities were the heart of the Renaissance; after all, patrons, most of whom lived in urban areas, supported artists and scholars. Indeed, without the cities—and their wealth—the Renaissance simply could not have occurred.

Cosimo de' Medici

Florence was the most prosperous of the cities on the Italian peninsula, a center of art, architecture, technology, and science. The renowned Medici family was extremely influential and spent much of their money showcasing the city to the outside world. Other large cities such as Venice, Genoa, and Milan also led the developing humanist worldview. Smaller cities also contributed, such as Urbino, which had a world-class library that featured ancient writers.

The giants of the arts, such as Michelangelo, Leonardo da Vinci, Brunelleschi, and Donatello, lived and worked in Italian cities. Architects built new roomy, airy houses. As drama was reestablished, theatre became a part of many cities' entertainment. The elaboration of the arts allowed for innovation, and new musical instruments such as the violin and harpsichord appeared.

In the 15th century, the Renaissance spread to other European countries. King Charles VIII brought Italian art and ideals back to France with him after he invaded Italy in 1494. The English Renaissance began with the Elizabethan Era and nurtured writers such as William Shakespeare and John Milton. The invention of the printing press around 1450, and the subsequent availability of reading matter, also helped spread Renaissance ideas across the continent.

Honoré de Balzac (1799–1850)

WHEN HE WAS 20 YEARS OLD, Honoré de Balzac decided he wanted to be a writer. Within a few short years, he made it happen, becoming renowned for his amazing richness of his works, as well as the sheer number he produced. He is generally known as a social observer and the father of realism in Western literature.

Balzac was born in Tours, France, on May 20, 1799, into a family that worked hard for their standing in society. They moved to Paris in 1814. Balzac's father wanted him to study law, but, much to his father's dismay, Balzac's passions were stirred by writing.

Success did not come easily for Balzac. Living in a poor sector of Paris, he was continually in debt and ran an unsuccessful publishing business and print shop. His early attempts at writing were considered failures. In the beginning, he wrote under pseudonyms, and his works were ignored. It was not until several years later that Balzac's skill as a writer became apparent.

But then things began to pick up. The philosophical *Louis Lambert* (1832) was well received, and success made him ambitious. In 1834, he decided to undertake the enormous task of compiling his work—nearly 2,000 characters from more than 100 novels. Balzac then set about combining them to create a new series that would depict the day-to-day culture, customs, and habits of the French bourgeoisie.

This major compilation became known as *La Comédie Humaine* (*The Human Comedy*). Just as Balzac adapted *Le Pere Goriot* from William Shakespeare's *King Lear,* the title of *The Human Comedy* was adapted from Dante's *The Divine Comedy.* It stands as a social mosaic of the time during the French Revolution and the era of Napoleon's rule. In it, Balzac presents a vivid picture of all classes of society, from the aristocracy to the criminal underworld, as they are affected by urbanization and technological growth. His descriptions of various areas of France became an integral part of the novel, featuring not only urban Paris but also the provincial parts of the country.

Balzac died on August 18, 1850, only five months after his marriage to longtime love Ewelina Hańska. By then, his legend was firmly in place. Novelist Victor Hugo served as a pallbearer at Balzac's funeral and delivered the eulogy. "Today," said Hugo, "we have a people in black because of the death of the man of talent; a nation in mourning for a man of genius."

The Boxer Rebellion

AS THE 19TH CENTURY WANED, Qing dynasty Empress Dowager Tsu Hsi began machinations to free her country. Chinese sovereignty had become a joke over the past several decades as Japan and European nations extracted humiliating concessions from the Chinese government.

The empress found her instrument in a secret society called the Fists of Righteous Harmony, whose members were known to Westerners as "Boxers" for their expertise in the martial arts. The Boxers originally hoped to overthrow the Imperial government and expel all foreigners from China. The empress encouraged the Boxers, focusing on their fervent antiforeign sentiment. The tactic worked, and soon thousands of disaffected Chinese joined the group.

Captured Boxers with their feet in wooden stocks

The unrest heightened in late 1899 and early 1900 as thousands of Boxers attacked Christian missionaries and their Chinese converts. Foreign ministers complained to the empress, who promised action but did nothing to stop the Boxers. Finally, in June 1900, the Boxers swarmed into the Chinese capital of Beijing. Several foreign ministers and their families were killed. Foreign diplomats and their families, along with about 400 troops from throughout Europe, Japan, and the United States, took refuge in the legation compound, throwing up hasty barricades.

The Boxers charged recklessly, believing they had mystical powers that protected them from bullets. An American recalled the scene as 20,000 red-turbaned Boxers "advanced in a solid mass," waving swords and stamping their feet. "Their yells were deafening, while the roar of gongs, drums and horns sounded like thunder," wrote a hostage. A volley of rifle fire knocked the Boxers back, but they soon resumed their attacks.

The legation siege dragged on for almost two months. Ammunition ran low, and food and medical supplies were running out. On August 14, an international relief force fought its way through from Tientsin to lift the siege. About 66 defenders had been killed and 150 wounded.

The outcome was a disaster for the Chinese. Huge reparations were levied on the government by the Western powers, and Chinese sovereignty was weakened even further. The ill-fated rebellion hastened the Republican Revolution of 1911 that eventually ended the Imperial government.

George F. Kennan (1904–2005)

BORN IN 1904, Wisconsin native George F. Kennan graduated from Princeton University and embarked on a foreign policy career. He served as a minister-counselor to Moscow (1944–1946), deputy commander of the National War College (1946–1947), and director of the Policy Planning Staff of the Department of State (1947–1950).

During World War II the United States and the Soviet Union worked together as allies, but as the war wound down, Kennan was worried that the two countries would not get along in the postwar world. He recognized that Americans were unconcerned about the Soviets and generally ignored Soviet intentions in Europe under the guise of the alliance.

In February 1946, Kennan sent the now-famous 5,300-word "long telegram" from Moscow, in which he stated his concern for the future of Europe as well as U.S.–USSR relations. In the July 1947 article "Sources of Soviet Conduct," which appeared in the journal *Foreign Affairs,* Kennan (anonymously) wrote that the West must consider Russian history in order to understand its foreign policies. Stalin, Kennan noted, had to portray the outside world as hostile to the Soviet regime in order to legitimize his rule. Stalin thus mixed the traditional Russian fear of foreigners with Marxist ideology. To work with the Soviets, Kennan wrote, America must contain them from expansion and allow time for their country to either break apart or mellow into a more receptive regime.

Several prominent Americans jumped onto Kennan's "containment policy." Unfortunately, while Kennan had meant that the West must contain the USSR with a mix of economic, cultural, and political moves, Pentagon advisors thought that Kennan's containment policy would work better as a military buildup to keep the Soviets from expanding. As a result, the Cold War developed with both sides tried to build a more powerful military than the other. Kennan played a major role in the development of the Marshall Plan, a program to rebuild Western Europe (while repelling communism). But U.S. leaders fell back on old ways of thinking and became afraid of the USSR, leading them to form NATO. In response, the USSR established the Warsaw Pact, and the Cold War escalated.

Kennan's criticisms of American military policy continued through successive presidencies. Although his presidential influence fell after 1948, he often publicly voiced his distaste for President Ronald Reagan's statement that the USSR was the "evil empire," and for the rapid buildup of military might by both superpowers. He died at age 101 in 2005.

The Seven Years' War

THE SEVEN YEARS' WAR, which ran from 1756 to 1763, is known in North America as the French and Indian War. Whatever the name, the war resulted from the British and French race for colonial supremacy and the rivalry of Frederick II of Prussia with Hapsburg Austria.

By the middle of the 18th century, the worldwide competition between Britain and France was escalating. In North America, the French chain of outposts from Quebec to Louisiana prevented British colonists from moving west. Disputes erupted over sugar islands in the West Indies and trade in West Africa, while in India, British and French trading companies confronted each other in a succession of battles in their struggle for privileges and territory. In May 1756, France attacked the British naval base at Minorca. Britain retaliated and declared war on May 18.

That year, the so-called Diplomatic Revolution had overturned longstanding alliances. By the time Britain declared war, Europe was divided into two power blocs ready to fight: Austria, France, Spain, Russia, Sweden, and Saxony stood opposed to Prussia, Britain, and Portugal.

In August of that year, Frederick the Great of Prussia ensured the alliances would move into action by invading the Austrian province of Saxony. France, Russia, and Sweden honored their defensive treaties with Austria and declared war on Prussia. In 1761, Spain sided with France in reaction to British victories in North America and the Caribbean.

Two separate peace treaties ended the distinct but overlapping wars. The Treaty of Paris, signed on February 10, 1763, redistributed the colonial possessions of Britain, France, and Spain. Britain was established as the preeminent colonial and maritime power, which kept France from actively settling North America.

The Treaty of Hubertusburg, signed five days after the Treaty of Paris, restored the territorial status quo in Europe and acknowledged a fundamental realignment of European powers. With a combination of luck and military ability, Frederick forced Prussia into the ranks of the Great Powers. France remained an important European country in terms of population and military resources, but the war destroyed its position as the arbiter of Europe. In the years following the war, Austria, Prussia, and Russia dominated the affairs of continental Europe.

Together the treaties set the stage for the Napoleonic wars at the turn of the century.

Women Gain Equal Voting Rights

E VEN THOUGH EQUAL VOTING RIGHTS had been advocated by women, and some men, for nearly a century before the amendment's ratification, the 19th Amendment to the U.S. Constitution giving women the right to vote was finally ratified in 1920.

The women's suffrage movement was part of a larger movement to establish equal rights for women. The first concerted efforts to promote women's suffrage began when Elizabeth Cady Stanton and Lucretia Mott organized a convention to discuss women's rights. The first Women's Rights Convention was held in mid-July 1848, in Seneca Falls, New York. The convention's mission was guided by the Declaration of Independence, which had been adapted by Stanton in her *Declaration of Sentiments and Resolutions*. Stanton's resolution regarding women's duty to "secure to themselves their sacred right to the elective franchise" was passed by convention members and became a major focus in their program to gain equality for women.

Susan B. Anthony, a New York resident and Quaker, became involved in the women's suffrage movement after meeting Stanton in 1851. Anthony worked as a headmistress at a school for women, and she was a staunch supporter of temperance and the abolition of slavery. When she joined with Stanton, she became a spokesperson for the crusade for women's suffrage.

Suffragists demonstrating

At the conclusion of the Civil War, Stanton and Anthony formed the American Equal Rights Association and campaigned for both Negro and women's suffrage in Kansas, where voters were deciding the issues. Their efforts were not rewarded when the voters cast their ballots but, undaunted, the women forged ahead and formed a new organization, the National Woman Suffrage Association, which condemned the passage of the 14th and 15th amendments—they provided for equal protection and male Negro suffrage, but the amendments were unjust to women.

Wyoming gave women the right to vote in 1869, but it was not until 1918 that Congress began to seriously consider the issue. Two congressional attempts to pass an amendment met with failure, but in 1919, both the House and Senate passed the measure, paving the way for its ratification in 1920.

Establishing the Colony of Jamestown, Virginia

IN 1606, a joint venture company known as the Virginia Company of London organized an expedition to settle the region known as Virginia. On December 20, 105 men and boys left London in three wooden ships. Inspired by tales of Spanish gold mines, the settlers hoped to find riches. Instead, they found virgin wilderness.

The settlers reached Chesapeake Bay on April 26, 1607. After two weeks of exploration, they chose to settle on a small peninsula on the James River. They thought the location would be easy to defend from attack and would have a good supply of fresh water. Both the river and their settlement were named after their king, James I.

Life at Jamestown was difficult. Only a handful of the men were able, or willing, to do the manual work needed to build the new colony, the rest being "gentlemen," who had led idle lives. The ground was swampy, and the drinking water was tainted. Relationships with the neighboring Indian nations, under the leadership of Chief Powhatan, were often violent. About two-thirds of the men died of malnutrition and disease.

Captain John Smith held the colony together from 1608 to 1609. He forced the gentlemen-settlers to work, and he opened trade relations with the Indians. When an accident forced Smith to return to England in 1609, the colony was left without a strong leader. The winter that followed his departure, known later as "the Starving Time," was a low point for the colony. Due to a severe drought, the colony's crops failed, and Powhatan's Indians had nothing to trade. Of the 500 colonists still living in Jamestown at the time of Smith's departure, fewer than 100 were still alive by the spring of 1610.

The settlement was saved by the arrival of Governor Thomas West with new settlers and supplies. The marriage of Chief Powhatan's daughter Pocahontas to John Rolfe in 1614 brought eight years of peace between the two groups. By 1619, the colony was a success. The colonists were shipping tobacco back to England at a profit. The Virginia Company sent a number of "young, handsome and honestly educated maids" as potential brides for the settlers, hoping men would make the colony their permanent home.

On July 30, 1619, the first representative legislative assembly in the New World met in the town church, signaling that the settlement was a true colony—and not just a commercial venture.

The Tiananmen Square Protests

IN THE EARLY HOURS OF JUNE 4, 1989, thousands of Chinese were congregated in Tiananmen Square. Most were there as part of the ongoing protest that had started two months earlier.

The gathering began in April with the death of the former general secretary of the Chinese Communist Party, Hu Yaobang. Liberals regarded Hu Yaobang as a hero, and when he died many chose to honor his passing by holding peaceful prodemocracy demonstrations. The group initially started with a few hundred passionate students, but it soon swelled to thousands. The Chinese government was less than happy with the protesters, and new leader Deng Xiaoping issued a warning: Quit protesting by April 20.

The demonstrators ignored the warning, and the movement continued to grow, reaching more than 100,000 people in the square. On May 20, the Chinese government declared martial law against the protesters. Finally, on June 4, the government sent tanks into the square. They also sent in the army, wearing full battle gear and bearing automatic weapons. Soldiers with sticks and iron bars beat anyone not cooperating. Shots were fired, and within minutes hundreds of unarmed people were dead. More than 10,000 protesters were injured and rushed to nearby hospitals in bicycle-drawn rickshaws. The total number of fatalities was never ascertained; estimates range from 300 to 3,000.

China did not realize the world was watching. Foreign correspondents from around the world were on site covering an impending visit to the capital by Soviet leader Mikhail Gorbachev. The media happened upon the massacre, and the ensuing pictures and stories were released worldwide. Until then, China had been seen as an ally; now it was seen as a government with no respect for human rights. There was instantaneous worldwide condemnation of the Chinese government.

Almost 20 years later, the phrase "4 June" is still not allowed on the Chinese news or Internet.

The Fall of Rome

HISTORIANS HAVE HOTLY DEBATED for centuries just why the Roman Empire fell. Did the wealthy Romans become sterile after using water from lead-pipe aqueducts? Or was it simply the overwhelming number of barbarian tribes that inundated the empire? Many historians examining the fall of Rome also neglect to note the fact that the eastern half of the empire went on for another 1,000 years. For this reason, the decline of the empire is an excellent example of how despite their best efforts, historians can often only speculate; in the end, we may never know exactly what happened.

In his famous 1776 book, *The History of the Decline and Fall of the Roman Empire,* Edward Gibbon postulated that Christianity played a part. Christians were more interested in an eternal life in heaven than in paying obeisance to the emperor. It was a loss of civic virtue, he wrote, that destroyed the empire. Gibbon also established the date A.D. 476 as the year the Roman Empire collapsed, which many historians have accepted.

Arnold Toynbee, in his great study of civilizations around the world, *A Study of History,* concluded that any empire's decline is inevitable, so it was no surprise that Rome fell. Gibbon, however, pointed out that one should also contemplate why the empire lasted as long as it did.

Most historians agree that it was a combination of factors that destroyed the empire. In William McNeill's *Plagues and Peoples,* it is noted that the recurring plagues that struck Europe after A.D. 165 greatly weakened the empire. Others pointed out that the Romans never had a state budget and wasted much of their wealth. When the empire stopped expanding after the second century, its wealth began to dry up because the empire depended on plundering its opponents to accrue wealth. Roman technology fell behind its opponents, said others. For example, mounted tribes from central Asia had the stirrup long before the Romans, which changed how calvary rode.

Other historians pointed to a series of weak emperors: Many of these rulers were military men with very little political background, who often had no experience running an enormous empire. Between A.D. 186 and Diocletian's ascension in 284, there were 37 emperors, most of whom were assassinated. Add the rise of Sassanid Persia and larger groups of barbarians moving westward in a domino process from central Asia, and the makings of collapse are easily recognizable.

The Development of Radio

Although Guglielmo Marconi is usually considered the inventor of the radio, he should more accurately be credited with originating wireless telegraphy. The Italian electrical engineer was studying the propagation of electromagnetic waves when he realized the waves could transmit information through the air. By 1895, he was sending and receiving radio signals over a mile and a half. In 1901, Marconi's wireless transmitter delivered messages in Morse code across the Atlantic.

Guglielmo Marconi (left) *and assistant*

A scientist named Reginald Aubrey Fessenden first devised wireless telephony, or audio communication, over continuous radio waves. On December 24, 1906, he made his climactic demonstration, relaying messages from the Massachusetts coast. Fessenden spoke, read scripture, and played the violin into his radio telephone. Shipboard telegraph operators at sea and newspaper reporters in New York were able to pick up his messages.

The earliest application of wireless technology was in 1907 maritime communication for navigation, rescue, and naval operations. On land, thousands of amateur experimenters seized the air, using fabricated transmitters and receivers. The amateurs made crucial contributions to the development of the medium, but they also interfered with naval transmissions. As a result, the Radio Act of 1912 divided the radio spectrum into separate jurisdictions. When the United States entered the First World War in 1917, the armed forces shut down amateur radio and took control of all transmitting stations.

Radio production boomed during the war. Wartime collaboration among the leading producers led to patent-sharing arrangements after the armistice. The government assisted in General Electric's formation of a new company, the Radio Corporation of America (RCA).

In 1916, Frank Conrad, a Westinghouse engineer, began experimenting with wireless telephony. He received a license to commercially broadcast in October 1920. Six days later, station KDKA went on the air. The first broadcast announced Warren Harding's presidential victory over James Cox. By the middle of 1921, the age of radio broadcasts had begun.

The United Nations Is Formed

IN JUNE 1941, with the Axis powers controlling most of Europe and nine exiled European governments taking refuge in London, representatives from 14 governments signed a joint declaration. "The only true basis of enduring peace," the statement read, "is the willing cooperation of free peoples in a world in which, relieved of the menace of aggression, all may enjoy economic and social security."

Even though the United States had not yet entered the war, President Franklin D. Roosevelt's administration was already considering an international security organization to replace the collapsed League of Nations. Roosevelt wanted principles of human rights and freedom to guide the postwar order. These were stated in the Atlantic Charter of August 14, 1941, a joint declaration by Roosevelt and British Prime Minister Winston Churchill. The charter provided a beacon of hope to occupied Europe. Roosevelt and Churchill, along with representatives from China, the Soviet Union, and 22 other nations, signed the United Nations Declaration on January 1–2, 1942, committing to the Allied war effort and to the principles in the Atlantic Charter.

Following D-Day, American, British, Soviet, and Chinese diplomats worked out a sketch for the United Nations organization at Dumbarton Oaks in Washington, D.C. Their blueprint included a General Assembly of all members, a smaller Security Council, an International Court of Justice, and a Secretariat. The plan stipulated that member states would make armed forces available to the Security Council to buttress its capacity to deter aggression. Just how Security Council voting would occur was decided at the Yalta meeting with Roosevelt, Churchill, and Joseph Stalin in attendance in February 1945.

The United Nations founding conference opened in San Francisco on April 25, 1945, with delegates from 50 countries attending. Roosevelt had died two weeks before the conference began; days after it began, Benito Mussolini and Adolf Hitler would also be dead, and European victory would be at hand. The San Francisco conference drafted the United Nations Charter, which was adopted unanimously on June 25.

On October 24, 1945, the United Nations was established. Meanwhile, the war in the Pacific had ended after the United States dropped atomic weapons on two Japanese cities. The bombings presented a challenge to the new global organization. The U.N. General Assembly, in its very first resolution, called for the eradication of atomic weapons from the arsenals of all nations.

Russia's Bloody Sunday

WHEN RUSSIAN PEASANTS LEFT their St. Petersburg church on the morning of Sunday, January 22, 1905, none of them knew that in a matter of hours, their world was going to be turned upside down with anger, violence, and loss. But they all knew that they could not go on any longer the way they were—it was finally time to speak out.

Led by Russian Orthodox priest Father George Gapon, more than 150,000 Russians, many of them women and children, headed to Czar Nicholas II's Winter Palace. In hand was a petition pleading with the czar for help.

For a year, Russia had been embroiled in the Russo-Japanese War over the control of land in China. But Russia was losing, and its people were paying the highest price of all. They needed the czar to step in and make things right again. They were weary of being treated as slaves and were so exhausted by poverty that they felt "death would be better than the prolongation of our intolerable sufferings."

The unarmed crowd was met by the *okhrona*, the czar's secret police, who soon began firing on the peasants to prevent them from moving forward. A correspondent for the Paris newspaper *Le Matin* described the panic and cruelty that followed as more than 150 people fell, mostly women, young people, and children. "Blood flows on all sides," he wrote. "The people, terror-stricken, fly in every direction. Scared women and children slip, fall, rise to their feet, only to fall again further on."

The citizenry of Russia responded with anger and shock. People went on strike, refusing to go to work, and businesses shut their doors. Some soldiers even mutinied. Uprisings and revolts took place around the country, and Russia effectively shut down. In that defining moment, all faith was lost in the czar, and Russia took its first step toward the long and bloody Revolution of 1905. Armored with the people's discontent with their government, St. Petersburg revolutionaries called the Soviet (council) of Workers' Deputies seized upon the situation and demanded change.

POSTSCRIPT

Russian composer Dmitri Shostakovich memorialized Bloody Sunday and the Revolution in his Eleventh Symphony. The third movement is an homage to those who lost their lives that day in St. Petersburg.

The Founding of the State of Israel

E VER SINCE THE ROMANS had expelled them from Palestine in the second century A.D., many Jews longed for a return to what they considered their ancestral homeland, given to them by God. The belief that the Jews are a nation and deserve the right to return to Israel is called *Zionism*.

A Jewish family after the British Mandate

Zionism's most important proponent was an Austrian named Theodor Herzl, who, in 1896, published *Der Judenstaat,* or *The Jewish State.* Before then, most Zionists had been Russian Jews, concerned about the czars' anti-Semitism. As Herzl broadcast the message to Jews in Western Europe, the movement grew. The First International Zionist Congress took place in Switzerland in 1897, during which Zionists expressed the goal of colonizing Palestine.

Jewish immigration to Palestine was slow at first. The Ottoman Empire frowned on Jewish immigrants, even after the 1905 Russian Revolution, which led to an increased Jewish exodus from that country. During World War I, England expressed interest in helping the Jews move to Palestine as long as they did not disrupt the region's Arab population. More Jews tried to escape to Palestine with the rise of Hitler in Germany, but the British, given a mandate over Palestine by the League of Nations, tried to restrict such immigration. England wanted to retain Arab support for the coming war with Germany, and as a result, Jews and Arabs began to fight as more Jews moved into Palestine.

After World War II, England declared that it was giving up Palestine. The new United Nations voted to partition Palestine into two states, one Arab, one Jewish, but the compromise satisfied no one: The Jews reluctantly agreed, and the Arabs threatened war. Still, on May 14, 1948, the Jewish region of Palestine declared its independence as the new state of Israel. David Ben-Gurion was named Israel's first prime minister, and ever since its inception, Israel has had to contend with continuous tension with Palestine, a growing Palestinian refugee population, and criticism from other countries.

Montesquieu Publishes
The Spirit of the Laws

CHARLES-LOUIS DE SECONDAT was born near Bordeaux, France, in 1689, the son of an aristocratic family. He studied law at the University of Bordeaux and in Paris. In 1716, he inherited the title of Baron de La Brède de Montesquieu and a position in the Parliament of Bordeaux from his uncle. He spent years traveling throughout Europe gathering material for his numerous works on political philosophy and law.

Montesquieu's first major work, *The Persian Letters,* is a novel featuring two Persians traveling through Europe writing letters about their experiences. Filled with humorous observations about these strange European creatures and customs, *Letters* also illustrates Montesquieu's views on European politics and laws, some of which he saw as antiquated and absurd.

His 1748 magnum opus, *The Spirit of the Laws,* is an attempt to explain the human laws and societies he pokes fun at in *Persian Letters.* No doubt the most famous and influential aspect of the book is the author's discussion of the separation of executive, legislative, and judicial powers. According to Montesquieu, such division is crucial because "constant experience shows us that every man invested with power is apt to abuse it." He writes, "It is necessary from the very nature of things that power should be a check to power." This point influenced the framers of the U.S. Constitution, who built such checks and balances into the American system. Indeed, virtually all modern democratic governments embrace at least some form of separation of powers.

Perhaps even more importantly, Montesquieu argued that governments must be viewed empirically and comparatively. His most controversial notion stated that climate actually made some areas less likely to support particular forms of government. Although such reductionism has been criticized as simplistic and deterministic, the underlying point is illuminating: Political structures depend on a variety of factors, including geography, social customs, and past traditions. Many variables must be considered before determining the viability of particular forms of government in different areas of the world.

POSTSCRIPT

The Spirit of the Laws was considered subversive by the Catholic Church and was placed on the Index of Forbidden Books in 1751.

The Long March

ON OCTOBER 16, 1934, Mao Zedong and a Communist army of 80,000 men, 35 women, 5,000 porters, and hundreds of teenagers began a year-long march over 6,000 miles of difficult terrain and obstacles. By the time they reached their destination, the northwest province Shaanxi, the army numbered only 9,000.

The Nationalists under Sun Yat-Sen had joined with the Soviet Union in 1919 after the Allies allowed Japan to keep territories seized during World War I. The Soviets, who were not present at the signing of the peace treaty at Versailles, saw an opportunity to introduce Communism to China. Sun Yat-Sen was succeeded by Chiang Kai-shek, who eventually turned against the Communists in order to gain the support of wealthy Chinese people and foreign powers.

A five-year fight ensued. At the start of Chiang's Fifth Final Extermination Campaign against the Chinese Communists, the Central Committee guided the Red Army. By the time they gave control to Mao, the only options left for the Communists were surrender or retreat. Choosing to retreat, the Red forces left on a march that would last 368 days, cross 18 mountain ranges and 24 rivers, and elude armies of half a million men. Mountain travel resulted in frostbite, which required amputation without medical supplies. The Great Grasslands provided no safe drinking water or dry wood for fuel. Hundreds of marchers sank into bogs.

One of the most remarkable events occurred while crossing the Tatu River, as a group of Communists crossed hand-over-hand along a half-destroyed iron-chain suspension bridge across a vast gorge. The Nationalists fired at the group the entire time they crossed.

Once Mao and his army reached Shaanxi Province, the Nationalists were unable to mobilize enough troops and popular support in Northwest China to defeat the Red Army. By 1949, Mao's forces had driven Chiang Kai-shek into exile in Taiwan.

POSTSCRIPT

■ When the march started, each member had a limited supply of rice. By the end, they had eaten the grain, wild vegetables, the horses, and finally their leather belts, ultimately leaving them to march on empty stomachs.

■ If caught during the march, Red Army scouts were instructed to pretend to be one of the many professional ear-cleaners traveling around China.

Consumerism and Its Critics

KARL MARX's view of modern civilization rested on the hypothesis that those who control the means of industrial production accrue social power. Alongside Marxist theory was a separate, but no less important, strand of critical thought that focused more on the consumption of goods than on their production. Economist Thorstein Veblen was a leader in this intellectual tradition.

In 1899, Veblen coined the phrase "conspicuous consumption" in *The Theory of the Leisure Class,* which skewered the peculiar behaviors of the upper classes. He perceived the ostentatious display of wealth through expensive goods and the cultivation of refined tastes and manners as evolutionary vestiges of the earliest barbarian civilizations. Some reviewers lauded Veblen's book under the mistaken assumption that it was intended as satire; within the field of economics, his ideas were roundly rejected.

Half a century later John Kenneth Galbraith took up Veblen's strain of social criticism. A Canadian economist who came to the United States, Galbraith brought attention to the perennial gap between rich and poor and the contrast between "private affluence and public squalor" in his 1958 book *The Affluent Society.* Woven into his critique was a protest against the assumption prevalent among mainstream economists that a healthy economy requires, above all else, constant growth. Galbraith argued that this assumption led to the proliferation of artificial consumer needs and the withering of the public sector.

The countercultural movements that arose in the 1950s and '60s amplified these arguments. From the New Left to the Beat poets and the tribal love-rock hippies of the musical *Hair,* '60s radicals proclaimed the emptiness and sterility of consumer culture and sought to puncture the slick veneers of advertising and the mass media. Their challenge to business as usual led to significant cultural change.

Opposition to mass consumption has become a worldwide phenomenon in the early 21st century. The collapse of Soviet Communism, the rise of transnational corporations and brands, and the deterioration of the planet's ecological systems have given rise to a global protest campaign against unrestricted free trade and "corporate globalization." Among the North American chroniclers of this movement are thinkers and writers such as Naomi Klein, Benjamin Barber, Thomas Frank, Kalle Lasn, and Joseph Stiglitz. In their own way, they are all descendants of Thorstein Veblen.

Aztec Society

O VER 600 YEARS AGO, a Mesoamerican civilization arose, one that would be remembered for its agricultural and architectural innovations—and its penchant for human sacrifice.

The word *Aztec* refers to the native culture that flourished in the Valley of Mexico in the 15th and early 16th centuries. The Aztecs consisted of a number of tribes, including the Tenochca, or Toltec. Their chronicles tell of a warlike people who moved into the Valley of Mexico beginning in A.D. 1168.

In fact, the Aztecs were driven there around 1300 by the Culhuacán, who kept the Aztecs as vassals. As the Aztecs became more militarily skilled, however, they became the ally of choice during battles between other warring tribes in the Valley. They eventually became independent by 1440.

Aztec stone mask

Over the next 80 years, the Aztecs established a rigid social hierarchy and government and conquered surrounding tribes. At its height, their capital, Tenochtitlán, supported a population between 100,000 and 300,000—many of whom worked farms on the mainland and lived in the island city. Stunning architecture, a sophisticated calendar and religious structure, and above all, a system of writing were among the major accomplishments of this culture.

On the other hand, many of the laws and customs of the Aztecs would be considered harsh by modern standards. Most crimes were punishable by death, and slavery was common. Although all males were required to attend school, the women did not since they were considered inferior and subordinate to men.

From a modern perspective, the most noted and reviled Aztec ritual was human sacrifice. Usually practiced to appease or thank a god, some sacrifices were minimal, involving a single person, while a few were mammoth, including the killing of 20,000 captives by King Ahuitzotl after a military campaign in the late 15th century. The most common form of religious sacrifice was voluntary bloodletting.

Spanish conquistador Hernán Cortés vanquished the Aztec nation between 1519 and 1521. What was once a flourishing civilization was all but destroyed, leaving spectacular ruins in modern Mexico City.

Britain Abolishes Slavery

COMPARED WITH PORTUGAL AND SPAIN, Great Britain entered the slave trade rather late. But Britain made up for lost time, and by 1713 it was the principal transporter of slaves across the Atlantic Ocean to the Caribbean and West Indies.

In 1807, the same year the United States ended slave importation, Britain passed the Slave Trade Act, which outlawed the slave trade but not slavery itself. Severe financial penalties of 100 pounds per slave were slapped on British captains caught transporting slaves. But the law did little to stop the lucrative, if nefarious, trade. Slavers were sometimes willing to pay the fines, but they often simply had the slaves thrown overboard to avoid capture.

The demand for slaves still existed, and other countries were eager to pick up the slack: Spanish and Portuguese slavers transported slaves to Brazil, Cuba, and other parts of Latin America. Instead of obeying the law, British slavers just conspired to continue trading.

Britain's next step was to end the institution of slavery once and for all. In 1823, Thomas Clarkson, William Wilberforce, and others formed a new Anti-Slavery Society and campaigned against slavery for more than a decade. Slavery and slave-produced products had been waning as a source of revenue for decades, and a number of prominent advocates of laissez-faire capitalism had written editorials urging its abolition on economic, rather than humanitarian, grounds.

The campaign against the cruelties of the slave trade laid the groundwork, and the 1833 Abolition of Slavery Act immediately freed all slaves under the age of six. Slaves older than the age of six were to undergo a period of government-supervised rehabilitation. During this time, they were to be paid a partial wage as free laborers.

Owners of freed slaves were compensated. The Bishop of Exeter received more than ten thousand pounds when his 665 slaves were freed. In all, 20 million pounds were paid to British slave owners who lost their property.

The plan for gradual emancipation often failed as many former slaves refused to work for their old masters. The freed men and women left in search of their own land; they sought to escape any and every form of coercive labor that reminded them of their former enslavement. As a result, most plantations folded.

The Prohibition Era

Before the 1800s, it was possible that milk and water could be contaminated, so many people believed it safer to guzzle beer, rum, or wine. By the turn of the 19th century, however, opinions began to change. Both physicians and ministers started to worry about the effects of alcohol on the body and soul.

Later in the 19th and early 20th centuries, the United States was undergoing a revived interest in religion. The idea of *temperance,* or using alcohol in moderation, seemed reasonable. Surely, temperance proponents argued, if alcohol led to broken families, ill health, and great poverty, people would willingly stay far away from it. But temptation won out in the end. The movement was abandoned, and *prohibition*—the legalized banning of alcoholic beverages—was implemented instead.

Organizations, both politically and religiously based, came together quickly against alcohol. They worked to convince the American people that alcohol was a true danger. Slowly, the nation began to agree. At the beginning of the 20th century, three states had adopted statewide prohibition. By 1917, half of the nation had banned alcohol. Many people felt that with the removal of alcohol from the country, crime would end. Some small towns even sold their jails. In 1920, the 18th Amendment went into effect banning the manufacture, transportation, and sale of alcoholic beverages.

Unfortunately, crime remained, and the nation's morals were no greater. Saloons slyly became speakeasies, so named because passwords were required to get in the door. Some people became rumrunners and bootleggers who secretly transported alcohol to bars. Once-petty criminals, such as Al Capone, sold liquor and soon became rich and powerful gangsters who frequently took over entire sections of cities. Farmers went bankrupt as the need for barley and hops, the key ingredients in beer, disappeared.

Did people drink less? Perhaps, but in the long run forbidding alcohol only created more crime and trouble. In 1933, President Franklin D. Roosevelt repealed the 18th Amendment with the 21st Amendment, which made liquor, beer, and wine legal once again.

Alexander the Great (356–323 B.C.)

A LEXANDER THE GREAT created an empire that spanned the known ancient world from Greece to the Indian Punjab, from the Danube to Egypt—and all by the time he was 26 years old.

Alexander's father, Philip II of Macedonia, set a precedent for his son by transforming the northern Greek kingdom of Macedonia from a small divided state into the principal power of ancient Greece. In 336 B.C., he was struck down by an assassin while he prepared for an expedition against the Persian Empire. Twenty-year-old Alexander succeeded his father, and with the enthusiastic support of the army, he quickly asserted his authority. He executed not only the suspected sponsors of the assassin, but all possible rivals and opposition factions in Macedonia, marching south to squash uprisings in Thessaly and Thrace. Turning west, he defeated a coalition of Illyrians who had invaded Macedonia.

With Greece firmly under control, Alexander set out to conquer Persia, crossing the Dardanelles in the spring of 334. After visiting the ruins of Troy, a gesture inspired by Homer's *Iliad,* he defeated his first Persian army at the Granicus River, near the Sea of Marmara. He led his troops to victory against the Persians in Asia Minor, Syria, and Egypt without a single defeat, pursuing Emperor Darius III to the Caspian Gates in Bactria. Finding that the *satrap,* or governor, of Bactria had murdered Darius, Alexander sent the Persian ruler's body back to Persepolis for burial in the royal tombs.

Once he accepted the surrender of Darius's army, Alexander continued to advance east, crossing the Hindu Kush Mountains into Sind and the Punjab. In June 326, he fought his last great battle against Porus in India. He had reached the river Hyphasis (probably the Beas River in modern Pakistan) when his army refused to go further. Alexander agreed to turn back, later claiming that the only military defeat he ever suffered was at the hands of his own men.

In 323, Alexander died in Babylon at age 32, following a prolonged bout of drinking and banqueting. His empire died with him, crumbling into independent Hellenistic kingdoms ruled by generals.

POSTSCRIPT

- Alexander founded 70 cities in his march across Central Asia, including one named after his favorite horse, Bucephalus.
- Alexander was educated by the philosopher Aristotle.

Emily Dickinson (1830–1886)

IF YOU HAD THE CHANCE to sit down to tea with Emily Dickinson one-and-a-half centuries ago, it would be practically impossible to believe that she would later be known as one of the most original and influential poets in American history. After all, this person was very reserved, with a

tendency to jot quick verses on grocery lists. She would be more than hospitable, but don't ask her to leave the grounds; in her later years, Dickinson became virtually agoraphobic.

Appearances are deceiving, however. Dickinson was a person of deep emotion and unconventional style. Born in 1830 in Amherst, Massachusetts, she was raised in a quiet, sober home. Her family was highly educated, and her father was involved in local politics. As odd and reclusive as her personal life was, her poetry was full of profound musings about life, death, love, and religion. Dickinson was a brilliant student, but after one year at Mount Holyoke Female Seminary, she was too homesick to continue her education and returned home.

Dickinson wrote an amazing number of poems—1,775 in all—each one using extremely unusual patterns for the time, such as randomly capitalized words, unexpected dashes, and unique rhyming meters. By using these styles, she broke all of the era's rules of poetry. Not that any of her peers would have known it: She did not share her poems with anyone, neither friends nor family, instead choosing to keep them bundled together, tied with a string and hidden inside a locked box. Although a handful of them were published during her lifetime, the majority never saw print until after she died.

She died at age 56 from Bright's Disease, an illness of the kidneys. It caused years of pain and may have been one of the reasons she was so reclusive. Only after her death did her sister Lavinia discover the treasure trove of verses. She turned them over to an editor who immediately "fixed" the grammar and meter before publishing them. It was not until years later that the poems were returned to their original state.

The Stonewall Riots

THE 1969 STONEWALL RIOTS in New York City are considered a turning point in the gay rights movement.

The riots began on June 27, when police raided the Stonewall Inn, a gay bar in Greenwich Village. Gays had been officially discriminated against for years; until 1966, a New York City bar could lose its liquor license for serving a group of three or more homosexuals. Many restrictive laws aimed at homosexuals had been relaxed by 1969, but gays continued to endure police harassment.

The Stonewall Inn was no palace. Consisting of two large rooms, it had previously been burned out, reopening after some minor repairs and a coat of black paint over the soot. Rumors circulated that the Mafia owned it. The Stonewall catered to a largely gay clientele, as well as hippies, underage youths, drag queens, and street people. It also operated without benefit of a liquor license.

The New York Police had been conducting a series of raids on illegal clubs, and at 1:20 A.M. on Saturday, June 28, they showed up at the Stonewall. The eight officers ordered everyone out of the bar and arrested the employees for selling liquor without a license. Outside, the crowd of evicted patrons milled around in a seemingly festive mood.

The mood changed when police attempted to shove some of the bar employees and patrons into a police vehicle, including the bartender, a doorman, and three drag queens. Shouting, "Pigs!," the crowd pelted the police with coins and eventually bottles. As the crowd pressed in, the police took refuge inside the Stonewall. The crowd—estimated at as many as 400 people—battered the outside walls and then tried to burn the police out. Inside, the police had drawn their weapons for a last stand when reinforcements finally arrived.

The riot had only lasted about 45 minutes. But in that time, the gay community felt a new sense of unity, and a willingness to finally fight back after years of persecution. The crowds returned the next night, and the rioting resumed with shouts of "Gay Power!" The battle raged up and down Christopher Street for hours before police could clear the area.

The gay community had changed. The following month saw the formation of the Gay Liberation Front in New York. A movement was born, one that would soon spread across the nation as the gay community asserted itself in America.

The Wisdom of Hillel the Elder

Hillel the Elder is among the most revered sages in Jewish history, famous both for his new flexibility in the interpretation of traditional Jewish law and for his simple moral maxims.

His two best-known statements are probably: "If I am not for myself, who will be? If I am only for myself, what am I? And if not now, when?" and "That which is hateful to you, do not do to your fellow. That is the whole Torah; the rest is explanation; go and learn."

Born in Babylon around the first century B.C., Hillel went to Jerusalem to study. He eventually settled in what is now Palestine. The final third of his 120-year life was spent as a spiritual leader of the Jewish people. He was the head of his own school, and he associated with the scholars Menachem and Shammai. Shammai later became Hillel's peer in teaching Jewish law.

The House of Shammai was continually at odds with the House of Hillel. Shammai advocated a strict, rigid interpretation of traditional law, while Hillel and his disciples advanced a milder, more flexible approach. The difference also seems to have extended to their personalities. "Let a man always be humble and patient like Hillel, and not passionate like Shammai," went one popular saying.

One of the most famous examples of Hillel's wisdom was his practical solution to a law involving the cancellation of debts during the Sabbatical year. Hillel engineered an interpretation that protected the creditor against loss while also ensuring that those in need of a loan would not be refused out of fear that repayment would subsequently be canceled.

Hillel was known as a man who practiced the highest morality in all aspects of his life and dealings with others. His sagacity forms the basis for modern-day rabbinic tradition.

However, his maxims are what have ensured his great popularity. For Hillel, the three keys to the righteous life were love of peace, love of man, and dedication to knowledge of religious law. His maxims imparted his wisdom and moral view with pointed brevity.

As he said on study: "Say not, 'When I have free time I shall study'; for you may perhaps never have any free time."

Chaucer Writes *The Canterbury Tales*

Sometimes called the father of English literature, Geoffrey Chaucer is best remembered today for his masterpiece *The Canterbury Tales.*

Born around 1343, little is known of his early life, though his family appears to have been well-to-do and politically connected. During Chaucer's lifetime, he served as a page, courtier, diplomat, and civil servant. He was known to have traveled widely, and his experiences are reflected in his writing. Around 1366, Chaucer married Philippa (de) Roet, a lady-in-waiting to King Edward III's wife, Philippa of Hainaut. By the next year, he was a member of the royal court.

Geoffrey Chaucer

Chaucer's first major literary work was *The Book of the Duchess,* written between approximately 1369 and 1374. Other early works include *Anelida and Arcite* and *The House of Fame.* His most prolific creative period appears to have been from 1374 until 1386 when he served as customs comptroller for the port of London. *Parlement of Foules, The Legend of Good Women,* and *Troilus and Criseyde* date from this period.

It is believed that Chaucer began work on his most famous book, *The Canterbury Tales,* toward the end of his life. This collection of tales, related by various pilgrims on their way to Canterbury, differed from traditional works in its lack of literary stiffness or formality. The stories and language reflect the social standing and vernacular of the tellers—indeed, they were obviously based on real people. This approach and the inclusion of bawdy jokes and sly humor made *The Canterbury Tales* a popular read among the general public.

Chaucer's prose and poetry received acclaim during his lifetime, and the veneration continued following his death in 1400. *The Canterbury Tales* was one of the first books printed in England, an estimated 150 years after his death. His books were printed more than those of any other English author during the 16th and 17th centuries, and he was the first author whose collected works were issued in a single volume edition. His popularity and stature as an English literary giant remain unshaken today, more than 600 years after his passing.

The Trail of Tears

U NLIKE NATIVE AMERICANS on the northern and western frontiers of the new United States, the Cherokee responded to the arrival of European settlers by adopting European customs and intermarrying with the white immigrants.

However, assimilation and treaties were not enough to protect the Cherokee from the expansion of white settlers into their territories, as a larger movement advocated the relocation of Native Americans. In his 1829 inaugural address, Andrew Jackson announced a policy of relocating all Native American peoples to land west of the Mississippi. The policy became law in 1830 with the passage of the Indian Removal Act. That same year, gold was discovered on Cherokee lands. Georgia ignored federal treaties with the Cherokee and held lotteries to give Cherokee land and gold rights to white settlers.

Georgia state laws forbade the Cherokee from conducting tribal business, signing contracts, testifying in court against whites, or mining for gold. In 1832, in *Worcester v. Georgia,* the Supreme Court upheld Cherokee treaty rights and tribal autonomy.

A minority of Cherokee felt their only chance to survive as a people was to sign another treaty with the United States. This group, comprised of several hundred Cherokee (but not one elected Cherokee official), signed a treaty at New Echota, Georgia, in December 1835, ceding Cherokee lands east of the Mississippi to the United States in exchange for five million dollars and land in the Oklahoma Indian Territory. Fifteen thousand Cherokee protested the illegal treaty; the Senate ratified it by one vote.

The forcible removal of the Cherokee from their lands began in May 1838. Federal troops and state militia rounded up the Cherokee into stockades. Despite official orders that the Cherokee were to be treated "kindly," families were separated and people were given only minutes to gather their belongings.

More than 15,000 Cherokee were sent to the Indian Territory, driven by 7,000 U.S. Army troops on what became known as the "Trail of Tears." Bad weather, neglect, and limited food supplies turned the 800-mile march into a horrific trek, during which more than 4,000 Cherokee died. The survivors reached Oklahoma in March 1839.

The Battle of Hastings

FOR YEARS, the Normans had dwelled among the English people. While some intermarriage and merging occurred to soothe political tensions, it did not completely assuage them. The 1066 Battle of Hastings proved to be a major turning point for both groups.

When Duke Robert of Normandy died in 1035, his young son William inherited Normandy. As he grew into adulthood, he earned a reputation as a tough fighter by campaigning against neighboring kingdoms and fending off attacks by royal French armies.

William was cousin to England's King Edward the Confessor. In 1064, Edward named William as his successor, but while the king was on his deathbed, the succession was changed over to Edward's brother-in-law, Harold Godwinson. Meanwhile, William was on a campaign in Brittany. Edward died on January 5, 1066, and the next day Harold was crowned as king of England in the newly consecrated Westminster Abbey. William was enraged when he heard the news, and he began to gather an army and build a fleet to invade England.

Meanwhile, Norwegian King Harald Hardrada, one of the fiercest Viking leaders, invaded England. He defeated the local army near York on September 20. Harold quickly marched his own army northward and engaged the Vikings, destroying them but suffering heavy losses in the process. William wanted to take advantage of Harold's recent battle, and so on September 28 he landed on England's southeast coast. After fortifying two bases, William and his troops began ravaging the countryside for supplies as Harold's force marched south to confront them.

The climactic battle took place on October 14, seven miles from Hastings. Harold formed his 7,000 foot soldiers in a shield wall up to 12 ranks deep on the crest of Senlac Hill. William, who also had 7,000 troops, moved to attack. The daylong battle saw the Normans assault the Saxon line many times, only to be repulsed. But the Saxons had heavy casualties and as the battle went on, they began to weaken. When Harold was killed, his army disintegrated. William won a decisive victory, and he was crowned king of England on December 25.

POSTSCRIPT

▦ After the battle, Bishop Odo of Bayeux commissioned a pictorial tapestry to commemorate the battle. The resulting Bayeux Tapestry is 77 yards long.

Germany Invades Poland

IN 1938, British Prime Minister Neville Chamberlain returned from Munich, armed with an agreement to prevent hostilities between Britain and Germany. "I believe it is peace for our time," he declared triumphantly. A year later the world was at war.

Chamberlain's mistake was to trust Hitler. For the past three years, the German *führer* had been flexing his territorial muscles in Europe. In 1936, the German army reoccupied the Rhineland. Encouraged by the lack of opposition, he proceeded to absorb Austria. By late 1938, he was proclaiming Germany's right to annex the Sudetenland, part of Czechoslovakia.

In an effort to appease Hitler and preserve peace in Europe, Chamberlain negotiated the 1938 Munich Pact, accepting Hitler's claim to the predominantly German Sudetenland. Hitler, in turn, promptly seized all of Czechoslovakia and set his sights on Poland.

On March 31, 1939, Chamberlain announced that Britain guaranteed Poland's sovereignty, a pledge joined by France. But Hitler was not impressed. On August 23, he announced that Germany had signed a non-aggression treaty with the Soviet Union. Unknown to the world, a secret part of the treaty called for the division of Poland between Germany and the USSR.

England and France continued to attempt negotiations with Hitler, but their attempts just convinced him that neither nation would actually go to war. At midnight on August 29, German Foreign Minister Joachim von Ribbentrop presented the British ambassador with a list of demands, including the return of the Polish city of Danzig to Germany, a vote by the common people in the Polish Corridor, and a proposed exchange of minority populations. He demanded that a Polish representative with full powers come to Berlin and accept the terms by noon the next day. But Hitler was already intent on war. When the Polish ambassador arrived the next day and told Ribbentrop he did not have full powers to accept or reject the offer, the Germans announced that Poland had rejected their terms. Negotiations were broken off.

On September 1, Germany invaded Poland. After Hitler ignored ultimatums to withdraw, France and Britain declared war on Germany on September 3. It was far too late for Poland, however, and by September 17, Polish defenses were broken, overwhelmed by more than 1.5 million German troops. The coup de grâce came that same day when the Soviet army invaded from the east.

Vincent van Gogh (1853–1890)

Vincent van Gogh was the first great Dutch master since Rembrandt in the 17th century. Although he was a contemporary of Cézanne and Seurat, he chose not to paint in an Impressionistic style, as he felt it did not give the artist enough freedom to express emotion.

Van Gogh did not begin painting until age 27, in 1880. During his brief career, he produced thousands of paintings and drawings, including some of the best-known and most powerful paintings of the 20th century.

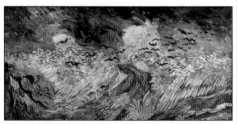

Van Gogh's Wheatfield with Crows

He worked for two years as a lay preacher among the poverty-stricken coal miners of La Borinage, the poorest part of Belgium. For the first five years of his painting career, he produced somber, rather primitive works that recorded the hardships suffered there, including his famous piece, *The Potato Eaters*.

In 1886, his brother Theo, who ran an art gallery in Paris, made it possible for van Gogh to receive formal art training. In Paris, he met Degas, Seurat, and other French artists. His canvases began to show his distinctive style: bold brushwork, thick layers of paint, and explosions of color.

In 1888, on Toulouse-Lautrec's advice, van Gogh left Paris and went to Arles, in the south of France, where he found what he described as a "kingdom of light." In Arles, he concentrated on landscape painting, depicting a countryside filled with ecstatic movement, each brushstroke vibrant with color and energy. Van Gogh's letters to his brother from this period show in detail how color had emotional meaning for him.

Van Gogh eventually invited Paul Gauguin to join him in Arles. The friendship between the two artists was tumultuous and ended in a violent quarrel, during which van Gogh threatened Gauguin with a razor. Shortly thereafter, van Gogh cut off his own ear and asked to be placed in a psychiatric hospital. Released in May 1890, he went to live at Auvers-sur-Oise, near Paris, under the supervision of a physician.

While in the asylum, van Gogh received his first public recognition, in an article by A. Aurier. It came too late. He shot himself on July 27, 1890, at the scene of one of his last paintings, *Wheatfield with Crows*.

The Outbreak of AIDS

IN THE MIDDLE of the 14th century, the Black Death swept through the world. Before it was done, it had killed around 25 million people in Europe alone. Centuries later, another pandemic has developed that affects millions of lives: the killer known as acquired immune deficiency syndrome, or AIDS.

The public first became aware of AIDS in a July 1981, *New York Times* article that reported a rare type of cancer among gay men in New York and California. Later, the disease was identified as Kaposi's Sarcoma. At the time, gay men were also reporting an odd combination of flu-like symptoms and a rare pneumonia. Soon, the condition was called gay-related immune deficiency, or GRID. Because the first cases were typically reported within the homosexual community, the illness soon developed a stigma of being a "gay disease." Eventually doctors and scientists realized the disease also affected heterosexuals, and it was renamed AIDS.

In 1983, researchers at the Pasteur Institute isolated a retrovirus believed to be related to AIDS and named it the human immunodeficiency virus, or HIV. It was known to be transmitted in three ways: sexually, via blood, and from mother to child. The following year, "patient zero" was identified as a Canadian flight attendant and was credited with spreading the virus to the general population. At the time, there were approximately 8,000 confirmed cases of AIDS in the United States and 3,700 confirmed deaths.

After the virus was identified, Retrovir, or AZT, the first medication to fight AIDS, was given FDA approval in 1987. The number of diagnosed HIV and AIDS cases was then up to 150,000 and would reach one million only three years later. Soon a debate raged among researchers as to the effectiveness of AZT. More medications and inhibitors were added to the drug arsenal, but in 1997 studies showed that HIV hides in the body, making it impossible to completely eliminate. The news was devastating. Two years later, the first human trials in the United States for an AIDS vaccine began. More than a decade later, a vaccine has yet to be found.

By 2001, approximately 31 million people worldwide were living with HIV, mostly in Africa. In 2005, a daunting 4.9 million individuals became infected and 40.3 million were living with either HIV or AIDS. To date, more than 25 million people have died of AIDS.

Jean-Jacques Rousseau Publishes Two Classics in One Year

A GREAT DEAL IS KNOWN about Rousseau's life, in part because of his autobiography. He was born a watchmaker's son in 1712. He had an introspective, sexually charged childhood; failed in two apprenticeships; took a mistress; left a tutoring position; and wrote his first book—all between 1725 and 1751. In 1762, he had to leave France to avoid arrest for his allegedly seditious writings. He returned to France five years later and lived there until his death in 1778.

His two major works, both written in 1762, were revolutionary in both ideas and impact. In *The Social Contract,* Rousseau begins with one of the most famous sentences in political theory: "Man was born free, but everywhere he is in chains." In other words, he says that people were "free" in their natural state before governments were formed, but that governments were instituted by a minority and thus became oppressive.

Since it would be impossible to return to a state of nature, Rousseau said that in order to live without oppression from the state (or from each other), people should create a "general will" through a collective agreement with each other. In giving up individual autonomy to the general will, a government by the people could then work for the common good. Although this form of radical democracy was never put into practice, it did become part of the modern view that government must be created by the people governed and be responsive to those people.

Rousseau's novel *Emile: or On Education,* applies his belief in natural freedom to education. First, he says that children pass through a variety of stages, thus each stage requires a different sort of educational method. However, because different children may vary within stages, education must be individualized. Above all, children must draw conclusions based on their own experiences rather than on the dictates of the teacher.

Both of these seminal works emphasize nature and freedom and have become part of the intellectual environment that helped create the modern world.

POSTSCRIPT

- *Emile* was banned in Switzerland and France, where it was burned.
- Rousseau had five illegitimate children, all of whom he placed in foundling homes.

The Byzantine Empire

THE BYZANTINE EMPIRE never existed, at least, by that name. In fact, the term was coined by French historians during the Renaissance who needed a word to describe the Greek-speaking Roman empire based in the capital city of Constantinople.

After the end of the Roman Empire's civil wars, the victorious Emperor Constantine founded a new capital for the empire's eastern half in the Greek colony of Byzantium. Dedicated in May 330, the city was named Constantinople in his honor.

Constantinople soon became one of the greatest cities in Western civilization. Its great walls defied scores of invaders for centuries. As the western half of the Roman Empire declined and eventually ceased to exist in A.D. 476, the eastern half went on, perpetuating Roman civilization with a Greek twist. This Greek-speaking "Eastern Roman Empire," as some called it, was the bulwark of Western civilization.

Ottoman Turks sack Constantinople

The Byzantines fought with a revived Persian Empire until 627, when Emperor Heraclius defeated the Persians. But the war had weakened both empires. When Arab armies emerged out of the desert just a few years later to spread the new faith of Islam, the Byzantines lost Egypt, Palestine, and North Africa to the invaders. Thereafter, until the tenth century, the Byzantines fought the Arabs to protect Anatolia, part of the empire's heartland. On the Balkan Peninsula, waves of invaders occupied much of the land. Later, under Macedonian rule, the Byzantines restored the Danube River as their northern frontier.

However, a subsequent series of weak emperors neglected to maintain the strength of the Byzantine army, and in the 11th century, Turks, Normans, and other invaders attacked the empire. In 1204, the Fourth Crusade captured and sacked Constantinople, and although the Byzantines recovered their capital in 1261, the empire was but a shadow of its former self. The end came on May 29, 1453, when the Ottoman Turks captured the city after a long siege. Renamed Istanbul, Constantine's city became the capital of the expanding Ottoman Empire.

The Battle of Vimy Ridge

DURING THE FIRST WORLD WAR, German-held Vimy Ridge was a key position on the Western Front northeast of Arras, France. The ridge had been the subject of multiple attacks by French and British troops. All had failed, with 150,000 men dead as a result.

In April 1917, the Canadians got their turn. They knew it would not be easy. After seizing the seven-kilometer-long height in September 1914, the Germans had constructed formidable defenses with bunkers, caves, protected trenches, and concrete machine gun emplacements. The efficiency of their work was evident in the still-unburied French and British corpses lying between the lines. Many Allied commanders thought Vimy Ridge was impregnable.

The Canadian troops planned the assault for months. Replicas of the terrain and detailed maps were compiled; careful observation located 80 percent of the German gun positions. Miles of tunnels were dug so troops and supplies could be moved forward without being spotted. The assault would be conducted by the Canadian Corps, which had four divisions of about 100,000 men, under the command of General Julian Byng.

The infantry would attack behind a rolling curtain of high-explosive shells, cleaning out the Germans before they had a chance to man their defenses. Timing was crucial. "Chaps, you shall go over exactly like a railroad train, on time, or you shall be annihilated," Byng instructed.

For two weeks, Canadian and British artillery hammered away at the German defenses, firing 2,500 tons of ammunition a day. More than 1,000 artillery pieces were moved in to support the assault. Easter Monday, April 9, arrived with a cold rain. At 5:30 A.M., the Canadian divisions attacked as a deafening artillery barrage sent mud cascading skyward.

Their plan worked. The infantry overran the German forward defenses, continuing to advance even as the enemy began to recover and return heavy fire. Hill 145, the highest point of the ridge, was taken with a bayonet charge. The fighting dragged on for three days, but the Canadians prevailed, and the battle was declared a victory on April 12. It was a stunning success, but it did not come cheaply: 3,598 Canadian soldiers died and 7,000 were wounded.

The Battle of Vimy was more than a military victory, it marked the first time all four Canadian divisions had attacked together. Men from all parts of Canada sacrificed themselves for the victory. "In those few minutes, I witnessed the birth of a nation," remarked a Canadian general.

Einstein's Theory of Relativity

PEOPLE WHO SPEND TIME riding public transportation often find themselves with extra time to ponder. Such was the case in May 1905, when 26-year-old Albert Einstein rode a streetcar in Bern, Switzerland.

Born in Germany in 1879, Einstein is considered one of the most brilliant and innovative men of the 20th century, even though in school he was scolded by professors who found him disruptive and disobedient. He was educated to be a teacher, but unable to find a post, he took a job in the Swiss Patent Office. Here, he did much of his best work.

As Einstein later described it, while riding the streetcar, he looked back at the clock tower slowly fading into the background. He imagined what it would be like if the streetcar moved closer to the speed of light. Einstein suddenly realized that it would appear as if the clock had stopped since light could not catch up to streetcar, but his own watch would continue to tick away.

He also realized that this image held the solution to a problem he had been working on for more than a decade. He knew that Newtonian mechanics and Maxwell's equations, two of the foundations of physics, were essentially incompatible. If one was right, the other had to be wrong. For years, he had been trying to understand how Newton's ideas of absolute space and time could fit with Maxwell's constancy of the speed of light.

With his observation in the streetcar, as Einstein later described it, "A storm broke loose in my mind." The solution was actually simple: Time could move at different rates throughout the universe, depending on how fast an object was moving. "The solution came to me suddenly with the thought that our concepts and laws of space and time can only claim validity insofar as they stand in a clear relation to our experiences," he explained. "By a revision of the concept of simultaneity into a more malleable form, I thus arrived at the theory of relativity."

Einstein spent several weeks committing his theory to paper, which ran to more than 30 pages. He sent the paper off to the physics journal *Annalen der Physik* for publication in the fall of 1905. Weeks later, he realized he had left something out and hurriedly mailed a three-page supplement to his paper, including his now famous "$E = mc^2$" formula that would forever change how scientists view the universe.

The Battle of Marathon

IN 499 B.C., the Greek cities in the district of Ionia in Asia Minor revolted against the Persian Empire. They requested help from mainland Greece, and Athens readily sent what aid it could. However, the Greek rebels were not able to present a united front and were defeated by the Persians by the end of 494 B.C.

Persian Emperor Darius I decided to seek revenge against the Greeks by sending an expedition against the Athenians. The initial expedition turned back from Macedonia after the Persian fleet was wrecked in a storm, but the emperor was undaunted, sending a second force of approximately 50,000 men straight across the Aegean Sea toward Athens. Once the Greeks learned of the Persian expedition, they sent word to Sparta and asked for help. Unfortunately, the Spartans were in the middle of a religious festival; their aid would be delayed by two weeks.

The Persians landed at the bay of Marathon, 26 miles from Athens. General Datis alone had 20,000 Persian troops; the others had remained on their ships and were moving closer toward Athens. When the Athenian commander Miltiades learned about the Persian plan, he decided to attack at once. Lacking the Spartans, he gathered about 9,000 Athenian hoplites (heavily-armed infantry), along with some men from the city of Platea, to confront the enemy.

The Greeks advanced downhill to the narrow plain of Marathon where they formed their lines. Miltiades placed most of his infantry on the flanks, leaving a smaller number in the center. As the Greeks slowly advanced, Persian archers had time to fire before retreating behind their main line. When the two armies crashed together, the Greek center was driven back a short distance, but the Greek wings, which contained more soldiers, drove in their opponents to complete a classic double envelopment.

The Persian line collapsed, and their men began to run for their ships. Datis managed to organize a rear guard and held off the Greeks long enough for most of his men to get aboard their ships and escape. The Greeks suffered a loss of 192 men, while the Persians reportedly lost more than 6,400 men.

As Miltiades re-formed his men and began the march back to Athens, he sent the runner Pheidippedes ahead to announce the victory. Pheidippedes entered the city and delivered his message: "Greetings, we have won." He then dropped dead from exhaustion; his 26-mile journey was the first marathon run.

The Haitian Revolution

THERE HAVE BEEN many revolutions throughout history, but only one successful slave revolt. The Haitian Revolution of 1791–1804 threw off French colonial rule and established Haiti as the first independent black state in the New World.

In the mid-1700s, Haiti was known as the colony of Saint-Domingue, a major supplier of the world's sugar. In order of social standing, whites ruled, followed by free blacks, who were usually of mixed blood and referred to as "persons of color." At the bottom of society were the black slaves, who did most of the labor.

Toussaint L'Ouverture

The slaves were treated brutally, but they did have an advantage in numbers. By 1789, the slave population outnumbered whites and free blacks by a ratio of ten to one. Clashes were not unusual. Bands of runaway slaves, called *maroons,* conducted raids on plantations. On August 22, 1791, thousands of slaves suddenly rose up against their masters, demanding liberty and vengeance. Angry rebels murdered 2,000 whites and burned nearly 1,000 sugar plantations. Within ten days, they controlled the entire northern province.

A former domestic slave, Toussaint L'Ouverture, emerged as the leader of the revolt. L'Ouverture was charismatic, with a genius for political maneuvering. He played British, Spanish, and French interests in the colony against each other. Finally, allying himself with France, his rebel forces were able to gain control of the island.

In 1801, he declared Haitian autonomy. Napoleon Bonaparte responded by sending French troops to Haiti; L'Ouverture was apprehended and later died in captivity. Jean Jacques Dessalines then took up the cause against the French. The conflict degenerated into barbarism as both sides indulged in mass atrocities.

Ravaged by yellow fever and weakened by a British naval blockade and Napoleon's reluctance to send reinforcements, the French colonial army was finally defeated at the Battle of Vertières on November 18, 1803. On January 1, 1804, Dessalines declared the former colony independent.

The Founding of the NAACP

T HE NATIONAL ASSOCIATION for the Advancement of Colored People (NAACP) stands as America's oldest civil rights organization. The organization traces its founding to the Niagara Movement, named after a 1905 meeting organized by Harvard scholar W.E.B. Du Bois. Because white hotels refused blacks admittance, Du Bois arranged for blacks to meet at a hotel situated on the Canadian side of Niagara Falls—a sly nod to the Underground Railroad and earlier abolitionist movement. But the group was not exclusively for blacks. NAACP members included Mary White Ovington, Henry Moskowitz, and William Walling, all of whom were white.

The Springfield Race Riot of 1908 in Abraham Lincoln's hometown in Illinois sparked many of the initial respondents to see the urgency in creating a national organization to combat racial injustice. On May 30, 1909, the Niagara Movement met in New York and formed the National Negro Committee with Du Bois presiding. At a second meeting the following year, the group was again renamed and the National Association for the Advancement of Colored People was born.

Ironically, although the NAACP was created to "promote equality of rights and eradicate caste or race prejudice," its initial leadership was largely white. Du Bois was eventually added to the executive board as editor of *The Crisis* magazine, but an African American was not elected president of the organization until 1975.

Early on, the NAACP was small, weak, largely northern and urban, and dependent on white philanthropy. It failed in its initial protest of President Woodrow Wilson's racial segregation of the federal government. But, by 1914, the group had 6,000 members and 50 branches and successfully lobbied for the right of African Americans to serve as officers in World War I. It also had considerable success in organizing a boycott against D.W. Griffith's racist film, *Birth of a Nation.*

But its principal successes would come through the courts. In the 1917 case of *Buchanan v. Warley,* the NAACP prevented state and local governments from formally segregating African Americans in separate residential districts. It later went on to battle "white primaries," grandfather clauses, restrictive covenants, and lynching. The NAACP would eventually play a central role in passing civil rights legislation in the 1950s and '60s.

John Muir (1838–1914)

IF NOT FOR A LOCUST TREE, a case of malaria, and a Scottish immigrant named John Muir, Yosemite National Park might not exist. Today Muir is hailed as "The Father of Our National Parks" for his achievements as a naturalist and conservationist.

In 1849, Muir immigrated to the United States from Scotland with his family and grew up on a farm in Wisconsin. He attended what is now the University of Wisconsin, where one day a student picked a flower from a locust tree and explained to Muir its relationship to the pea plant. The lesson, wrote Muir, "charmed me and sent me flying to the woods and meadows in wild enthusiasm." It kindled his lifelong fascination with nature.

In 1867, Muir's plans to go to South America were interrupted by a bout of malaria. He decided to go to California instead. Arriving in San Francisco, he inquired as to the way out of town. When asked where he wanted to go, he replied, "To any place that is wild." He made for Yosemite, and the experience changed his life. He was enthralled. "No temple made with hands can compare with Yosemite," he said.

Muir would devote the rest of his life to the study and preservation of the Yosemite area and the Sierras. He wrote prolifically about his adventures and travels, the awesome beauty of the wilderness, and the need to protect its irreplaceable wonders from development. His letters, essays, and books found a wide audience, and contributed to the beginnings of a new movement to create Yosemite, Sequoia, Mount Rainier, Petrified Forest, and Grand Canyon national parks. During a camping trip with president Theodore Roosevelt, he persuaded the president of the need to involve the federal government in expanding the Yosemite area.

In 1892, Muir founded the Sierra Club with the mission of preserving the Sierra Nevada and making it accessible. He served as president and mentor of the club for some 22 years.

On December 24, 1914, John Muir died of pneumonia in a Los Angeles hospital, but his legacy remains in the natural heritage he preserved for all generations and in the continuing effort to follow his example.

The Monroe Doctrine

IN HIS MESSAGE to Congress on December 2, 1823, President James Monroe declared that European nations must stay out of the Americas.

In 1823, America itself was hardly in the position to dictate terms to powerful countries such as France, Prussia, and Russia. The United States fleet was tiny, and the army was not large enough to attack other countries. Still, Monroe said that there would be no new colonies established, and no European nation would be allowed to intervene in any North or South American country. He went on to state that the United States was uninterested in Europe and would in turn remain neutral in any future European conflict. European powers were expected to stay out of the western hemisphere, but the United States would accept existing European colonies in the Americas.

While the declaration sounded presumptuous, there was strength behind it. Britain's Foreign Secretary George Canning was completely in agreement with Monroe, and he had the British Royal Navy, the world's largest and most powerful fleet, to back him up.

The political intrigue behind the Monroe Doctrine started when the French under Napoleon invaded Portugal and Spain in 1807 and 1808. The warfare in Europe weakened their hold on their colonies in the New World. As a result, independence movements flared up in almost every colony in Central and South America. By 1823, under the leadership of generals such as Simón Bolívar and José de San Martín, many former colonies had declared their independence.

During this process, the English had established several highly successful economic relationships with the new American countries. They heard that Spain and France were jointly considering sending troops to reconquer the colonies, but if that happened, the English would lose their new trading agreements. With this in mind, the English foreign minister suggested to his American counterpart that England and America issue a joint warning to European powers to stay out of the Americas. Monroe was interested in the British proposal, but others were not so sure—after all, America had just fought against England in the War of 1812.

And thus, Monroe took the initiative to proclaim his doctrine. With British naval assistance implicit in his message, any threat of European intervention quickly dissipated. The Monroe Doctrine became a cornerstone of American foreign policy and remains so to this day.

The Salem Witch Trials

IN SALEM, MASSACHUSETTS, during the late 17th century, the Puritans believed the devil was lurking around every single corner. He was a constant source of temptation, trying to lure hearts, minds, and souls from the righteous paths they were following. The Puritans were on constant lookout for a devil in their midst. If people were spotted talking or muttering under their breath, or were argumentative or overly friendly, they could be witches. If the crops failed, the temperature turned unusually hot or cold, or a person suddenly sickened and died, a witch must be to blame.

As history has proven time and again, if a person looks hard enough for something, it will be found. This was certainly true in Salem. In January 1692, several young girls began to scream, drop to the ground, writhe around, and shake. The physician could find nothing wrong, and so the minister was called in—he was sure the devil was to blame. The townspeople believed the devil had crept into their community via a witch; he or she had to be found immediately and punished.

When asked what was wrong, these young girls, including Betty Parris, age 9, and Abigail Williams, age 11, accused community members of practicing witchcraft, including Tituba, a slave who had entertained the children with stories of magic from her homeland of Barbados. Claiming possession, the girls played into what is now thought to have been a combination of mass hysteria and a love of being the center of attention in a culture that usually ignored children.

Those accused as witches, primarily women, were rounded up and thrown in jail. They were tortured for information, and in the end, 19 "witches" were hanged, one was crushed to death under heavy stones, and others died in prison while awaiting trial. The combination of gullible children, fanatic religion, and intense fear culminated in one of history's darkest moments.

The Vikings

SOMETIME IN THE EIGHTH CENTURY, the Norse peoples of Scandinavia began to produce light, fast ships that made it possible to navigate the open seas and sail up the inland rivers of Europe using either oars or sails. Soon afterward, Viking raiders began to harry the coastlines of Western Europe. The first documented attack was on the monastery at Lindisfarne, off the British coast, in A.D. 793.

Eventually, spring raids on the coastal settlements of Britain became an annual event. The shallow hulls of the dreaded "dragon ships" meant the raiders could land small bands of armed men directly at the mouth of a river or on a beach. Noted for their lightning-fast attacks, the raiders pillaged isolated settlements on the coasts and navigable rivers, with wealthy monasteries a favorite target.

From about 800 to 1050, raiders, explorers, traders, and colonists poured out of Scandinavia and across the known—and unknown—world. They traveled westward over the open seas as far as modern Newfoundland, which, according to some accounts, Icelandic explorer Leif Ericsson reached in the 11th century. Raiders from Norway and Denmark attacked Britain and Ireland, ravaged the coasts of France and Spain, and entered the Mediterranean. Archaeological finds of silver Arabic coins in Scotland suggest the Vikings even got as far as the Middle East.

By the middle of the ninth century, the Vikings began to settle in the areas they raided. At first, the settlements were just winter camps where raiders could refit their ships for the coming year's expeditions. With time, the camps developed into farming communities and permanent commercial centers with craftsmen and industry.

By the end of the ninth century, the Danes had conquered most of England and established the kingdom of Normandy in France. Swedish Vikings, called the Rus, founded a new Russian state, with its capital at Kiev. Viking Dublin ruled over a substantial portion of the British Isles and served as the center of a Scandinavian trade network that ranged from Greenland to the Mediterranean. By the end of the tenth century, the Viking kingdoms in Ireland had become integrated into Irish society, creating a hybrid civilization known as Hiberno-Norse.

POSTSCRIPT

▓ The name *Viking* comes from an Old Norse word meaning "pirate raid."

Sukarno (1901–1970)

THE SON OF A SCHOOLTEACHER, Sukarno (Indonesians traditionally use one name) developed nationalist sentiments while studying civil engineering in secondary school. In 1927, he became head of the pro-independence party Partai Nasional Indonesia. The young activist was arrested by Dutch authorities in 1929 and spent two years in prison. Other arrests followed over the next decade.

Sukarno's situation improved with Japan's seizure of the Dutch East Indies two months after Pearl Harbor. By then he was a well-recognized figure. He collaborated with the Japanese in the belief it would hasten Indonesian independence, but Japan lost the war before that could happen. On August 17, 1945, Sukarno took the initiative and declared the independence of the Republic of Indonesia. The new parliamentary government named him president of the primarily Islamic country.

It was a tumultuous time. Various Indonesian factions engaged in political infighting while resistance grew toward the Dutch, who attempted to reassert control over their prewar possession. By 1956, Sukarno had grown disenchanted with parliamentary democracy. Continual squabbles led to a series of unsuccessful coalition governments.

His solution was "guided democracy," modeled after the Indonesian tradition of discussion and consensus under the guidance of village elders. Select groups representing the main powers in Indonesian politics—primarily the army, Islam, and the Communists—would govern by reaching consensus under Sukarno's guidance. Backed by the military, he implemented the new system in 1957.

Sukarno gradually tightened his grip on the country even further: He replaced the elected assembly with an appointed body that named him president for life in 1963. Opposition was suppressed, especially rightist movements, and government controls were established over the media. Sukarno also drifted further to the left. Dutch companies were nationalized. He brought more Communists into his government, strengthening ties with China and North Korea. In 1961, he joined the Non-Aligned Movement with India, Egypt, Ghana, and Yugoslavia.

Despite these efforts, rightist groups, led by army General Suharto, toppled Sukarno's regime in 1966. Sukarno was forced to turn over power to Suharto and was stripped of his presidential title on March 12, 1967. The Father of the Nation was held under house arrest until his death three years later from kidney disease.

Hitler Comes to Power

A DOLF HITLER first gained attention in 1923 for his failed attempt to seize the Bavarian state by force. While imprisoned for high treason, he penned his manifesto *Mein Kampf* (*My Struggle*). In it, he declared his intention to acquire dictatorial power and called for a new German regime based on racial purity and eugenics.

While the book espoused an ideology associated with the fanatical fringe, it also contained a program for building a powerful movement through a combination of propaganda, disciplined party organization, and violence. Hitler's Nazi party rapidly established itself in the aftermath of the New York stock market crash of 1929. His paramilitary group, the thuggish

Hitler (left) *at a parade with President von Hindenburg*

Sturmabteilung (aka Brown-shirts or storm troopers) intimidated all opponents. Meanwhile, Hitler's propaganda chief Joseph Goebbels engineered colossal election campaigns in 1930 and 1932, bringing the National Socialists to the brink of power.

A striking feature of the Nazi takeover of Germany is that it required no overt constitutional violations. The nation had been in a state of emergency since 1930 under a series of appointed chancellors who could not keep a governing coalition together. Hitler was offered the post of vice chancellor in 1932 but refused it, gambling that the ongoing crisis would yield him a better opportunity. In late January 1933, another coalition collapsed, and he was offered the chancellorship.

On February 27, 1933, a few days before scheduled parliamentary elections, an unknown arsonist set fire to the Reichstag parliament building in Berlin. Hitler, who had been in office less than one month, seized the moment to declare a Communist insurrection and arrest thousands of suspects—from a list that had already been drawn up. He then convinced President von Hindenburg to sign an emergency decree suspending constitutional liberties, freedom of speech, and freedom of the press. Cowed by the threat of terrorism, the Reichstag swiftly passed an Enabling Act, which granted the chancellor the dictatorial powers he sought. These statutes would not be lifted until the demise of Hitler's Third Reich in 1945.

The Fall of Constantinople

In 1451, Mehmet II became sultan of the Ottoman Empire; as new leader of the Turks, he resolved to put an end to what remained of the Byzantine Empire. He moved quickly, and by the summer of 1452, Mehmet had a fortress constructed on the western shore of the Bosporus to prevent supply ships from the Black Sea from reaching Constantinople. The sultan also occupied all surviving Byzantine territory outside of the city.

Mehmet's army, of an estimated 100,000 men, arrived in front of Constantinople's formidable walls on April 2, 1453. By contrast, the Byzantines could only muster about 6,000 men, many of them Genoese and Venetian mercenaries, to defend the city. The walls stretched for miles, some of them protecting the city's sea approaches. The land walls, built 1,000 years earlier by Emperor Theodosius II, consisted of a *foss* (a dry ditch) and three layers of walls, each higher than the one before it.

The Ottomans used a variety of artillery to smash into the brick walls of the city. Mehmet obtained the services of a Hungarian engineer named Urban who built immense cannons, one of which was more than 26 feet long and fired cannonballs weighing as much as 1,200 pounds. This monster could only be fired seven times each day because of the time needed to load it and the heat it generated with each blast. Meanwhile, the Byzantines rarely used their own cannons because of the danger their reverberations posed to the city's walls.

After giving his army a day of rest, Mehmet ordered the great assault to begin before dawn on May 29. The first wave of lightly armed troops was repelled after two hours of fighting. Mehmet then sent in his *sipahis,* the main force of Turkish soldiers. They, too, failed.

Then came the famed Janissaries, the sultan's shock troops. These slaves had been recruited for military service and were fanatically loyal. By now the city's defenders had suffered losses and were tired. Some Janissaries found a small gate that had been left open in the confusion and used it to get inside. The city was doomed as Turks poured into the breach. Byzantine Emperor Constantine XI perished in the fighting, and his body was never found; Greek legend has it that he was spirited away into a cave below the city and will rise again to reconquer the city on some unspecified future date.

It was then that Constantinople (renamed Istanbul) became the new capital of the Ottoman Empire.

Tocqueville Travels in America

IN APRIL 1831, Alexis de Tocqueville embarked on a sojourn in the United States. It wasn't a typical sightseeing trip—he wanted to visit American prisons.

Tocqueville served as a magistrate at Versailles in France. After an insurrection in Paris had deposed the conservative Bourbon monarchy and shifted power in favor of the middle-class bourgeoisie, Tocqueville and a colleague, Gustave de Beaumont, took leave from their duties for a research project across the Atlantic.

Their official purpose was to study prisons, which were under reform in France. Beneath that pretext, however, they aimed to observe the American political experiment in action. He wondered what the French could learn from the successes and failures of American democracy.

The travelers saw America at a moment of democratic ferment. President Andrew Jackson was at the height of his popularity, defending the common man and railing against the corrupt influence of bankers. Between 1820 and 1830, property restrictions on voting had been lifted in most states, doubling the number of American men eligible to vote. Wherever the Frenchmen went, they were impressed by the engagement of ordinary citizens in public affairs.

Tocqueville and Beaumont visited 17 states during their nine-month visit, meeting with politicians and thinkers in New York, Philadelphia, and Washington, D.C. They witnessed the forced removal of Indians along the Mississippi River and observed the deleterious effects of slavery on social life in the South. Everywhere they went, Tocqueville was struck by "the general equality of condition among the people."

In his two-volume masterpiece, *Democracy in America,* Tocqueville evaluates what he saw with evenhandedness and keen insight. He perceived distinct advantages and disadvantages in the culture of democracy. On the positive side, he noted, the majority of citizens understood their rights and participated in public life. Thus, he wrote, public policy was likely to benefit the many rather than the few.

However, the power of majority opinion, if left unchecked, can produce a stifling conformity. For all the lively political debates he encountered in the United States, Tocqueville still noted, "I know of no country where there is so little independence of mind and real freedom of discussion as in America."

The Excommunication of Elizabeth I

Pope Pius V's excommunication of Queen Elizabeth I was the climax of a long struggle for control of the church in England that had started with Elizabeth's father, King Henry VIII, who had split from the

Catholic Church in 1534. The break made the English king head of the church and clergy. and enabled Henry to confiscate the church's monasteries and redistribute its land. This continued until Henry's daughter Mary I came to the throne in 1553, and she returned to the Catholic Church.

Elizabeth, meanwhile, had been raised as a Protestant, and when she became queen in 1558, she chose that path for England. The Anglican Church was officially established in 1563: Protestant in dogma, but Catholic in pomp and hierarchy.

The pope excommunicated Elizabeth in 1570, citing the queen's "illegitimate" birth as well as her heretical religious beliefs and demands that her subjects observe them. The excommunication allowed Englishmen to disobey their queen and return to the true Catholic faith.

Scores of agents were sent to England to assassinate Elizabeth while hundreds of Jesuit priests secretly went to England in an attempt to subvert the monarchy. But Elizabeth's superior security measures negated their efforts. Although the foreign attempts to unseat the ever-popular queen created a surge in English nationalism, there was still unrest in England, however, much of it centered on the queen's Catholic cousin, Mary Stuart, the "Queen of Scots." After being forced out of Scotland, Mary lived in England, where the crown kept a close eye on her—rumors abounded that Mary desired to oust her cousin. After a 1587 plot against the throne revealed Mary's complicity, Elizabeth had no choice but to order Mary's execution.

Although at one point he had tried to marry Elizabeth, Philip II of Spain used Mary's execution, along with Elizabeth's Protestantism, to declare a religious war on England. Boasting the pope's support, Philip gathered the Spanish Armada to clear the seas of English warships, after which his soldiers would land on English soil. The Armada's subsequent defeat signaled the rise of English naval superiority and the decline of Spanish power.

The 1980 Olympic Boycott

AMERICA'S BOYCOTT of the 1980 Olympics came as a shock to athletes across the country. Thousands of hours of training and countless dreams and hopes came to a sudden halt. On March 21, 1980, President Jimmy Carter stood in front of more than 100 athletes and coaches and explained why. "What we are doing," he said, "is preserving the principles and the quality of the Olympics, not destroying it."

It was not an easy decision for anyone, but Carter, the U.S. Olympic Committee, and Congress felt they needed to make a stand. In December 1979, Soviet tanks and paratroopers invaded Afghanistan with the announced intention of aiding Afghanistan's government but meaning to take control. The U.S. response was immediate, as Carter suspended arms negotiations with the Soviets and banned the export of grain. He condemned Russia's actions to the United Nations and threatened to boycott the upcoming 1980 Olympic Games held in Moscow. The Soviets had until February 20, 1980, to withdraw from Afghanistan. When the Soviets refused, Carter followed through with his threat. America would not be participating in the games, and American athletes refusing to cooperate would have their passports revoked.

Athletes were understandably devastated. "As citizens, it is an easy decision to make—support the president. As athletes, it is a difficult decision," said one competitor. Distance runner Dick Buerkle found out while watching the nightly news. "I don't think I saw it coming, no. It was kind of a shock. I was angry," he said.

The United States wasn't the only country to participate in a boycott. "It should be remembered that in the United States and other free countries, the national Olympic committees were independent of government control," Carter said. "In a few countries, including Great Britain, governments supported the boycott, but Olympic committees made the final decision about whether to send athletes to Moscow."

Sixty-five countries joined in the boycott, including Japan, West Germany, China, and Canada. Great Britain, France, Italy, and Sweden sent smaller teams than usual, and other countries did not send teams but did not punish athletes who chose to compete. When these athletes appeared in the games, the Olympic anthem and flag were flown rather than their national ones.

While the world reacted boldly, the boycott did nothing to hasten change in the Soviet policy in Afghanistan—Russian soldiers did not leave the country for almost another decade.

The California Gold Rush

IN 1839, an immigrant of Swiss descent named John Sutter arrived in California. Several years later, he obtained Mexican citizenship and received a nearly 50,000-acre land grant east of Sacramento. In early 1848, he hired carpenter James Marshall to supervise the construction of a lumber mill along the American River. On January 24, Marshall noticed some yellow specks in the water flowing in a tailrace of the mill. "It made my heart thump," recalled Marshall, "for I was certain it was gold."

He was right. Sutter and Marshall tried to keep the discovery secret, but rumors began to circulate. Soon scores of hopeful miners descended to try their luck at finding the precious metal. California had recently become an American territory as part of the peace treaty that ended the Mexican-American War. Now thousands of people swarmed into the area hoping to find their fortunes; boomtowns sprang up as men fought for their share of a riverbank to pan for gold.

In August, the *New York Herald* became the first east-coast newspaper to report the gold rush. Word spread, and soon men across the country began to concoct ways to get to California. Some organized wagon trains across the Great Plains and Rocky Mountains. Others went by sea to Panama, where they trekked through the jungle to the Pacific, to board another vessel bound for San Francisco. Still others went by sea around Cape Horn and up the Pacific coast of South America. But underneath all the hype was a feeling of unease that the legend of gold in California could be just that—a rumor. On December 5, President James Polk verified the gold story.

Although most miners never struck it rich, that didn't stop prospectors from trying. Throughout 1849, tens of thousands of men, dubbed "forty-niners," came to California, lured by the prospect of becoming rich in a flash. The population of the territory rose so quickly that by the end of the year there were more than 100,000 people living there. In 1850, for instance, San Francisco's population went from 800 people to more than 20,000. In response to California's rapidly growing population, the lawmakers organized a legislature, elected representatives, and applied for statehood. California became the 31st state on September 9, 1850, as part of the Compromise of 1850.

POSTSCRIPT

By 1855, $200 million worth of gold had been mined.

The Phoenicians Found Carthage

THE ANCIENT CITY OF CARTHAGE is one of history's great mysteries. According to one legend, it was founded in 814 B.C. after Queen Dido of Tyre fled her home following her husband's murder.

The history of Carthage suffers a serious case of spin: Because the city and its culture were completely destroyed by the Romans after the Third Punic War in 146 B.C., everything we know about Carthage is based on other sources, primarily Greek and Roman writers. And because the Carthaginians warred with both peoples, these historians generally made few favorable comments about their enemy.

The Phoenicians were responsible for the founding of Carthage. Phoenicia is the name given to the narrow coastal strip on the eastern Mediterranean Sea in what is parts of modern Lebanon, Syria, and Israel. The people of this region were descendants of Canaanites, who had founded several cities along the coast. Their coastal

Phoenicians establishing trade

position led the Phoenicians to develop a trading empire after Carthage's birth in 1200 B.C. The Phoenicians also founded many colonies along the North African and Spanish coasts, settling Sardinia and other islands. A wide network of trading partnerships was developed. When Phoenicia was conquered by Assyria and later, Persia, Carthage became an independent city-state and developed its own trading empire.

Carthage was located in present-day Tunisia. It was ruled by two annually elected officials called *suffetes,* who were supported by a 300-man senate and a 104-man council. The Carthaginians worshipped a pantheon of deities, with Tanit and Baal Hammon as their two chief gods.

Carthage's massive trading fleet dominated western Mediterranean trade. The Carthaginians exported tin, lead, and silver to Spain and manufactured a raisin wine favored in Rome and Greece. They produced a purple dye called Tyrian purple that was worth its weight in gold. They also dealt in slaves and wheat from their farms in North Africa. Carthage developed a superb agricultural program; when the Romans destroyed the city, they salvaged an agricultural manual and had it translated into Latin.

The Great Fire of London

THE NIGHT OF SATURDAY, September 1, 1666, bakery owner Thomas Farynor made a simple oversight: He forgot to douse the fire in his oven, igniting what would become known as the Great Fire of London.

Soon after Farynor went to bed, a journeyman living above the bakery awoke to find the house filled with smoke. As the flames spread, Farynor and his family escaped through an upstairs window. A maid, too frightened to climb out, stayed in the house and became the first victim of the fire. Five days later, London lay in ruins.

Accidental fires were common in 17th-century London, but this blaze was aggravated by high winds. Flames ignited hay at the nearby Star Inn, then spread to the inn itself. Windblown sparks then set the Church of St. Margaret alight, and the fire proceeded to race through the city's closely packed buildings. The structures, many of them built of highly flammable wood and pitch, went up like tinder.

London had no central fire-fighting organization. Citizen efforts to create firebreaks by demolishing buildings in the path of the fire began too late. Fast-moving flames jumped the gaps before the firebreaks could be completely cleared. By morning, the fire had spread halfway across London Bridge.

The fire continued to burn for four days and nights, devastating the city. Londoners fled en masse, often after burying their valuables. As old St. Paul's cathedral burned, molten lead from the roof ran down the street in a stream. The Tower of London was saved by blasting large firebreaks.

The winds finally began to diminish on Wednesday, and the conflagration weakened. The last of the fire was extinguished Thursday night. Farynor's run-of-the-mill kitchen fire burned four-fifths of London and left up to 200,000 people homeless. More than 13,000 houses, 87 churches, and most of London's main buildings were gone. Miraculously, only five deaths were documented.

The fire actually had some benefits. It finally put an end to the Great Plague epidemic that had killed 100,000 Londoners the previous year. The fire also prompted long overdue changes in construction, city planning, and fire safety. Brick and stone replaced wood. Insurance companies, hoping to reduce future losses, created fire-fighting units. Impressive new structures, including the new St. Paul's Cathedral designed by architect Christopher Wren, were built. A new London rose from the ruins.

The European Union

Wһile тһe Soviet Union and Yugoslavia were breaking apart in the 1990s, the nations of Western Europe were fusing together into the European Union: a supranational, intergovernmental organization, designed to overcome nationalism.

The devastation Europe faced at the close of the Second World War, and the immediate rise of the Cold War, produced a desire for political and economic cooperation during the rebuilding process. Reconciliation between France and Germany, whose rivalry had been central to both world wars, was especially vital. Two French statesmen, Jean Monnet and Robert Schuman, proposed to institutionalize peace through policy coordination. Taking the first step toward that end, six Western European nations—France, West Germany, Italy, Belgium, the Netherlands, and Luxembourg—pooled their coal and steel production in 1951 to create a free trade area for these key industrial and military resources.

The European Coal and Steel Community proved a success, and the six states took more cooperative steps in 1957. Two treaties established a cooperative atomic energy policy (EURATOM) and eliminated trade barriers over goods and services (the European Economic Community). Gradually, more joint policy was developed, and more nations joined. The process culminated in the Treaty on European Union, also called the Maastricht Treaty, which took effect on November 1, 1993, officially founding the European Union.

The Brussels-based EU is run by a body of governing entities, which roughly parallels most democratic governments. Some of its institutions, including the Council of the European Union, are comprised of ministers who represent their governments officially. On the other hand, the elected members of the European Parliament and appointed officials of the European Commission act independent of their national governments.

The most visible achievement of the EU is the common European currency, the euro, which was introduced to the public in 2002. Equally far-reaching has been the elimination of border controls, allowing the free movement of people between European countries. European courts have accepted the EU's legal authority; in most cases, laws adopted by the EU supersede national laws with which they conflict. The continent's unification was brought closer by the inclusion of ten formerly Communist countries in 2004. However, French and Dutch voters rejected the proposed European Constitution, and it remains unclear how much sovereignty nations will be willing to surrender to the supranational group.

The Celts

T HE HISTORY OF THE CELTS abounds with myth, mystery, and contradiction. The forebearers of the Celts are believed to have come from what is now western Russia, migrating into central Europe by around 3000 B.C. Over the centuries, they occupied a vast area in what is now modern Europe: Greece, Spain, England, Wales, Scotland, and Ireland.

The Celts had no written language until late in their history. Their culture and tradition instead were preserved via oral tradition. They are first noted by the Greeks and Romans beginning about 500 B.C. The Celts were generally described as having dressed in bright colors. They were fair skinned with gold or red hair. The women wore their hair in complex braids and were seen as technically equal to men. They could own property, choose their own husbands, and even serve as war leaders.

A Celtic Wicker Man

The Celts were said to have held religious ceremonies in groves of trees or near sacred wells and springs. Druids, who appear to have been a class of priests and sages, acted as ambassadors, advisors, healers, and arbitrators in Celtic society. Though sharing a similar language, religion, and culture, the Celts did not have a central government. They settled for a loose tribal organization and were as content to fight among themselves as they were to battle outsiders.

Classical writers tended to depict the warlike Celts as barbarians, happiest when fighting and seeking glory and plunder, though the objectivity of these accounts is often suspect. Charging forward in light chariots, they would hurl spears, then dismount and slash at their enemies with swords. They were also enthusiastic collectors of enemy heads, displaying them on their doorposts and even carrying them on their belts.

According to lore, when they weren't fighting, the Celts were farmers. Their metalwork was highly advanced, and they were responsible for bringing ironworking and the iron plough to Britain.

In later years, the Celts were highly romanticized. The influence of their culture is felt to this day. However, it did contain a fatal flaw: The Celts simply could not stop fighting among themselves. Their inability to unite against common enemies, such as the Romans, prevented them from establishing a stable framework that might have saved them from being overwhelmed by more organized societies.

The Agricultural Revolution

A T THE BEGINNING of the 18th century, farming was based on a medieval system: large open fields where individual farmers cultivated strips of land and shared pastures for small numbers of domestic animals. Seed was scattered by hand. Higher yields were dependent on animal manure and leaving fields fallow on a two- to three-year cycle.

In England, the new spirit of innovation caused by the Enlightenment spilled over into agriculture and was encouraged by King George III, mockingly called "Farmer George." Inventors such as Jethro Tull introduced horse-drawn equipment including the seed drill. New fodder crops, including turnips and clover, were introduced, making it possible to increase the amount of livestock a farmer could keep and consequently the amount of manure. Experimentation with crop rotation meant that fields no longer needed to remain uncultivated for long periods of time. Robert Bakewell pioneered scientific stock-breeding, producing sheep that he described as "machines for turning grass into mutton," but that his detractors claimed were "too dear to buy and too fat to eat." Large landowners including Viscount "Turnip" Townsend and Thomas Coke (later Earl of Leicester) enthusiastically introduced new methods to their estates.

All of these developments required the highly controversial practice of fencing in formerly common lands, known as enclosure. This allowed progressive farmers to work on a larger scale, enjoy the benefits of mechanization, and implement extensive land drainage projects, making more land arable. Between two and three million acres of open fields and wasteland were enclosed in central Britain alone between 1760 and 1799, usually by act of Parliament rather than voluntary agreement. As fields were enclosed, woods and waste disappeared.

The merits of improved farming were widely publicized, most notably in Arthur Young's *Annals of Agriculture,* which began publication in 1784. The county of Norfolk, home of the so-called "new husbandry," was held up as a model of increased productivity and prosperity.

But increased productivity had social costs. Small farmers who depended on access to common lands no longer had the ability to keep a cow or pig. Contemporaries such as Oliver Goldsmith mourned the transformation of small, self-sufficient farmers to landless agricultural laborers and machine knitters. However, the Agricultural Revolution of the 18th century made the Industrial Revolution possible by increasing agricultural productivity and freeing the people from the land.

Charlemagne Crowned in Rome

THE WESTERN HALF of the Roman Empire was fairly over after A.D. 476. A Frankish kingdom emerged by the end of the fifth century, uniting much of modern-day France, Belgium, the Netherlands, and western Germany.

In 771, Charles assumed control of the entire Frankish kingdom. He fought a 32-year war with the Saxons in northwestern Germany before finally annexing their land by 805. When Pope Hadrian asked for help against the Lombards, Charles moved into what is modern-day northern Italy and defeated them, taking their territory. His troops also annexed Bavaria, and in the 790s his troops defeated the Avars in eastern Europe.

In 794, Charles built a new capital at Aachen, bringing craftsmen and artisans from throughout Europe to work there. He reformed the noble estates into a system that would be the basis for feudalism. He also kept tabs on his large territory by assigning commissioners to rove about the empire and report back on what they encountered. As time went on, he became known as Charles the Great, or Charlemagne in the vernacular.

On Christmas Day 800, Pope Leo III crowned Charlemagne emperor of the Romans. Charlemagne's coronation placed the pope under his protection and conferred great distinction on Charles, who was named the first Holy Roman Emperor.

The coronation also meant a decisive break with the Eastern Roman Empire, which considered itself the real Roman Empire. Despite the fact that it was ruled by Empress Irene at the time, a female ruler was considered anathema in the West. Thus, instead of looking east for stability, the pope decided to make a westerner heir to the glory of Rome. Thereafter, Greeks in Constantinople considered Charlemagne a usurper.

When Charlemagne died in 814, his son Louis inherited the empire. But Louis was weak, and the landed gentry became stronger, foreshadowing the development of feudalism. Slow transportation and a lack of bureaucracy to administer the empire, along with increasing Viking raids, led to the demise of Charlemagne's empire by the end of the ninth century.

The Ancient Hebrews and Monotheism

THE POLITICAL HISTORY of the ancient Hebrews is relatively unre- markable, as it was similar to that of the small desert kingdoms that surrounded their land. But it was their religion, characterized by belief in a single God, that gave them a prominent role in world history.

The Jews were one of the Semitic peoples who moved into Palestine in the 14th century B.C. during the decline of Pharaonic Egypt. Threatened by the formidable Philistine state, the confederation of Hebrew tribes formed the kingdom of Judea around 1000 B.C. under the leadership of Saul and, later, David. The kingdom reached its height under David's second son, Solomon. After Solomon's death, the kingdom divided into two states, Israel and Judah.

Scholars disagree about when monotheism became part of the Hebrew culture. According to tradition, Abraham made a covenant with his god, Yahweh, around 1800 B.C. Approximately 600 years later, Moses led a group of Hebrew tribesmen out of Egypt. He also renewed the covenant with Yahweh, binding his people to observe the divine decrees known as the Ten Commandments—including a promise that the Jewish people would worship only Yahweh. This move to monotheism was considered odd at a time when most religions and cults featured many deities.

As the Jews occupied Palestine and made the transition from nomads to farmers, their worship of Yahweh competed with local fertility cults. In response to this perceived threat, a series of prophets denounced the worship of other gods. Yahweh had always been a jealous god, the proph- ets said, and he is the only god. They asserted Yahweh's power over all mankind, Jewish or otherwise. They referred to the social injustices that had occurred throughout the development of the Judean monarchy and interpreted the fall of the Hebrew kingdoms as Yahweh's punishment of a faithless people.

Judaism took its definitive form a century after the Babylonian exile, when leaders Nehemiah (ca. 444 B.C.) and Ezra (ca. 347 B.C.) reorganized the worship of Yahweh. Today, monotheism is the crux of other major religions; Christianity and Islam share the worship of a single god with their Hebrew brethren.

The Montgomery Bus Boycott

O N DECEMBER 1, 1955, four blacks sat in the fifth row of a bus in Montgomery, Alabama—the first four rows were reserved for whites. When a white man expressed that he wished to sit in their row, the bus driver ordered the four blacks to move back. Three complied, but the fourth did not.

Rosa Parks being fingerprinted in 1956

The dissenter was Rosa Parks, a seamstress who also was the secretary of the NAACP's Montgomery chapter. She was arrested, fingerprinted, and fined a total of $14. Her refusal spawned a social movement that ultimately toppled America's edifice of legal white supremacy.

A boycott actually had been planned by the president of the local chapter of the NAACP prior to Park's arrest. Earlier, 15-year-old Claudette Colvin had been arrested for refusing to give up her seat, the chapter refused to press her case when she was found to be pregnant.

An organization called the Montgomery Improvement Association was created, and Rev. Martin Luther King, Jr., was chosen as the leader. King endorsed a compromise proposal that accepted black and white sections for the bus but demanded that when the white section was oversubscribed, whites would have to stand. Blacks would not be forced to give up their seats to whites. They also demanded more courteous treatment from bus drivers and that blacks be employed as bus drivers.

Instead of riding the bus, boycotters biked, walked, hitchhiked, and organized carpools. Across the nation black churches raised money and collected shoes for the Montgomery protesters. The boycott lasted 381 days.

In retaliation for the boycott, four black churches were firebombed, as were some homes, including King's. Under a 1921 law, 156 blacks were arrested for "hindering" a bus. On June 4, 1956, the federal district court ruled that Alabama's racial segregation laws for buses were unconstitutional. Although an appeals court kept the law intact, on November 13, 1956, the Supreme Court upheld the lower court's ruling. A city ordinance was passed allowing blacks to sit anywhere they wanted, and the boycott officially ended December 21, 1956.

Buffon's *The Epochs of Nature*

SCHOOLCHILDREN THE WORLD OVER recognize the name of famed naturalist Charles Darwin. Fewer are probably familiar with Darwin's predecessor, French naturalist Georges-Louis Leclerc, Comte de Buffon. A naturalist, mathematician, biologist, cosmologist, and author, Buffon's work helped change the way science views the world.

Buffon was born in 1707 at Montbard, Cote-d'Or, the son of the Lord of Dijon and Montbard. His first accomplishments were in the mathematical field, joining the French Academy of Sciences at age 27. His studies were wide-ranging: He kept wild animals at his home to research their behavior, he examined microscopic organisms, and he conducted experiments to determine the age of Earth.

Some of his conclusions were considered startling for the time. He considered the possibility of common ancestry between humans and apes and disputed the common theory that humankind consisted of different species. He also noted that different regions have distinct plants and animals and speculated that species were capable of change—an early step toward the theory of evolution.

He wrote about the solar system in 1778's *Les Époques de la Nature* (*The Epochs of Nature*). Using his experiments with heating and cooling iron spheres, he publicly stated that he determined that Earth was at least 75,000 years old—although privately he believed it to be older. "For 35,000 years our globe has only been a mass of heat and fire which no sensible being could get close," he wrote. "Then, for 15,000 or 20,000 years, its surface was only a universal sea." Humans were relative newcomers, he maintained.

Not all of Buffon's theories were on the right track, and many were considered radical. He deduced, for instance, that the planets had been formed from debris after a comet crashed into the sun. This nonbiblical theory of creation brought about pressure from the Faculty of Theology of Paris for him to recant. Buffon obliged, remarking to a friend, "It is better to be humble than hung." Still, his theories offered a transition point and foreshadowed some of the most important theories in the natural sciences—including those of Charles Darwin.

His life's work was included in the multivolume *L'Histoire Naturelle,* in which he hoped to cover everything known about the natural world at the time. Though he worked 14-hour days into his old age, he managed to publish only 36 of the proposed 50 volumes before his death in 1788. Another eight volumes were published posthumously.

Building the Berlin Wall

WHILE MANY COUNTRIES FACE the problem of trying to limit the intake of new citizens, during the mid-20th century East Germany had the opposite problem. In 1961, East German leader Walter Ulbricht watched as thousands of his people fled to West Berlin. People had been running to the West for years, especially after the 1953 crackdown on a workers' uprising. The West offered far more cultural and economic choices, as well as more freedoms. Within the first seven months of 1961, more than 160,000 refugees were counted crossing over.

The concept of the Berlin Wall dated back to the beginning of the Cold War, not long after the end of World War II. Germany was divided up into four zones, each one controlled by an Allied Power: American, British, French, and Soviet. The city of Berlin, deep in the Soviet zone, was also divided by the four parties.

As the Cold War escalated, however, the French, British, and American zones formed the Federal Republic of Germany, taking West Berlin with them. At the same time, the Soviets formed the German Democratic Republic, taking East Berlin. The city was divided—first geographically, and then culturally and economically.

Although Ulbricht said in June 1961 that he had no personal knowledge of any plan to build a wall dividing Berlin, two months later the government began putting up barbed wire and antitank obstacles. Streets were dug up, and stone barricades were put into place. Railway service between the East and West stopped. The government announced its plan for an "Anti-fascist protection wall," which evolved into the Berlin Wall. The tall, concrete wall had a lighted control area known as the "death area," where any refugee caught approaching it was shot on sight. A trench was built so vehicles could not crash through the wall. The entire area was monitored by watchdogs, watchtowers, and guards.

Life in East Berlin was very harsh. People could not own property, and food was scarce. Families became desperate and often risked their lives in an attempt to get past the wall. People tried to reach the other side in many creative ways, including hiding inside secret compartments in cars, flying in hot air balloons, swimming Berlin canals, or tunneling underground. Very few succeeded, and many died. Although estimates vary widely, historians believe that between 1961 and 1989 as many as 1,000 people were killed at the Berlin Wall.

Attila the Hun Defeated at Chalons

B Y THE EARLY FOURTH CENTURY A.D., the western half of the Roman Empire had been overrun by barbarian invasions. Gaul (France) was occupied by Burgundians, Franks, and Visigoths (who had also moved into Spain). Meanwhile, the Vandals conquered North Africa.

In the 430s, Roman general Aetius returned to Italy after a self-imposed exile, during which he had stayed with a Hun tribe. A large army of Huns accompanied him back to Italy to support the Roman leader Johannes. Aetius was restored to his former rank and given command of the Roman army.

Meanwhile, Attila coruled the Huns along with his elder brother, Bleda. In 445, Attila killed Bleda, securing his place as king. His leadership united several feuding Hun tribes into a larger entity. Using their military might, Attila brought together an enormous empire in Eastern and Central Europe. The Huns swept into the Eastern Roman Empire on two occasions, ravaging the Balkans before the Romans finally paid tribute to end the attacks.

Attila then set his sights on the West. Through a series of misunderstandings, Attila demanded that Roman Emperor Valentinian III's sister be his bride. The emperor refused, and using the rejection as one of many pretexts for battle, Attila's massive army of Huns attacked in early 451. All opposition was swept aside as his horde swept through northern Gaul. In retaliation, Aetius gathered an army of Roman infantry and cavalry, aided by thousands of Germanic soldiers, specifically Franks and Visigoths.

Attila was attacking Orleans when Aetius approached with Theodoric, king of the Visigoths, on a mid-June day. The Huns withdrew until their entire army was assembled and took position near the town of Chalons on the Marne River. A bloody battle ensued. Theodoric was slain during the fighting, but his men rallied and helped drive the Huns back to their fortified camp. The fighting ended at nightfall, and Attila withdrew his troops entirely the next day.

Attila's reputation as the leader of an invincible army was shot. He died in 453, and his empire quickly fell apart as his sons fought for control. By the 470s, the Huns had ceased to exist as a separate people.

The Communist Takeover of China

THE BEGINNING OF THE CHINESE CIVIL WAR dates to 1927 when Chiang Kai-shek purged the Communists from the Kuomintang (KMT) party following the death of Sun Yat-sen. Concerned about the rising influence of the Chinese Communist Party in his organization, Chiang ordered hundreds of Communists and KMT leftists arrested and executed.

Chiang's government received international recognition when the KMT captured Beijing in 1928. Communist leader Mao Zedong retreated to remote Jiangxi Province, where he established a Soviet Chinese Republic. In late 1934, faced with defeat at the hands of Chiang's forces, Mao and 80,000 others fled in the subsequent "Long March."

Chiang's domination seemed assured. However, when the Japanese seized Manchuria and subsequently invaded China in 1937, the Communists and the KMT reluctantly suspended hostilities to form a Second United Front against the Japanese. There wasn't much "unity," as both sides knew the civil war would eventually resume and were not anxious to expend resources fighting Japan. In the end, the agreement benefited Mao more than Chiang. The Communists had a chance to recoup, while the KMT, closer to the coastal areas, suffered more heavily from Japanese operations.

By the time Japan surrendered in 1945, the KMT military had been badly weakened. Popular sentiment had also warmed toward the Communists, whose guerrilla warfare in rural areas was the only noticeable opposition to Japanese brutality. The corruption and inefficiency of Chiang's government was also a factor in the shift. Communist strength also grew to tens of thousands thanks to disaffected Nationalist troops—many from the armies of toppled Chinese warlords—who joined Mao in large numbers. The collapse of Japanese forces on the mainland ensured there would be no shortage of weaponry for the new recruits.

American efforts to arrange a cease-fire between the two sides and build a coalition government failed, and full-scale war broke out again in June 1946. Despite American aid, the demoralized Nationalists were on the run by late 1948. Beijing fell without a fight on January 31, 1949. The Nationalist capital of Nanjing fell April 23.

On October 1, Mao proclaimed the People's Republic of China. Chiang, along with 600,000 troops and two million civilians retreated to the island of Taiwan where the Republic of China remains today.

William Penn (1644–1718)

WILLIAM PENN was the most famous member of the Religious Society of Friends, or Quakers, during the American colonial era. At the time, the Quaker religion was fairly new. It taught that everyone had an inner light, which allowed followers to find their own way to God. They had no ordained clergy, and anyone could speak at a church meeting. Men and women were considered equal. Quakers were pacifists, refused to take oaths in court, and wore plain clothing. They were also heavily persecuted by the Anglican Church.

According to some accounts, Penn asked King Charles II to be awarded a colony in North America for his family's service to the crown. Penn named it Pennsylvania, which means "Penn's Woods," in honor of his father Sir William Penn. He viewed the colony as a "Holy Experiment" where there would be religious tolerance for all. The first settlers began arriving in 1681; Penn arrived a year later to establish the colony's new capital, Philadelphia. The city was a model with streets arranged in a grid and named for trees rather than famous people. It was also a green city, featuring large parks for the benefit of its residents.

Penn advertised his new colony across Europe, and as a result, a wide variety of people immigrated to Pennsylvania. Large numbers of Welsh immigrants and Scots-Irish Presbyterians arrived and went out to the expanding western frontier of the colony. Thousands of Amish and Mennonites left Germany, settling to farm the rich soil west of Philadelphia.

Penn also respected the Native Americans. He entered into treaties to purchase land from them, listened to their concerns, and treated their leaders with respect. Because of this, Pennsylvania avoided the armed conflicts with Native Americans that were prevalent in many other English colonies. The Penn family kept ownership of Pennsylvania until its induction into statehood in 1787.

POSTSCRIPT

■ The 37-foot-tall bronze statue of William Penn atop Philadelphia City Hall is the tallest statue on top of any building in the world. It was also the tallest point in the city until 1987, when the One Liberty Place skyscraper exceeded the statue's height.

■ The boundary between Pennsylvania and Maryland was long disputed and was finally surveyed in 1763. The resulting Mason–Dixon Line was long considered the dividing line between the North and South.

Mikhail Gorbachev (1931–present)

BORN INTO A PEASANT FAMILY, Mikhail Gorbachev earned his law degree at Moscow University and joined the Communist Party in 1952. He gained the attention of high-ranking Soviet officials as head of the Stavropol region's agriculture department. In 1971, he was elected to the Central Committee and became a full Politburo member in 1980. In March 1985, he was elected general secretary, making him the de facto head of the USSR.

Gorbachev was disillusioned with the traditionally structured Soviet approach to the economy, feeling that it only perpetuated stagnation. He was determined to make the Soviet system less rigid and more democratic and efficient. His policies were reflected in two famous phrases: *glasnost* (openness or liberalization) and *perestroika* (reform).

Glasnost relaxed previous restrictions on freedom of speech and the press. It also brought about the release of thousands of political prisoners and dissidents held by the old regime. Gorbachev hoped open discussion and debate would help garner popular support for his reforms. Among his most radical economic reforms was the 1988 Law on Cooperatives. The law allowed private business ownership in certain sectors and permitted more autonomy, sowing the seeds of capitalism in the Soviet economy. Gorbachev also recognized that the arms race was a huge drain on the Soviet economy and called for arms control agreements with the West.

In 1990, Gorbachev received the Nobel Peace Prize. He was also elected as the first president of the Soviet Union by the Congress of People's Deputies. Ironically, he would also be the last president. Though he was hailed in the West for his reforms, Gorbachev's efforts were not well received by the old-school Soviet members of the Communist party. Meanwhile, radicals felt reform was not moving fast enough. Perhaps Gorbachev's biggest mistake was his failure to recognize how glasnost would contribute to breakaway nationalist sentiment in the Soviet Union's member states.

By this time the Soviet Union was in the process of collapsing. The Eastern Bloc had already disintegrated, and the core Soviet states were breaking away, caught in the grip of ethnic and nationalistic movements. During a single month in 1991, 11 states declared independence. The Soviet Union was doomed. Gorbachev resigned on December 25, 1991. The USSR formally dissolved the next day.

Today Gorbachev remains an outspoken figure on domestic and foreign affairs.

Saint Loyola and the Jesuits

IGNATIUS LOYOLA was one of the great Catholic thinkers who helped change the church in response to the Protestant Reformation. Born in Spain in 1491, Loyola was of noble birth and trained for military service. Influenced by the religious reading he had done while recuperating from a wound, Loyola decided in 1522 to make a pilgrimage to Montserrat, near Barcelona. During his stay, he had a vision and decided to dedicate his life to God and the church.

Loyola was inspired to write *Spiritual Exercises,* a 200-page book that detailed a four-week course in meditation and prayer designed to bring the reader closer to the Catholic Church. Historians have called Loyola's manuscript a textbook for militant Catholicism, and, indeed, as the Catholic Counter-Reformation got underway, Loyola became one of its leaders.

Loyola began attending the University of Paris in 1528. Six years later, Loyola and five companions took vows of poverty and celibacy; Loyola became a priest, serving the poor and needy and helping in hospitals. Loyola and his friends approached the pope, placed themselves at his disposal, and began creating plans for a formal society called the Company of Jesus. The papacy officially recognized the society in 1540, and Loyola set out to help reform the church.

Initiates into the society worked through the *Spiritual Exercises.* After two years, they took vows of poverty, celibacy, and obedience, after which they were called *scholastici.* The best of the scholastici were sent to learn in colleges founded by the order. The Jesuits, as they came to be known, stressed education as a way to improve the clergy, which would in turn lead to more effective priests.

After 12 years in the Company of Jesus, scholastici were ordained as priests, taking a fourth vow of absolute obedience to the pope. Loyola became the first superior general of the Jesuits and supervised the rapid growth of his order. Jesuit missionaries traveled to the New World, Africa, and Asia, and had a profound influence on the reforms of the church. Loyola was canonized in 1622. Today there are more than 4,000 Jesuit-run schools and colleges worldwide.

The Travels of Marco Polo

IN HIS BOOK *The Travels of Marco Polo,* Polo tells of his extensive travels to and around China during the rule of Kublai Khan in the 13th century. Since then, it has remained an international best seller.

In 1260, Marco Polo's father and uncle left Venice on a routine trading voyage to the Crimea. Caught in a war between two Mongol rulers, the brothers found themselves stranded in Bukhara for three years. A Mongolian diplomat eventually rescued them and took them to the great Mongolian military leader Kublai Khan, who was curious about the West. After a year at Khan's court, they returned to Europe with the Khan's passport in the form of a golden tablet and a letter asking the pope to send Khan 100 European scholars.

In 1271, the brothers returned to China, this time taking along 17-year-old Marco. Traveling overland along the Silk Road, they arrived at the Chinese court four years later. Marco became a favorite of the Khan, who sent the young Venetian on diplomatic missions to Persia, India, and Southeast Asia. Marco traveled throughout China on the Khan's business, served on the Privy Council, and was the tax collector for the city of Yanzhou for three years. Although he never learned Chinese, he became fluent in both Persian and Mongolian, the languages of the ruling classes.

After 17 years, Khan reluctantly allowed the Polos to leave China. Again, with the golden passport as protection, they traveled as escorts for a Mongol princess. First they sailed to Persia by way of Sumatra and southern India and then traveled overland to Constantinople. The Polos finally reached Venice in 1295, carrying with them a fortune in precious stones.

The next year, Marco was captured by the Genoese, and he spent a year in prison. One of his fellow prisoners was a writer of romances, who urged Marco to record the story of his travels. Known at the time as *Il Milione* (*The Million Lies*), Marco Polo's *Travels* became one of the most popular books in medieval Europe.

Marco Polo described it best himself when he wrote, "I believe it was God's will that we should come back, so that men might know the things that are in the world, since, as we have said in the first chapter of this book, no other man, Christian or Saracen, Mongol or pagan, has explored so much of the world as Messer Marco, son of Messer Niccolo Polo, great and noble citizen of the city of Venice."

The Founding of the Dominion of Canada

AN INDEPENDENT COUNTRY often gets its start when an empire gives up governing control of a colony—usually after a bloody battle. The 1867 founding of the Dominion of Canada proved a notable exception.

As a result of losing the French and Indian War to England in 1763, France gave up virtually all of its North American colonies. Thousands of resentful French Canadians suddenly found themselves living under minority British rule.

In response to thousands of pro-British colonists fleeing to Canada and settling there at the conclusion of the American Revolution, the British split the country into Upper and Lower Canada in 1791. This created two territories: one primarily English speaking and the other French Canadian (now Ontario and Quebec, respectively). The dividing line was the Ottawa River.

Unhappiness over this system resulted in a rebellion in both Upper and Lower Canada in 1837, and another in Lower Canada in 1838. Although they were suppressed, they pointed to an underlying need for political change. That year, Britain appointed Lord Durham governor general and high commissioner of Canada. In a report, he recommended the two territories be reunited and encouraged British immigration so that English culture would assimilate the French. He also suggested a legislative assembly elected by the people (and dominated by English-speaking peoples) and that the governor general be reduced to a figurehead.

In 1840, Canada was reunited. On July 1, 1867, the Constitution Act of 1867 (also known as the British North America Act) united the British colonies of New Brunswick, Nova Scotia, and Canada into the self-governing Dominion of Canada. The act divided power between the national parliament and the provinces in a combination of England's parliamentary governmental model and federalism. In addition, although no specific Bill of Rights was included in the act, it was held to contain an Implied Bill of Rights that said provincial legislation couldn't intrude on freedoms of speech, religion, association, or assembly. It was considered that protection of these rights, though not specified, was implied by Canada's Constitution, as per the 1867 act.

Thus governing power was transferred bloodlessly from mother country to former colony.

The Stalin Purges

AN EARLY ACTIVIST in the Bolshevik movement, Joseph Stalin triumphed over his rivals for control of the Communist Party following the death of Vladimir Lenin in 1924. Within four years, he had emerged as the supreme Soviet leader and launched his Five-Year Plans

to collectivize agriculture. When farmers in Ukraine resisted, Stalin engineered a famine by raising grain quotas to unattainable levels. Between six and seven million people died. Other opponents disappeared into Soviet *gulags (*labor camps).

Stalin's methods were opposed by many, including party leader Sergei Kirov, who was assassinated in December 1934. Afterward, Stalin launched a purge of supposed spies and counterrevolutionaries, taking advantage of the opportunity to remove anyone who might present a threat to his authority. Several show trials speedily disposed of many prominent former revolutionaries, now deemed "enemies of the state," including Lev Kamenev, Grigory Zinoviev, and Nikolay Bukharin. Most of those prosecuted were executed.

Fearing resistance from the military, Stalin extended the purge to the army in 1937. The victims included eight top Red Army commanders, all of whom were accused of plotting with Germany against the state. Thousands in the lower ranks also fell victim to Stalin's paranoia, including about half of the officer corps.

The purges spun out of control as ordinary citizens were swept up in the madness. Tens of thousands were accused of treasonable thoughts and executed or sent to gulags by the dreaded NKVD (secret police). Farmers, priests, and people who had relatives living abroad were all targeted. More than a third of the party members in Ukraine—as many as 170,000 people—were "purged," as were the top 17 ministers of the Ukrainian Soviet government.

The exact toll will never be known, but it is estimated that about 500,000 people were executed just between 1937 and 1939, and somewhere between 3 and 12 million people were sent to labor camps. Ironically, the top leaders of the NKVD, who had worked so enthusiastically on Stalin's behalf, were among the last victims of the purges.

The 1918 Influenza Epidemic

BY 1918, millions of soldiers had died in the carnage of the First World War. They were soon to be joined by millions of other men, women, and children who would not be the victims of bullets but of a mysterious plague that became known as the Great Influenza Epidemic.

The first signs of trouble appeared in March at U.S. Army Fort Riley in Kansas. In less than two weeks, many officers and men stationed there had mysteriously fallen ill, and large numbers were dying.

The disease spread rapidly across the country. So many people died in Philadelphia that by mid-October the city issued an appeal for volunteer grave diggers. More than 2,300 Chicagoans died in one week. The New York phone company asked subscribers to use the telephone only for emergencies since many of its operators were either sick or dying. Morgues overflowed, and there were not enough coffins for the sheer numbers of dead.

In a situation reminiscent of the Black Death of the Middle Ages, the influenza refused to respond to any known medical treatment. An exposed person typically became sick within three days and suffered a fever for up to five days. The killer, it later turned out, was not the flu itself, but the complications—usually pneumonia—that attacked the weakened immune system. With none of today's wonder drugs or vaccines to combat the initial infection or resulting complications, victims of the sickness were doomed. "They actually drowned in their own fluids," recalled a nurse.

The epidemic killed an estimated 550,000 Americans. But it was not confined to the United States—victims died in European cities, Eskimo villages, and remote parts of Africa. The numbers are staggering: India, 1.9 million dead; England, 200,000; Japan, 250,000; Italy, 350,000; Spain, 165,000; Mexico, 500,000; and Canada, 44,000. The disease finally reached its peak in November and then vanished just as mysteriously as it came.

In 1933, using an electronic microscope, the deadly organism was identified as a filterable virus capable of many mutations. Its exact origin is unknown, though it was widely called Spanish Influenza due to early outbreaks in that country. Whatever its origin, in less than a year it killed at least 40 million people worldwide—more than twice the estimated number of casualties from World War I.

The Birth of Buddhism

B UDDHISM BEGAN IN INDIA sometime between 550 and 450 B.C. It was initially one of a number of ascetic sects that challenged the religious authority of the Brahmans, the Indian religious texts known as the Vedas, and the inevitable cycle of rebirth based on *karma* and *dharma*.

Siddhartha Gautama (ca. 560–482 B.C.), known as the *Buddha* or "enlightened one," was the son of a chieftain in what is present-day Nepal. He gave up family life to become an ascetic when he was age 29. Several years later, he became the leader of a group of wandering mendicants who pursued a "Middle Way" between extreme asceticism and worldly life. He spent the next four or five decades teaching a small group of followers.

Buddha taught that the way to end suffering was to follow the Eightfold Path: the right view, right intention, right speech, right action, right livelihood, right effort, right mindfulness, and right concentration. The ultimate goal is *nirvana*: the extinction of individual desires and the absorption of the self into the infinite.

Between the time of the Buddha's death and the conversion of Ashoka, the great Buddhist emperor of India, Buddhism developed from a small sect of ascetics into a religion with numerous lay followers. A canon of sacred texts developed and stories regarding the life of the Buddha grew. Buddhist monks began to settle in monasteries.

The spread of Buddhism received a great impetus under Ashoka. During his reign, Buddhist monasteries flourished and missionaries carried the Buddhist message throughout India and into Sri Lanka. With time, Buddhism expanded beyond the Indian subcontinent to Tibet, Southeast Asia, China, and Japan.

Buddhism in India was destroyed by the waves of Muslims who invaded north India, beginning around A.D. 1000. Mounted raiding parties in search of plunder sacked the wealthy monasteries, and thousands of monks were killed or driven into Tibet. Buddhism did not reappear in India until 1956, when the *dalit* (untouchable) leader, Dr. Bhimrao Ramji Ambedkar, and several thousand of his followers converted to Buddhism as a means of stepping outside the caste system. Today those who follow Buddhism number in the millions.

The South Sea Bubble

To give it a modern comparison, one could refer to the South Sea Bubble as the "Enron of England."

One of history's most notorious market collapses, the South Sea Bubble had its roots in Britain's huge national debt of the early 1700s. In 1711, the government struck a deal with the South Seas Company; the company would finance the national debt in return for 6 percent interest and exclusive trading rights in the South Seas. Company directors believed they would be able to monopolize the slave trade and market British goods in South America for gold and jewels.

Stock was issued, and the shares were quickly snapped up by eager investors. More stock was issued and it, too, sold rapidly. Speculation—buying and selling despite high risk—was rampant, encouraged by hype and misinformation from the company management.

By 1718, Britain and Spain were again at war, interrupting trade with South America. Investors continued to scramble for South Seas Company stock, but management now realized that company operations weren't generating any profits—all the money coming in was from the sale of stock, which was stupendously overvalued. Company leaders got out while the getting was good and quietly sold their stock.

As word leaked out, panicked investors tried to sell their stock, as well. But now there were no buyers, only sellers. Fortunes disappeared overnight. The disaster brought about a general stock market crash.

An investigation uncovered large-scale fraud and corruption, including fictitious entries in the company books. Among those implicated was Chancellor of the Exchequer John Aislabie, who was expelled from the House of Commons and imprisoned. The estates of the company directors were confiscated with most of the proceeds going to the victims of the bubble, but the money was only a fraction of what had been lost.

Victims included everyone from members of Parliament to pensioners who had traded their government annuities for stock. The scandal became inspiration for countless satires, cartoons, and songs about knavery and greed. Among the victims of the bubble was Jonathan Swift, who went on to satirize English society in his classic work *Gulliver's Travels*. Another famous victim was Sir Isaac Newton, who lost 20,000 pounds of his fortune.

It took the British economy 100 years to fully recover from the collapse.

The First Punic War

BLAME IT ON THE MAMERTINES. Sometime in the 280s B.C., this group of Italian mercenaries seized control of the city of Messana in Sicily, igniting the first war between Rome and Carthage. Their exploits garnered the attention of neighboring Syracuse, who attacked them sometime between 270 and 264. The Mamertines called for help from both Rome and Carthage. The Carthaginians sent troops in a timely manner; the Romans also intervened because they did not want Carthage to control the straits between Italy and Sicily. Years later, Roman troops moved into Sicily and defeated the Carthaginians, whose Latin name was *Punici.*

Rome had the better army, but initially Carthage had the better naval fleet. In response, the Romans invented the *corvus,* a long wooden plank with an iron spike underneath its far end. When adjacent to a ship, this plank was lowered, and the spike stuck into the enemy vessel to allow Roman soldiers to board and capture their opponents.

After defeating the enemy fleet, the Romans invaded Africa in 256. Carthage was forced to seek peace, but the Roman commander's terms were harsh, and the war continued. Carthage eventually hired a mercenary general from Sparta named Xanthippus, who, in 255, defeated the Romans and captured their commander at a battle southwest of Tunis. A Roman fleet rescued the remnants of the army but was ultimately destroyed in a storm on its way back to Italy.

The war dragged on with neither side being able to drive the other off of Sicily. One Roman fleet was defeated; other fleets were decimated due to storms. But Rome had more resources to draw upon than did Carthage, and so it simply built another fleet. Despite Rome's setbacks, Carthaginian commander Hamilcar Barca still did not have enough men to conquer the island.

In 241, the Romans besieged two Sicilian cities, forcing the Carthaginians to send a fleet with reinforcements. This time, the Romans won a decisive victory off the Aegates Islands near Sicily's northwest coast. Carthage sought peace terms by surrendering Sicily and agreeing to pay tribute to Rome for the next 20 years.

POSTSCRIPT

■ The Roman navy improved after a beached Carthaginian vessel was seized by the Romans and used as a model for future warships.

The Construction of Versailles

L OCATED JUST A FEW MILES outside Paris, the Palace of Versailles—known for its magnificent grounds and fabulous Hall of Mirrors—was the creation of King Louis XIV, the so-called "Sun King."

Louis had been enthralled with Versailles since childhood, when the palace was still a small royal hunting lodge. In 1669, he decided to transform it into a decadent palace surrounded by fountains and expansive gardens. Thousands of laborers drained swamps and graded the land. Architect Louis Le Vau oversaw design of the palace, and gardener Andre Le Notre created the lavish gardens. A 70-acre artificial pond called the Grand Canal was created. A hydraulic machine pumped water from the Seine River to an elaborate system of underground reservoirs and aqueducts to feed the hundreds of fountains.

One highlight was the Hall of Mirrors. Measuring more than 73 meters long, the hall featured 17 windows opening onto the gardens. The inside wall was lined with beveled mirrors—an expensive luxury—to reflect the view.

Work on the palace would continue for years. On May 6, 1682, Louis moved the royal court and government to Versailles, transforming the palace into the political and administrative center of France. The Sun King's motives went beyond his love for Versailles itself. By bringing the nobility to the new palace, Louis was able to keep a watchful eye on potential rivals. Stripped of any real political power, the nobles passed their time on empty diversions and devoted their energies to an elaborate —and vacuous—system of courtly etiquette for social advancement.

Versailles also served to remove Louis from the French people, though the palace was open to the public on various days of the week. Citizens could come and gape at the art and even watch the king have supper.

Meanwhile, "the other France" was much less resplendent. Beyond Versailles existed hunger, poverty, and social unrest directed toward a tax system that placed the heaviest burden on those who had the least. Louis, who died in 1715, would not pay the price for his many extravagances—that would be done by Louis XVI, on the guillotine during the French Revolution decades later.

The First Transatlantic Cable

IN THE MID-19TH CENTURY, it took six weeks by ship to get a message from the United States to England. Then American businessman Cyrus Field got the idea of laying a telegraph cable across the Atlantic.

Field's interest was sparked when Canadian engineer Frederick Gisborne proposed a telegraph line connecting New York and Newfoundland. Field noticed how close Newfoundland was to Ireland, and wondered if putting a cable across the Atlantic Ocean was possible. He founded a company to lay the cable, but by the time the cable was finally in place in 1856, the company had spent all its resources.

Undaunted, Field secured support from the British government and began selling stock in the Atlantic Telegraph Company. He then contracted for 2,500 miles of coated copper submarine cable. Sheathed in tarred hemp and iron wire, the cable weighed more than one ton per nautical mile. Initial efforts to lay the cable from Ireland's southwest coast began in August 1857 but were abandoned after the cable broke.

Field tried again the next summer, this time using the cable-laying vessels USS *Niagara* and HMS *Agamemnon,* which met in the mid-Atlantic on June 26. The cable was spliced together and the ships headed their separate ways, one toward Ireland and one toward Newfoundland. Once again, the attempt was foiled by breaks in the cable. Finally, on July 29, the vessels tried once more; this time the cable went out smoothly. The ships went their separate ways with their load of cable; the *Niagara* arrived in Newfoundland on August 4, and the *Agamemnon* arrived at Valentia Island, Ireland, on August 5.

On August 16, Queen Victoria sent a congratulatory telegram to U.S. President James Buchanan over the line. The president replied, calling the achievement "far more useful to mankind, than was ever won by conqueror on the field of battle."

The jubilation, however, was short-lived. The cable was poorly designed—it took more than 16 hours to transmit the Queen's message—and over time the quality continued to deteriorate. Field's chief electrical engineer tried to improve transmission by sending more electricity through the wire, but only succeeded in burning it out. By September, the cable was dead.

The cable became an object of derision. Some writers even insinuated the whole thing had been a hoax. Field did not give up and worked to raise more funding. In 1866, an improved cable was successfully laid. Others soon followed; by 1900, there were 15 cables crossing the Atlantic.

Bauhaus

IN 1919, the Grand Duke of Saxe-Weimar invited German architect Walter Gropius to start a school of design in Weimar. Originally named the Staatliches Bauhaus Weimar, it became known as the Bauhaus. Its curriculum embraced all the applied and visual arts, as implied by its name, simply translated as "House of Building."

Gropius believed that the base of all art began in handcraft, and he sought to create a new guild of craftsmen. In its early years, the Bauhaus specialized in teaching art, design, and the applied arts in a workshop system that required students to make objects as well as design them. The Bauhaus was unique for using well-known artists as instructors—most notably Paul Klee and Vassily Kandinsky—in what was essentially a school of architecture and design, with a policy that intended to break down the distinction between fine and applied arts.

In 1923, the Bauhaus moved beyond its original "Arts and Crafts" roots to embrace industrial technology and explore its implications for design. The school's workshops began to create prototypes for mass production.

In 1925, Gropius's bold use of new building materials and innovative architectural methods was condemned as "architectural socialism," and the Bauhaus was forced to move from Weimar to Dessau. The move provided an opportunity to create a new building more appropriate for its activities. Designed by Gropius, the structure is an asymmetrical combination of "boxes" that pushed prewar techniques of industrial construction to new limits.

When Hitler came to power, Mies van der Rohe, the school's director at the time, moved the Bauhaus to Berlin; he finally closed it in 1933 rather than submit to Nazi interference. Many teachers from the Bauhaus fled to the United States, where László Mooly-Nagy founded the New Bauhaus in Chicago in 1937, a precursor of the Illinois Institute of Technology.

The Bauhaus had an immediate effect in Germany through its method of teaching and through the production of domestic items designed in its studios. The Bauhaus International Style of architecture became influential after World War II, especially in the United States.

The Jones Act

THE 1917 JONES ACT supposedly settled the issue of Puerto Rico as it relates to the United States. Yet, almost a century later, the relationship between the United States and Puerto Rico remains cloudy.

Puerto Rico was a Spanish colony until the brief Spanish-American War in 1898. In the peace that followed, the victorious United States received several Spanish land possessions, including the island nation of Puerto Rico. Some Puerto Ricans were hopeful that the United States would follow the same route with Puerto Rico as it had with territories such as Wyoming and Utah, both of which became states.

However, those hopes were dashed when the United States passed the Foraker Law (officially known as the Organic Act of 1900), which established a limited civil government in Puerto Rico. The U.S. president appointed the island's governor and all cabinet officials. An elected assembly called the House of Delegates was limited to debates and making recommendations, and it was able to pass laws. Puerto Rico could send one elected delegate to the U.S. House of Representatives, but the delegate's power was limited to speech-making and recommendations.

Puerto Rico's single delegate, Luis M. Rivera, made the most of it. He served from 1911 to 1916, and in his numerous speeches he eloquently pled for greater rights. In 1917, Congress passed the Jones-Shafroth Act (commonly known as the Jones Act) to give Puerto Rico more say in its governing. Most significantly, it bestowed statutory American citizenship on Puerto Ricans and allowed island citizens to elect members to both its legislative houses. It also revised the island's governmental structure.

Still, nationalistic fever continued in Puerto Rico. In late October 1950, nationalist rebels tried to launch an armed revolt in Puerto Rico. Though the rebellion was quickly defeated, two nationalists who wanted to highlight the plight of Puerto Rico made their way to Washington, D.C., in a failed attempt to assassinate President Harry Truman. In 1952, Puerto Rico became a self-governing Commonwealth of the United States.

Today Puerto Rico is a curious hybrid as a governmental entity within the United States. In many respects, it is the same as a U.S. state, but because Puerto Rico is not actually a state, U.S. citizens residing there are not enfranchised. Though its citizens do not usually pay federal income tax, they do pay federal payroll taxes. Puerto Ricans are eligible for Social Security, but they are excluded from Supplemental Security Income. The debate over Puerto Rico's status continues to this day.

The *Iliad*

Composed sometime around 750 B.C. by the blind Greek poet Homer, the *Iliad* tells the story of a few weeks during the ninth year of the Trojan War.

The war had begun between approximately 1190 and 1180 B.C., when Paris, a Trojan prince, stole Helen, the beautiful wife of Menelaus, king of Sparta. In retaliation, the Greek city-states elected King Agamemnon of Mycenae leader of the expedition, and attacked Troy. After eight long years of fighting, the war was at a stalemate.

The *Iliad* centers on the Greek hero Achilles, whose father was King Peleus of Myrmidons and mother was the goddess Thetis. Wishing to make her son immortal, Thetis dipped Achilles in the River Styx but held him by the heel, which became the only vulnerable part of his body.

Although Achilles knew he was fated to die if he joined the Greek army, he chose to sacrifice immortal life for military glory. Slighted by Agamemnon, Achilles withdrew from battle; because of this, the Greeks were defeated. In his stead, Achilles's friend Patroclus put on Achilles's armor and charged into battle but was slain by the Trojan hero Hector, son of King Priam of Troy. In turn, an enraged Achilles sought revenge and killed Hector. Achilles then tied Hector's body to his chariot and dragged it around the battlefield. Eventually, he yielded to Priam's pleas and returned Hector's body to him. The *Iliad* ends with Hector's funeral.

Achilles did not survive much past Hector's death, dying when Paris shot an arrow into his only vulnerable place—his heel. The Greeks' morale was failing when another hero, Odysseus, came up with the plan of building a giant wooden horse and hiding soldiers inside. Suspecting nothing, the Trojans accepted the gift. That night, the Greeks inside the horse came out and opened the city gates. The waiting army surged inside, killing the Trojans and burning the city.

To this day, scholars argue over the authenticity of the *Iliad*'s authorship: Was Homer a man who worked on his own, or was the story actually written collectively? What is known is that nearly 3,000 years later, the *Iliad* is still one of the most widely read epic poems ever written.

POSTSCRIPT

■ In 1870, German businessman Heinrich Schliemann, using the *Iliad* as a guide, began digging in Turkey and found the remains of more than nine different cities, each built on top of the ruins of the previous one.

The Great Depression

EVERYONE HAD AN EXPLANATION for the Great Depression. Some pronounced it biblical prophecy; Henry Ford blamed it on laziness. Economist Charles Kindleberger, however, said it was a global event caused by a lack of any nation exerting economic leadership.

Some governments could not survive the depression. Weimar Germany faced hyperinflation and massive unemployment—more than five million people were out of work by 1932—helping the Nazis become the country's chief political party by mid-1932. Sweden also faced rising unemployment and shrinking wages, resulting in communist agitation and worker revolts.

Crowds of unemployed men wait outside a charity shop

In France, unemployment reached 15 percent by 1932. French Premiere André Tardieu dangled the threat of communism as his main campaign issue and won the election on the platform of belt-tightening and low taxation. Great Britain, whose economy was still suffering from World War I, also reshuffled its government, but in a more conservative direction. Thriftiness was the order of the day. However, thanks to Britain trading within its own empire, the country was able to insulate itself from the rest of Europe and the United States. By 1935, its industrial output had returned to 1929 levels. In America, Franklin Delano Roosevelt routed President Herbert Hoover in the 1932 presidential election and then launched his "alphabet soup" New Deal programs. America's involvement in World War II helped put it on the mend.

In Italy, Benito Mussolini made contradictory economic decisions because he lacked expert advisers. However, the public considered this genius. Because of tactics such as government involvement in industry, the Italian economy was recovering by 1934.

Thanks to a planned economy and quick yen devaluation, Japan suffered less from the Depression than other nations. But in 1936, a failed military coup led the shaken civilian government to cede power to the armed forces. Thus the German, Italian, and Japanese military all emerged from the chief Depression years strong, setting the stage for World War II.

George Orwell (1903–1950)

IN HIS TWO MOST FAMOUS NOVELS, *Animal Farm* and *1984,* George Orwell gave the world a vocabulary for criticizing totalitarianism: "Big Brother;" "All animals are equal, but some animals are more equal than others;" "He who controls the present controls the past."

Born Eric Blair, Orwell hated social inequalities, the British Empire, the regimentation of the welfare state, and the Communist Party. Everything he wrote, from the grimly comic *Keep the Aspidistra Flying* to the chilling distopia *1984,* was based on his passions and personal experience.

Orwell was born in India, the son of a minor official in the Indian Civil Service. A member of what he described as the "lower-upper middle class," he was educated at Eton on scholarship, where he developed what would be a lifelong inferiority complex and became, in his own words, "an odious young snob." Instead of moving on to Oxford or Cambridge with his classmates, Orwell spent five years as an officer in the Imperial Police in Burma, where he learned to despise both the British and the Burmese.

Disgusted with his own imperial role, Orwell left Burma in 1927 to become a writer. He spent several years living with the poor in London and Paris, picking up odd jobs. In 1933, he published his first book, *Down and Out in London and Paris*, which described his years of living hand-to-mouth. It was at this time that he took the name George Orwell in an attempt to reinvent himself.

Already an independent-minded socialist, Orwell spent the next several years writing novels and social documentaries. In 1936, he went to Spain to report on the Civil War and fight for the Republicans. He was shot in the throat while on the front in Aragon and barely escaped with his life from the 1937 communist purge. In his essay *Why I Write,* Orwell claimed that his experiences in Spain forever shaped his work.

Orwell was rejected for military service in World War II, as he was already fighting the tuberculosis that would ultimately kill him. But he was eager to enter the fight against fascism, and so he spent two years producing propaganda for the BBC. Between 1941 and 1946, Orwell wrote both *Animal Farm* and *1984,* though neither was published until after the war.

Orwell summed up his own literary career in the preface to *Animal Farm*: "If liberty means anything at all it means the right to tell people what they do not want to hear."

Bentham and Utilitarianism

JEREMY BENTHAM was the creator of the political and ethical theory of "Utility," summed up in his famous sentence, "It is the greatest happiness of the greatest number that is the measure of right and wrong."

A child prodigy, Bentham was found reading a multivolume history of England when he was still a toddler. In 1760, he was sent to Oxford at age 12 and began reading for the law school's bar exam at age 16. Although Bentham trained as a lawyer, he was more interested in the theory of law than the practice.

Bentham first laid out his theory of "utility" in *The Introduction to the Principles of Morals and Legislation,* published in 1789. According to Bentham, pleasure and pain rule man's conduct. The moral quality of an individual act can be determined by the pleasure and pain brought on all members of a community as a result of that act. The goodness of a law can be determined by how strongly it serves the happiness to which each individual is equally entitled. Believing that pleasure and pain can be quantitatively measured according to their "intensity, duration, certainty, and propinquity," Bentham worked out their values with the intention of giving scientific accuracy to discussion of morals and legislation.

John Stuart Mill described Bentham as "the great questioner of things established." Although he never held office or led a political movement, Bentham regularly proposed legal and social reforms based on his "felicific calculus" of morality. He was an early proponent of animal welfare, arguing that the ability to suffer was more important in determining how we treat others than the ability to reason. He also argued for universal sufferance and the decriminalization of homosexuality. Less appealing to the modern mind is his design for a prison called the Panopticon, which would allow a central observer to see prisoners without the prisoners knowing they were being watched. Bentham described the Panopticon as creating an atmosphere of "invisible omniscience"—modern critics have described it as "Bentham as Big Brother."

Bentham died in June 1832. He bequeathed his remains to be dissected, having long been interested in the value of direct study of the human body. His skeleton, dressed in his own clothes and topped with a wax head, is displayed in a box he called his "Auto-icon" at University College in London, an institution which embodied many of his ideas about society and education—particularly his belief that education should be more widely available.

The Harlem Renaissance

T HEY WERE THE "NEW NEGROES"; the brash young voices of the exuberant Roaring Twenties.

It had many names: the Harlem Renaissance, the black Literary Renaissance, the New Negro Movement. It was actually an unexpected confluence of writers, dramatists, musicians, artists, and sociologists in the New York neighborhood of Harlem—as well as their wealthy white patrons—who instigated an intellectual revolution. In the end, it affected not only black Americans but Africans throughout the Diaspora, including African and Caribbean intellectuals living in Paris.

Langston Hughes

The Renaissance was born of the Great Migration of African Americans during and after World War I. It was nurtured by a mixture of the exhilaration that many African Americans felt on arriving in New York and the resolve of those disillusioned by scores of race riots that scarred the country during the "Red Summer" of 1919.

Some argue that it was born in 1926 with *The Nation*'s publication of Langston Hughes's defining essay "The Negro Artist and the Racial Mountain," a response to George Schuyler's attack on black art, "The Negro Art Hokum." The artists and literati of this new generation intended to speak for themselves, Hughes wrote, and they intended to create a new, authentic art, born of the passion of the African American struggle for social justice and set to the rhythm of inextinguishable African beat. These Renaissance men and women were often criticized for revealing their race's "dirty laundry," for the luridness of their art, and the "primitiveness" of their music and performances. Still, they represented the birth of a new defiance and established a new canon.

The principal artists are well known, including Langston Hughes, Zora Neale Hurston, Claude McKay, Jean Toomer, and Alaine Locke, the first African American Rhodes scholar. Others insist that it cannot be understood without Duke Ellington and Marcus Mosiah Garvey.

The Harlem Renaissance marked a transition in African American history and society. American culture would never be the same.

Thirty Years' War

BEGINNING IN 1618, this long and bloody war over rival claims to the throne of the Kingdom of Bohemia is known for being the first conflict to affect most of Europe.

The war occurred primarily on German soil, involving both Catholics and Protestants. Although most of the German states were part of the Holy Roman Empire, opposing princes had created two rival organizations, the Protestant Union and the Catholic League. Ferdinand II, the emperor, was unable to promote unity between them.

At first, Catholic armies quickly overran Bohemia and forced the population to convert to Catholicism. By 1621, the conflict had spread across Germany. In 1625, Christian IV of Denmark intervened on the side of the Protestants, but four years later, his troops were defeated and Denmark was knocked out of the war.

Eventually, the fighting in Germany attracted the attention of France. Although they were Catholic, King Louis XIII and his advisor, Cardinal Richelieu, opposed the rising might of Catholic Spain and its connection to the Hapsburg Empire in Austria. In response, Richelieu brokered peace between Sweden and Poland so that Protestant Sweden could assist the beleaguered Protestants in Germany. In 1630, Swedish troops entered the war under their warrior king, Gustavus Adolphus. The Swedish enjoyed some victories, but their gains were negated after the Battle of Nördlingen in 1634.

In 1635, France leapt in and officially declared war on Spain. French armies fought against the Spanish in Germany and Italy, defeated a Spanish invasion, and assisted Protestant armies in Germany. The Netherlands also entered the war against the Spanish.

The Peace of Westphalia in 1648 ended most of the war and resulted in territorial gains for Sweden and France, general amnesty for princes throughout Germany, and a guarantee of religious equality for Protestants and Catholics. Still, France and Spain continued fighting until 1659.

But the war had left its mark—mostly on Germany. For 30 years, armies had crisscrossed German territory; many armies had been poorly supplied, and the men had resorted to taking what they needed from the countryside. As a result, harvests were disrupted, thousands of civilians were killed, and many cities were sacked and destroyed. Plague and famine ruined the countryside and led to wide areas of devastated territory.

William Gladstone (1809–1898)

WILLIAM GLADSTONE was the "Grand Old Man" of Liberal politics in Victorian England, serving four terms as Prime Minister of Great Britain between 1868 and 1894.

He began his political career as a Tory Member of Parliament in 1832 and held a seat in Parliament for the next 62 years. Making his mark from the start, he held junior offices in several Conservative governments, eventually rising to Chancellor of the Exchequer. Gladstone was disturbed by Tory support of the Corn Laws that protected British agriculture against the import of cheap grain at the expense of the poor, and he began to drift toward liberalism and social reform. In 1859, he joined the Liberal Party and became its leader in 1867. His ministries were notable for the introduction of a series of social and political reforms, including national elementary education.

Gladstone's primary concern was with social and political reform at home, but he commonly focused on Ireland. He de-established the Irish Protestant church in 1869, and he passed land acts designed to give Irish tenants "the three F's"—fixed tenure, fair rents, and free sale of land. Not everyone agreed with his actions, however, and his campaigns in favor of Home Rule for Ireland in 1886 and 1894 led to the defection of the Unionists from the Liberal Party and the fall of his third government.

Unlike his political rival, Benjamin Disraeli, Gladstone had a troubled relationship with Queen Victoria. They disagreed on policy, especially in terms of foreign affairs. Worse, Gladstone lacked Disraeli's knack for mild flirtation. The queen complained that he addressed her as if she were a public meeting and at one point described him as "this half-crazy and in many ways ridiculous, wild, and incomprehensible old fanatic."

Gladstone's interest in social reform was not limited to his political career. Having a charitable interest in "fallen women" was common at the time, and in 1840, he began his lifelong work of "rescuing" London prostitutes and rehabilitating them through employment, marriage, or emigration.

POSTSCRIPT

▪ Gladstone's favorite form of exercise was cutting down trees, which he did regularly from 1852 to 1891. Cartoonists often drew him with an ax in hand.

The Rise of Arabic Culture

THE ABBASID CALIPHS, who ruled the Islamic world from around A.D. 750 until their final defeat by the Mongols in 1258, presided over an expanding Arabic era of learning and science. During this time, Baghdad was the both the political and cultural capital of the Islamic world.

Detail from a mosque

Instead of conquest, the Abbasids focused on cultural consolidation and assimilation. From the mid-eighth to the ninth centuries, it was an imperial priority to translate the important works of the displaced languages of conquered peoples. Manuscripts were collected throughout the empire and brought together at translation centers. The best works of literature, philosophy, and science were translated into Arabic from Sanskrit, Greek, Latin, Syriac, Coptic, and Persian, making them accessible to the Arabic-speaking world.

This period of translation was followed by one of extreme creativity. In the 10th and 11th centuries, Muslim scholars first adapted and interpreted classical learning within the framework of Islamic theology and philosophy, then moved beyond the classical into purely Islamic learning. The mathematician al-Khwarizimi used Indian numerals (known today as "Arabic numerals") to develop new forms of accurate calculation, including the algorithm. The doctor al-Razi wrote a treatise on smallpox and measles and compiled a vast encyclopedia summarizing Greek, Persian, and Hindu medical knowledge. The philosopher Abu Nasr al-Farabi was devoted to reconciling Platonic and Aristotelian philosophies.

The philosopher and physician Avicenna's medical works, *The Book of Healing* and *The Canon of Medicine,* served as the standard medical textbooks in Islamic and European universities through the 18th century. The philosopher Averroës expounded the Koran in terms of Aristotle, creating a Muslim philosophy of religion. Countless Arabic experimenters developed important scientific devices, such as accurate balances, alembics, and the astrolabe, constructed by Ibrāhīm al-Fazari.

During the 12th and 13th centuries, many classical works, as well as Arabic scientific studies were translated into Hebrew and Latin, thus laying the foundation for the European Renaissance of the 15th and 16th centuries.

Independence for Cuba

IN 1902, the island nation of Cuba finally received the independence it had long worked toward. In reality, however, Cuba had just exchanged one master for another.

Ever since the early 16th century, Cuba had been almost continually ruled by Spain. Revolts and revolutions took place over the years, but all had failed. Finally, in 1895, the Cuban War of Independence began. Harsh Spanish efforts to quell the rebellion created sympathy for Cuba in the United States, which led to the 1898 Spanish-American War. When America won the war, it seemed as if Cuba had finally achieved independence. In April 1898, the U.S. Senate passed the Teller Amendment, which stated that America would not establish permanent control over Cuba. But after the war, the United States continued to occupy Cuba.

In July 1900, the Cuban Constitutional Convention began, only to be notified the United States intended to attach an amendment to the document. As drafted by American Secretary of War Elihu Root, the Platt Amendment (named after Connecticut Senator Orville Platt) authorized the United States to intervene in Cuba as necessary, forbade the Cuban government from borrowing money without American permission, and forced Cuba to lease land to the United States for naval bases.

Cuba reluctantly accepted the Platt Amendment. In May 1902, the country became "independent," but just four years later, the United States intervened in Cuba following a disputed election. Cuban resentment bubbled for years over the Platt Amendment. On May 29, 1934, the Amendment was repealed as part of President Franklin D. Roosevelt's "Good Neighbor Policy" toward Latin America. The United States, however, continued to maintain a naval base at Guantánamo Bay.

By then, Cuba was suffering through a period of governmental instability that did not end until Fulgencio Batista y Zaldivar, who had been the military power behind the throne for several years, was elected president in 1940. After completing his term in 1944, he stepped down and was replaced in a free and democratic election. However, in 1952, he overthrew the government. This time he played the part of corrupt dictator, and organized crime elements began moving into the city of Havana.

A small but insistent insurgency led by Fidel Castro continued to fight Batista's gradually weakening army. Seeing his military and political support crumbling, Batista fled Cuba on December 31, 1958. Castro took over in 1959, but he quickly saddled Cuba with a totalitarian Communist regime. Once again, Cubans were denied democracy.

Friedrich Nietzsche (1844–1900)

IT'S IRONIC THAT the German son of a Lutheran minister would later pronounce the death of God. But in his philosophical masterpiece *Thus Spake Zarathustra,* philosopher Friedrich Nietzsche did just that.

Nietzsche was passionately religious as a boy, but he later abandoned the study of theology in favor of philology. He was such a brilliant scholar that, as a student at Leipzig, he was offered the professorship of classical philology before he had even graduated. While working as a professor of classics at Basel, Nietzsche wrote his first major work, the study of aesthetics known as *The Birth of Tragedy,* in which he developed the theory that Greek tragedy arose from a fusion of what he called the Apollonian and Dionysian dichotomy, combining restraint and passion.

Beset by ill health, he resigned from his post in 1879. Nietzsche produced his most important works over the next ten years, including *Thus Spake Zarathustra, Beyond Good and Evil,* and *On the Genealogy of Morals.*

Much of Nietzsche's work searched for meaning and morality in the absence of God. Believing that only the strong should survive and that compassion perpetuates the weak, he rejected Christianity as not only false but as harmful to society. Nietzsche argued that Christianity leads people's thoughts away from this world and into the next, making them less capable of coping with life. He suggested in its place the "will to power," a variation on Schopenhauer's "will to live"; that is, that everything in the universe has an innate fear of death, and thus a will to live.

Nietzsche is probably most famous for the Nazi interpretation of his theory of the *Übermensch,* commonly translated as "superman." In Nietzsche's formulation, the Übermensch would not be the product of evolution but would emerge when a man of talent mastered himself, abandoned the values of society, and created his own set of values rooted in life on earth. Although Nietzsche was opposed to nationalism and anti-Semitism, his writings were used by Nazi political theorists, who twisted the concept to suggest that self-discipline and racial purity could produce a race of superior Aryan beings.

In 1889, Nietzsche suffered a mental breakdown and spent a year in an asylum. He spent the last ten years of his life cared for by his family.

The Babylonian Captivity

THE BABYLONIAN CAPTIVITY is the name given to the time in the sixth century B.C. when the Jews were exiled from their homeland and deported to Babylon.

The Jews lived under the Assyrians, who held the part of Asia closest to the Mediterranean Sea. But the Assyrian empire began to crumble during the 700s B.C.; they were eventually defeated and replaced by the Babylonians under King Nebuchadnezzar. The Babylonians in turn defeated the Jews in 586 B.C. and captured the city of Jerusalem.

In revenge for their support of the Assyrians, the Babylonians destroyed the sacred Temple of the Jews (built by Solomon and also known as the First Temple) and sent thousands of Jews into exile in Babylon. Thus began the Babylonian Captivity and the Jewish Diaspora.

Despite the pain and hardship of being ripped from their homeland, the banished Jews found that there were other Jews who had previously settled in Babylon and established a Jewish infrastructure there. And so, the new arrivals were able to remain true to their culture and heritage.

Two prominent religious leaders emerged: Ezra and Nehemiah. They wondered why God would allow such misfortune to befall the Jews, and they determined that their people had not observed the Ten Commandments carefully enough. And so Ezra and Nehemiah persuaded many Jews to be more stringent. The Babylonian Captivity was also a time of miracles. According to the Book of Daniel, a group of young Jewish men refused to eat nonkosher food or bow to idols and thus were thrown into a fiery furnace by Babylonian King Nebuchadnezzar. They miraculously survived, which prompted Nebuchadnezzar to forbid anyone to blaspheme the god of Israel.

The Babylonian Captivity had been prophesied to last 70 years: "when the seventy years are fulfilled, I will punish the king of Babylon," said God. When the time was nearly up, the current Babylonian king, Belshazzar, was understandably nervous. But he miscalculated, figuring the time by one year too few, and when the year passed without incident, he decided the prophecy was not going to be fulfilled. Belshazzar threw a great feast in celebration and brought out vessels stolen from the First Temple. Suddenly, a disembodied hand appeared and wrote on the wall that God had brought Belshazzar's kingdom to an end. That night, the Persians attacked, killed Belshazzar, and ended the Babylonian reign. The Persian ruler, Cyrus the Great, allowed the Jews to return to Palestine.

The Voyage of the *Mayflower*

THE SEPARATISTS (who became known as the Pilgrims) were a sect of dissident Protestants who lived in England in the 1500s and 1600s. For years they had been persecuted by the monarchy. In the 1590s, many fled to Holland to be able to freely practice their religion, but life there proved to be difficult. In 1619, the English government issued a patent of land in northern Virginia, and many Separatists decided to sail to America in hopes of finding a better life.

Pilgrims arriving at Plymouth Rock

The *Mayflower* sailed from England for the New World in September 1620. One hundred and two passengers were on-board the *Mayflower*, which had a crew of around 25 men. Christopher Jones, one of the owners of the ship, captained the *Mayflower* during its multi-week voyage across the Atlantic.

The ship was a cargo ship that had been used in the wine trade between England and France; its small capacity left little room for personal belongings. Some brought straw and canvas to make mattresses; others brought chests in which to store personal belongings. Many of the passengers suffered seasickness as they braved fierce storms. During one of these tempests, one of the ship's main beams cracked, and some feared for their safety. Resolute, they continued their journey, believing God would guide them to their destination.

On November 21, 1620, the Separatists landed on the shores of North America. When they realized they had reached Cape Cod, Massachusetts, rather than Virginia as authorized, many became concerned that their leaders might no longer have the authority to guide them. They decided to stay together as a group, and it was agreed to follow their leaders as they would have done in Virginia.

To that order, they drafted what is known as the Mayflower Compact. The document was short and signed by 41 males, who indicated they were loyal subjects of King James of Great Britain. The signers agreed to further the purposes of colonization, enact just laws, and abide by the laws they enacted. The document, signed while onboard the *Mayflower*, before anyone set foot ashore, is considered to be the beginning of democratic government in America.

The White Rose

IN MID-1942, two years before the Allied landings at Normandy, a handful of German students began a secret campaign against Adolf Hitler's Third Reich. The movement began among medical students at the University of Munich, who referred to themselves as the White Rose. Medical student Hans Scholl, age 24, coined the title. Its significance, if any, is unknown.

Though not Jewish themselves—Scholl had been a member of the Hitler Youth—they were disillusioned with the tyranny of the Reich, the brutal treatment of the Jews, and the progress of the war.

The students typed up and mimeographed antigovernment leaflets, which were distributed between June 27 and July 12. The leaflets were surreptitiously left in phone booths, mailed to professors and students, and left in public buildings. Soon afterward, Hans's sister Sophie, a biology student, joined the group.

Bearing the title "Leaves of the White Rose," the leaflets were directed primarily at students and intellectuals. They commented on the liquidation of the Jews and other atrocities and called for resistance to the Nazis. "We shall not be silent—we are your bad conscience. The White Rose will not leave you in peace."

Thirty-five of the first 100 leaflets ended up in the hands of the secret police, but the White Rose was not deterred. The student group managed to obtain a duplicating machine, and in early February 1943 they produced 5,000–6,000 copies of their fifth leaflet, now called "Leaflets of the Resistance Movement in Germany."

Their luck ran out with the production of a sixth leaflet, which referred to the disaster at Stalingrad, calling the Reich "the most abominable tyranny that our people has ever endured," and urging the people to rise up in opposition. Hans and Sophie were observed dumping leaflets in a university courtyard on February 18 and were taken into custody.

A "People's Court" quickly convicted the Scholls and fellow White Rose member Christoph Probst. All three were guillotined that same day.

More than 80 people were subsequently arrested, imprisoned, or executed in connection with the White Rose group: a sad ending to a gallant expression of conscience.

Sputnik

SPUTNIK WAS THE RUSSIAN SPACE LAUNCH that shook up the Cold War. On October 4, 1957, the tremendous roar of a rocket engine lifting off shook the Baikonur Cosmodrome in the Soviet country of Kazakhstan. Within minutes, the rocket's 264,000 pounds of thrust had pushed it more than 500 miles above the earth's surface. Then an aluminum sphere emerged from the rocket's third stage. Four antennas popped up from it, and the sphere started emitting a steady beeping sound. Sputnik, the world's first artificial satellite, had just been launched by the Soviet Union.

The USSR had just taken a huge leap forward in the Cold War. "People of the whole world are pointing to the satellite," exulted Soviet leader Nikita Khrushchev. "They are saying the U.S. has been beaten."

Today, many people assume that the launching of Sputnik electrified America and sent a stunned United States scrambling to catch up to the Soviets. However, on the day after the launch, many U.S. newspapers apathetically ran a small Sputnik story on their inside pages.

Over the previous few years, Russia had announced plans to go into space nearly two dozen times. The Pentagon and the CIA knew the precise status of the Soviet space program. President Eisenhower was even pleased, since Sputnik's launch cleared the way to implement the "Open Skies" program, which allowed countries to do aerial reconnaissance of one another. The Soviets couldn't complain about the United States sending up satellites when they had already done the exact same thing. The United States had been in no hurry to get into space, anyway; Eisenhower initially had selected the navy to develop the country's first space rocket, later switching the project to the army.

One month after Sputnik, the Soviets launched Sputnik II. Now people started talking. Senators such as William Fulbright discussed the possible danger to American society. Newspapers and politicians were suddenly full of indignation: "Sputnik outrage" had begun.

Sputnik did push America to create the National Aeronautics and Space Administration (NASA) in 1958. Sputnik also lit a fuse under the space race, leading to the American rocket programs that culminated with the Apollo program and the 1969 moon landing.

POSTSCRIPT

■ Sputnik weighed just 184 pounds.

The First Opium War

BEGINNING IN THE LATE 18TH CENTURY, opium was the center of a thriving three-way trade between Britain, India, and China. The British East India Company was one of many companies that grew opium in India and auctioned it to licensed traders. The opium was sold in China to pay for the purchase of teas, silks, and porcelains, which were then shipped to London. By the 1820s, the British were shipping enough opium to China to supply approximately one million addicts.

The Chinese government was alarmed at the economic and moral consequences of the growing opium market. Opium destroyed individuals and their families, and the drug's high price led to violence and corruption. The drain of silver payments for imported opium threatened government and private incomes. The Chinese had made the import and production of opium illegal in 1800, but previous attempts to enforce the ban had been unsuccessful.

Britain was equally unhappy with the nature of its restricted trade with China. European trade was limited to Canton where merchants were permitted to reside from October to March. A British diplomatic mission sent to establish more open trade with China was refused with a written explanation to King George III from the Chinese Emperor: "We have never valued ingenious articles, nor do we have the slightest need of your country's manufactures."

In 1838, the emperor sent Imperial Commissioner Lin Zexu to Canton to stop the opium trade. The commissioner successfully suppressed Chinese opium sellers, but he had to barricade the foreigner merchants in their warehouses before they surrendered their merchandise. In all, Lin Zexu confiscated and destroyed 20,000 chests of illegal opium from British warehouses.

In response, Britain sent 16 warships, "four armed steamers," and 28 troop ships and transports to China. Over the course of three years, the British attacked and blockaded Chinese ports, sank their ships, occupied Shanghai, and sailed up the Yangtze River to threaten Nanjing.

The 1842 Treaty of Nanjing opened five ports to Europeans, gave the British what was then the barren island of Hong Kong, paid reparations to British merchants, and made concessions to Western ideas of trade. The most important of these granted extraterritoriality to foreign merchants, making them subject to their own laws rather than Chinese law. But it did not discuss opium at all. In the end, neither side was happy with the provisions of the treaty, leading to a second trade war from 1856 to 1860.

Frederick the Great (1712–1786)

FREDERICK II OF PRUSSIA, known as Frederick the Great, transformed the Hohenzollern states of Prussia and Brandenburg into a leading European power, later replacing Austria as the dominant German state.

Although Frederick received a rigorous military education, he hated it, preferring the study of literature and music. At age 18, he tried to escape to the court of his English cousin, George II, but was caught. Frederick's father saw this as an act of treason and threatened his son with the death penalty. Frederick was ultimately spared but was forced to watch the beheading of the friend who had helped him escape.

Frederick was kept in close confinement until his marriage in 1733. Allowed to establish a court at Rheinsberg, he surrounded himself with musicians, scholars, and artists; composed sonatas for the flute; and began a lifelong correspondence with Voltaire.

In May 1740, Frederick became King of Prussia and Elector of Brandenburg. In October, the accession of Maria Theresa to the Austrian throne led to the War of Austrian Succession. Frederick seized the opportunity to revive Prussia's claim to the province of Silesia, an area rich in minerals and metal ores. The so-called Silesian Wars, which were more accurately campaigns in the War of Austrian Succession, gave Prussia sovereignty over Silesia and established Frederick's reputation as one of the best military commanders of his day.

Frederick spent years preparing Prussia for impending war. He introduced new tax systems, encouraged industrial growth, and increased the size of his army. In 1756, Frederick began the Seven Years' War by invading Saxony. "Old Fritz" fought a brilliant defensive war on two fronts, but every battle drained his manpower reserve. Prussia was saved when Russia switched sides following the death of Czarina Elizabeth in 1762.

Frederick continued to expand Prussia's territory and power. He acquired Polish Prussia in the First Partition of Poland, making the Hohenzollern lands contiguous for the first time. In 1778, he seized the Franconian duchies. One of his last political actions was the formation of the Fürstenbund, or "League of Princes," which served to protect the liberties of the German states against Holy Roman Emperor Joseph II's ambitions.

By the time of his death in 1786, Frederick had more than doubled Prussia's territory, built a strong economic foundation, and transformed it into one of the most powerful states in Europe.

The Defeat of the Spanish Armada

Eᴺɢʟᴀɴᴅ's Qᴜᴇᴇɴ Eʟɪᴢᴀʙᴇᴛʜ I had already rejected Spanish King Philip II's offer of marriage, but tensions rose when she further offended His Most Catholic Majesty in 1559 by reconfirming the 1534 Act of Supremacy, which established the Church of England as an institution separate from Rome with the British ruler at its head. The conflict

reached an apex in 1587 with Elizabeth's execution of her cousin, Mary, Queen of Scots.

It took more than two years for Philip to prepare to invade England and overthrow the "heretic queen." One hundred and thirty ships set out from Lisbon in May 1588, carrying about 19,000 infantrymen under the command of the inexperienced Duke of Medina Sidonia. An army of about 30,000 men, under the command of the Duke of Parma, waited in the Spanish Netherlands for the fleet to arrive. The plan was for the Spanish fleet to secure a landing area on the Kentish coast and then ferry the invasion army across the Channel.

The English navy first spotted the Armada on July 19. The fleet harassed the Armada with long-range guns as it sailed up the Channel, causing little damage. Unable to connect with the Duke of Parma's forces, Medina Sidonia decided to anchor off Calais until contact could be made. At midnight on July 28, eight British fireships sailed into the tight Spanish formation. The Spanish ships scattered, closely followed by the lighter British vessels. Then the British provoked the Spanish into firing on them while they were still out of range, then closed in and fired repeated broadsides at the Spanish fleet at close range.

The next day, a strong wind drove the remaining Spanish ships into the North Sea. They were forced to make their way back to Spain on the treacherous route around the north of Scotland and west of Ireland. Thirty-five ships foundered or ran aground on the way—barely half the original Armada returned to port.

The defeat of the "Invincible Armada" by the smaller, more maneuverable British ships marked the emergence of England as an important maritime power.

Chinua Achebe (1930–present)

ONE OF THE FIRST pieces of advice often given to new writers is the adage, "Write what you know." In his first novel, *Things Fall Apart,* Nigerian author Chinua Achebe did exactly that.

He was born Albert Chinualumogu Achebe in the Igbo village of Ogidi in southern Nigeria in 1930. Achebe was the son of a Christian missionary teacher, and as he grew older, he straddled the teachings of his culture along with the religious lessons from his parents.

Achebe went to college, studying religion and African culture. After he graduated, he rejected his first name, which had been chosen by his parents to honor England's Prince Albert. He renamed himself Chinua. Through his work with the Nigerian Broadcasting Service, Achebe traveled throughout Africa and America. By the 1960s, he was the director of External Services in charge of the Voice of Nigeria. Achebe's various writings reflected his overall unhappiness with what was happening in Nigeria after it gained its independence in the Nigerian Civil War.

Things Fall Apart, published in 1958, described the life of Okonkwo, an Igbo leader. Set in the 1890s, it highlights a time when missionaries and colonial government began interfering strongly with Igbo society, eventually bringing about the Nigerian independence of which Achebe so strongly disapproved. In the second part of the novel, Okonkwo commits suicide when the world he knows is altered into one he refuses to accept.

The exploration of colonialism and the transformation of his culture were continued in Achebe's other novels, *No Longer at Ease, Arrow of God,* and *Anthills of the Savannah.* He has also published collections of short stories, poetry, and even children's books. He has received a number of awards for his writings, including the 2007 Man Booker International award.

In 1983, Achebe was elected deputy national president of the People's Redemption Party; the following year he founded a bilingual magazine called *Uwa ndi Igbo,* a resource for Igbo studies. In 1990, Achebe was in a serious car accident while on the Lagos-Ibadan expressway, and he was paralyzed from the waist down. Despite this adversity, he continues to write and, as his words clearly convey, he truly writes about what he believes, feels, and knows.

The First Man on the Moon

IN HIS MAY 25, 1961, speech to a joint session of Congress, President John F. Kennedy made it quite clear that he had an important point to make to the American people. He did not mince his words as he asked for an enormous amount of money from the federal budget to give to the development of the space program. "I believe that this nation should commit itself to achieving the goal, before this decade is out, of landing a man on the Moon and returning him safely to Earth," he said.

Even though Russia had already put a man in space, to many, the idea of traveling to the moon still seemed like an idea straight out of a science fiction novel. It was hard to imagine the enormous amount of advanced technology and knowledge this project would require, yet the president believed it was all entirely possible and attainable within a relatively short amount of time.

Sadly, Kennedy was assassinated on November 22, 1963, long before his goal was reached. The Apollo 11 mission took off on July 16, 1969, with crew members Neil Armstrong, Edwin "Buzz" Aldrin, and Michael Collins inside. Four days and about 250,000 miles later, Armstrong stepped down the ladder from the lunar module, the *Eagle,* and onto the moon's surface, uttering, "That's one small step for man, one giant leap for mankind." For the next two-and-a-quarter hours, he and Aldrin walked around the surface, later saying it was like walking in powdered charcoal. They collected rocks and dirt, jumped around a bit, and planted the American flag in the ground. Finally, they rejoined Collins, who had remained in orbit in the *Apollo 11* capsule, and made their way back to Earth. They were regaled as the country's heroes—and most exotic travelers. Someone even took the time to place a handwritten note on President Kennedy's grave, simply reading, "Mr. President, the *Eagle* has landed."

By being the first country to put a man on the moon, the United States won the Space Race against the Soviet Union. It also provided an important ego boost for the United States during the Cold War era.

King Alfred Defeats the Vikings

IN A.D. 878, England was divided into numerous kingdoms, some of which were ruled by separate kings. Vikings, who had a deserved reputation for being fierce and ruthless, controlled other kingdoms.

At the time, the Vikings held much of the north and east of England. King Alfred ruled Wessex, the land of the West Saxons, which constituted a large part of southwest England. He is also regarded as England's first king. After numerous battles with the Vikings, in 871, Alfred paid them to leave Wessex alone.

Five years later Danish Viking King Guthrum returned with his army. Alfred and his men held strong, but the Vikings returned for another surprise attack in January 878, this time intent on conquering the West Saxons. The Vikings routed the surprised Alfred at Chippenham, sending him scurrying for safety into the marshes of Atheiney at Somerset with a few of his followers. The once-great king hid throughout the winter while he tried to figure how to defeat the Vikings.

Come spring Alfred and his *fyrd,* or army, met at a place called Egbert's Stone. Meanwhile Guthrum and his Vikings moved south from Chippenham to high ground on the Edington ridge. Here the two sides met in May. Alfred ordered his men to form a shield wall—a tactic used successfully by the ancient Romans. Shields were placed side by side to create a solid wall, with spears thrust through small openings. Groups of attackers could then be sent out from it to attack vulnerable spots in the enemy's defenses. In another tactic, the formation of the shield wall could be altered into a "V" shape that could punch into the enemy's defense.

The West Saxons proved victorious. The Vikings were chased back to Chippenham. Once he had them surrounded in the fortress there, Alfred and his men simply waited for the Vikings to starve or surrender. Fourteen days later, Guthrum sued for peace.

Under terms of the Peace of Wedmore, Guthrum agreed to withdraw to the territory under Viking control where Danish law and custom applied—an area known as the Danelaw. Afterward, Guthrum and his captains were baptized and became Christians. Alfred also later developed a string of fortified border towns as an early defense against future Viking incursions.

POSTSCRIPT

■ In 2002, Alfred ranked 14th in a poll of 100 Greatest Britons.

The Sinking of the *Titanic*

EVEN THOUGH THE SINKING of the *Titanic* happened almost a century ago, the story of what occurred that icy night continues to fascinate.

Ironically, the *Titanic* was known as an unsinkable ship. The British luxury liner—also the largest passenger ship in the world at the time—set out on its maiden voyage from Southampton, England, to New York City on April 10, 1912.

Only days later, on April 14, the Titanic hit an iceberg shortly before midnight, about 400 miles from the shore of Newfoundland. A massive tear was ripped across the ship, rupturing five of its watertight compartments. Just after 2 A.M., the ship began sinking as water poured inside. Despite the severity of the collision, very few passengers noticed it. Those who did only felt a slight shuddering and thought little of it.

An SOS for help was issued to neighboring ships. The *Carpathia* picked up the call and headed straight for the *Titanic,* but unfortunately, by the time it arrived an hour and 20 minutes later, the only thing left was a handful of lifeboats holding confused, frightened survivors.

While the *Titanic* was lavish in its luxuries, including a heated swimming pool, a squash court, two barbershops, and two libraries, it lacked a sufficient supply of lifeboats. Management from the ship's owners, the White Star Line, felt the sight of so many lifeboats ruined the overall beauty of the vessel, and so the ship was only outfitted with enough to hold half the total number of passengers on board. When the lifeboats were finally deployed, many were lowered to the water at half capacity.

The *Titanic* originally held 2,228 people. Of those, 1,523 died, including Captain Edward J. Smith, who was planning to retire after the *Titanic*'s voyage. Several years before this fateful voyage, the captain had said, "When anyone asks me how I can best describe my experiences of nearly forty years at sea, I merely say, uneventful. Of course there have been winter gales, and storms and fog and the like. But in all my experience, I have never been in an accident of any sort worth speaking about."

POSTSCRIPT

■ Things lost during the sinking of the *Titanic* include 3,364 bags of mail, 50 cases of toothpaste, 30 cases of golf clubs and tennis rackets, and 5 grand pianos.

The Emancipation Proclamation

WHEN PRESIDENT ABRAHAM LINCOLN asked for a 75,000-man, three-month militia to suppress the Southern rebellion in April 1861, his sole desire was to reunite the country. The actual abolishment of slavery was secondary.

Lincoln had won only 40 percent of the vote in the 1860 presidential election, and his coalition included Democrats who were lukewarm supporters of the war effort. He also did not wish to alienate the Union border states, including Delaware, Maryland, Kentucky, and Missouri.

But the issue of slavery arose again and again. By mid-1862, Lincoln had concluded that restoring the Union to its prewar state was impossible. He began working on a draft of a proclamation abolishing slavery, but he decided not to issue it until his army won a battlefield victory. That came on September 17 at the Battle of Antietam. Although not a decisive Union victory, Robert E. Lee's retreat gave Lincoln the opportunity to announce a preliminary emancipation proclamation five days later. Lin-

Lincoln the President

The Noblest Deed of all

coln stipulated that unless the Southern states came back into the Union, all slaves in Confederate-controlled areas would be freed on January 1, 1863.

As promised, Lincoln signed the permanent Emancipation Proclamation on that day, and except in Tennessee and the parts of Virginia and Louisiana that were in Union hands, all slaves in the Confederate states were considered free. Critics complained that Lincoln's proclamation did not free slaves in loyal states such as Kentucky, but his supporters realized that Lincoln could only use his power as commander in chief to affect the rebellious states. It would take a constitutional amendment to abolish slavery throughout the United States.

The Emancipation Proclamation changed the course of the war: In addition to suppressing rebellion, it was now a fight to end slavery. European nations such as England and France, who had already abolished slavery themselves, would now be unable to intervene on behalf of the Confederacy, lest they appear to be supporting slavery.

The Dreyfus Affair

THE DREYFUS AFFAIR was arguably the most famous political scandal in late 19th-century France, if not all of Europe. It began in 1893, when Charles Dreyfus, a French artillery captain who was also Jewish, was charged with providing secret information to the German government. He was found guilty in 1894, stripped of his rank, and sentenced to the squalid French penal colony on Devil's Island for life.

Two years later, George Picquart, the head of French intelligence, found evidence suggesting that Major Marie Charles Esterhazy was the actual spy. The army, hesitant to admit an error, fired Picquart; then, in a mockery of a court-martial, they found Esterhazy innocent.

Picquart's successor admitted he had forged evidence against Dreyfus. An outcry ensued, spearheaded by French novelist Emile Zola, which led to a new trial for Dreyfus in 1899. He was again found guilty, but he received a reduced sentence. A new, more sympathetic government pardoned Dreyfus shortly after the trial. A French court finally cleared him of all charges in 1906. He was reinstated in the army, made a major, and awarded the French Legion of Honor. Esterhazy, who had emigrated to England, finally admitted his guilt.

This complex and embarrassing series of events showed severe fault lines in French politics and society. After the first verdict, elements of the French press launched a vitriolic anti-Semitic campaign. Prior to the second trial, some Catholic leaders—already hostile to what they saw as a secular republic—hinted at a conspiracy between Jews and Freemasons.

If the affair helped unify right-wing elements, it also brought a number of liberals and radicals together to defend the Republic. Novelist Anatole France and poet Charles Peguy denounced the initial verdict. But the most important voice in the outcry was that of Zola. His 1898 letter to the press, *J'Accuse,* was a passionate attack on the forces of conservatism and a defense of Dreyfus that helped bring worldwide attention to the case.

Finally, the affair led directly to the fall of the French government that was implicated in railroading Dreyfus. Under the new, more liberal government, anticlerical laws were passed that, in effect, provided for the separation of church and state in France.

POSTSCRIPT

■ Lieutenant Colonel Hubert Joseph Henry, who admitted forging evidence against Dreyfus, committed suicide while in prison.

The Composition of the Four Gospels

ALTHOUGH THE FOUR GOSPELS of the Christian New Testament deal with the life, person, and teachings of Jesus of Nazareth, they are not a biography of the man. The gospels use stories and examples from the life of Jesus in order to interpret the Christian message in terms of its historical context. The one element shared by all four is the story of Jesus's suffering, death, and resurrection, which is the center of Christian worship.

Early Christians repeated Jesus's parables and teachings, creating an oral tradition centered on the tale of his crucifixion and resurrection. Over time, stories were written down, and there were many variations of the *gospel*, or "good news," of Jesus. The four gospels known as Matthew, Mark, Luke, and John became part of the Christian canon in the second and third centuries when the text of the New Testament was established. Although they are attributed to disciples of Jesus, there is some debate among scholars as to who actually wrote them.

Written many years after the death of Jesus and shortly after the war between Rome and Judea that destroyed the temple in Jerusalem, the Gospel of Mark is the earliest of the gospels. It told the life of Jesus in story form, beginning in Galilee and ending with his death in Jerusalem.

The gospels of Matthew and Luke expanded on Mark's framework. They used other sources from the early Christian tradition, including a hypothetical collection of the sayings of Jesus that scholars call *Q*, from the German word *Quelle* (source). The Gospel of Matthew was written for Jewish Christians, explaining Old Testament prophecies in terms of Jesus, whose ancestry is traced back to Abraham, and placing Jesus's teachings within the tradition of Judaic law. Written slightly later, the Gospel of Luke was aimed at an audience concerned with integrating Christian belief with Roman citizenship. According to tradition, Luke was a Greek physician who traveled with the apostle Paul and who also wrote the Acts of the Apostles.

Each of the four Gospels reflects its author's social context and consequently depicts Jesus in slightly different ways. Together, the gospels of Mark, Matthew, and Luke are known as the "Synoptic Gospels" because they see things in the same way. The Gospel of John is sometimes called the "spiritual gospel." It is different in incident, style, and symbolism from the other three, emphasizing the meaning of Jesus's life and death rather than the events themselves.

Literature During World War I

THE POET WILLIAM WORDSWORTH once said, "Poetry is the sponta-
neous overflow of powerful feelings." For those who fought during
World War I, coping with war certainly involved strong emotions. As the
war raged on, a number of poets came forth, their words reflecting the
vivid scenes around them, as well as the fragile condition of the mind and
heart. From immense tragedy came words reminding everyone, on both
sides, that behind each soldier's face was a human soul.

One of the most famous poems to emerge during this period was "In
Flanders Fields" by John McCrae. A surgeon in the Canadian army, when
the words did not come out as intended, McCrae tore the paper from his
notebook and tossed it in the mud. An officer
spied it, read it, and sent it to the press. The
first line is easily recognized: "In Flanders
fields the poppies blow/between the crosses,
row on row."

Wilfred Owen was one of the more famous
war poets. While recuperating from trench
fever during the war, he met fellow poet Sieg-
fried Sassoon, who encouraged him to keep
writing. Tragically, Owen was killed during
the last week of the war. In his poem "Anthem
for Doomed Youth," he wrote, "What passing-
bells for these who die as cattle?/Only the
monstrous anger of the guns."

Rupert Brooke

Rupert Brooke was an English poet known
for his good looks as much as his poetry.
When he died of blood poisoning from a war injury, he became a hero
and symbol of the gifted and beautiful young people who gave up their
lives for their country. His most famous poem was "The Soldier" in which
he wrote, "If I should die, think only this of me: That there's some corner
of a foreign field/That is forever England."

Men were not the only poets of the era; many women, such as Rose
Maccaulay, Edith Nesbit, and Edith Sitwell, also put pen to paper to write
about their perspectives and experiences. While they did not write of
battlefronts and pervasive death, they did describe the war effort at home,
from making weapons and nursing the wounded to coping with the loss
of loved ones.

Quebec Separatism

THE CANADIAN PROVINCE OF QUEBEC was a colony of New France until it was ceded to the British in 1763 at the end of the Seven Years' War. Questions arose almost immediately as to whether to integrate the French-speaking population into British institutions or maintain the French seigniorial system. The territory was divided and split between Lower Canada (present-day Quebec) and Upper Canada (present-day Ontario) in 1791. Later, the territory was redivided, and it joined the Canadian federation as the Province of Quebec in 1867, but the anomaly of a French-speaking province was never resolved.

In the 1960s, Quebec had become the most urbanized province in Canada, and the growing French-speaking professional class began to voice long-standing minority grievances. French-speaking nationalists formed new political parties, ranging from the Quebec Liberal Party, which believed that reforms could be accomplished within the federal system, to the secessionist Parti Québécois.

During the same period, the terrorist Front de Libération du Quebec launched a bombing campaign to secure the separation of Quebec province from Canada. FLQ terrorism received little support from French-speaking separatists, who preferred the nonviolent approach of the Parti Québécois. In 1976, the Parti Québécois won a plurality of the seats in the Quebec legislative assembly. During its first four years in power, the separatist party restricted the use of English in schools and required the use of French as the official language of business and government. In 1980, the Parti Québécois called a referendum to make the province an independent country, but Quebec voters rejected it.

The question of Quebec's independence became a national issue in 1982, when the province refused to ratify the Constitution Act. The government negotiated a constitutional amendment known as the Meech Lake Accord, which recognized French-speaking Quebec as a "distinct society" within Canada and transferred extensive powers to all the provinces. The House of Commons passed the amendment in 1987, but English-language provinces refused to ratify it. A second attempt was made in 1992. The Charlottetown Agreement, which included concessions for greater autonomy for Quebec and the Inuit and Indian populations, as well as decentralizing federal power, was defeated with 54 percent opposed.

Most recently, the Parti Québécois brought another referendum on secession to Quebec voters in 1995. It was defeated by less than half of 1 percent.

Auguste Rodin (1840–1917)

REGARDED DURING HIS LIFETIME as Michelangelo's equal, sculptor Auguste Rodin failed the entrance examinations for the famed French art school Ecole des Beaux-Arts no less than three times. Rodin instead earned his living as a craftsman, doing ornamental stonework and modeling while taking classes from sculptor Antoine-Louis Barye.

In 1875, a trip to Italy shook Rodin out of academic formalism. Inspired by the work of Michelangelo and Donatello, he created his first truly original work: a large bronze statue of a single male figure, *Age of Bronze*. The piece was more realistic than those of his contemporaries—so much so that Rodin was accused of making life casts from a model instead of creating a clay form. His next major piece, *St. John the Baptist Preaching,* exhibited in 1880, established Rodin's reputation as a sculptor.

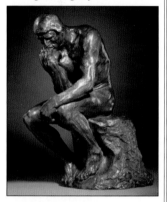

Rodin's The Thinker

Shortly thereafter, Rodin received his first official commission—a pair of bronze doors for the proposed Museum of Decorative Arts. Inspired by the *Gates of Paradise* by 15th-century sculptor Lorenzo Ghiberti, Rodin chose to illustrate scenes from Dante's *Inferno,* creating a piece that came to be called *The Gates of Hell.* The construction of the museum was canceled in 1885, but he later used the piece as a framework for creating individual sculptures, including two of his most famous pieces, *The Thinker* (originally intended as a portrait of Dante) and *The Kiss.*

Rodin's career was marked by the violent controversies surrounding the public monuments he was commissioned to create. The unveiling of statues commemorating landscape painter Claude Lorrain and President Domingo Sarmiento of Argentina caused riots. The patrons who commissioned him to do statues of Victor Hugo and Honoré de Balzac ultimately rejected the final products: the statue of Hugo because it was nude; the statue of Balzac because the figure was enveloped in a cloak with only the face defined.

Rodin remained popular despite his quarrels with patrons. A special pavilion at the Exposition Universelle in Paris in 1900 displayed 150 of his sculptures and drawings.

Christopher Columbus (1451–1506)

CHRISTOPHER COLUMBUS was born in 1451, in Genoa, Italy. At age 14, he began a life at sea. By 1477, he was living in Lisbon, Portugal. There he married Filipa Moniz, who lived only long enough to give Columbus a son named Diego in 1481.

Columbus based his plan to reach the east by sailing west on centuries-old information, including *The Travels of Marco Polo.* After his idea was turned down by Portugal in 1484, Columbus tried Spain's King Ferdinand and Queen Isabella. His plan was repeatedly rebuffed, but finally the monarchs agreed to fund Columbus's endeavor in 1492.

He set out on his first voyage on August 3, 1492, from Palos, Spain. He took three ships, the *Niña,* the *Pinta,* and the *Santa María.* On October 12, Columbus and his crew reached what was most likely San Salvador. He explored Hispaniola, left a settlement there, and sailed along the coast of Cuba before returning home. Back in Spain, he exhibited gold, colorful parrots, and islanders to the fascinated king and queen.

Columbus's second, larger expedition consisted of 17 ships. He left on September 25, 1493, but when he reached Hispaniola, he found the settlement burned down and its inhabitants exterminated. Columbus searched for gold but found little. He enslaved the native peoples to work on a new settlement. He returned home, leaving his brothers Bartholomew and Diego in charge on the island.

He returned to Hispaniola for a third time in 1498, but he found his colony in revolt. Unable to stop it, he asked for a judge to be sent from Spain. When the judge arrived, he stripped Columbus of his titles of viceroy and governor. He arrested Columbus and his brothers and sent them home in chains. Columbus reached Spain in 1500; the monarchs removed the chains but did not restore the titles. Powerless, he languished in Spain for two years.

Although giving some credence to the idea of a new continent, Columbus still clung to the idea that the islands he found were part of Asia. Instead of retiring, Columbus undertook a fourth voyage in 1502, which resulted in his being marooned on Jamaica for many months. He finally returned home in November 1504.

POSTSCRIPT

■ During the first voyage, Columbus kept the reward for being the first to spot land for himself, instead of giving it to the lookout.

Child Labor in America and England

INDUSTRIAL COMPETITION, a large class of working poor, and an abundance of children all combined to create the conditions of child labor in 19th-century England and the United States. By 1821, nearly half of the British population was under the age of 20. Employers saw advantages in hiring children—they generally were paid up to one-third the wages of a man, were more easily "trained," and could move under the machines.

By 1838, a large percentage of the workforce in England's cotton mills was under the age of 18, with children as young as seven working 12- to 15-hour days, six days a week. Falling asleep, working too slowly, or misbehaving could result in beatings. To prevent them from running away, children were sometimes chained to machines. Accidents, poor diet, and lack of exercise and fresh air often caused children to become crippled and even die.

Children working in coal mines found cave-ins, explosions, and gas fumes part of daily life. With tunnels only three to four feet high, they crawled on their hands and knees, dragging heavy loads of coal. Children worked in virtual darkness and continuously inhaled soot from the coal.

Windows in fabric mills were often nailed shut to seal in humidity, since this was believed to prevent threads from breaking.

An eight-year-old gold miner

Smoke from whale oil lamps mixed with cotton dust, which made breathing even more difficult. Children often worked barefoot to make it easier to climb onto the huge machines.

Working on the streets outside offered no relief. Newsboys, working in even the worst weather, had to be ready to start selling the morning edition by 5:00 A.M. and finished the evening edition around midnight. Long hours standing on sidewalks hawking papers caused orthopedic defects and chronic throat problems. Some children even froze to death in the delivery wagons.

Conditions began to improve in the United States in 1938 with the Fair Labor Standards Act, which contained a minimum wage provision that applied to both adults and children. This, in effect, removed some of the benefits of employing child workers in place of adults.

The Civil Rights Act of 1964

THE CIVIL RIGHTS ACT OF 1964 was the landmark legislation that outlawed segregation in U.S. schools and public places. It also highlighted discrimination against people because of their religion, national origin, or sex.

As time passed, the 1957 Civil Rights Act was proving inadequate. The chorus of protests against racial injustice, led by the NAACP and Martin Luther King, Jr., was growing louder. On June 11, 1963, President John F. Kennedy called for legislation that would provide "the kind of equality of treatment which we would want for ourselves." He later proposed a new bill that included provisions to ban discrimination in public accommodations; it also enabled the U.S. Attorney General to sue city and state governments that operated segregated school systems.

Its initial reception in the House of Representatives was favorable. The House Judiciary Committee, chaired by New York's Emanuel Cellar, added provisions to ban discrimination in employment. But the bill quickly faced resistance among conservative Southern Democrats, primarily Howard W. Smith, chair of the powerful House Rules Committee. Washington insiders feared that if any bill emerged at all, it would be watered down beyond recognition.

On November 22, 1963, everything changed when Kennedy was assassinated in Dallas and Vice President Lyndon B. Johnson ascended to the presidency. Using the nation's grief and his considerable persuasive powers, Johnson identified the civil rights bill with Kennedy's legacy in order to promote the cause. Smith was threatened with a discharge petition, which, if signed by half of the Senate, would allow the bill to move directly to the House floor. He backed down on the issue, and on February 10, 1964, the bill passed 290–130 and was sent to the Senate for debate.

The Senate proved to be even more difficult. Precedent dictated that after its second reading, the bill would be referred to the Senate Judiciary Committee, chaired by arch-segregationist Senator James O. Eastland of Mississippi. Senate Majority Leader Mike Mansfield took the unusual step of proposing that the bill bypass the Judiciary Committee and go immediately to the floor. After a 75-day filibuster, the bill came before the complete Senate on March 30, 1964, and was passed on June 19, 73–27. President Johnson signed the bill on July 2.

The Yangtze Flood of 1931

CHINA'S YANGTZE RIVER is the longest river in Asia and the third longest in the world. It is also a killer: Over the past 2,000 years, Yangtze River floods have taken millions of lives.

The most catastrophic of these disasters occurred during the summer of 1931, when heavy flooding affected more than 51 million people—a quarter of China's population. An estimated 3.7 million people died from drowning, disease, and starvation.

Heavy monsoon rains began in May and June and continued into the summer, swelling the Yangtze and overwhelming China's protective dykes and levees. Where the river was ordinarily a mile wide, it was now 20 miles. Water poured into the lowlands. One of the worst disasters occurred at Gaoyou, where thousands of sleeping inhabitants were swept to their deaths when the levees broke in the early morning hours.

By August, water covered 35,000 square miles. The Wuhan, Hankow, and Hanyan areas were hit especially hard. In places, water ranged from

4 to 18 feet deep. Flat-bottomed boats, called *sampans,* navigated former streets riddled with floating bodies. Refugees clung to rooftops, makeshift rafts, the muddy remnants of broken levees, and even floating coffins wrenched from their resting places.

Crops were washed away. There was no food and little prospect of obtaining any. Even as the waters gradually receded in the weeks and months that followed, millions succumbed to starvation, typhoid, cholera, dysentery, malaria, and other diseases. Many survivors simply gave up hope. Newspapers worldwide reported the mass devastation. Relief agencies reported a situation beyond their capacity to help.

Modern China has taken steps to prevent a recurrence of the disaster, building levees, and a series of dams along the Yangtze, but the river remains dangerous. Major floods occurred in 1954 and again in the late 1990s, although none has matched the magnitude of the 1931 disaster.

Samuel Gompers and the AFL

SAMUEL GOMPERS was just a child when he began making cigars with his father in London. When he was about 13, his family immigrated to New York in 1863. There he continued making cigars—first at home with his father and then for a local union of cigar makers.

He eventually joined a branch of the United Cigar Makers' Union where he developed ideas of social reform through unionism. After a failed cigar-makers' strike, Gompers and another union leader restructured the Cigar Makers' International Union. He eventually became its president. After socialists defeated him in an election for the presidency of the union, Gompers helped establish the Federation of Organized Trades and Labor Unions (FOTLU) in 1881.

The FOTLU was organized on Gompers's principles that unions should be organized for specific industries and should focus on economic, rather than political, reform. When political action was needed, Gompers urged trade union members to vote for those supporting a labor agenda rather than directly participating in politics. The FOTLU struggled; competing interests caused dissatisfaction among members. Membership declined, and Americans struck out against unions and unionism.

In 1886, Gompers and some loyal members of FOTLU met to reorganize their ranks. The result was the American Federation of Labor (AFL), which focused on the betterment of workers rather than challenging the actions of owners. Gompers was elected president, and he began building a national federation of trade unions within the umbrella of the AFL. Within a short time, membership in the AFL mushroomed.

In 1908, the U.S. Supreme Court applied the Sherman Antitrust Act to organized labor, and it ruled that boycotts across state lines were conspiracies in restraint of interstate commerce. The decision threatened the existence of unions, but the AFL launched a campaign to elect union members and union-supporting candidates to office as a way to remove unions from the antitrust law.

In 1900, the AFL had grown to approximately one million members. Gompers was a practical leader who promoted realistic goals for the organization. Except for one year, he served as president of the union until his death in 1924.

The Amiens Cathedral

During the early Middle Ages, the church was a unifying force, as nearly everyone in Europe, regardless of class, was Christian. The church was often all-encompassing; it served as a social outlet, the town's babies were baptized there, and a church's stained windows related stories

to those who could not read. People attended church regularly and paid church taxes. Many gave gifts to the church; the wealthy gave land, crops, and even serfs. As a result, the church became very wealthy and powerful.

While European villages had parish churches, in the cities, where the rich congregated and churches flourished, bishops often built grand cathedrals.

The Cathedral of Our Lady of Amiens, or the Amiens Cathedral, is an excellent example of 13th-century High Gothic style. Located in the French city of Amiens, construction started on the cathedral in 1220 to house the head of St. John the Baptist, which had been brought back from a Crusade earlier in the century. The main construction was finished in about 1269, though work on other elements, such as the cathedral's labyrinth, continued for decades afterward.

Of the three great Gothic cathedrals constructed in France during the 13th century (including the cathedrals at Chartres and Reims), the Amiens cathedral is the tallest and largest, at 476 feet long.

Earlier Romanesque cathedrals were noted for their wooden roofs and interior darkness. Gothic cathedrals, by comparison, emphasized light and featured sturdy stone roofs that were supported by arched flying buttresses. The cathedral at Amiens was constructed using stone and lightweight masonry, and the exterior's exquisitely carved facade featured three large arched openings. The cathedral's interior height, 139 feet, is accentuated by a narrow nave and side aisles, and the light is provided by the large rose window and numerous stained glass windows in each arm of the transept.

Such construction was not cheap, but by then the Catholic Church had gathered enough money to handle the expenses for such opulence.

Margaret Thatcher Becomes Prime Minister of England

IT IS HARD TO IMAGINE that the daughter of grocery store owners living in a small railroad town would one day become one of the most honored and respected politicians in the world, but in the case of Margaret Hilda Roberts, that is exactly what happened. She was born in 1925, in the town of Grantham, England. Her rise in politics was at least partially inspired by her father, who held a number of community positions including preacher, justice of the peace, town alderman, and mayor.

In 1943, Roberts began college. After getting a degree in chemistry, she began working as a research chemist. While she was still in her 20s, she ran as the Conservative candidate for the Labor seat at Dartford. She lost both times she ran. While she was campaigning, she met Denis Thatcher and in 1951, they were married. In 1953, she both became a barrister and gave birth to twins Mark and Carol. Finally, she was selected as a candidate for Finchley in 1958.

When Thatcher was only 34 years old, she became the youngest woman in the House of Commons. She quickly established a reputation for having extremely strong—and often unpopular opinions—about the quality of education. In 1979, she became the first female prime minister of the United Kingdom. As she said, "If you want anything said, ask a man. If you want anything done, ask a woman."

Thatcher was a popular leader, and when she ran for a second term in 1983, she won the election by a landslide. Known as "The Iron Lady," a term she reportedly enjoyed, Thatcher became an internationally recognized figure. She was a close personal friend of President Ronald Reagan and a respected colleague of Soviet leader Mikhail Gorbachev.

However, not everything in Thatcher's years as prime minister went well for her. Her Foreign Secretary, Sir Geoffrey Howe, resigned from his post in 1990 because he strongly disagreed with her attitude about Britain's overall role in Europe. By then, dissatisfaction with Thatcher's decisions about government taxation and high interest rates had grown; Howe's resignation just made matters worse. Finally, after three terms in office, Thatcher withdrew from the upcoming election and resigned on November 28.

To this day, Thatcher and her years as Britain's prime minister are a topic of immense controversy.

The Spanish-American War

THE SPANISH-AMERICAN WAR lasted just 100 days (from April to August 1898). It also proved to be a uniting cause for a country still divided over the outcome of the American Civil War.

For years, Cuba had been clamoring for independence from Spanish rule, and the United States began to be concerned about a revolt. Sensational "yellow journalists" such as William Randolph Hearst whipped up public opinion against the Spanish. But when the U.S. battleship *Maine* mysteriously blew up in Havana harbor on February 15, 1898, the cry became "Remember the *Maine*!" War was declared on April 25.

The Americans struck first. Commodore George Dewey's Asiatic Squadron steamed in from Hong Kong and entered Manila Bay in the Philippines, a Spanish colony at the time. On May 1, his ships engaged and wiped out the Spanish vessels in the harbor. American troops arrived in July, and the city surrendered in August.

Meanwhile, Admiral Pasqual Cervera's fleet steamed into Cuba from Spain. His ships eluded the American Atlantic Fleet and safely entered the harbor at Santiago in late May. On June 22, 16,000 American troops led by General William R. Shafter landed east of Santiago, skirmished with the Spanish, and approached the city's defensive line. On July 1, the Americans attacked the defenses at El Caney, Kettle Hill, and San Juan Hill. After a bitter fight, including the celebrated charge of the Rough Riders led by Theodore Roosevelt, the Spanish retreated. Cervera's fleet attempted to escape on July 3, but the American fleet pursued them and sank every Spanish ship. Santiago soon surrendered.

An armistice followed as peace negotiations opened. On December 10, the treaty was signed: Spain ceded Puerto Rico and Guam to the United States and the U.S. paid $20 million for the Philippines. The United States also recognized Cuba's independence. The war brought the U.S. onto the world stage as an imperial power while effectively ending the era of the Spanish empire.

POSTSCRIPT

■ When an American fleet arrived off Guam and fired a warning shot, the Spanish commander there sent out a note apologizing that he could not return the salute because he was out of gunpowder for his cannon—he had not learned that his country was at war. Needless to say, the Americans seized Guam without a fight.

The Crash of 1929

THERE'S A SAYING THAT GOES, "The bigger they are, the harder they fall." That is precisely what happened to America in October 1929.

The Roaring Twenties was one of the country's best decades. World War I was over, and prosperity returned. Industrialization was increasing; new technologies such as the car and radio were entering people's daily lives. To increase their newfound wealth, hundreds of thousands of people invested in the stock market. The Dow Jones skyrocketed from 60 to 400 as the decade progressed, and those who bought stocks became millionaires virtually overnight. With an air of assuredness, Americans mortgaged their homes and invested their entire savings accounts.

On October 24, 1929, the financial bubble burst, and the Dow Jones plummeted. People went bankrupt just as quickly as they had become millionaires. Billions of dollars were lost in a matter of days. On Monday, the stock market dropped 12.8 percent. The next day, Black Tuesday, it dropped an additional 11.7 percent. By 1932, it was down 89 percent from its peak in 1929.

People rushed to their banks to pull out their money, but it was too late—the banks had taken customer deposits and invested the money in stocks. When people came to empty their accounts, they found them already bare. More than 10,000 banks failed; countless people committed suicide over their losses. This devastation ushered in the Great Depression of the 1930s. Describing the event, a journalist wrote, "Wall Street was a street of vanished hopes, of curiously silent apprehension and of a sort of paralyzed hypnosis.... It was the consensus of bankers and brokers alike that no such scenes ever again will be witnessed by this generation."

Another ramification of the crash involved the Dawes Plan. In 1924, President Calvin Coolidge focused on foreign policy. Germany was struggling to pay reparations to France and England in the war's aftermath. Vice President Charles Dawes created a plan to help Germany make payments: U.S. banks issued long-term loans to Germany, who in turn, paid the money to France and England. Those two countries then gave that money back to the United States to pay off the billions they had borrowed to fight the war. It was a win-win arrangement for everyone—until the crash. Suddenly, the United States needed that money and halted the loans. Germany could not pay England and France any longer, and they had to default on their U.S. loans, worsening America's Depression.

The Mughal Invasion of India

THE FIRST MUGHAL EMPEROR, Babur, was a descendant of Timur and Genghis Khan, the two great conquerors of Central Asia. After he was driven out of the Central Asian kingdom of Ferghana in 1501, Babur seized the kingdom of Kabul in Afghanistan. He then turned his attention to the rich lands of northern India.

Babur the Conqueror

Between 1519 and 1524, Babur led four raids into what is now Pakistan. In 1524, Daulat Khan Lodi, the governor of the Punjab, invited Babur to intervene in a civil war that had developed in the Lodi Sultanate of Delhi. Daulat Khan wanted Babur to defend the Punjab against Sultan Ibrahim Lodi, but Babur had different ideas. In his autobiography, the *Babur-nama* (*Book of Babur*), he wrote, "From the year 910 [1504–1505] when Kabul was conquered, until this date, I craved Hindustan [India].... Finally all such impediments had been removed."

That year, Babur overthrew Daulat Khan. He defeated Sultan Ibrahim at the battle of Panipat on April 20, 1526, declared himself emperor at Delhi, and proceeded to conquer a territory that extended from Afghanistan to Bengal and the Rajput desert. Babur's empire was lost by his son, Humayan, who was driven into exile in 1540 by a confederation of disaffected Afghani nobles. Humayan retook Delhi in 1555.

When Humayan's 13-year-old son, Akbar, inherited the empire, it was little more than a title and a claim. But he made the most of it. Known as the Great Mughal, Akbar was the real architect of Mughal India. During his 50-year reign, Akbar expanded the boundaries of the empire from Afghanistan to the Deccan Plateau in southern India. His reign was characterized by the unification of the empire and a policy of religious tolerance toward non-Muslims.

Mughal power began to crumble with the death of Emperor Aurangzeb in 1707. In 1739, the ruler of Persia invaded India and sacked Delhi. Thereafter, the Mughal emperor was nothing more than a figurehead.

Margaret Sanger (1879–1966)

THIS RENOWNED ADVOCATE for the dissemination of birth control information was born Margaret Higgins in Corning, New York. Her father was a working-class nonconformist who encouraged her to rebel against prejudice and intolerance. Her mother died from tuberculosis after experiencing 18 pregnancies and 11 live births, which focused Sanger's rebellion on the issue of women's control of their own bodies.

Sanger began working as a nurse on New York City's impoverished East Side in 1912. After witnessing firsthand a reprise of her mother's plight among hundreds of young girls, in 1914 she started a newspaper, *The Woman Rebel.*

Sanger's life as a radical reached a turning point in 1916 when she opened the first birth control clinic in United States. The clinic was in the Brooklyn neighborhood of Brownsville, and there she dispensed birth control devices and related information. She also quickly ran afoul of New York's anti-birth control law. She fled to Europe to avoid severe criminal penalties but returned the next year when the charges against her were dropped.

In 1917, she started a new journal, *Birth Control Review,* and in 1921 founded the American Birth Control League. Two years later, following a New York Appellate court decision that allowed contraceptives to be dispensed for therapeutic reasons, Sanger founded the Clinical Research Bureau, the first legal birth control clinic in the United States. In 1940, the Bureau changed its name to the Margaret Sanger Research Bureau. In 1942, the American Birth Control League became the Planned Parenthood Federation of America.

Sanger lived to see the introduction of a birth control pill in the early 1960s. She also saw the end of all state laws forbidding the sale of contraceptive devices and the dissemination of birth control information after the Supreme Court struck down Connecticut's anti-birth control statute in 1965.

To many historians and feminists, Sanger's reputation for progressive reform is somewhat tainted by the fact that in the 1920s she published articles in *Birth Control Review* that advocated sterilization of the insane and feebleminded. But for many Americans, Margaret Sanger remains an icon. For them, the most famous statement of her ideals rings true: "No woman can call herself free who does not own and control her body."

The Baby Boom

WORLD WAR II was over at last! In 1945, thousands of men returned to the United States, Canada, and Australia, after spending years serving their country overseas. They were ready to put bloody battles behind them and focus on the future. Often this future included getting married and starting a family. The nation, too, was experiencing postwar economic growth. Together, these two facts resulted in one of history's biggest jumps in population—the Baby Boom.

In the United States, the Baby Boom lasted from 1946 through 1964. In that time, 79 million babies were born. The children born during this era were a new generation that openly voiced their different values. The "boomers" grew up listening to the bands of Woodstock, protesting in the era of war and Civil Rights, and watching the assassinations of John F. and Robert Kennedy and Martin Luther King, Jr. The Vietnam War was a defining issue for the generation that was characterized by its rebelliousness. They often rejected the conservatism of the previous generation and fought against issues such as discrimination and the use of nuclear weapons. Illegal drug use was rampant and, with the advent of the birth control pill, so was promiscuous sex. Baby boomers also had a huge influence on popular culture, shaping everything from television shows and music to fashion.

While the Baby Boom may seem like a population fluke, it has actually strongly affected the world as it is today. With so many extra people being born, there was a much higher demand for consumer products and services. With the population growth, there was a spike in families moving out of cities and into suburbs. Schools opened, jobs were relocated, and the economy shifted to accommodate all of the new people.

Today, the boomers, now in their 40s, 50s, and 60s, make up about 27 percent of the American population. They remain one of the most influential age groups in the country and are a major influence in elections and business trends. As more baby boomers get closer to retirement age, they will have a significant impact on government programs such as social security—especially as life expectancy continues to increase.

The Destruction of Pompeii and Herculaneum

WHEN THE FIRST SIGNS that the volcano Vesuvius was active appeared during mid-August, A.D. 79, no one in the area around Pompeii was particularly alarmed. The volcano had been quiet for many years, and minor earthquakes were common. Even if a major earthquake occurred, the city would rebuild and go on. No one realized just how devastating an eruption could be.

A victim of Vesuvius

A vivid eyewitness account of the disaster exists in two letters written by Pliny the Younger, who watched the eruption from across the Bay of Naples. Pliny tells us that the volcano erupted in the early afternoon of August 24, and a cloud of smoke "like an umbrella pine" billowed into the sky. Volcanic cinder and ash rained down. By the time Pliny and his mother decided to evacuate, "a dense black cloud was coming up behind us, spreading over the earth like a flood."

Within 48 hours, the two Roman cities of Herculaneum and Pompeii ceased to exist. Their fates were very different but equally horrible. An avalanche of volcanic ash and lava poured over Herculaneum until it covered the city. In Pompeii, the disaster began with a light fall of ash, which accelerated into a hail of pumice that drove residents back into their homes. Clouds of ash and poisonous gases settled over the city. Roofs collapsed under the weight of falling rock. Those who were not buried alive choked to death on the fumes.

Unlike other ancient ruins, Herculaneum and Pompeii were perfectly preserved, protected for 17 centuries from vandalism and decay by more than 20 feet of volcanic debris. Excavation of the sites did not occur until ordered by the king of Naples, who had been intrigued by fragments of statuary uncovered by workmen. Herculaneum was excavated in 1738, and Pompeii in 1748. The ruins provide a vivid picture of both the life and death of these cities. Excavators not only uncovered public buildings but also private homes, shops, mosaics, furniture, and graffiti. The remains are as domestic as a loaf of bread abandoned in the oven and as horrible as the imprints of victim's bodies, preserved by lava and hardened volcanic ash.

Slavery Ends in Brazil

THE HISTORIES OF SLAVERY in the United States and Brazil share some similarities. In both countries, slavery existed from the colonial stage through their emergence as independent nations. Although both the United States and Brazil faced governmental crises over slavery, the American government survived while the Brazilian monarchy did not.

Brazil's slave-holding period was significantly longer (1532–1888) than that of the United States (1619–1865). During the 17th century, America used indentured servants as laborers in addition to African slaves. However, Brazil relied heavily on slavery. Almost 40 percent of the African slaves brought to the Americas were taken there. The importation of slaves was outlawed in the United States in 1808. By contrast, as many as 60,000 slaves were imported into Brazil annually by 1848.

In 1850, British warships went into Brazilian ports and burned ships that were suspected of transporting slaves. Their reasons weren't entirely beneficent: Because Britain had ended slavery in its West Indies colonies, they wanted to ensure that Brazil did not gain an advantage in world sugar sales by producing cheaper sugar than the West Indies. A year later, Brazil abolished slave trading—though not the use of slaves.

By the middle of the 19th century, slavery in the Western world existed only in Brazil, Cuba, Puerto Rico, and the southern United States. Prior to the invention of the cotton gin and the expansion of the cotton industry, many U.S. leaders expected slavery to die out. However, only the American Civil War in the 1860s and subsequent 13th Amendment to the Constitution in 1865 abolished slavery in America.

Brazil was slower to act. In 1871, slavery was abolished for newborns, and for senior citizens in 1885. In 1886, Cuba ended slavery, which left Brazil increasingly isolated as a slave nation. On May 13, 1888, while her father Emperor Dom Pedro II traveled in Europe, Princess Isabel of Brazil abolished slavery by signing the Golden Law of Emancipation—with no compensation to owners. Landowners, unwilling to replace slaves with free workers, revolted; the emperor was asked to leave the country. A republic structured after the United States government was established in 1889.

POSTSCRIPT

■ Emperor Dom Pedro II invited defeated American Confederates to cultivate cotton in Brazil. Between 1867 and 1871, 3,000 Confederate families went to Brazil, but about 80 percent eventually returned to the United States.

The Miracle on Ice

IN 1980, America had just emerged from the depressing '70s—the decade of Watergate, inflation, the energy crisis, and South Vietnam's collapse. Americans had been taken hostage in Iran, and the Soviet Union had rekindled the Cold War by invading Afghanistan. The country's spirit was low. But when the American hockey team beat the Soviet team in the 1980 Winter Olympics at Lake Placid, the win sent the entire United States into a frenzy of patriotic pride.

At the outset of the Olympics, it appeared that no one could take down the mighty Soviets; the year before, they had crushed a team of National Hockey League All-Stars 6–0. The Soviets had a team of professionals, with stars including Boris Mikhailov, Valeri Kharlamov, and Vladislav Tretiak in the goal. Instead of gathering an all-star cast, the United States sent an amateur squad of college and semi-pro players. True, American coach Herb Brooks had drilled and conditioned them into peak form, but the reality was that it was like sending a sandlot team against the 1927 Yankees dream team of Babe Ruth and Lou Gehrig.

A reality check was in order when, in an exhibition game prior to the Olympics, the Soviets annihilated Team USA 10–3. Then, in their first Olympic contest, the Americans seemed certain to lose to Sweden. But a last-second goal salvaged a tie, and the team turned a corner. Victories over Czechoslovakia, Norway, Romania, and West Germany sent Team USA into the medal round against the invincible Soviets.

For most of the first period the Soviets led, but Tretiak misplayed a shot and the United States converted it for a 2–2 tie. The second period ended with the Soviets on top 3–2. In the third period, Team USA stunned reserve Soviet goalie Vladimir Myshkin with two goals. American goalie Jim Craig repeatedly turned back the Soviets. When the game ended with the American win 4–3, the arena erupted in pandemonium. The crowd screamed deliriously and waved American flags as the players piled on top of one another. Team USA completed its memorable run by topping Finland 4–2 for the gold medal.

The Miracle on Ice was more than just a hockey game—it marked the day Americans started to feel good about themselves again.

POSTSCRIPT

■ American Coach Herb Brooks gave would-be players psychological tests as part of tryouts.

The Nazi Camps

THE TERM "CONCENTRATION CAMP" is often used as an all-inclusive label for Nazi camps during World War II. But actually there were four categories of camps: concentration, labor, transport, and death.

Concentration camps were established in 1933 for the dual purpose of incarcerating Hitler's political opponents and striking fear in the German population. Those opposing Hitler were subjected to brutal treatment then released to spread word of their experiences. By 1937, Dachau, Sachsenhausen, Buchenwald, and Lichtenburg had replaced the 40 to 50 improvised concentration camps scattered around Germany.

Around this time, citizens considered to be asocial—such as criminals, drunks, Gypsies, and members of some religious groups—were being imprisoned along with political opponents. After Kristallnacht on November 9–10, 1938, when Jews and their homes and businesses were attacked, Jews were arrested and sent to Dachau, Buchenwald, and Sachsenhausen. Most were only held for a few weeks in an effort to intimidate them into leaving Germany and its occupied territories.

In the summer of 1941, most camp internees were political opponents and foreign prisoners of war. By that winter, anticipating a protracted war with Russia and England, the concentration camps changed from detention centers to slave labor camps. Military and civilian companies were able to hire camp laborers to replace German workers who had gone off to fight. As Germany encountered more military failures, Jews began to replace the dwindling numbers of political prisoners and prisoners of war who died from starvation, bitter cold, illness, and brutal treatment.

As Germany headed toward the Final Solution—the mass extermination of the Jews—death camps were built at Chelmno, Belzec, Sobibor, and Treblinka. Other camps at Majdanek and Auschwitz were reconstructed as both labor and death camps. Transit camps to hold Jews waiting for cattle cars to Auschwitz or Sobibor were set up throughout Nazi-occupied Europe. While there were deaths at all of the camps, only the death camps had extermination of the Jewish population as their primary purpose. It is estimated that six million Jews died during the Holocaust.

The People's Charter

ENGLAND IN THE 1830s was no bastion of popular democracy. Although the Reform Act of 1832 expanded the franchise, only about 700,000 people were eligible to vote out of a population of about 14 million. The lower middle class and working class were essentially disenfranchised.

Frustrated that political and social power lay in the hands of the aristocracy and landed gentry, working-class organizers decided to take action. In 1836, the artisans of the London Working Men's Association began considering a charter—essentially a formal petition—detailing the political concessions they felt were due. "The People's Charter," drafted in 1838, contained six demands, including universal suffrage for all men over the age of 21, equal-sized electoral districts, voting by secret ballot, an end to a property qualification to be able to serve in Parliament, annual election of Parliament, and pay for members of Parliament.

The petition was widely circulated and met with an enthusiastic response, garnering more than one million signatures in what may well have been the first working-class movement in history. A convoy of horse-drawn wagons transported the documents to the House of Commons in London in the summer of 1839, where it was introduced by Thomas Attwood, M.P.

Attwood's colleagues were not impressed. The charter was rejected by a vote of 235–46. The rejection sparked several violent outbreaks by frustrated workers. Chartist leader John Frost led a march through South Wales to Newport, Monmouthshire. A confrontation between Frost's Chartists and about 60 soldiers ended in disaster when 22 Chartists were killed and another 50 were wounded.

There is some evidence the confrontation at Newport was intended to ignite a general uprising if successful. Instead, Chartism suffered a major blow. Many of its leaders were arrested and imprisoned, causing the movement to fragment.

In 1842, another petition, this one with more than three million signatures, was rejected by Parliament. In 1848, yet another Chartist petition was turned down. This one bore six million signatures. The government cracked down severely on unrest and demonstrations, and the Chartist movement gradually faded away.

But while the Chartists did not achieve their aims, change was to come. By 1872, most of the six points of the People's Charter had become law.

The de las Casas Debate

DOMINICAN PRIEST BARTOLOMÉ DE LAS CASAS, who was known as the "Apostle of the Indians," criticized the conquest and exploitation of the indigenous peoples in the Spanish colonies of Latin America.

He had firsthand knowledge of the Spanish experience in America, having sailed with Columbus's third voyage in 1498. He had also been a settler in Hispaniola in 1502 and participated in the pacification of Cuba in 1513. After witnessing a massacre of the native population in 1514, de las Casas gave up his own slaves and spent the next 50 years traveling between Spain and the colonies advocating reform and the abolition of Indian slavery. He proposed that the colonists be allowed to import African slaves to replace the indigenous peoples and that those people be placed under the protection of the Catholic Church. He attempted to bring in Castilian peasants as colonists; worked as a missionary in Mexico, Nicaragua, Peru, and Guatemala; and wrote books arguing the rights of Indians as subjects of the Spanish king, including *A Brief Account of the Destruction of the Indes.*

In 1550, de las Casas argued his position in a public debate with Spanish historian Juan Ginés de Sepúlveda before the council of Charles V in Valladolid. Sepúlveda appeared first. For three hours, he argued for the "civilizing mission" of Spain on the grounds that Indians were "natural slaves" in the Aristotelian sense of the phrase, "inhuman barbarians who thought the greatest gift they could offer to God was human hearts." Their art and sculpture, which was brought back to Spain as treasure, was proof of neither their civilization nor their humanity, "for do not even bees and spiders make works which no human can imitate?"

De las Casas's rebuttal lasted for five days, using a lifetime's collection of firsthand reports. "The savage peoples of the world may be compared to uncultivated soil that readily brings forth weeds and useless tares," he argued, "but has within itself such natural virtue that by labor and cultivation it may be made to yield sound and beneficial fruit." Even that the Indians practiced human sacrifice could be explained as a rational step in the development of religious thought. His defense ended with the statement, "All the world is human."

The debate had no effect on the treatment of Indians in the Spanish colonies. Modern scholars see de las Casas's arguments in the Valladolid debate as the forerunner of modern positions on human rights and an inspiration for the UN Universal Declaration of Human Rights of 1948.

Formation of the Arab League

THE ARAB LEAGUE, an alliance of Arab states in the Middle East, was officially announced on March 22, 1945. By May it included Egypt, Jordan, Iraq, Lebanon, Saudi Arabia, and Syria. The league's main goal was to "draw closer the relations between member states and coordinate their political activities with the aim of realizing a close collaboration between them, to safeguard their independence and sovereignty, and to consider in a general way the affairs and interests of the Arab countries."

Although the countries' differences meant that there would be many difficulties to overcome, there was one thing all the members agreed

Delegates sign the Arab League Charter

upon: They did not want more Jewish settlers in Palestine. When Britain announced that it was giving up control of Palestine, the United Nations voted to partition the territory between Jews and Arabs. The Arab League announced that they would fight the partition. When the state of Israel was announced on May 14, 1948, all six league members attacked Israel. The league secretary announced that the Arabs would wage "a war of extermination and a momentous massacre which will be spoken of like the Mongolian massacres and the Crusades."

The resulting Arab–Israeli conflict became a central focus of the Arab League. Although at first the league did not consider the plight of the Palestinian people, the very fact that Israel continued to exist influenced the league to create the Palestinian Liberation Organization in 1964, expressly to attack the Jews. The league voted to expel any member that signed a peace treaty with Israel. When Egyptian president Anwar al-Sadat did sign such a treaty in 1979, the league expelled Egypt and moved its headquarters from Cairo to Tunis. Egypt was readmitted a decade later, and the league's headquarters was moved back to Cairo.

Presently the Arab League has 22 members whose lands stretch from Morocco to Sudan and Somalia to the Comoros islands. The league has supplied peacekeeping troops in Lebanon, started literacy campaigns across the region, helped preserve cultural heritage, worked to preserve the rights of immigrant workers, and is currently working on a free trade agreement between member states.

Confucius (551–479 B.C.)

ACCORDING TO LORE, Confucius was born in 551 B.C. into a poor, hardworking family in the Lu State in China (now Shandong Province). Although not many facts are known about his life, he grew up to become one of the world's most famous philosophers: His words have inspired both criticism and praise from generations of thinkers.

Confucius taught that each person had a span of existence, determined by fate, that could not be altered. Within that span, each person could determine his or her own accomplishments and the things for which he or she would be remembered. He also taught that presenting oneself in a false or self-aggrandizing manner was the opposite of love and compassion and thus was considered improper.

Confucius's teachings were based on ancient beliefs, though many of his ideas and teachings were original. His ideas later formed the basis of Chinese education. His views were focused on the ideal man—how he should live, how he should interact with others and to what extent, and how he should participate in society and government. Confucius believed that education kept people from straying ethically. It was important that education be open to all classes of people, he said, because everyone could accomplish great things during his or her life, regardless of status.

The *Five Classics* served as the basis of Confucius's educational program. Students became educated through memorization and rote learning and were discouraged from questioning what they learned. History, poetry, and the study of rituals were part of the classical program.

Students who aspired to government service were required to take a civil service examination. Since, theoretically any male in China could enter government service, the civil service examination was used to maintain cultural unity and societal values. Students wanting to prepare for government service were trained in Confucius's *Five Classics*.

Confucius taught that self-discipline was about compassion and respect for others. He also taught that only careful study of a subject would bring about thorough understanding. Confucius is probably best remembered for his sayings, many of which relate to morality and principles of living. As Confucius said, "Our greatest glory is not in never failing, but in rising every time we do."

The Discovery of the Double Helix

IN 1953, two young scientists named James Watson and Francis Crick made a discovery that would change medical science forever. They first wrote about their discovery of the double helix—the very structure of DNA—in a scientific paper, in what would be a gross understatement: "This structure has novel features which are of considerable biological interest." Nine years later, they won the Nobel Prize in Physiology or Medicine.

The discovery of the double helix was, in essence, "the secret of life." It opened the door to modern technologies such as gene therapy, DNA fingerprinting, cloning, stem cell research, genetically engineered crops, and DNA-based medications. In 2002, even Watson modestly marveled at how their discovery changed the world, saying, "We didn't envision any consequence except knowledge."

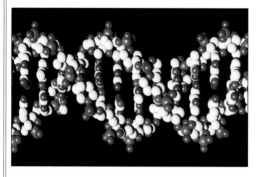

The concept of DNA and its importance had been determined in 1944 by American scientist Oswald Avery. The scientific community accepted that DNA was probably the "molecule of life," but they could not figure out its structure. Until they could understand its biochemical makeup, they couldn't comprehend how it affected heredity and reproduction. Crick and Watson knew that developing a three-dimensional model of DNA was critical. Instead of doing additional experiments, the two men immersed themselves in what had already been done, looking into many scientific fields such as genetics, biochemistry, and X-ray crystallography. Combining this knowledge with their own scientific backgrounds—along with a lot of intuition and a little luck—they created a cardboard model of the elusive DNA.

When they published their evidence, important as it was, it actually did not cause the gasp of amazement throughout the world that some might have thought. In fact, most newspapers gave it little attention. It was not until the team won the Nobel Prize that they achieved any kind of notice. From that point onward, however, their names were familiar to geneticists and, eventually, the entire world.

The Scopes Monkey Trial

IN 1914, a biology textbook was published that was meant to teach high school students, not create a nationwide controversy. In the textbook, a line stated that evolution was "the belief that simple forms of life on the earth slowly and gradually gave rise to those more complex and that thus ultimately the most complex forms came into existence." This statement fueled what would become one of the most famous and pivotal trials in U.S. history.

In early 1925, the Butler Bill was passed in Tennessee, making it illegal to discuss the theory of evolution in any classroom. Indeed, according to the bill, teachers were forbidden to teach, "any theory that denies the story of the Divine Creation of man as taught in the Bible, and to teach instead that man has descended from a lower order of animals."

In response, the American Civil Liberties Union announced it was looking for teachers who would be willing to challenge this law. Twenty-four-year-old science teacher and football coach John Thomas Scopes was willing to do it, even though he had only briefly taught biology and wasn't sure he had even mentioned evolution.

Scopes was indicted on April 24. The trial began on July 10 in Dayton, Tennessee. It received a massive amount of press, and the topic brought together some of the best-known names in the history of American law, including Clarence Darrow for the defense and William Jennings Bryan for the prosecution. Both sides argued the definition of the word *evolution,* and the details of the Old Testament. A mere 11 days later, the jury found Scopes guilty after only nine minutes of deliberation. He was fined $100 and made his only statement, declaring that he would "oppose this law in any way I can. Any other action would be in violation of my ideal of academic freedom—that is, to teach the truth as guaranteed in our constitution, of personal and religious freedom."

The Butler Act was finally repealed in 1967. Meanwhile, in 1955, the sensational trial was turned into a Broadway play, *Inherit the Wind.*

POSTSCRIPT

■ In reference to the fact that evolution implies humans came from apes, Dayton was nicknamed "monkeytown" by journalist H. L. Mencken.

Virginia Woolf (1882–1941)

VIRGINIA WOOLF'S FAMOUS 1929 ESSAY *A Room of One's Own* took the early feminist position that the under-representation of women in the arts was not the result of lack of ability but lack of financial independence. According to Woolf, "A woman must have money and a room of her own if she is to write fiction." Unlike many of her contemporaries, she had the luxury of both.

Woolf grew up surrounded by literature and learning. Her father was renowned British literary critic and biographer Leslie Stephen, and she was related to some of the most distinguished scholarly families of the day, including the Darwins. After the death of her father in 1904, Woolf moved to the London district known as Bloomsbury with her sister and two brothers. There she began to entertain a circle of writers and intellectuals very different from the Victorian luminaries she met in her father's house. This group of avant-garde writers, artists, and philosophers became known as the Bloomsbury Group.

She married journalist and critic Leonard Woolf in 1912. With him, she founded the Hogarth Press in 1917, a single handpress that became a successful publishing house. In addition to Woolf's first short stories, Hogarth Press published works by Katherine Mansfield, E. M. Forster, and T. S. Eliot and introduced Dr. Sigmund Freud's writings to English readers.

Woolf began her literary career writing well-regarded essays and criticism but is best known for her experimentation and innovation in the form of the modern novel. She rejected what she called the "materialism" of contemporary novelists such as Arnold Bennett and John Galsworthy in favor of a style that combined psychological insight with the rhythms and imagery of lyric poetry. In novels such as *Mrs. Dalloway, Jacob's Room,* and *To the Lighthouse,* she used techniques including inner monologue and stream of consciousness to reveal the personalities and relationships of her characters and to explore issues of memory, time, and change. Novelist E. M. Forster, a fellow member of the Bloomsbury Group, summed up Woolf's accomplishments when he said she "pushed the light of the English language a little further against darkness."

Throughout her life, Woolf was troubled with depression. She spent time in nursing homes on "rest cures," heard voices, and openly referred to herself as "mad." On March 28, 1941, depressed and afraid that another nervous breakdown would leave her a burden on her husband, Woolf filled her coat pockets with rocks and drowned herself in the River Ouse.

Genghis Khan (1162–1227)

Born in central Mongolia in 1162, Genghis Khan was first known as Temujin. At a young age, Temujin killed his older half-brother in an argument and later survived capture and enslavement by another Mongol tribe. Although at first he had very few followers, Temujin methodically conquered and absorbed neighboring tribes, building alliances as he went. Eventually, he united most of the feuding Mongol tribes.

It was around this time that Temujin took the name Genghis, meaning unshakable and fearless. He formed a mighty mounted army that relied on speed. When the Mongols overran much of the Chin empire, they added the empire's engineering knowledge to produce a superb corps of engineers who manned a vast array of siege machines. The Mongols were thus able to capture walled cities everywhere they went.

Within 25 years, Genghis Khan's Mongol army conquered an area much larger than the Roman Empire, which had taken 400 years to develop. Alongside his sons and grandsons, Genghis conquered much of the civilized world, which included China, Korea, and parts of India, central Asia, Russia, and the Middle East.

Genghis Khan's views were remarkably advanced for his time. He allowed religious tolerance as long as his subjects were loyal to him. He issued new laws that softened the Mongols' hard life. His conquests led to a melding of civilizations and ideas that long had been separate. His engineers built numerous bridges, facilitating transportation and communication across the empire. Because of this, the Silk Road was made safe from bandits, which led to European and Chinese exchanges of goods and ideas.

The Mongols did not establish a new religion or create any new technologies, barely wrote anything for future historians to read, and had no works of great art or building. In fact, there were no contemporary images made of Genghis Khan, and after he died in 1227, the Mongols buried him in a secret place with no monument to mark his grave. Though later in history the Mongols were regarded as savages, Genghis Khan's influence was far-reaching: The longest story in *The Canterbury Tales* is about the Mongol leader.

The Assassination of Martin Luther King, Jr.

FOR 13 YEARS, Dr. Martin Luther King, Jr., was the model for nonviolent social change. King was universally known and broadly admired. For many, he had become America's moral conscience. But on April 4, 1968, his voice was stilled by a sniper's bullet while he stood on the balcony at the Lorraine Motel in Memphis, Tennessee.

King had entered the national stage as the leader of the successful 1955 Montgomery Bus Boycott. He was a Baptist minister and a gifted orator; his message resonated with African Americans across the country. King was also a committed disciple of *satyagraha*, the nonviolent strategy associated with India's Mohandas Gandhi. King expanded his focus from the noneconomic liberalism of racial integration to include issues of class and poverty. But just as some older leaders of civil rights organizations criticized his opposition to the Vietnam War, many younger members of the movement were moving away from nonviolence.

Initially, King had been invited to Memphis to show his support for striking sanitation workers. The strike had only been going on for a few weeks, but morale was low, and King saw an opportunity to meld his crusade for racial justice with his growing concern for issues of class and poverty. He had been warned that there might be violence if he led a march, but he pressed on. When some younger members of the march and some hangers-on began to smash windows and loot stores, he called for calm but to no avail.

That evening, clearly distressed, King delivered his "I've Been to the Mountaintop" speech. He clearly sensed his own mortality. "Like anybody, I would like to live a long life—longevity has its place," he said. "But I'm not concerned about that now. I just want to do God's will." He was assassinated the next day.

Nationwide grief over King's murder quickly turned to rage. Riots erupted in numerous cities and towns, and more than three dozen people were killed. Controversy soon surrounded the assassination. The FBI investigated the murder, but many remembered J. Edgar Hoover's personal antipathy toward King and questioned the department's motives. When James Earl Ray was arrested, many people, including members of King's own family, believed that he was innocent. Questions of a cover-up and suspicion of a conspiracy remain.

The New Weapons of War

As World War I broke out in August 1914, the armies of Europe still operated in a 19th-century mind-set. Outdated attitudes about warfare clashed heavily with the realities of modern technology. The resulting bloodshed brought about dramatic change in the methods of waging war.

A French air torpedo circa 1914

Few images better sum up the shift in technology and thinking than that of French soldiers charging across open fields in the initial weeks of the war—only to be mowed down by German machine guns. Cavalry was suddenly obsolete, replaced by the first tanks, which could negotiate the broken ground of no-man's-land and protect crews against the hail of gunfire. In 1915, invisible death arrived with the German introduction of poison gas. Phosgene could kill its victim within hours; mustard gas inflicted painful burns.

Fast-firing artillery and lethal high-explosive shells drove soldiers into trenches and underground bunkers protected by lavish barbed wire entanglements. Attackers resorted to flamethrowers and hand grenades to dig them out. Even the soldiers' uniforms changed: Soft caps were replaced by steel helmets; brightly colored uniforms were discarded in favor of subdued colors that better concealed the wearer.

Airplanes assumed an increasingly important role on the battlefield. Used at first for reconnaissance, aircraft developed into a means of dropping bombs on ground troops. As air superiority became increasingly important, fighter planes were introduced to destroy enemy aircraft. Blimps floated high in the sky as observers studied enemy positions. Zeppelins motored hundreds of miles to drop bombs on London, as civilian populations became a legitimate military target.

The war also expanded to beneath the seas with the German U-boat campaign against Allied shipping. Submarines attacked without warning, a strategy widely condemned as immoral, though it later became routine during World War II. In 1915, the German sub *U-20* sank the British passenger liner *Lusitania*. The loss of 1,198 civilian lives marked yet another departure in the accepted rules of warfare.

The Hundred Years' War

THE HUNDRED YEARS' WAR was neither a 100 years long nor was it a war, per se. It was actually a series of smaller conflicts between England and France, punctuated by numerous truces, from 1337 to 1453. The war saw the decline of mounted knights on the battlefield and an increase in foot soldiers.

At the beginning of the war, England controlled much of modern-day France. The French were concerned about the size of the English territory, which threatened both countries' sense of nationalism. The war was also ignited by French support of Scotland's fight against English domination.

In 1337, King Philip VI of France announced that he would seize all English territory south of the Loire River. In response, English King Edward III landed in France with an army of 15,000 soldiers, more than half of them longbowmen. He marched through Brittany and Normandy, down the Seine River toward Paris, and placed his troops in a defensive position near the village of Crecy. The French attacked late on August 26 with an army of 60,000. The muddy ground hampered French cavalry charges, but they persisted. The attacks were all repelled, mainly by English bowmen. The French lost between 10,000 and 20,000 men, while Edward's army suffered only 200 casualties.

The fighting continued. Truces were made and broken. War erupted yet again in 1415 when Henry V of England took advantage of chaos in France to reconquer Normandy and assist the Burgundians in seizing Paris. That same year, the Battle of Agincourt was another major English victory and was later immortalized in the play *King Henry V* by William Shakespeare.

In 1429, a 17-year-old French peasant girl, Joan of Arc, rose to fame when she commanded a French relief force that successfully ended the English siege of Orleans. However, despite Joan's victories for France, King Charles VII was jealous of her success and allowed the Burgundians to capture her. Joan was sold to the English and burned at the stake in 1431. The war continued, and the French recaptured Paris five years later.

A truce went into effect from 1444 until 1449, during which time the French reorganized their army and established an effective artillery force. During the next four years, the French captured one English-controlled town after another. Finally, on October 19, 1453, Bordeaux fell to the French, effectively ending the long war, as the English now held only the city of Calais.

Warsaw Ghetto Uprising

IN 1940, the Germans began concentrating Poland's three million Jews in designated urban ghettos. The largest was in Warsaw: Approximately 400,000 Jews were herded into a 3.5-square-mile area sealed off from the rest of the city by guards and an 11-mile-long glass-topped brick wall. Thousands died of disease and starvation.

Jews surrender after the uprising

In 1942, the Nazis began deporting Jews from the Warsaw Ghetto to the Treblinka extermination camp. About 300,000 Jews had already been removed before the remainder realized they were being taken to their deaths. Instead of accepting their fate, some decided to retaliate. The first armed resistance took place on January 18, 1943, when the Nazis tried to resume the deportations. The move surprised the Nazis, and after four days of clashes, they pulled back.

But the fighting wasn't done yet. The Jewish Military Union (ZZW) and Jewish Combat Organization (ZOB) organized defense efforts in the ghetto. The fighters scrounged up a few pistols and rifles, supplementing them with homemade explosives and gasoline bombs.

On April 19, the eve of Passover, General Jurgen Stroop sent a force into the ghetto. Although about 750 Jewish fighters resisted, they were heavily outgunned. Supported by artillery and armored vehicles, German troops began systematically burning houses. Thousands of civilians perished in the flames, while others were simply shot on sight.

The ZOB command post was overrun on May 8, and most of its fighters were killed or committed suicide. The Nazis declared victory on May 16, though sporadic resistance continued for weeks. The Nazis concluded by blowing up the Warsaw Synagogue. "The former Jewish quarter of Warsaw is no longer in existence," reported Stroop, who received the Iron Cross First Class for his efforts.

During the uprising, more than 40,000 Jews died or were sent to death camps. Casualties reported by the Nazis were far lower—only 16 killed and 85 wounded—though the total is thought to be higher.

Benedict Establishes Monastic Rules

ALTHOUGH CHRISTIAN MONASTICISM had begun a few centuries earlier in Egypt, Palestine, and Asia Minor, Benedict of Nursia established the guidelines by which monks live. His adherence to such rules, however, almost cost him his life.

Little is known about the life of Benedict, but what information is available comes from Pope Gregory the Great, who wrote about the monk in his *Second Book of Dialogues.* It is thought that Benedict was born in 480 in Nursia, a mountain village northeast of Rome. His parents sent him to Rome for a classical education, but he found the city too decadent and fled to Subiaco, east of Rome. There he lived a hermitlike, spiritual existence in a cave for three years. This attracted the attention of a local group of monks, who asked him to become their leader. Although he knew of the monks' dubious virtuousness, Benedict nevertheless agreed.

Benedict had his own ideas how monastic life should be lived, but his stringent rules did not sit well with the less-pious monks, who decided to kill him by poisoning his food. According to legend, when Benedict said a prayer over a cup of poisoned wine, the cup shattered. When he said a prayer over some poisoned bread, a raven came and snatched it away. Finally, Benedict left the monks.

Benedict's reputation for holiness and virtue spread, and many people came to live under his guidance. He then established 12 monasteries, each with a superior and 12 monks. In 529, Benedict moved to Monte Cassino, about 80 miles southeast of Rome. After destroying a temple dedicated to the Greek god Apollo, he built his premier monastery on the grounds. There he wrote his famous *Rule of Benedict,* developing it for use at Monte Cassino but also realizing it could be used at other monasteries. Benedict died there on March 21, 547, and was canonized in 1220.

The *Rule of Benedict* eventually became the guideline for monastic living throughout the Western world. Written for laymen who want to become monks, not clerics, the *Rule of Benedict* contains 73 chapters that combine spiritual doctrines such as, "Go to help the troubled and console the sorrowing," with routine explanation of how to operate a monastery. The document has become venerated as one of the finest in Christianity.

POSTSCRIPT

■ In an attempt at standardization, Charlemagne ordered that all monasteries follow *The Rule of Benedict.*

India Gains Independence

O N September 3, 1939, India was informed that the British Empire was at war with Germany. On September 14, the Indian National Congress, led by Mohandas Gandhi, responded that it could not support the war without British commitment to Indian independence.

Britain was not prepared to discuss Indian independence. In protest, Congress members immediately resigned their government posts as provincial ministers. On October 17, 1940, Gandhi adapted the technique of *satyagraha,* or nonviolent noncooperation, to protest India's involvement in the war through individual acts of civil disobedience. Within seven months, 25,000 *satyagrahis* had been arrested.

India eventually became an important base for the Allies, and Britain made another attempt to gain national cooperation. In March 1942, Sir Stafford Cripps arrived to negotiate a constitutional settlement with Indian leaders. Instead of self-rule, Cripps offered dominion status "upon the cessation of the hostilities." Gandhi described the offer as "a post-dated cheque on a bank that was failing." Indian nationalist organizations unanimously rejected the offer.

On May 3, Gandhi announced a new satyagraha campaign, the "Quit India" movement. For the remainder of the war, nationalists yelled "Quit India" at the British in the streets. The British treated the campaign as open rebellion, and more than 60,000 nationalists were arrested by the end of the year. Nonviolent demonstrations turned into riots. British soldiers and police fired into crowds of satyagrahis.

The end of the war brought with it a trial of Indian prisoners of war who had joined the Japanese to fight for Indian independence. Defended by Nationalist barristers, the "rebels" emerged as popular heroes. Even Indian servicemen who had fought for Britain began to question their own loyalty. On February 18, 1946, the Royal Indian Navy mutinied at Bombay. The next day, leaders in the British Parliament announced that it was time to resolve India's "constitutional problems."

Lord Mountbatten presided over the transfer of power into Indian hands. Faced with conflicting demands from the largely Hindu Congress Party and the Muslim League, Mountbatten decided to create a separate state for Indian Muslims. On August 14, 1947, India and Pakistan became independent nations in a solution known as the Partition. Muslims and Hindus migrated between India and Pakistan, creating enormous refugee populations in both countries—as well as violence that resulted in nearly one million deaths.

Wounded Knee

THE FAMOUS CLASH between the U.S. cavalry and Lakota Sioux at Wounded Knee Creek in South Dakota on December 29, 1890, is considered the last major armed conflict between the United States and Native Americans.

The confrontation came as 500 troops from the U.S. 7th Cavalry Regiment attempted to round up some 350 Lakota, hoping to disarm all Sioux warriors. Half-starved and without a home, the Lakota were reluctant as the cavalrymen surrounded them with rapid-fire artillery pieces.

The frozen body of Chief Big Foot

The military was already wary of the situation. Chief Sitting Bull had been killed earlier that month, and his followers had sought protection with his half-brother Big Foot. The government also knew of Ghost Dance practitioners among the Lakota. The Lakota believed the Ghost Dance was a means of ridding the land of all white people—through chanting and dancing, not violence. Young warriors donned specially consecrated Ghost Shirts, which they believed would make them immune to bullets in a battle with whites. Whites often wrongly interpreted the ritual as a war dance.

The Lakota were ordered to give up their weapons. While the soldiers gathered firearms, a medicine man named Yellow Bird began to perform the Ghost Dance. As tensions mounted, a deaf Lakota named Black Coyote refused to give up his rifle unless he was compensated for the weapon. Failing to understand, the soldiers grabbed him roughly, and Black Coyote's rifle discharged.

Chaos erupted as soldiers opened fire. Soon the cavalrymen and the Lakota fought at point-blank range. As the Lakota attempted to flee, the troops shot men, women, and children indiscriminately. One on-the-scene newspaper reported that 250 Lakota died, including Big Foot.

General Nelson Miles denounced the events at Wounded Knee as a "massacre" and relieved the colonel in charge of command. A court of inquiry subsequently reinstated the officer and determined that the soldiers had generally attempted to avoid killing noncombatants. That claim has been hotly disputed, and the controversy remains both sensitive and highly political more than 100 years later.

The End of Apartheid

ALTHOUGH SEGREGATION had been part of South African life since European settlers arrived in the 17th century, the policy of legalized segregation known as *apartheid* (Afrikaans for "apartness") was not formalized until 1948.

The Nationalist Party, which took office on a ticket of racial separation, passed apartheid laws that institutionalized segregation in every aspect of life. Under the Population Registration Act of 1950, people were assigned to one of three racial groups: Black, White, and Coloured (mixed race). In 1952, apartheid laws were tightened further with the introduction of Pass Laws, designed to limit the movement of nonwhites in certain areas.

Protests against apartheid escalated in the '60s, beginning with the 1960 "Sharpeville massacre," in which police killed 69 demonstrators during a protest against the Pass Laws. Increased demonstrations triggered official repression. Black nationalist organizations such as the African National Congress (ANC) were banned, and ANC president Nelson Mandela was sentenced to life imprisonment for treason in 1964.

On June 16, 1976, antiapartheid protest entered a new stage. Police in the Johannesburg suburb of Soweto fired on students who were marching against the teaching of Afrikaans in language schools. The result was a months-long uprising that spread to more than 80 cities. By the '80s, political violence in South Africa had reached a crisis point. Rioting, protests, and work stoppages led the government to declare a state of emergency and deploy units of the South African Defence Force in the cities. At the same time, international pressures to end apartheid began to mount; 25 nations imposed trade sanctions on South Africa.

In 1985, President Pieter Willem Botha began to respond to growing militancy and tightening international economic sanctions by lifting some apartheid restrictions, creating subordinate parliamentary chambers for Coloureds, and abolishing the Pass Laws. The reforms were not enough, however, and continued violence forced white South African leaders to the bargaining table.

In July 1991, President Frederik de Klerk repealed all remaining apartheid legislation. In December, the government and 18 political groups, including the ANC, formed the Convention for a Democratic South Africa. In 1993, the government ratified a transitional constitution that enfranchised all South African adults. South Africa's first multiracial elections were held in 1994, resulting in the Government of National Unity, with Nelson Mandela as president.

The Han Dynasty

THE FOUNDER OF THE HAN DYNASTY was Liu Bang, a Chinese peasant who became a bandit leader and commander of one of the major armies that destroyed the repressive Qin dynasty in 206 B.C. Taking the imperial name Gaodi, Liu Bang reigned until 195 B.C. He established the capital at Chang'an, which, at one time, was the largest city in the world, with more than 240,000 people. He reorganized the government, established recruitment of civil servants based on Confucian principles, and unified the country.

During the reign of Wudi (141–87 B.C.), the Han dynasty reached its height. Wudi's armies pushed southward into northern Vietnam, conquered Korea, and pushed back the steppe nomads in Mongolia. Wudi established a national academy and opened trade routes with the West, the beginning of the storied Silk Road. But his many campaigns bankrupted the empire and led to widespread unrest. A slow, steady decline began, culminating in the reign of Wang Mang, who briefly seized the throne from A.D. 9 to 23.

After Wang Mang's Xin dynasty was overthrown, the Han reestablished control over their empire and moved the capital east to Luoyang. The first emperor of the Eastern Han was Guang Wudi, who had to defeat 11 other claimants for the throne. He quickly stabilized the empire and left it in capable hands, but after A.D. 88 there was a series of child-emperors who were controlled by landed families. In A.D. 220, the last Han emperor abdicated, and China split into three kingdoms.

During their 400-year rule, Han emperors oversaw important cultural achievements. The Chinese invented paper and began mass-producing it in the second century A.D. Calligraphy developed into an art form, and the first dictionary of the Chinese language was compiled. Other inventions included the compass and seismograph.

POSTSCRIPT

▓ During his reign, Wang Mang tried to corner the gold market. He is reported to have gathered five million ounces of gold.

▓ Chinese alchemists discovered gunpowder in the second century A.D., but it was not until the tenth century that it was mixed with carbon to produce an explosive.

▓ Chinese authors were the first to use what we now call "footnotes," which were inserted into commentaries on the *Five Classics*.

Horace Walpole and the Gothic Revival

B Y THE MIDDLE OF THE 18TH CENTURY, the reign of neoclassicism was drawing to a close. Small bursts of the eccentric and frivolous began to appear in the arts. Chinese garden pavilions and picturesque grottoes disturbed the precision of previously formal, Western-style gardens. In England, Horace Walpole made his own highly artificial version of Gothic style fashionable.

An example of Gothic vaulting

In 1747, Horace Walpole purchased a former coachman's cottage on the Thames at Twickenham, which he expanded and transformed into "a little Gothic castle." Decorated with fake pinnacles, miniature battlements, and gargoyles, Walpole's Strawberry Hill kicked off a fad of using Gothic style in English country houses. Walpole's version of Gothic was charming and whimsical: a playful use of Gothic forms closer in spirit to *chinoiserie,* using Chinese elements, than to Victorian Gothic Revival. The house became a tourist attraction almost immediately. Walpole claimed that he showed more than 4,000 visitors through his home and ultimately had to issue tickets to manage the flow.

Walpole's Gothic tastes extended into literature as well. His popular 1764 horror novel, *The Castle of Otranto, A Gothic Story,* ushered in a host of similar tales characterized by horror, violence, and supernatural events, usually set against a backdrop of Gothic architecture. The genre reached its height with Mary Wollstonecraft Shelley's 1819 Gothic masterpiece, *Frankenstein.* Jane Austen satirized the genre in her novel *Northanger Abbey.*

Throughout the century, critics suggested that the popular taste for the Gothic, and other exoticisms, was somehow vulgar. Walpole himself said, "One must have taste to be sensible of the beauties of Grecian architecture; one only wants passions to feel Gothic."

After 1800, with the growth of Romanticism, Gothic Revival entered the architectural mainstream.

The Oka Crisis

D URING THE SUMMER OF 1990, the Canadian town of Oka, Quebec, was the scene of a violent showdown between police and the Mohawk Nation. The clash was ostensibly over the expansion of a golf course, but the actual causes went far deeper.

The roots of the Oka Crisis date back to 1717, when the governor of New France granted lands—including a sacred pine grove and Mohawk burial ground—to a Catholic seminary. The seminary leaders were to hold the land in trust for the Mohawk Nation, but eventually they began to sell the property. As early as 1869, some Mohawk protesting the sales were jailed. In 1936, the seminary sold the last of the land.

In 1961, developers built a nine-hole golf course on part of the land. Again the Mohawk protested; again they were ignored. In 1977, they filed a land claim with the federal Office of Native Claims. It took nine years for the claim to be processed—only to be rejected. Nearly 300 years of bad feelings peaked in 1989, when Oka Mayor Jean Ouellette announced the remaining pine trees would be cleared to expand the members-only golf course. No one bothered to consult the Mohawk.

A number of armed Mohawk responded by erecting a barricade to deny access to the disputed area. Quebec's Minister for Native Affairs supported the protestors and wrote, "These people have seen their lands disappear without having been consulted or compensated, and that, in my opinion, is unfair and unjust, especially over a golf course." Another government official suggested the protestors should be sent off to the eastern region of Labrador "if they wanted their own country so much."

On July 11, 1990, a SWAT team attacked the barricade with tear gas and flash-bang grenades. The Mohawk fired back. After a 30-second skirmish, the police retreated, but the dispute had claimed its first casualty: A 31-year-old police corporal had been shot and killed. It was never clear who had fired the fatal shot. The standoff escalated as sympathizers from Canada and the United States joined the protestors. The authorities attempted to blockade the Mohawk, but the protesters responded by blocking highways, causing massive traffic jams. In August, the army was called in after Canadian Mounties were unable to resolve the situation.

The confrontation finally ended on September 26. The Canadian government agreed to buy the disputed land for $5.3 million, and plans for the golf course expansion were canceled. The Oka Crisis was over, though the historic grievances remained.

The Lewis and Clark Expedition

IN 1803, Napoleon Bonaparte sold the Louisiana Territory to the United States for $15 million. With this addition of approximately 828,000 square miles (or 530 million acres, which works out to about three cents per acre), the young country suddenly doubled in size.

To explore the new territory, President Thomas Jefferson turned to his correspondence secretary, former army captain Meriwether Lewis, to assemble a "Corps of Discovery." Lewis in turn asked his friend Lieutenant William Clark to act as the primary record keeper of the group. The voyage would be the first American expedition by land to the Pacific coast.

Jefferson, who advocated further exploration of the West, had Congress allocate $2,500 to cover the cost of the trip. On May 19, 1804, Lewis, Clark, 23 soldiers (from the onset, the party was a military expedition), three interpreters, and one slave set out from St. Louis, Missouri. They brought with them one large keelboat and two canoes. The group traveled about 1,600 miles up the Missouri River and wintered among the Mandan Indians in present-day North Dakota.

After sending a boat back to St. Louis with the information and specimens they had collected so far, the expedition departed again in the spring of 1805, toiling up the Missouri River and then across the rugged Rocky Mountains. During their travels, they were accompanied by a young Shoshone woman named Sacagawea, who acted as translator and smoothed relations between the travelers and Native Americans. On November 7, 1805, the expedition first sighted the Pacific Ocean in present-day Oregon.

After wintering on the coast, Lewis and Clark led their men back over the Rockies and reached St. Louis on September 23, 1806. In all, the Corps of Discovery had traveled more than 8,000 miles. Their accurate mapping showed where the Missouri River originated, and that North America was more than 1,200 miles wider than previously believed. They learned that there was no fabled Northwest Passage and that the Rockies were not a single, massive mountain chain. Their expedition also furthered Western science, bringing back 122 new species of animals and 178 new plants.

POSTSCRIPT

■ Although Congress allocated $2,500 to the expedition, its actual cost was almost $40,000.

■ Lewis died mysteriously in 1809. Some say he was murdered.

The Origins of Mormonism

JOSEPH SMITH, JR., lived in upstate New York when he began having visions and heavenly visitors in the 1820s. According to Smith, in 1823, the angel Moroni instructed him to obtain a document written by ancient peoples and translate it.

The story continued as Moroni led Smith to a hillock, where Smith dug up several ancient gold plates. On the plates was a story written in Egyptian. Once Moroni gave him the means, Smith translated the tale, written by the ancient prophet Mormon. It told of a tribe of Israelites who departed from Palestine for North America in 600 B.C. According to the tale, some of the Native American tribes descended from this band of Israelite settlers. Once Smith finished copying the plates, they were taken back to heaven.

Using what he had read as inspiration, Smith wrote *The Book of Mormon* in 1830. The scripture became the bedrock of Smith's new religion, which he called the Church of Jesus Christ of Latter Day Saints, more commonly known as the Mormon Church. Smith had already begun converting neighbors when rising hostility from others necessitated a move away from New York. Smith's growing band migrated west to Ohio, then to Missouri in 1838. They moved again and founded the city of Nauvoo, Illinois, in 1839.

Smith ruled as a virtual monarch and controlled his own militia to protect his people. Some people opposed Smith's opulent lifestyle and his decision to allow *polygamy*, the practice of being married to more than one wife at a time. In 1844, widespread hostility from neighboring towns led to Smith's arrest and incarceration in nearby Carthage. On June 27, a mob broke into the jail, killing Smith and his brother Hyrum.

Brigham Young became the new leader of the Mormons and, in 1846, he led his followers west on a trek across the Great Plains. They reached the shore of the Great Salt Lake, where in 1847 they founded Salt Lake City, the new capital of the Mormon faith. There the Mormons had increasing problems with the U.S. Army and the federal government. Although there were enough people to move the Utah territory into statehood, the government refused. Utah was finally admitted as the 45th state in 1896. Today, there are more than five million Mormons in the United States.

Florence Nightingale Reforms Hospitals

Florence Nightingale believed she had a mission in life. She was born into an upper-class English family in 1820. Although her mother was concerned about her daughter's marriage prospects, Nightingale pursued her goal to study nursing and help others. This particularly distressed her mother, since nursing was a profession with a rather poor reputation at the time. But Nightingale persevered, and in 1853 she became superintendent of a women's hospital in London. When England became involved in the Crimean War, Nightingale convinced British military leaders to allow her to take a group of women to Turkey to help care for the sick and wounded.

When Nightingale and her nurses arrived in Turkey in November 1854, she found the hospitals in deplorable condition; the facilities were unsanitary, and the soldiers' clothes weren't clean. All around, soldiers were dying of cholera and dysentery. Nightingale and her nurses were met with great resistance from the military commanders, but they soon took control of the situation and began boiling clothes and cleaning to eliminate the filth in which the soldiers lived. British officers resented the women's intrusion into camp management, but some soldiers appreciated Nightingale's efforts, nicknaming her "the lady with the lamp." It was not until she began writing articles for London newspapers that conditions really improved for the British soldiers stationed in Turkey.

After the Crimean War, Nightingale returned to England in August 1856. By then, she was convinced military hospital conditions needed to be improved overall, and she began to advise others on reforming and bettering the facilities. She recorded statistics, kept records, and began a writing campaign. As Nightingale studied new designs for modern hospitals and reviewed conditions in military hospitals, she began promoting her ideas and stressed that reform was needed in civilian hospitals as well.

Nightingale published two books, *Notes on Nursing* and *Notes on Hospitals*. The latter focused on civilian hospitals and the need for increased sanitation and better means of health care. She wrote that hospitals needed to be better ventilated and less cramped. Hospitals, she pointed out, should be for the purpose of saving lives rather than just a place to die. Her books charted hospital statistics, citing hospitals' mortality rates to make her point that they were neither clean nor helping the sick. Both of her books helped reform health care worldwide.

The Khmer Rouge

THE KHMER ROUGE, which ruled Cambodia from 1975 to 1979, began as an orthodox communist party that opposed colonial rule. As it evolved, its doctrine strayed from traditional Marxism and held up the rural peasantry as the true proletariat.

A Khmer Rouge soldier

In 1968, Khmer Rouge forces launched a widespread insurgency. With help from the Vietnamese, they gained strength over the next two years and emerged as the Communist Party of Kampuchea (CPK). By 1973, CPK forces, led by Pol Pot, controlled large parts of the country. Two years later, the Cambodian government, headed by Lon Nol, collapsed.

Many Cambodians supported the Khmer Rouge against Lon Nol, thinking they were fighting on behalf of the popular former head of state, Norodom Sihanouk. They soon discovered their mistake. Under Pol Pot, the Khmer Rouge isolated Cambodia from the outside world. Schools and hospitals were closed. Banking and currency were abolished. Religion was banned, and private property was confiscated.

The cities emptied as residents were forced en masse into rural labor camps. Under the new regime, all citizens were to become farmers. The transplants, or "New People," could obey or die. "To keep you is no benefit," observed a Khmer Rouge slogan. "To destroy you is no loss."

Death was also the fate of anyone viewed as a threat to the new classless society, including anyone with ties to the old government, members of other ethnic groups, professionals, Buddhist monks, teachers, and intellectuals. Virtually anyone with an education—even someone who wore glasses, which was considered an indication of literacy—was thought to be a threat.

In December 1978, the horror finally ended when the Vietnamese army invaded Cambodia and toppled the regime. Pol Pot and a small cadre disappeared into the jungle where they held out for years. Pol Pot died of natural causes in 1998; the remaining leaders surrendered in 1999. During its reign, the Khmer Rouge is believed to have killed between 1.2 and 1.7 million people.

Andrew Carnegie (1835–1919)

ANDREW CARNEGIE was born on November 25, 1835, in the town of Dunfermline, Scotland. His father was a weaver who was put out of work by the spreading Industrial Revolution, and so in 1848 the family immigrated to Pennsylvania. Andrew followed in his father's footsteps, working in a large textile mill at $1.20 per week.

He swiftly rose through the business ranks until 1853, when he joined the rapidly growing Pennsylvania Railroad. In one year, his shrewd business sense garnered him an annual income of nearly $40,000 from investments alone. Carnegie learned the value of iron from his experience building iron railroad bridges. In 1870, he began construction of a blast furnace in Pittsburgh; within two years, it was up and running.

While on a business trip to England, he met Sir Henry Bessemer, who had invented a cheap way to make high-quality steel. Carnegie switched to making steel, and by 1878 his Pittsburgh-based steel mill was producing more steel than any other company in America.

Carnegie became a sought-after public speaker and writer whose liberal views touched a chord with the American people. In 1889, he wrote his most famous magazine article, "Wealth," in the *North American Review*. In it, Carnegie explained his philosophy of the rich distributing their income back into society so as to give people the tools to better themselves. "The man who dies . . . rich dies disgraced," he said.

In 1881, he hired Henry Clay Frick to run his business. But in 1892, with Carnegie on vacation in Scotland, Frick oversaw the bloody Homestead strike. The episode destroyed Carnegie's reputation as the worker's friend.

Carnegie sold his company for $480 million in 1900, of which his share was about $225 to 250 million. In February 1901, Carnegie Steel and seven other companies merged to form the U.S. Steel Corporation, the world's first company valued at more than $1 billion.

For the remainder of his life, Carnegie concentrated on using his fortune to build libraries, music halls, and art museums, and to support countless other endeavors. His philanthropic gifts totaled more than $350 million, which amounted to more than 90 percent of his fortune.

POSTSCRIPT

During the initial days of the American Civil War, Carnegie brought the first line of troops to Washington via railroad to protect the city.

David Alfaro Siqueiros (1896–1974)

DAVID ALFARO SIQUEIROS was a Mexican muralist and activist, along with Diego Rivera and Jose Orozco. Siqueiros was probably the most politically radical of the three.

He was born in Chihuahua City, Mexico, in 1896. While the 15-year-old Siqueiros was a student, he led a successful strike aimed at improving teaching methods, effectively launching his life-long commitment to activism. In 1913, he served in the army of the Constitutionalist movement opposing military dictator Victoriano Huerta.

For the next 13 years, Siqueiros combined art and politics in ways that often put him at odds with public officials. In 1918, he helped organize a group called the Congress of Soldier Artists. Three years later, he painted his first important mural, *Los Mitos* (*The Myths*), at the National Preparatory School. In the 1920s, he served as a union organizer. He was put under house arrest for his union activities and eventually was expelled from the country in 1932. After a sojourn in Los Angeles, Siqueiros returned briefly to Mexico in 1934 when a more radical government took power. Two years later, he went to Spain to fight against fascist forces there.

When he came back to Mexico in 1939, art and politics again merged, as he painted another mural, the famed *Portrait of the Bourgeoisie*. He became involved in Communist politics and later led an unsuccessful assassination attempt on Leon Trotsky, who was living in Mexico after being expelled from the Soviet Communist Party. During World War II, Siqueiros painted several works trumpeting themes such as anti-fascism (*Death to the Invader*) and black rights (*Fraternity Between the Black and White Races*).

After the war, Siqueiros painted and politicked, with 70 paintings displayed in a 1947 exhibit. From 1959 to 1964, he was jailed for practicing "social dissolution." After he was released, he spoke out in support of Fidel Castro in 1964 and finished his most ambitious mural, *The March of Humanity*, in 1971.

Charles V and the Hapsburg Empire

Under Charles V's watchful eye the Hapsburg dynasty reached its peak, accumulating the largest conglomerate of lands since Charlemagne's rule in the ninth century, including Austria, Sicily, Naples, the Netherlands, the Iberian peninsula, and Spain's American colonies.

The son of Philip I and Joanna of Spain, Charles was the heir of four European ruling families. He inherited his father's Burgundian properties in 1506 and became joint ruler of the throne of Spain in 1516, when his mother's madness left her unable to rule. He united his Spanish possessions with the German Hapsburg empire, which he inherited in 1519 from his grandfather, Emperor Maximilian I. That same year, he was elected Holy Roman emperor, a title that brought formal prestige as the first prince of Christendom, but little else.

Charles's reign was marked by almost continuous warfare. He survived revolts in Spain and the Low Countries, overcame papal resistance to the establishment of Spanish hegemony over the Italian states, and defended Vienna against the Ottoman Turks in 1529. He fought four controversial wars against Francis I of France, who had competed with Charles for election as Holy Roman emperor and whose kingdom was surrounded by the Hapsburg empire.

Charles's greatest failure was in war-torn Germany, as German princes broke away from Rome. In 1531, a number of the princes formed the Schmalkaldic League of Protestant States in response to Charles's opposition to their conversion to Lutheranism, and his subsequent loss of control over the church in their own territories, including Hesse, Saxony, Wurttemberg, the Palatinate, and several imperial cities. Charles managed to crush the combined forces of the Protestant rulers of Hesse and Saxony at the Battle of Muhlberg in 1547 but was unable to check the spread of Protestantism. In 1552, the Protestant princes rebelled in Germany, led by Maurice of Saxony and supported by Henry II of France. That same year, Charles was forced to concede the right of the secular estates of the empire to adopt the Lutheran reforms at the Peace of Passau and to reaffirm the settlement at the Peace of Augsburg in 1555.

Charles abdicated as the Holy Roman emperor in 1556 and retired in Spain. He handed over Naples, Spain, and the Netherlands to his son, Philip II, and the Austrian empire to his brother Ferdinand. After Charles's death, the Hapsburg dynasty remained divided between the Spanish line, which died out in 1700, and the Austrian line, which remained in power until 1918.

The Chinese Cultural Revolution

THE CULTURAL REVOLUTION in 1966 was engineered by Communist Party Chairman Mao Zedong, who hoped to reinvigorate the Chinese Revolution. Mao was concerned that the bureaucratized Soviet style of Communism was infecting China. He also saw danger from political rivals and in a growing sentiment for moderation in the Communist party.

In response, Mao turned directly to China's youth. He closed schools and invited children to join Red Guard units to fight the so-called bourgeois influences. Brandishing red books of Mao's quotations, the youths responded to the call by the millions. He was supported by his wife Jiang Qing and her three powerful associates, who became known as the Gang of Four.

Students with a picture of Mao

Mass chaos ensued as the Red Guard destroyed temples, burned books, and persecuted anyone perceived as an impediment to Mao's will and the revolution. Chinese president Liu Shaoqi, a moderate who had once been Mao's designated successor, was accused of being a traitor. He died in prison in 1969. Other victims were humiliated, tortured, imprisoned, or forced to do menial labor. Thousands died or committed suicide.

The movement spun out of control as the Red Guard split into factions, each claiming Mao's blessing. Schools and universities remained closed for three years. There was mass economic disruption, and industrial production dropped 12 percent in just the first two years. In 1967, Mao called in the army to restore order.

Still not satisfied, in 1969, he introduced the "Campaign to Purify Class Ranks." Urban residents, intellectuals, youths, and government officials were forced into the countryside to perform hard labor and "learn" from the peasants. Many Chinese remained in exile for years as Mao tried to close the economic gap between urban and rural areas.

The worst of the Cultural Revolution was over by the mid-70s, though its ramifications continued even after Mao's death in 1976. The Gang of Four were arrested that same year and sentenced to long prison terms. The Communist Party, led by the more moderate Deng Xiaoping, condemned the Cultural Revolution.

The Quebec Act

DURING THE 18TH CENTURY, the religion of French Canada and Quebec was generally Catholic, and the economy centered on fur trading. The area was under French control until the end of the French and Indian War in 1763: The Treaty of Paris transferred the territories to the victorious British.

The British parliament at this time was having trouble ruling its overseas colonies. It had begun to regulate activities in the American colonies, and when colonists participated in the Boston Tea Party, Parliament passed a series of retaliatory acts, known as the Intolerable Acts. One act closed the port of Boston, and another placed the government of Massachusetts under the direct control of the British. In Canada, French inhabitants were able to hold public office under British rule, but they first had to renounce their Catholic faith.

Nervous about Canadians rebelling like the American colonists, Parliament passed the Quebec Act in 1774. The act affected people living in Canada as well as the colonists living in what would become the United States. The act gave the new British colony of Quebec control of all lands west of the Appalachian Mountains and north of the Ohio River. It also made concessions in favor of Roman Catholicism.

In response, the American colonists added the Quebec Act to the list of Intolerable Acts. The colonists were infuriated because they had been settling in the land of the Ohio Valley as they moved west. The Ohio Valley had valuable resources because of its widespread fur trading, and the settlers were not eager to relinquish them. The act also gave the British governor of Quebec control over settlers' access to the area. The colonists were concerned that the governor of Quebec might decide to either close the area to settlers entirely or take measures to monopolize the lucrative fur trade for Canada. Protestants in the American colonies also worried because of the act's stance toward Roman Catholicism.

Although the act was not enforced outside Canada, its provisions provided yet another reason for the angry American colonists to declare independence from Great Britain. When the final break came between the colonies and Britain, the Quebec Act was listed in the Declaration of Independence as one of the colonists' grievances.

Roe v. Wade

NORMA L. MCCORVEY (aka "Roe") was a pregnant, single woman in Texas who brought a class action suit against Dallas County District Attorney Henry Wade in 1970.

Roe, represented by Linda Coffee and Sarah Weddington, challenged the constitutionality of the state's abortion legislation, which provided that abortions could only be sanctioned for the medical purpose of saving the mother's life. The plaintiff argued that the Texas law violated her constitutional rights set forth in the Ninth and Fourteenth amendments.

On January 22, 1973, the U.S. Supreme Court presented its decision, with a 7–2 majority vote in favor of the plaintiff. Justice Harry Blackmun, representing the Court, described attitudes concerning abortion dating from ancient times and discussed abortion in terms of the Hippocratic Oath, common law, English statutory law, American law, the American Medical Association's views, and the position taken by the American Public Health Association. Blackmun also recognized the emotional and sensitive nature of the case and detailed the history of abortion legislation in the United States to explain the rationale behind the Court's decision.

Part of the problem was the vagueness of the Texas legislation. In *Roe v. Wade,* the court ruled that in restricting legal abortions, the Texas Penal Code was too broad since the statute made no distinction between abortions performed early in pregnancy and those performed later. It also found the Texas law invalid because it limited the legal justification for the procedure to a single reason, that is, saving the life of the mother.

While the Court did not resolve the difficult question of when life begins, it did recognize the state's important and legitimate interest in protecting the health of a mother. The *Roe* decision also held that the state had a compelling interest at a point in time to interfere with a mother's decision to terminate her pregnancy; in other words, states might be able to restrict late-term abortions. Despite the ruling, the decision has been challenged many times. To this day, abortion remains a hot topic in the United States.

Cicero (106–43 B.C.)

Marcus Tullius Cicero was a staunch defender of the dying Roman Republic. Born in the town of Arpinum in 106 B.C., Cicero studied law in Rome and then went to Greece to study rhetoric under Apollonius, the greatest Greek orator of the day.

After he returned to Rome, Cicero developed a reputation as a defense lawyer. Members of his profession were not paid directly but were given gifts; the amount Cicero received allowed him to purchase a home on Palatine Hill. In 70 B.C., he prosecuted the former governor of Sicily, Gaius Verres, who went into exile without waiting for the verdict.

Cicero became one of Rome's two consuls in 64 B.C. As consul, Cicero was charged with keeping the treasury solvent. One of his first acts was to defeat a measure by Crassus and Caesar that called for redistribution of state lands among their political supporters.

Soon thereafter, Cicero learned of a conspiracy being hatched by Catiline, an unsuccessful candidate for consul. Catiline was from a family of little influence—he was a self-made man trying to move up in politics. He was also involved in a plot to kill those who defeated him in his bid for consul. Catiline and his supporters were conspiring to violently seize control of Rome. Although Catiline himself fled Rome, his supporters continued to plan and were eventually betrayed to Cicero. A Senate bill advocated the execution of Catiline's followers, and Cicero carried it out at once—in spite of remonstrance from Caesar that a death sentence required prior approval by a popular assembly. Catiline perished in battle as he tried to escape from Italy.

When Caesar occupied Rome in 49 B.C., Cicero sided with Pompey. However, after Pompey's defeat, Caesar pardoned Cicero and held no grudge against him. In turn, when Caesar was assassinated, Cicero spoke out against Antony in what has been labeled as his 14 "Philippic orations." Anthony at first contended with Octavian over Caesar's legacy, but in November 43 B.C., Antony, Octavian, and Lepidus joined forces to create the Second Triumvirate. Their troops occupied Rome late that month. Cicero tried to flee but was caught and slain on December 7. His head was nailed to the *rostra* (speaker's platform) in the Forum. Cicero tried to save the Republic, but being a part of it, he was unable to see its corruption and inevitable decline.

Cicero is remembered today for his great orations. During the Renaissance, the humanist Petrarch discovered a manuscript copy of Cicero's private letters and edited it for publication.

Oliver Cromwell (1599–1658)

OLIVER CROMWELL was born on April 25, 1599. While part of the English land-owning gentry, he ranked near the bottom of the landed elite. He studied at Cambridge University but left without getting his degree after his father's death.

When King Charles I summoned a new Parliament in 1628, Cromwell was elected to the House of Commons. He built a reputation as the voice of the oppressed for his stand against government interference in matters of conscience. When the king led troops into Parliament to arrest radical leaders, Cromwell found himself on the side of the Parliamentary supporters, or Roundheads, in the English Civil War.

England had experienced peace for about 70 years, and Cromwell, like most of the English, had little knowledge of military matters. Only the aristocrats, who mainly made up the opposing forces, or Cavaliers, were trained in fencing, riding, and shooting. As the civil war began, Cromwell learned about military tactics from books and from observing battles. He formed a cavalry of disciplined, well-trained men of faith. Under Cromwell's guidance, his New Model Army defeated the Cavaliers in decisive battles at Marston Moor and Naseby.

After the 1649 trial and beheading of Charles, the House of Commons abolished both the monarchy and the House of Lords and declared England a Commonwealth. Cromwell was to be the nation's leader. But disorder in England and fear of foreign invasion resulted in Cromwell's elimination of perceived enemies. His army put down uprisings by supporters of Charles II in Ireland and Scotland, slaughtering more than 40 percent of the Irish population. When Parliament refused to follow his directives, Cromwell forcibly dissolved it and called for a Parliament of Puritan saints. In 1655, he dissolved this Parliament, too, and chose to rule under the title Lord Protector of the Realm. Under Cromwell, Puritan social values resulted in the closing of theaters. He was also a strong supporter of education.

Cromwell became less popular as time passed. He died on September 3, 1658. By 1660, a newly elected Parliament had invited Charles II to return to England as its king.

POSTSCRIPT

Cromwell's head was reportedly displayed for years on a pole above Westminster Hall. In 1960, it was entombed in a wall at Cambridge University.

Brown v. Board of Education

O N MAY 17, 1954, the Supreme Court overturned a 1896 court ruling, *Plessy v. Ferguson,* that declared that states were permitted to enforce "separate but equal" statutes segregating blacks and whites in virtually every avenue of public life. They unanimously decided in *Brown v. Board of Education* that "separate but equal facilities are inherently unequal." According to the ruling, state laws that established and maintained separate public schools for black and white children denied black students equal educational opportunities. The court ruled that segregation in law was a violation of the Equal Protection Clause of the 14th Amendment.

The Brown sisters

Times had changed since the *Plessy* decision. Americans united across color lines in the war against Nazi Germany's Aryan supremacist doctrines. Growing international condemnation of American racial practices also spurred heightened sensitivity among American leaders in an increasingly non-white world.

For their part, blacks had never passively accepted racial marginalization; a variety of organizations had been initiated, most notably the National Association for the Advancement of Colored People (NAACP), which sought to use the courts to overturn Jim Crow laws. The NAACP legal department, headed by Charles Hamilton Houston and his protégé Thurgood Marshall, spent decades challenging racial segregation in state professional schools and on the college level.

Emboldened by these victories, in 1951, they filed a class action suit against the Topeka, Kansas, Board of Education. The plaintiffs were 13 black Topeka parents headed by Oliver L. Brown, on behalf of their children. Brown's daughter Linda, a third grader, had to walk six blocks to catch a bus to a segregated school a mile away. The nearest white school was only seven blocks away.

Despite the desegregation rulings, not everyone complied right away. In Virginia, public schools closed entirely rather than desegregate. In Arkansas, Governor Orval Faubus called the National Guard to prevent black students from entering Little Rock Central High School in 1957. President Eisenhower, in turn, federalized the Arkansas National Guard and ordered them back to their armories.

Catherine the Great and the Cossack Insurrection

CATHERINE II became empress of Russia in 1762 after deposing her husband, Peter III. As insurance against Peter's return, Catherine's lover, Aleksey Orlov, then allegedly murdered the former czar.

Catherine embarked upon a reign as an enlightened monarch, determined to bring much-needed reform to Russia. She attempted to codify Russian law, introducing Western political and legal thinking to the archaic system. She also sought to make government administration more effective with increased centralization.

Her move toward reform was interrupted by war with the Ottoman Empire from 1768 to 1774. Among the veterans of that war was Emelyan Pugachev, who served as a junior officer in the first Russo-Turkish War. After he either deserted or was sent home in 1770, Pugachev returned to his Ural Cossack home to find considerable social unrest. Discontent stemmed in part from the loss of autonomy caused by Catherine's attempts to centralize government, as well as unrest among Russian serfs. In the autumn of 1773, Pugachev instigated a revolt against the central government. Within weeks, this local uprising became a widespread rebellion. Serfs, mine workers, Tatars, and other disaffected minorities flocked to the cause.

Due to the Russo-Turkish War, there were few government troops in the area to combat the insurrection. Pugachev proclaimed himself emperor. He established his own court, announced the liquidation of former government officials and landowners, and abolished serfdom, taxation, and compulsory military service. He and his disciples planned elections to establish a government in the freed territories and attempted to form a regular army.

Government troops were sent to destroy the revolt, but they suffered a series of defeats. Finally, in August 1774, the rebels were crushed in a battle near Tsaritsyn, losing 10,000 men due to capture or death. Pugachev escaped but was handed over by his own Cossacks. He was sent to Moscow in a metal cage, where he was quartered in the public square on January 10, 1775.

Though brief, the revolt had long-lasting consequences, pushing Catherine toward a more conservative outlook and prompting her to abandon other potential social reforms such as emancipation of the serfs.

Nicolaus Copernicus (1473–1543)

Nicolaus Copernicus was born on February 19, 1473, in the Polish city of Toruń. After their parents died, he and his siblings were raised largely by their uncle, who was a church canon and later worked as Prince-Bishop governor. In 1491, Copernicus studied at the university in Krakow, Poland, where he first became involved in astronomy—a field of study that he would one day change forever.

Back then, astronomy courses were similar to mathematics because they introduced information about the universe and methods of calculating dates on the calendar. They also provided information about ways of applying astronomy, such as in navigation. Copernicus even learned about astrology and ways to calculate horoscopes.

After Copernicus completed his studies in Krakow, his family urged him to study canon law to continue in his uncle's footsteps in the church. With his uncle's funding to back him, Copernicus agreed and enrolled at the University of Bologna in Italy. There, in addition to his church studies, he continued to study mathematics and astronomy. During this time he made many astrological observations and saw the moon eclipse a star. A year later, while he was in Rome lecturing scholars on mathematics and astronomy, he observed another lunar eclipse.

In 1514, he distributed an unsigned book to friends called the *Commentariolus* (*Little Commentary*) in which he outlined his theory that the sun was the center of the universe—a revolutionary thought at the time. This mode of thought became known as Copernican heliocentrism. It is believed that the following year he began writing *De Revolutionibus Orbium Coelestium* (*On the Revolutions of the Celestial Spheres*).

That book would be Copernicus's masterpiece. In it, he continued his original heliocentric theory by explaining just why the sun would be at the center of the universe, and he offered the hypothesis that heavenly bodies, including Earth, rotated around the sun. His book included the most accurate scientific knowledge that existed about the movement of heavenly bodies. It also was the most controversial. *On the Revolutions* would not be published until Copernicus was on his deathbed in 1543.

Thoreau Writes *Walden*

MORE THAN 150 YEARS before contemporary author Jon Krakauer wrote about a man shedding all of his material possessions in his book *Into the Wild,* author, naturalist, and philosopher Henry David Thoreau went on a similar journey of self-discovery.

After graduating from Harvard in 1837 and briefly teaching in Concord, Massachusetts, Thoreau found himself restless. His older brother John, with whom he had opened a grammar school, died in 1841, and Thoreau found himself questioning life's purpose. His friend and mentor, poet Ralph Waldo Emerson, encouraged Thoreau to write. And so he did, penning essays and articles about self-reliance, simplicity, and the American Transcendentalist ideas of the universality of all creation.

By 1845, 28-year-old Thoreau had had enough with civilization. He felt he needed to escape the materialism surrounding him, and so he built a cabin in the woods by Walden Pond outside of Concord. On July 4, 1845, he moved in and began a 26-month adventure that would be chronicled in a collection of essays, *Walden, or Life in the Woods.* He took only a few basic clothes and seeds with him, believing that by stripping himself of everything but the bare essentials, he would learn the real meaning of life. His goal, he wrote, was "to live deliberately, to front only the essential facts of life, and see if I could not learn what it had to teach, and not, when I came to die, discover that I had not lived."

During his time at Walden Pond, Thoreau not only explored the philosophy of simplicity but also the natural world around him, which he described in great detail in *Walden.* In "Solitude," he wrote, "This is a delicious evening, when the whole body is one sense, and imbibes delight through every pore. I go and come with a strange liberty in Nature, a part of herself."

When Thoreau returned from his retreat in 1847, he continued to write. He gained notoriety for the essay *Resistance to Civil Government* (known also as *Civil Disobedience*) in 1849, and he worked on *Walden,* revising and editing it a number of times before publishing it in 1854. Thoreau died from tuberculosis on May 6, 1862, but his words continue to ring true as a reminder to slow down in life: "If a man does not keep pace with his companions, perhaps it is because he hears a different drummer. Let him step to the music which he hears, however measured or far away."

Darwin's *Origin of Species*

Hᴏᴡ ʟɪꜰᴇ ᴅᴇᴠᴇʟᴏᴘꜱ and changes over time is a question that everyone from scientists to philosophers to clergy has tackled from one
perspective or another. The name most associated with the origins of the
human species is British naturalist Charles Darwin. He developed the
theory of evolution, which states that all life on Earth, human and otherwise, evolved over millions of years from common ancestors.

Decades of studying fossils and other specimens led Darwin to four basic
conclusions: Evolution does happen; it happens gradually over thousands
to millions of years; it happens through a process called natural selection;
and the millions of species alive today came from a single ancestor.

Natural selection refers to the idea that,
over time, species undergo genetic mutations. The mutations that help a species
survive are kept while the ones that don't
are eventually eliminated. This concept
turned into the well-known phrase,
"survival of the fittest," which, put simply,
means the species best able to adapt to
its environment is the one most likely to
survive. Darwin summarized his findings
in 1859 in his classic book, *On the Origin
of Species by Means of Natural Selection.*

The scientific world was fascinated by this
theory, and many professionals went on to
expand on it. Religious institutions, however, were less thrilled. They interpreted

A caricature of Charles Darwin

his ideas as saying that humans were simply another kind of animal that
most likely evolved from apes, as opposed to Christian creationist beliefs.
Darwin very carefully stayed away from applying evolution to theology,
but he was still accused of using his theory to deny the existence of God.

More than 100 years later, the controversy still exists as American public
school systems continue to debate what theory should be taught in the
classroom. In 2005, Darwin's theories were put on trial by the Kansas
State Board of Education. The board fought hard to get the theory of
"intelligent design," or the creationist's perspective, taught in schools as
an equivalent to evolution. They lost—but the debate rages on in school
board meetings, churches, and even around the family kitchen table.

Salvador Allende Gossens (1908–1973)

SALVADOR ALLENDE GOSSENS, the controversial socialist president of Chile, was born in Valparaiso, Chile, in 1908. His family was deeply involved in social and political activism. Shortly after Allende received his medical degree, his father died. At his father's funeral, he proclaimed his vision of his own future: "I [will] devote my life to the social struggle, and I believe that I [will] fulfill that promise."

In 1933, he was a founding member of the Socialist Party of Chile. Four years later, he was elected to the national legislature and served as minister of health in 1939 and 1941. From 1945 until his election as president in 1970, Allende served in the Chilean Senate. He was impressed with Cuban leaders Fidel Castro and Che Guevara, who praised Allende for trying to bring about Marxist socialism through nonviolent means.

After three previous attempts, Allende finally succeeded in his quest for the presidency in 1970, when his left-wing coalition won a plurality— 36 percent of the vote—and the endorsement of the national legislature. His ruling party embarked on a path to nationalize the country's major industries, banking system, and natural resources.

Many centrist and conservative Chileans opposed the move, but the most powerful opposition came from the United States. The Nixon Administration was worried that Allende could become another Castro, further destabilizing Latin American relations. Indeed, National Security Advisor Henry Kissinger said, "I don't see why we have to let a country go Marxist just because its people are irresponsible."

For the next three years the United States, through overt and covert means, tried to undermine Allende's government. Credits from the Export-Import Bank were canceled, while the Agency for International Development withdrew its help from the country. The CIA secretly funded a number of anti-Allende political groups in Chile. By the summer of 1973, members of the military were disturbed by the decline in the economy and feared that Allende might use his power to diminish theirs.

With CIA encouragement (but apparently no direct involvement), a military coup overthrew the government in September. Allende was either killed or committed suicide, and General Augusto Pinochet became Chile's dictator—to the dismay of the many Latin Americans who had trusted the United States' commitment to democracy.

The Return of Charles de Gaulle

IN 1958, Charles de Gaulle emerged from a five-year retirement to once again take the reins of power in France. His nation was in the throes of a political and military crisis as it fought an increasingly violent battle to retain Algeria, its most important colony. The French people believed that this legendary hero would somehow save the country.

Born in 1890, young de Gaulle graduated from the prestigious St. Cyr military academy in 1912 and fought with distinction in World War I. In the years after the war, he rose steadily in the ranks of the military and wrote several important works on the reorganization of the French military. When France fell to Germany early in World War II, de Gaulle, by then a brigadier general, escaped to London. In December 1940, he created his famous Free French Movement, asserting, "France has lost a battle; but France has not lost the war."

As Allied forces continued their slow advance against the Nazis and Fascists in North Africa and Italy, de Gaulle's stature rose among the French people. After the successful 1944 D-Day invasion of Nazi-occupied France and liberation of Paris in August of that year, de Gaulle made a triumphant entrance into the capital city. In November, he was named head of the Provisional Government of France. Upset by the French legislature's resistance to his desire for a strong presidency and by the failure of his newly created political party, de Gaulle retired in 1953.

When he returned to power in 1958, the National Assembly granted him broad powers as head of the Fourth Republic as he sought to end the Algerian crisis. When he ran for president in December, he received an overwhelming 78 percent of the vote. By 1962, de Gaulle had brokered peace in Algeria, offering the nation independence from France, which was approved in a referendum. He also successfully pushed for a new constitution that guaranteed universal suffrage.

In 1968, he was able to put down massive strikes and demonstrations by a worker-student coalition, winning an unexpected majority for his party in the National Assembly. His last experiment in national democracy failed, however, when a referendum voted down his plans to reform the French legislature in 1969. He retired once again and died a year later.

The GI Bill

THE SERVICEMEN'S READJUSTMENT ACT, signed into law by President Franklin D. Roosevelt on June 22, 1944, ensured that returning veterans would be taken care of as they readjusted to civilian life. The veterans of World War I had been poorly treated when they returned home; FDR and many others did not want to make the same mistake twice.

Roosevelt had suggested this legislation in a speech almost a year earlier. Harry W. Colmery, former national commander of the American Legion and Republican party chairman, is credited with writing the first draft. House and Senate members fought about one key provision, unemployment, before passing it along to the president to sign.

The GI Bill, as it was popularly known, had three main sections: First, the bill contained education and training for returning veterans. Those who wanted to attend college would receive a stipend that would cover tuition, books, and housing. Veterans could receive on-the-job training or take specialized classes to acquire necessary skills. Within the first seven years, more than 9 million of the 16 million veterans had taken advantage of the perk. Of these men and women, 2.3 million went to college, 3.5 million underwent school training, and 3.4 million received job training. In 1947, 49 percent of those admitted to college were veterans under the bill.

Another section of the GI Bill allowed veterans to apply for low interest, zero-percent-down loans to purchase homes. Through this section's termination in 1952, 2.4 million home loans were approved by the Veterans' Administration.

Finally, the most controversial section of this bill stipulated that any veteran looking for work could receive $20 per week in unemployment compensation, capped at 52 weeks. Congress fought over the provision, opponents arguing that unemployment payments might influence some veterans to not look for work. But less than 20 percent of the funds allocated for unemployment compensation were paid out; most veterans actively looked for and received jobs.

The GI Bill democratized higher education by allowing veterans the opportunity to attend college, which, prior to 1945, was considered the bastion of the rich. Colleges had to build new dorms and classroom buildings, which stimulated the economy. The bill also helped suburban America to grow by giving veterans and their families the means to move out of cities. Although the bill's provisions ended in July 1956, Congress has continued to fund similar legislation to help take care of America's veterans.

The Samurai

SAMURAI WERE PROFESSIONAL SOLDIERS who dominated warfare in Japan for centuries. Although the Japanese had an emperor, he was largely a ruler in name only. The real power lay in the hands of the land-owning families who were rich enough to have their own private armies. Samurai served these feudal lords and swore oaths of allegiance to their masters rather than to the emperor.

Up to about 1868, Japanese history is full of constant struggles between feuding lords and their samurai. During this period, the samurai were caught up in political instability and shifting alliances as local men used troops to retain control of their land and expand their power against adjacent lords.

Samurai warriors used swords and bows as their primary weapons. They could fight both on foot and on horse, and when Portuguese sailors introduced firearms to Japan in the 1540s, they easily made the transition to these weapons. However, the carnage that accompanied the introduction of guns to Japan resulted in the banning of firearms less than a century later. Samurai warriors used siege weapons to attack castles and adopted cannon for a brief period.

The samurai reached their apex under the leadership of Oda Nobunaga and his lieutenant, Toyotomi Hideyoshi, in the late 16th century. These two men reunited Japan by force, and their samurai-led armies were their main weapon. In 1585, new laws that stratified Japanese society placed the samurai warrior class at the top; three years later, only samurai were permitted to have weapons.

The samurai retained their elite status until the 19th century. As Japan opened up to the outside world, a leader named Takasugi Shinsaku conscripted a local force consisting of peasants and armed them with modern rifles. When a force of samurai armed with traditional swords and bows attacked, the rifle-armed peasants annihilated them. In 1868, Emperor Meiji regained imperial power in the so-called "Meiji Restoration." A forceful emperor, Meiji began to dismantle the power of the samurai. There were samurai revolts against Meiji's growing authority, but they were ultimately defeated. In 1876, the emperor forbade the wearing of swords, which, in essence, meant the end of the samurai.

King Francis I (1494–1547)

SOME KINGS ARE REMEMBERED for their brutality or prowess in war; Francis I is remembered as the "Father and Restorer of Letters" for the cultural advances he brought to France.

Considered France's first Renaissance monarch, Francis assumed the throne in 1515 following the death of Louis XII. Unlike his predecessors, Francis had been greatly influenced by the new intellectual movements emanating from Italy. His education inclined him toward humanism and his interest in art was passed on to him by his mother.

Upon ascending to the throne, Francis became an ardent supporter of the Renaissance movement in France and a major patron of the arts. He encouraged many of the greatest artists of the period, including Leonardo da Vinci, who moved to France during the latter part of his life. One of da Vinci's greatest paintings, the *Mona Lisa*, remained in France following Francis's death and is now in the collections of the Louvre.

When Francis came to the throne, the royal palaces contained only a rudimentary collection of art. That changed dramatically during his reign as Francis established what was to become one of the great art collections of the world—much of which can still be seen in the Louvre today. Francis also employed famed goldsmith Benvenuto Cellini and painters such as Rosso, Romano, and Primaticcio to decorate his palaces. His agents scoured Italy for art by the Italian masters, including Michelangelo, Titian, and Raphael. They even considered trying to move da Vinci's *The Last Supper* to France.

Francis also supported major writers of the period and expanded the collection of the royal library. His 1537 Ordonnance de Montepellier, directed that his library receive a copy of every book to be sold in France. He spent fantastic sums of money on building and renovating: He built the Louvre, began construction of the Chateau de Chambord, financed a new City Hall for Paris, built the Chateau de Madrid, rebuilt the Chateau de Saint-Germain-en-Laye, and reconstructed and expanded the royal chateau of Fonainebleau—which boasted a fountain of wine and water.

While remembered for his contributions to French culture, Francis was less successful on other fronts. His war against Holy Roman Emperor Charles V was a dismal failure, and his persecution of Protestants would bring years of civil war. In fact, his lavish spending on building projects damaged the French economy.

The Ratification of the 14th Amendment

THE 13TH, 14TH, AND 15TH AMENDMENTS to the U.S. Constitution are referred to as the Civil War Amendments. The 13th Amendment, ratified in 1865, ended slavery in the United States. The following year, Ohio Congressman John Bingham submitted language for an amendment to the Constitution to the Congressional Committee on Reconstruction. The language provided that no state could "deprive any person of life, liberty, or property without due process of law, nor deny to any person within its jurisdiction the equal protection of the laws." That language is now part of the 14th Amendment.

Bingham had intended that the proposed language refer to equal protection of all men before the courts, but not cities or other municipal departments. His intentions were framed in the historical background in which the words were written. The Civil War had just concluded, and thousands of blacks had been freed from slavery. The purpose of the 14th Amendment was to prevent Southern states from discriminating against the former slaves. The amendment proclaimed that all persons born on U.S. soil were citizens—thus enfranchising the vast majority of blacks.

In the years since the ratification of the 14th Amendment in July 1868, the amendment's equal protection clause has been the subject of much litigation. The term has been interpreted to mean "equal application" of the laws, and it applies to situations where a state has granted a class of people the right to participate in some activity while denying another class of people the same right.

The "equal protection" language of the 14th Amendment has been applied in civil rights cases and cases involving college admission programs and affirmative action. The 14th Amendment is applicable to actions by states but is not applicable to actions by the federal government. The "equal protection" language was utilized in *Brown v. Board of Education* where school segregation was held to be unconstitutional because separate facilities were not equal facilities.

In more recent years, in the case of *Bush v. Gore*, the Supreme Court decided that the different standards of counting ballots throughout the state of Florida in the 2000 presidential election violated the amendment's equal protection provisions.

The Final Solution

O N JANUARY 20, 1942, a small group of top Nazis gathered in Wann-see, an upscale Berlin suburb to discuss an ungodly subject: to determine the most efficient way to murder several million Jews—a program euphemistically referred to as the "Final Solution."

Anti-Semitism had a long history in Europe, but Hitler's government had taken it to a new level. Jews were stripped of their citizenship, beaten, persecuted, and hounded out of the country as part of a program to "purify" the Aryan nation.

Crematorium ovens at Dachau

The Nazi solution was brutally simple. Jewish men, women, and children were rounded up, herded to remote locations, and shot. By the time of the Wannsee conference, the Final Solution was well underway. Mass shootings in the East had been in effect for months. The gassing of Jews at Chelmno, Poland, had started in December 1941. In 1940, about 100,000 Jews were murdered. In 1941, the total was at about one million.

But dragging thousands of people out into the woods to be individually shot ran counter to the Nazi love of efficiency. With 11 million potential victims—including the Jews of England and Ireland—expected, a better mechanism was needed. Security Service (SS) Chief Reinhard Heydrich suggested a system allowing able-bodied Jews to be worked to death as slave laborers. Those unable to work—the old, young, and infirm—would be gassed in specially constructed death camps.

On January 30, Hitler declared that the results of the war would be "the annihilation of the Jewish race in Europe." Soon, Jews were streaming into death camps. In Poland alone, six killing centers began operation—Belzec, Auschwitz-Birkenau, Chelmno, Sobibor, Treblinka, and Majdanek—all located near rail systems that brought their doomed human cargo from concentration points in the West. In 1942, 2.7 million Jews were murdered. By war's end, the total would be at least 6 million.

After the war, the architects of this unimaginable horror showed no remorse. In his last will and testament, written just before his suicide on April 29, 1945, Hitler continued to exhort "a merciless opposition to the universal poisoner of all peoples, international Jewry."

Adam Smith
and *The Wealth of Nations*

ADAM SMITH was born in the small Scottish village of Kirkcaldy in 1723. Smith entered the University of Glasgow at age 14 and later studied at Oxford University, where, according to one biographer, he developed "an enduring contempt for English education."

He taught at the University of Glasgow from 1751 to 1764; afterward, he traveled through France as tutor to a young duke. He later moved to London, where he wrote his magnum opus, *The Wealth of Nations,* in 1776.

The Wealth of Nations was arguably the most influential book on economics written in the 18th century. Smith contends that in any society, people should, and do, act out of self-interest: "It is not from the benevolence of the butcher... or the baker that we can expect our dinner, but from their regard to their own interest." However, this pursuit of self-interest inevitably leads to the greater good of society as a whole. As if "led by an invisible hand," a person working for his or her own economic good actually promotes "an end which was no part of his intention"—that is, the general good of society.

This argument became the basis for classical economic theory, as best articulated by 20th-century economists Alfred Marshall and Friedrich Hayek. The economic good for all is maximized by a free market economy in which market forces determine prices and wages. In other words, government should not intervene in the economy in ways that artificially regulate the market.

Although Smith certainly opposed the 18th-century practice of mercantilism, in which European governments created a trade surplus by preventing colonies from competing with the mother country, he did not oppose all government interference in the economy. He favored government-sponsored public works such as building roads. Smith also believed in high taxes on imports if competing nations imposed them. He recognized the negative psychological effects of repetitive labor. Nonetheless, the theory of self-interest and the invisible hand remain his enduring contribution to economics.

POSTSCRIPT

■ Smith believed that it was in Britain's economic interest to free its American colonies.

Benito Mussolini (1883–1945)

BENITO MUSSOLINI grew up in a poor, socialist family in Predappio, Italy. He studied to become an elementary school teacher but was unable to find work. He eventually moved to Austria where he wrote for a newspaper. Mussolini's published views angered the authorities, however, and he was expelled from the country.

Upon returning to Italy, Mussolini joined the socialist party. Initially, he urged Italy's nonparticipation in World War I, but his political views changed over the years. He gained access to the political arena when he founded the Italian Fascist party in 1919.

In 1921, Mussolini was elected to parliament as a right-wing candidate. Meanwhile, his Fascist followers began confronting his former socialist colleagues. King Emmanuel III feared the country was headed for anarchy and asked Mussolini, who had the support of industrialists and farmers, to help form a government.

Mussolini agreed, and soon he dissolved political parties and parliament, and skillfully navigated his way into the position of dictator, which he held for 21 years. He deftly instituted programs of censorship and used propaganda to suit his needs. His personal takeover of the military and various government ministries, as well as the transfer of control of private industries to the state, kept rivals from obtaining power. Laws were rewritten; only writers approved by the Fascists were permitted to work as journalists.

Mussolini's aggressive policies included establishing a puppet regime in Albania while he pursued a plan to control the Mediterranean area. In 1935, he was condemned by the League of Nations for invading Ethiopia. Four years later, he became aligned with Nazi Germany. His military forces were unprepared to deal with Allied invasions, however, and his troops met defeat in Sicily in 1943.

On the night of July 24, 1943, a vote was passed to dismiss Mussolini from government service. He later organized a Fascist regime in northern Italy but was eventually captured by partisans as he and his mistress, Clara Petacci, were attempting to flee to Switzerland. On April 28, 1945, they both were executed and displayed in the public square in Milan.

Leonardo da Vinci (1452–1519)

LEONARDO DA VINCI was born on April 15, 1452, in the Italian village of Vinci and was primarily raised by his uncle Francesco. Around 1465, he left Vinci for the city of Florence, the epicenter of Renaissance culture. There he was apprenticed to Andrea del Verrocchio, a skilled artist, sculptor, goldsmith, musician, and mathematician.

The intellectual atmosphere surrounding Verrocchio undoubtedly stimulated the young da Vinci. In 1472, he became a master craftsman and joined the Painter's Guild. It was also around this time that he painted, in tandem with Verrocchio, his oldest surviving work, *The Baptism of Christ*. On January 1, 1478, da Vinci received a commission for a chapel altarpiece—his first work as an independent artist. Still, his interest in inventions, mechanical devices, and musical instruments began to distract him from his artwork.

In early 1482, he moved to Milan, where war and weaponry were valued as art, music, and literature had been valued in Florence. Although he supported himself as a painter, he filled stacks of notebooks with ideas and notes on a multitude of subjects, including the "science of painting." Da Vinci wrote backwards, in a style called mirror writing, which can only be read using a mirror. In 1482, he entered the service of Duke Ludovico Sforza, for whom he designed elaborate mechanical court festivals. He continued to design numerous other devices, including a tank with a spring-powered motor, doors that opened and closed automatically, and a flying machine. In 1495, he began the two-year task of painting the fresco *The Last Supper*.

In 1500, da Vinci returned to Florence, where he worked for a couple of years as a military architect and engineer for Cesare Borgia. It was also in Florence that he and his great rival, Michelangelo, were commissioned to create paintings on opposite walls—though neither man ever finished his painting. It is estimated that around 1503 he worked on his most famous painting, the *Mona Lisa*. While da Vinci had always had an interest in human anatomy, it was piqued late in life, as he spent hours examining the body from an artistic and scientific standpoint. He spent his last years in Rome and France, before dying on May 2, 1519.

POSTSCRIPT

■ Biographer Giorgio Vasari claimed da Vinci hired clowns and musicians to keep a smile on the model's face while he painted the *Mona Lisa*.

The Rise of Photography

FRENCHMAN JOSEPH NICÉPHORE NIÉPCE is credited with recording the first long-lasting photographic images. He apparently had success in 1824, though the earliest known surviving example of a Niépce photograph (or any other photographic image) dates to 1826.

Like other inventors on a similar track, Niépce sought a way to permanently fix the images cast by the *camera obscura*, a process that used lensed boxes, which projected an inverted image on the back. The boxes were often used by artists as a drawing aid.

Niépce experimented with a variety of light-sensitive chemical compounds on various backings before hitting on bitumen to coat his photographic "plates." The process, which he called *heliography* or "sun writing," worked, but it required many hours of exposure time. As a result, it could only be used to record images of buildings, landscapes, and inanimate objects.

An early photography studio

In 1829, Niépce formed a partnership with Jacques-Mande Daguerre. They developed a process called *physautotype* that involved lavender oil. Their efforts reduced exposure time to about eight hours, but they had not come up with a truly practical and reliable process by the time of Niépce's unexpected death in 1833.

Daguerre continued to work on the problem. Six years later he unveiled a process using silver-plated copper sheets that were sensitized with iodine vapors and exposed in a box camera. The image was then developed with mercury fumes and fixed with a salt-water solution. The new process reduced exposure time to only a few minutes.

Daguerre's process was quickly fine-tuned to make portrait-taking possible, and the daguerreotype became a sensation. The craze spread throughout Europe and to the United States.

Daguerre's name became a household word, while Niépce was generally forgotten. Only in modern times has Niépce's contribution to the discovery of photography gained the recognition it deserves.

The Rise of Robert Walpole

In 1714, England's Queen Anne, last of the Stuart monarchs, was quite ill. During her lifetime, she had suffered through the deaths of her five children and many miscarriages, and she had been in bad health for years. Her doctors had tried everything they could to cure her, including bleeding her and applying hot irons, but it was all to no avail.

After her husband, Prince George of Denmark, died in 1708, she had ruled alone. Anne knew she had to name a successor, but none of her children had survived. The true heir to the throne should have been her half-brother James, but he was a Roman Catholic living in exile in France. Through the 1701 Act of Settlement, the successor to the throne was determined to be German Prince George of Hanover. Queen Anne died on August 1, and George I was proclaimed King of Great Britain, even though he knew little about British politics. To this end, he relied on his chancellor, Robert Walpole, who is regarded as Britain's first prime minister.

Walpole was born in 1676, and although he originally intended to go into the church, he chose a life in politics instead. He was an ambitious man, attending Eton and Cambridge and becoming a member of Parliament— all by age 25.

In 1710–11, the Tories replaced the Whigs in Parliament, and Walpole found himself replaced as well. The Tories even convicted him of graft and sent him to prison in 1712, but Walpole was back in Parliament in 1713, where his influence grew.

After King George was crowned, Walpole made a comeback. He served as secretary at war and treasurer of the navy and held various offices under the king. In 1721, he became the first prime minister of England (although the title was not yet official) and was one of the country's most influential politicians for about two decades. Walpole's perspective was that a country's strength and power came primarily through material gain. To accomplish this, he encouraged business and sought to avoid war.

When war with Spain became inevitable in 1739, King George forged ahead and led his troops into battle. Walpole, however, did not agree with this decision. He acquired the nickname of "Sir Blustering" and began to lose the support of the British people as well as the House of Commons. Finally in 1742, he was forced to resign. Walpole held the position of prime minister for almost 21 years, the longest term of any British prime minister in history.

Joan of Arc (1412–1431)

JOAN, BORN IN LORRAINE in eastern France in 1412, was the daughter of peasant farmers. In 1425, around age 13, Joan first began receiving visions and hearing the voice of God. She was convinced the voices she heard were genuine messages; later the archangel Michael told her she was meant to lead French soldiers into battle against the English and Normans who claimed the French throne.

When she was about 17 years old, she traveled to the palace of the heir to the French throne, Charles VII, to ask permission to lead his troops. Clerics examined her to determine whether she was associated with the devil or evil forces. They found her to be pious, and after she made a prediction about a battle near Orleans, Charles permitted her to lead an army.

Disguised as a male soldier, Joan led her army to Orleans in 1429. She quickly learned the strategic wisdom needed to be a successful military leader and intuitively understood principles of military action. Her army overtook the fortress, and the sudden, unexpected victory led Charles to give her permission to advance. Joan and the French army proceeded to Reims, where Charles was crowned king. Getting to Reims was not easy, however, since they had to navigate miles of enemy territory to reach their destination.

Joan was captured at Compiègne while her troops were defending the city from a Burgundian attack. She was imprisoned, tried for heresy, and condemned to death by being burned at the stake. More than 20 years after her death, a court decided her trial had been politically motivated and illegal. They found Joan innocent of the charges, and in 1456 the death sentence was reversed—albeit far too late.

Joan was a masterful leader and has been used as a symbolic figure since the time of Napoleon. Her humble origins and support of nationalism have inspired the French people. In 1909, she was beatified, and in 1920, Pope Benedict XV canonized her as a saint. To this day, Joan is one of the most popular saints in the Roman Catholic Church.

Wilson's Fourteen Points

PRESIDENT WOODROW WILSON believed in the virtues of democracy and the right of self-determination for all people. His thinking was articulated in his 1917 "Peace Without Victory" address when he criticized European imperialism and militarism and advocated the creation of a "community of nations." This community, proposed Wilson, would include mechanisms for the arbitration of disputes and the reduction of armaments. It would promote respect for self-determination, freedom of the seas, and the equality and collective security of nations.

The speech received widespread praise. One commentator remarked that the president had rendered "a service to all humanity that is impossible to exaggerate." But from practical standpoint, Wilson's words had little impact on hostile nations. The war in Europe continued to drag on, and in April 1917, the United States also entered the conflict.

Wilson's idealism, however, remained intact. On January 8, 1918, he again articulated his views—what became known as the "Fourteen Points." The points mostly echoed his previous calls for the abolition of secret treaties, freedom of the seas, equality of trade, and similar guarantees. The most important was the last point, which called for "a general association of nations to be formed under specific covenants for the purpose of affording mutual guarantees of political independence and territorial integrity to great and small states alike."

Again, Wilson's speech was internationally lauded. Unfortunately, when he arrived at the Paris Peace Conference, Wilson found the Allies intent on business as usual. His hopes for international cooperation were battered by demands for monetary and territorial reparations, colonies, and indifference to the self-determination of all nations. Wilson eventually compromised on many points in order to gain acceptance for a "general association of nations," better known as the League of Nations.

He returned home to find his proposal opposed both by conservatives and by former supporters on the left who felt betrayed by his compromises. Despite Wilson's intense lobbying, the Senate refused to ratify U.S. participation in the League of Nations.

In an ironic postscript, Wilson was awarded the 1920 Nobel Peace Prize for his efforts. He was unable to attend the ceremony, having suffered a massive stroke. He died in 1924, and, 15 years later, the world was once again at war.

The Battle of Stalingrad

THE BATTLE OF STALINGRAD (August 19, 1942–February 2, 1943) was a major turning point in the European theater of World War II. It was also one of the bloodiest battles in human history.

German soldiers at Stalingrad

Before the summer of 1941, the German army had positioned itself throughout Western Europe with the intention of attacking the Soviet Union. On June 22, 1941, Hitler invaded, assuming a quick victory.

It did not go as Hitler had expected. As the war continued, Hitler realized his troops needed additional fuel. He launched an offensive to capture Soviet oil fields in order to revitalize his forces.

Hitler had scheduled an attack on Baku for September 1942; however, Stalingrad—a Soviet manufacturing and transportation center—was situated near the path of the German army's advancement. An initial German air assault on August 23 caused a firestorm in Stalingrad, killing thousands of civilians. Hitler's troops captured most of the city.

The Soviets were outnumbered, but the Germans had not anticipated the fierce determination of Soviet Marshal Georgi Zukov and the resistance of the Russian people. Zukov's forces trapped the Germans, and the soldiers fought hand-to-hand with knives and bayonets. The Soviets positioned their lines near the German armies to increase the loss of German life when the Luftwaffe bombed the city.

Hitler ordered the troops to hold their positions. Heavy October rains turned the roads to mud. By the end of November, although the Germans had captured most of the city, they also had to deal with the region's heavy snow. Ill equipped to deal with the cold and suffering from food and ammunition shortages, the Germans awaited the Luftwaffe's supply airdrops. Only a small fraction of what was needed reached the troops, and some of it—such as summer uniforms—was useless.

Against Hitler's orders, the German troops finally surrendered on February 2, 1943. The Axis forces suffered about 800,000 deaths, while the Soviets had upward of one million casualties.

Sitting Bull (ca. 1831–1890)

Tatanka-Iyotanka, better known as Sitting Bull, was part of the Hunkpapa Lakota Sioux nation in present-day South Dakota. When he was only 14 years old, Sitting Bull went on his first raid against the Crow. Years later, in June 1863, his war party attacked a detachment of the United States Army. The skirmishes became an annual event as his people warred against the advance of whites onto the Great Plains.

Thanks to his continued successes in war, Sitting Bull became the head chief of the Lakota nation in 1868. The Lakota soon became embroiled in hostilities with the United States over land rights after gold was discovered in the Black Hills of South Dakota in the mid-1870s. Hordes of prospectors descended on the area in spite of an earlier treaty that kept the hills off-limits to whites. The Native Americans considered the hills sacred ground, and they became openly hostile.

In 1876, the army took action. Several columns of troops moved into Lakota territory. On June 25, Lieutenant Colonel George A. Custer, commanding the 7th United States Cavalry, attacked Sitting Bull's encampment along the Little Bighorn River in the Montana Territory. By that time, thousands of Lakota had congregated there, and Custer was vastly outnumbered in what became known as "Custer's Last Stand." Custer died, along with more than 200 of his troops.

Custer's death spurred a major military backlash, and in 1877 Sitting Bull and his followers fled across the border into Canada to avoid capture. By then the region's buffalo had been hunted nearly to extinction: The Lakota and other Native Americans faced starvation. In 1881, Sitting Bull and his family finally surrendered and were incarcerated for nearly two years at Fort Randall, Missouri. Afterward, he lived at the Standing Rock Reservation before he was allowed to leave in order to join Buffalo Bill's Wild West Show. The once-mighty Sioux chief now earned $50 a week riding a horse around an arena. After four months with the show, he left and went back to Standing Rock, disgusted with white society.

In 1890, many of Sitting Bull's people joined the Ghost Dance movement, whose followers believed that they could rid the land of whites. Fearing that Sitting Bull would also join, authorities sent Lakota policemen to arrest the chief and move him elsewhere. On December 15, as they tried to move Sitting Bull through a crowd of his followers, a scuffle broke out, and the chief was shot and killed.

The Franco–Prussian War

THE BRIEF FRANCO–PRUSSIAN WAR changed the balance of power in Europe and helped unify Germany. At the time, Prussia was the most militarized of the fragmented German states, which Prussian Chancellor Otto von Bismarck was interested in uniting. It fought brief wars with Denmark in 1864 and Austria in 1866, solidifying its leadership of the North German Confederation. Bismarck's wily diplomacy endangered France, which was under the leadership of Emperor Napoleon III. Napoleon believed that war with Prussia was inevitable, as he objected to their plan to put a German prince on the Spanish throne. He declared war on July 19, 1870.

At the time, the French army was widely believed to be the best in Europe. However, its leadership was largely incompetent, and the war turned into a disaster. Napoleon organized his troops into two major armies, but thanks to the work of German chief of staff Helmuth von Moltke, both armies were outmaneuvered.

The German armies crossed the border, penetrating between the two French armies. The French Army of Bazaine fought two battles on August 16 and 18, suffered heavy casualties, and retreated into the fortress city of Metz. The second French army, accompanied by Napoleon, moved to Bazaine's aid but was confronted by German units at Sedan. Here, on August 31, the French were overtaken. They surrendered 83,000 men, including the emperor. Metz was surrendered on October 27 after a lengthy siege; the Germans captured 140,000 French soldiers.

The French government toppled on September 4, and the Third Republic was proclaimed. When the victorious Germans marched on Paris, it was defended by national guardsmen and fragments of the French army. The Germans besieged Paris on September 19; Paris surrendered on January 28, 1871. After France's defeat, from March to May radicals took over the city government in the form of the so-called "Paris Commune." When the government army retaliated, more than 25,000 civilians were killed in the fighting.

The Franco–Prussian War ended on May 10, 1871, with a peace treaty under which France ceded part of the provinces of Alsace-Lorraine to Germany and paid an indemnity of roughly one billion dollars. The war disgraced the French and left them with a bitter hatred of the Germans. It was this animosity that helped precipitate French entry into World War I and led to the harsh 1919 Treaty of Versailles.

The Maori Wars

THE MAORI WARS, a series of conflicts also known as the New Zealand Wars and the Land Wars, arose from the misappropriation of Maori land by white settlers and the government. The British assumed formal control of New Zealand in 1840, and, that same year, the Treaty of Waitangi guaranteed Maori tribes undisturbed possession of their lands. But pressure from land-hungry settlers encouraged the government to ignore the treaty, and whites were allowed into Maori areas.

The first clash occurred in 1843 when 22 settlers were killed while attempting to seize Maori land. More clashes were fought from 1845 to 1847. Eventually, an understanding was reached that English law would rule in the towns while Maori authority would prevail outside.

Relative peace prevailed for more than a decade, but English settlers began arriving in increasing numbers. This influx brought renewed grabs for land, which resulted in the First Taranaki War. The war lasted 12 months and ended in a draw, but the hiatus was brief. In 1863, the Waikato War broke out, culminating in the confiscation of four million acres of Maori land. The seizure brought about the Second Taranaki War.

Maori with tribal tattoos

Some whites saw the injustice of what was happening to the Maori; a few British settlers even fought alongside them. One of the best known was Kimball Bent, who later became a Maori *tohunga,* or priest. There was also an antiwar movement among British settlers who opposed the colonial government's policy toward the Maori. Prominent members included Anglican Bishop George Augustus Selwyn, Archdeacon Octavius Hadfield, and Sir William Martin.

But the Maori cause was doomed—their population was declining while the white population was exploding. The British could field full-time soldiers backed by a massive economic base, but the Maori were part-time fighters who needed to farm crops at home. No matter how hard the Maori fought, the settlers could outlast them.

In modern times, the government has apologized for its previous actions. Still the battle over Maori lands continues—but now it is fought in courtrooms and negotiating sessions rather than on battlefields.

Henry Kissinger (1923–present)

HEINZ ALFRED KISSINGER was born on May 27, 1923, in Bavaria. Concerned over what was happening to other Jewish families in their country, the Kissingers moved to London in 1938 and then to New York City. In New York, their son, renamed an Americanized "Henry," worked in a shaving brush factory during the day and attended high school at night. After being drafted into the army, he worked as an interpreter. Kissinger attended Harvard after the war, earning masters and doctorate degrees. As a professor at Harvard from 1954 to 1971, Kissinger wrote several books on foreign policy and diplomatic history.

When Richard Nixon was elected president in 1968, he asked Kissinger to be the assistant for National Security Affairs and later his secretary of state. After Nixon's Watergate scandal, Kissinger received a fair amount of criticism for being in Nixon's administration, although he was not involved in the scandal. He later served as secretary of state under President Gerald Ford. He continued to be criticized for his methods of diplomacy, which were often considered secretive.

Under President Ronald Reagan, Kissinger chaired the National Bipartisan Commission on Central America and was a member of the president's Foreign Intelligence Advisory Board. He was intensely involved with peace negotiations in the Middle East and Vietnam; helped ease Cold War relations, or *détente,* with the Russians; and established a relationship with China.

Kissinger authored several books on foreign affairs and international diplomacy, including *Nuclear Weapons and Foreign Policy* (1957). He has also been given many awards during his political life. Although he was initially a proponent of a hard-line course of action in Vietnam, over time he amended his ways. In 1973, Kissinger was awarded the Nobel Peace Prize for helping negotiate the cease-fire agreement during the Vietnam War, a prize that he shared with Le Duc Tho, a North Vietnamese peace negotiator (who refused to accept it). He has also been given the 1977 Presidential Medal of Freedom and the 1986 Medal of Liberty. Kissinger is also known for his humor: "Nobody will ever win the battle of the sexes. There's too much fraternizing with the enemy."

Today Kissinger continues to work as a writer, lecturer, international commentator, and consultant.

Solidarity

IN AUGUST 1980, a man climbed over a shipyard wall in Poland. Little did he realize that this simple action would change the world.

For years, Poland had been a reluctant member of the Eastern Bloc of Soviet satellite states. In 1970, a violent strike by Polish workers had ended disastrously with dozens dead. At the same time, 27-year-old shipyard worker and strike leader Lech Walesa realized that violence was not the solution. For ten years, he waited for his next opportunity.

It came on August 14, 1980, after government-imposed price increases led to a series of strikes in several Polish cities. On that day, a strike called at the Lenin Shipyard in Gdansk seemed to be fizzling out. Shipyard Director Klemens Gniech assured strikers that he would negotiate for their demands if they went back to work—a promise he had made before but had never followed through. Workers milled about, and many returned to work.

Suddenly Walesa, who had been fired from the shipyard several years before, scaled one of the shipyard walls and jumped onto a bulldozer. "We don't believe your lies," he shouted. The strike was reenergized. A bulletin called *Solidarnosc* (*Solidarity*) was printed. The workers soon adopted the name to describe their movement. They wanted the establishment of free and independent trade unions—a first in a Communist country.

Support poured in from around the world, including from fellow Pole Pope John Paul II. On August 31, 1980, the government agreed to the formation of the Independent Self-Governing Trade Union Solidarity. Over the next few years, through the imposition of martial law in December 1981, the Communist government of Wojciech Jaruzelski tried to destroy Solidarity—he even used terrorist tactics such as murder and made the group illegal, forcing it underground.

In March 1985, Mikhail Gorbachev came to power in the USSR, promoting tolerance for political differences. Solidarity regained legal status. In free elections held in June 1989, Solidarity won 99 out of 100 Senate seats in Poland. In August 1989, with Solidarity's backing, Tadeusz Mazowiecki became the first non-Communist head of government in the Eastern Bloc. This rapidly led to other Eastern European countries throwing off the Communist yoke. Walesa later served as President of Poland from 1990 to 1995, quitting Solidarity in 2006.

Harriet Tubman (ca. 1820–1913)

H ARRIET TUBMAN was born a slave in eastern Maryland around 1820. She was actually born Araminta Ross, but she was known by her mother's name, Harriet. When she was 13, she helped another slave who was being punished by their supervisor. The supervisor turned on Tubman, bludgeoning her with a two-pound weight. Her skull was fractured, and she suffered blackouts for the rest of her life.

In 1849, she escaped bondage after learning that she might be sold to another owner and be forced to leave her husband, a free black. Tubman made her way to Philadelphia, where she became associated with abolitionist William Still, who managed the local stations of the "Underground Railroad," a term for the men and women who helped escaping slaves reach freedom in either the North or in Canada.

Less than a year after her escape, Tubman began traveling back south to help other slaves reach freedom. She is reported to have made 19 such trips, rescuing more than 300 slaves in the process. Tubman became so notorious that Maryland slave owners posted a $40,000 reward for her capture. To aid her efforts, Tubman used money from her jobs as a domestic servant and donations from abolitionists. She earned the nickname "Moses" from those she helped to freedom. On one such mission, Tubman brought her 70-year-old parents north and out of slavery.

After the Civil War began, she went to South Carolina to help contraband slaves. Governor John Andrew of Massachusetts sent her to Hilton Head, South Carolina, after the region was captured by the Union army. Here on the coastal islands of South Carolina, Tubman helped slaves start new lives behind Union lines. She volunteered as a scout on army expeditions to the mainland and assisted with the rescue of thousands of slaves. When the 54th Massachusetts unsuccessfully assaulted Fort Wagner in July 1863, Tubman was on the scene to help bury the dead and treat the wounded.

Tubman moved to Auburn, New York, after the war. She remarried and became active in the women's rights movement. She also opened a home for aged and indigent blacks. She died in 1913 and was buried in Auburn.

The First and Second Continental Congresses

THE FIRST CONTINENTAL CONGRESS featured delegates from 12 of the 13 American colonies when it met in Philadelphia in 1774—only Georgia did not attend. The British Parliament had just passed a series of laws known in the colonies as the Intolerable Acts; the purpose of the Congress was to discuss the colonial relationship with Britain.

Samuel Adams and John Adams from Massachusetts attended the First Congress, as did George Washington and Patrick Henry from Virginia. The members of the Congress decided that the colonists needed to cut off trade with England and boycott British goods, and they passed resolutions asserting their rights as colonists to do so—unless Parliament abolished the acts. Thus the delegates accomplished the goals they had set for the Congress: defining their rights, identifying British violations of those rights, and devising a plan to convince England to restore the rights it was violating. In order to provide for continued action, members of the Congress decided to meet the following year if England had not made changes in colonial policy.

Their demands didn't sit well with England. Parliament punished the colonies for their actions and enacted legislation to limit colonial fishing rights in North Atlantic waters. They also dissolved the colonial legislatures. In 1775, the colonists met again in Philadelphia—this time with Georgia in attendance. The Congress convened approximately a month after colonists had participated in the battles against British rule at Lexington and Concord, both in Massachusetts.

The Second Continental Congress was extremely important for the nascent nation. The meetings continued for several months, and during that time, the Congress served as the colonies' government. It established the Continental Army and selected George Washington as its commander. The Congress also decided that the colonies needed to print paper money to support their war with Britain.

In May 1776, the delegates decided to formally break their relationship with England. A committee of five men was chosen to write a statement declaring the colonies' independence. Thomas Jefferson, known as an excellent writer, was selected as the primary draftsman. When the Declaration of Independence was completed, John Hancock, a delegate who had not attended the First Continental Congress, was the first to sign the document. He is said to have written his signature particularly large so that King George III could read it without his glasses.

Perón Dominates Argentina

WITH SUPPORT FROM LABOR UNIONS and agricultural workers, Juan Perón was elected president of Argentina in 1946. He advocated anti-imperialist and anti-American policies while promoting a nationalistic program that stressed the importance of economic self-sufficiency and industrialization. In the beginning, Perón's political program, "The Third Way," was somewhere between capitalism and communism, and the laboring classes welcomed his economic policies.

Perón devised a five-year plan to turn the economy around. The government purchased rail lines and built factories to produce iron and steel. It also began subsidizing the manufacture of farm machinery and provided paid vacations and free medical care for workers. Perón increased the size of the military and began manufacturing airplanes and ships. His country's economy blossomed, and so did his followers' support.

Then Perón met Eva Duarte, a young woman from rural Argentina who had come to Buenos Aires. She became his mistress, and later they married. Eva Duarte Perón, often referred to as Evita, captured the hearts of the poor and rural people. She was placed in charge of Argentina's welfare program and declared her vision of social justice and aid. Eva told women to follow the traditional roles assigned to them and give complete devotion to their families. Each day she listened to the plights of people who waited hours to see her, and she often paid for their trip home.

In 1949, the Peronists created a new constitution that allowed Perón to succeed himself as president of Argentina. As his reign continued, it became increasingly apparent that he was an authoritarian leader. Perón censored the press, controlled education, and imprisoned political opponents.

However, in 1950, the country was spending far more than it was making. After an attempted coup failed in 1951, Perón instituted more repression. When Eva died from cancer in 1952, he lost even more public support. Three years later, a military coup toppled Perón from his post. His administration, which demonstrated confidence, oppression, and luxury, had been extinguished.

The Kirov Murder

Sergei Mironovich Kostrikov's early life was not an easy one. He was born into poverty in 1886 in the Vyatka province of Russia; when he was a boy, his father walked out and never returned. The following year, his mother died. By the time he was seven, Kostrikov had been transplanted first to his grandmother's care and then to an orphanage.

Eventually things improved. In 1901, Kostrikov was given a scholarship, and he later earned an engineering degree. It was not long before his goals turned from education to politics. He became a Marxist and joined the Russian Social Democratic Labor Party. In 1905, he took part in the Russian Revolution.

Determined to get his opinions out, Kostrikov began handing out leaflets and going into factories to rally workers. Kostrikov, now calling himself Kirov, was repeatedly arrested for his actions. After Lenin came to power in Russia in 1917, Kirov was appointed Russian ambassador to Georgia, working his way up the ladder until he became secretary of the Communist Party of Azerbaijan. His was the most influential position within the Soviet government of the region. Even as the regime changed around him, Kirov participated in the destruction of the *kulaks,* or peasant class, resulting in the deaths of up to eight million people.

When Stalin purged Leningrad of his rivals, Kirov was made the new head of the Leningrad Communist Party in 1926. Many thought he would soon push Stalin out of his position of power and take over as party leader.

On December 1, 1934, Kirov's aspirations ended. While he was preparing to give a speech, Kirov was shot in the back of the neck by a party member named Leonid Nikolaev—despite his five bodyguards being present. Witnesses all claimed different stories as to what really happened. Many suspected the murder was not the act of a lone killer but ordered by Stalin. To protect his image, Stalin allowed a city in the Ukraine to be named after the victim, as well as a ballet and a warship.

Stalin used Kirov's death to set up new laws allowing him to essentially investigate and destroy anyone he chose. He proceeded to eliminate every single adversary in what became known as Stalin's Purge. Trials that had nothing to do with justice were held, with most of the guilty executed. In the end, Stalin used Kirov's death to murder countless innocent people.

The Black Death

DURING THE MIDDLE AGES, rats—more specifically, the fleas they carried—were the cause of widespread death and devastation in Europe.

The Black Death, or bubonic plague, was a pandemic of epic proportions that probably started in Asia in the early 1300s and was carried by the invading Mongol armies as they moved west. The plague hit Europe in 1347; as merchant ships traveled from East to West, they brought plague-infested rats harboring infected fleas. The plague was transmitted to people by the fleas or via contact with an infected person.

The plague spread across Europe like wild-fire. People abandoned homes and families to escape the sickness. The dead were often left in empty houses, unable to be given Christian burials. Churches closed and written language, mostly perpetuated by religious scholars, was nearly lost. Skeletons became part of artwork and paintings depicted the sad, ill, and dead. Lawlessness was at a high.

Trade and the economy were hit hard during the Black Death. People sank into despair, and many gave up hope. As a result, crops and animals were often not cared for. Priorities and attitudes about daily living changed, along with the status quo. Since so many people had died, anyone left living that had specialized skills could demand a greater income.

Some communities took measures to prevent and stop the plague with varying degrees of success. City officials in Milan, Italy, helped stop the spread of the disease by boarding up houses in which someone had contracted the deadly illness. Other Italian cities utilized quarantine and health measures. Port cities sometimes isolated incoming ships they feared might be carrying the plague. Other cities tried clanging church bells, firing cannons, and requiring people to cover their faces when in public. Individually, people wore charms, oils, and scents to keep themselves free from illness, to little avail.

Despite "cure-alls" and prevention, the plague returned through about 1400. During this time, an estimated one-third of Europe's population—or about 25 million people—died from the Black Death.

Simón Bolívar (1783–1830)

SIMÓN BOLÍVAR was born in Caracas, Venezuela, in 1783. The son of a wealthy Creole family, he was sent to Europe to complete his education, where he was exposed to the republican ideals of the American and French revolutions and witnessed Napoleon's coronation. He would later come to be known as "The Liberator of Latin America."

Bolívar's revolutionary career began in 1810 when the city council of Caracas took advantage of the turmoil in Napoleonic Europe and deposed the Spanish viceroy, declaring Venezuela an independent republic. Bolívar freed his slaves and joined the revolutionary forces as a lieutenant colonel. When the Spanish reconquered the country in 1812, he escaped to New Granada, now Colombia. The rebel government of New Granada authorized a force to liberate Venezuela, commanded by Bolívar.

Bolívar reentered Venezuela in May 1813, pitting his men against a large Spanish army. After six swift victories against small Spanish units, he built up his army; many of his new recruits were deserters from the Spanish army. The republican army entered Caracas on August 6. Bolívar declared himself the liberator and head of state of the new republic of Venezuela. It was not a long-lived victory, however. In 1814, he was driven out of Venezuela by repeated royalist attacks. In May 1815, the royalists regained control of Venezuela with help from thousands of recruited veterans.

In December 1816, Bolívar landed in Venezuela with a small band of rebels, planning to fight against the royal army with propaganda and guerilla tactics. Outmatched on the plains in Venezuela and aware that the Spanish guarded the frontier of New Granada very lightly, he marched into the Andes to attack the Spanish at their weak point.

Bolívar's first real success came in August 1819 with the republican victory at Boyacá. The Spanish began to evacuate New Granada, and as desertions from the royal army increased, formerly neutral citizens began to support the rebels. In December, the underground legislature of republican Venezuela created the republic of Gran Colombia, combining Venezuela, New Granada, and Ecuador. Bolívar was named president and military dictator. Bolívar's success in New Granada was followed by the liberation of Venezuela in 1821, Ecuador in 1822, Peru in 1824, and Upper Peru in 1825, which was renamed Bolivia in honor of its liberator.

Before Bolívar's death in 1830, Gran Colombia broke up into the modern states of Venezuela, Colombia, and Ecuador.

Napoleon Bonaparte (1769–1821)

NAPOLEON BONAPARTE was a devil to some and a saint to others, a leader who rose to power on the ashes of the French Revolution.

The man who became the greatest military genius since Alexander the Great was born on August 15, 1769, on the Mediterranean island of Corsica. At age ten he was sent to military school, where his leadership skills were so renowned that he was reportedly called on to command snowball fights. He became an officer in the French military at age 16. At age 24, he became a brigadier general. After Robespierre's faction was overthrown in 1794, Napoleon landed in prison, where he was nearly executed.

After his release, he met the bewitching Josephine de Beauharnais, a widowed Parisian socialite. His military career was rejuvenated in 1795 when he dispelled some Paris rioters. In the spring of 1796, Napoleon was given command of French troops in Italy. He married Josephine on March 9, leaving for Italy only two days later. Napoleon swept through Italy and then Egypt, where his troops uncovered the Rosetta Stone, by which Egyptian hieroglyphics could be deciphered.

France sought a strong leader after years of weak revolutionary governments. Napoleon stepped up and made himself First Consul on November 9, 1799.

Scholars argue as to whether Napoleon was the savior or the assassin of the French Revolution. Among other reforms, Napoleon changed some taxes, abolished serfdom, introduced religious tolerance, and established the *Code Napoleon,* a new civil code for France. Yet his dictatorial powers seemed to fly in the face of the revolution's commitment to equality and liberty for all. Initially, he was considered a great leader, but when he became emperor of France on December 2, 1804, he lost much of his public support worldwide.

"The only thing modern nations care about is property," Napoleon said, and by 1810 the vast Napoleonic empire was the largest since Rome. But England, Portugal, and other foreign nations had lined up against him. In 1812, he made a catastrophic blunder by invading Russia. Thrown back by the brutal Russian winter, Napoleon saw his empire slowly whittled down. In 1814, he abdicated from the French throne and was exiled to the island of Elba by the victorious Allies. Eleven months later, Napoleon escaped and reclaimed the throne in March 1815. But his July defeat at Waterloo ended his career. Napoleon lived the rest of his life in exile on the tiny island of St. Helena.

Frank Lloyd Wright and the Guggenheim Museum

IN 1943, American architect Frank Lloyd Wright received a letter from Solomon Guggenheim's art advisor asking Wright to design a new building to house Guggenheim's nonobjective paintings.

Wright was just the man for the job. According to Wright's design theory, known as Organic Architecture, the building and its surroundings should be integrated into one form. He was renowned for his design of Prairie Style residences, including Fallingwater and the Taliesin homes, all of which exemplify this idea of a unified whole. The Guggenheim Museum also exhibits the qualities of organic architecture for which he became famous.

From the beginning, the project was met with many obstacles. America was involved in World War II, and a building moratorium had been imposed. Finding a suitable site in Manhattan was also a challenge. Wright wanted the building to embrace nature and decided that a location near Central Park could give relief from the noise of the city.

The Guggenheim is unconventional in design, embodying modernism and organic architectural concepts. Wright constructed the building with reinforced concrete and created an expanding spiral with a continuous interior ramp. Modeled after an ancient winding pyramidal temple, the ramp permitted museum visitors to take an elevator to the top of the spiral and begin viewing the exhibits as they continued down the ramp without having to retrace their steps. Wright used an abundance of rigid, modernistic architecture throughout the museum by including oval-shape columns, circles, arches, triangles, and squares in his design.

Wright wanted the museum to have the appearance of a single, great space and his design took more than a decade to implement. Construction on the Guggenheim began in 1956. Wright's idea to make the building and the paintings merge into "an uninterrupted, beautiful symphony" was completed shortly after his death in 1959.

The First Commercial TV Broadcast

ALTHOUGH TV SEEMS LIKE a fairly modern invention, it actually dates back to the mid-19th century. In the mid-1800s, scientists began experimenting with electromagnetism and transmitting images over wires or through electronic signals. Inventors such as Alexander Graham Bell and Thomas Edison theorized about how to create a telephone that would not only transmit sound but also images.

Russian scientist Constantin Perskyi coined the word *television* at the 1900 World's Fair in Paris. The development of television soon became an international affair. Americans Philo Farnsworth and Charles Jenkins, along with German Paul Nipkow, Scot John Baird, and Russian Vladimir Zworykin, all worked on different aspects of what would eventually become the television. Some worked on creating spinning metal disks, while others focused on creating cathode ray tubes and iconoscopes.

On April 9, 1927, Bell Laboratories and the U.S. Department of Commerce joined together to present the first long-distance use of a television transmission from Washington, D.C., to New York City. Secretary of Commerce and future president Herbert Hoover said, "Today we have, in a sense, the transmission of sight for the first time in the world's history. Human genius has now destroyed the impediment of distance in a new respect, and in a manner hitherto unknown."

The next two decades brought enormous advances to television. In 1936, there were approximately 200 TV sets worldwide. Only 12 years later, that number soared to one million in the United States alone. Color was introduced in 1946. Shows such as *Kraft Television Theatre, Studio One,* and *Actor's Studio* were popular. In 1953, the programming magazine *TV Guide* was born. In 1949, a *Time* magazine reporter wrote, "As the clock nears eight along the Eastern Seaboard on Tuesday night, a strange new phenomenon takes place in U.S. urban life. Business falls off in many a nightclub, theatre ticket sales are light, neighborhood movie audiences thin.... A large part of the population has its eyes fixed on a TV screen."

Not everyone was thrilled with the new age of television. Radio shows, once the primary mode of electronic entertainment, suffered greatly after TVs came into homes. Radio comedian Fred Allen once said that television threatened to change Americans into creatures "with eyeballs as big as cantaloupes and no brain at all."

Today there are more than 1.7 billion television sets worldwide. Whether or not their role in people's lives is entirely positive is still being debated.

Anna Akhmatova (1889–1966)

ALTHOUGH MANY CONSIDER Anna Akhmatova to be Russia's greatest poet, her lyrical voice was stilled for years because of governmental repression.

She was born Anna Andreyevna Gorenko in June 1889 in Ukraine. She began writing at age 11; when her father discovered his daughter's poetic aspirations, he forced her to use a pen name to save the family from shame. She chose Akhmatova after her Tatar great-grandmother. At age 21, she joined the Acmeist circle of Russian poets, who emphasized clarity over symbolism. In 1910, she married Acmeist leader Nikolay Gumilyov. Two years later, Akhmatova published her first poetic collection *Vecher* (*Evening*), followed in 1914 by *Chyotki* (*Rosary*). The confessional style of these poems made her famous throughout Russia.

In 1921, the Bolsheviks took over Russia, and a reign of terror followed. By then, Gumilyov and Akhmatova had a son, Lev, and were divorced. That same year, Gumilyov was executed for supposed antigovernment activity. Things got worse when Joseph Stalin came to power in 1924; many writers were arrested and executed in an attempt to wipe all bourgeois elements from the new Communist society.

Akhmatova's poetry was banned from publication from 1925 to 1940. She survived by writing literary criticism. But poetry was in her blood; prior to 1940 she composed her masterpiece *Rekviem* (*Requiem*), a series of short poems about the horror of Stalin's rule, the difficulty in not being able to write under such a regime, and the agony of his victims. In 1940, a collection of her earlier works was published in *From Six Books*. It was abruptly withdrawn a few months later.

Plans were made for publication of her poetry, but in 1946, the Central Committee of the Communist Party deemed her "half nun, half harlot." She was expelled from the Writer's Union, which denied her a ration card and left her without any means of support. After Stalin's death in 1953, some of Akhmatova's work was finally allowed to appear, although in heavily censored form. Awards began to pour in, and she finally began to receive worldwide recognition. Akhmatova was even made president of the Writer's Union two years before her death.

POSTSCRIPT

Akhmatova considered *Requiem* so dangerous that she did not commit it to paper until the 1960s—until then, it existed entirely in her memory.

The Matabeleland Rebellion

THE MATABELE PEOPLE lived in what is present-day Zimbabwe. In 1888, British-born South African businessman and politician Cecil Rhodes negotiated an agreement with the Matabele to extract minerals from their land and permit the British to colonize the area. Rhodes and the Matabele also agreed that the Boers, or Dutch farmers, would not be permitted to colonize the area.

A year later, Rhodes was given a royal charter to establish the British South Africa Company to further colonize the Matabele region. The company established a police force, distributed land, formed banks, and traded with Africans. It also agreed to respect the laws and religions of the native peoples. However, in reality, the company disregarded local

laws, set up its own government and exploited mineral resources, and showed its strength through the use of military force.

In 1893, two of the Matabele groups began warring, and the British became involved in the First Matabele War. With their superior weaponry, the British prevailed. Three years later, the Second Matabele War, also known as the Matabeleland

Matabeleland chieftain (center) and his wives

Rebellion, took place. The Africans planned to attack and drive the British from the area and kill any remaining until the area was free of whites.

Chaos ensued; more than 200 settlers were killed. Those who decided to remain mounted an attack against the local Matabele. After several months of fighting, relief forces came to the assistance of the whites. One of the commanders of the relief unit was Colonel Robert Baden-Powell.

Baden-Powell and American Major Frederick Russell Burnham began their patrol of the area to find the rebel leader, Mlimo. After the patrol tracked down and killed Mlimo, Rhodes persuaded the remaining rebels to surrender. The Second Matabele War ended in 1897. The geographic area where the fighting had taken place was renamed Rhodesia, in honor of Cecil Rhodes.

Henrik Ibsen (1828–1906)

POPULARLY KNOWN AS the father of the modern drama, Norwegian playwright Henrik Ibsen discarded the formulas that ruled 19th-century theatre, replacing Victorian ideals and moral conclusions with realistic plays based on psychological conflicts.

Ibsen began his literary career at age 23 as the manager and official playwright for Ole Bull's new National Theater in Bergen, for which he wrote romantic dramas that combined Norwegian folklore and history with the conventions of 19th-century French theater. It was a valuable apprenticeship, giving Ibsen practical experience in every aspect of stagecraft. In 1857, he became the director of the Norwegian Theater at Christiana (now Oslo), where he remained until the theater failed in 1862.

For the next two years he struggled to make a living, supporting his family on a small folklore research stipend. At the time, most of the theater available tended toward light-hearted (and often empty-headed) entertainment. Ibsen sought to give something more to audiences. In 1864, financially desperate and angry at Norway and Sweden's refusal to support Denmark's struggle against Prussia, Ibsen went into voluntary exile. He lived abroad for 27 years, primarily in Rome, Dresden, and Munich. No longer called on to construct plays that fit the production needs of a provincial theater, Ibsen began to write for himself, beginning with the chamber dramas *Brand* (1866) and *Peer Gynt* (1867), a fantasy with an incidental music score by famous Norwegian composer Edvard Grieg.

Following the success of *Peer Gynt,* Ibsen received a small pension from the Norwegian government that gave him the financial security to experiment. He moved back to Norway in 1891. The resulting plays revolutionized European theater and earned him an international reputation: *A Doll's House* (1879), *An Enemy of the People* (1882), *Hedda Gabler* (1890), and *The Master-Builder* (1892). Placed against a realistic middle-class background, these plays considered controversial and often scandalous social issues, such as the hypocrisy of Victorian morality, women's rights, political corruption, and, in the case of 1881's *Ghosts,* venereal disease. Ibsen put a greater focus on character development than on plot; on a deeper level, his plays dealt with the individual's dreams and disillusions.

In 1891, Ibsen returned to Christiana, where he became an unlikely tourist attraction. He continued to write until a stroke in 1900 ended his literary career. He died six years later.

The Visigoths Sack Rome

WHEN AN ARMY of Visigoths seized Rome in A.D. 410, it was the first time since 390 B.C. that an armed enemy had entered the city.

The victor of the battle was Alaric, king of the Visigoths, a Germanic people who had migrated into the Balkans 20 years earlier. They had been allies of Rome previously, but Roman mistreatment led to an A.D. 365 revolt. Alaric's warriors ravaged Greece before moving across the Alps into Italy in 401. Stilicho, a general of mixed Roman-Germanic blood, defeated the Visigoths in a bloody battle and forced Alaric to retreat. Stilicho deflected two more incursions in 403 and 406, after which Alaric accepted a treaty under which he and his people became Roman allies.

Stilicho was assassinated in 408 by agents of Roman Emperor Honorius. His murder resulted in chaos; Alaric again crossed the Alps to take advantage of the situation. He bypassed Ravenna (then the capital of the western Roman Empire) and marched to Rome, putting the city under siege. Famine and plague devastated the city. Honorius did nothing to alleviate the situation, while the Senate paid Alaric a huge ransom to leave Rome.

The Visigoths moved to northern Italy while Alaric opened negotiations with Honorius. Insulted by the tone of the emperor's reply, Alaric again marched his troops to Rome in 409 and established a puppet emperor there to oppose Honorius. When his puppet started to become too independent, however, Alaric dethroned him and reopened negotiations with Honorius.

The negotiations were going well when a rival of Alaric attacked his camp near Ravenna. Alaric believed Honorius had sanctioned the attack and broke off negotiations. His troops again moved to Rome and placed the city under siege. On August 24, 410, some Visigoths entered the Salarian Gate at night and opened it to Alaric's army. Alaric allowed his troops to loot and sack the city. The barbarians killed, burned, and took whatever they wanted. Contemporaries reported that churches were spared because the Visigoths were Christians. When Alaric departed Rome, he took along Galla Placidia, the emperor's sister, as a captive.

Alaric died later that year as his troops were preparing to invade Africa. After his death, his men diverted the course of a river, buried their king in the riverbed, and then allowed the water to cover the spot. All those who worked on the tomb were slain so that no one would ever know where Alaric was buried and thus desecrate his burial place.

Flight at Kitty Hawk

IN THE LATE 1870S, two young brothers from Dayton, Ohio, received a toy from their father, a flying machine built with rubber bands, cork, bamboo, and paper, which they called the "bat." Wilbur and Orville Wright were thrilled, but after a while, the rubber bands lost their stretch, the paper tore, and the bamboo began to bend. The boys made copies of their old toy, to which they made some adjustments, designed a few improvements, and invented some new options. Soon, the bat was flying better than ever, and two brothers had found their life's mission.

Even though Wilbur and Orville ran a bicycle-manufacturing shop, flying was their passion; it was their dream to create the first flying machine. One of their first attempts was a pinewood glider, built in 1902. The brothers needed an exceptionally windy place to test it out, and they finally choose a remote fishing village in North Carolina called Kitty Hawk. It had the required wind for flying and soft sand dunes for landing.

The Wright brothers were quite a sight out on the beach, in suits and ties, struggling to control their glorified kite in the gusty coastal winds. One of the locals who helped them said, "I never saw men so wrapped up in their work in my life. They had their whole heart and soul in what they were doing."

That first year at Kitty Hawk, they managed to cover more than 300 feet in less than 20 seconds. It was an exhilarating moment. The Wright brothers returned to Kitty Hawk three years in a row. They'd analyze their data, fix flaws, and redesign blueprints. Eventually, they moved from making gliders to making a rudimentary airplane. Made of spruce wood, the plane had a 40-foot wingspan.

On December 17, 1903, the wind was just right. Orville climbed into the pilot seat and at 10:35 A.M. he took off. The plane only flew for 12 seconds, but it flew 120 feet the first time. Orville and Wilbur took turns, and by the end of the day, their new record was 852 feet in 59 seconds. Although other men had attempted to build an airplane at around the same time, the Wright brothers had done what no one else had been able to accomplish: sustained, powered, and controlled flight.

The Tet Offensive

THE MOST CRITICAL BATTLE of the American War in Vietnam, the Tet Offensive was a series of major attacks in South Vietnam initiated by the Communist North Vietnamese Army (NVA) and South Vietnamese Communist insurgents (Viet Cong) during the traditional Vietnamese Lunar New Year holiday (Tet) in late January 1968. Communist troops struck 36 of 44 provincial capitals, South Vietnam's largest airbase, and the American Embassy grounds and Presidential Palace in Saigon.

The leading North Vietnamese strategist, Vo Nguyen Giap, hoped the assault would encourage non-Communist South Vietnamese to over-throw the U.S.-backed government there. Although Giap's forces achieved some temporary victories, no general uprising occurred. In fact, by March 1968, U.S. and South Vietnamese troops had retaken all of the areas captured by the communists. Thus the offensive proved to be a tactical disaster, with an estimated 40,000 dead and untold wounded Communist troops.

Yet, most historians agree that Giap achieved a strategic victory, albeit an unanticipated one. By this time, many Americans had grown tired of the war. The main American goal was to convince Communist North Vietnam to cease attempts to take over non-Communist South Vietnam. The United States had supported anti-Communist efforts in Vietnam since 1946—initially with economic and military assistance, and, beginning in April 1965, an infusion of U.S. combat troops (some 485,000 by December 1967) and air attacks on Communist North Vietnam.

Many Americans were stunned by the size and geographical distribution of the Tet Offensive because the administration of President Lyndon Johnson had claimed the communists were losing the war. The mere fact that the enemy could launch such attacks seemed to reveal the lie in Johnson's rhetoric.

Growing public discontent, especially among business and political elites, ultimately led President Johnson to reduce the bombing of North Vietnam, call for a peace conference to end the war, and pull out of the 1968 presidential race. Some revisionist historians argue that if the United States had sent more troops and launched its own massive counteroffensive, the war could have been won. But most students of the war see the Tet Offensive as a tipping point, after which the chances for a military victory seemed remote. American ground troops remained in Vietnam until after a peace agreement was signed in January 1973.

Magna Carta

Aᶠᵗᵉʳ Rɪᴄʜᴀʀᴅ ᴛʜᴇ Lɪᴏɴʜᴇᴀʀᴛ died in 1199, his younger brother John was crowned the new king of England. About 16 years later, John was forced to sign Magna Carta, a charter that is still thought of as one of the premiere documents in the history of democracy.

Almost immediately after becoming king, John embroiled himself in financial and domestic upsets. In 1200, he involved England in a long-term war with France. John sought revenue from nobility to finance the wars, and eventually he instituted new taxes and increased existing taxes. Noblemen, meanwhile, resented additional financial commitments to the king and feared their feudal rights were eroding. John's continuous need for money and his reputation for greediness angered the barons. When the barons refused to continue supplying men and gold for his endeavors in capturing France, the tyrannical king began attacking baronial estates in England.

Sensing weakness, the barons began making demands of the king. In early 1215, the barons entered London and insisted John present them with a charter that enumerated their feudal rights. At first, John refused. Once again, the barons again approached John with more specific demands. Again, John refused to listen to their demands. Angry at the king's responses, the barons withdrew their allegiance to John and formed their own army. John asked the pope to intercede, but the barons refused to realign with the king. In retaliation, John attempted to crush the rebellious army, but the army instead attacked London. Finally, on June 15, representatives of the nobles and the king met out-side London at Runnymede.

At Runnymede, the barons presented *Articles of the Barons* to the king for his signature. John complied, but his representatives met again with the barons' representatives to make changes to the document to further delineate the role of the king and the rights of the nobility. The final document, Magna Carta (Latin for "Great Charter"), provided a means of enforcement if the king failed to comply with the terms. Magna Carta's main significance, however, was the limitation it placed on the king's authority—now England's rulers would be bound by law. The document later provided the basis for the constitutional government and estab-lished the monarch's fundamental obligation to observe common law.

Le Chambon-sur-Lignon: Haven from the Nazis

FRANCE DID LITTLE to resist Nazi persecution of Jews during World War II; in fact, the Vichy government declared informing on Jews a patriotic duty. One notable exception was the French village of Le Chambon-sur-Lignon. Located in the hilly southeastern region 350 miles from Paris, the villagers of Le Chambon-sur-Lignon defied the Nazis and their own government to save 5,000 Jews over the course of the war.

The moral force behind this defiance was the village's Protestant pastor, André Trocmé, who was descended from Huguenots and Germans. In 1938, he helped found the International Pacifist School in Le Chambon for the education of Jewish children.

Around 1940, under Trocmé's direction, hundreds of fleeing Jews were sheltered and sent to safety in Switzerland or Spain via an underground escape network. Others found permanent shelter in the village until the end of the war. The villagers, themselves the Protestant descendants of the much-persecuted Huguenots, risked their lives to hide the fugitives. Refugees were hidden in private homes and on farms; there was scarcely a farm in the area that did not shelter a Jewish family. By mid-war, several safe houses outside the village were being funded by Protestant groups, the Quakers, Catholic clergy, the Red Cross, and Sweden.

It was impossible to hide so much activity. The Nazis referred to the village as "that nest of Jews in Protestant country." Vichy authorities searched houses and demanded a halt to the activity. Trocmé refused. "I do not know what a Jew is," he replied. "I know only human beings."

During Nazi sweeps, the Jews hid in the woods. "As soon as the soldiers left, we would go into the forest and sing a song," recalled a villager. "When they heard that song, the Jews knew it was safe to come home."

A few residents were arrested. Trocmé's cousin was arrested and later died in a concentration camp. Trocmé himself was forced to go into hiding, but his wife carried on his work. He survived the war. Thanks to Le Chambon, so did 5,000 Jewish refugees.

In 1990, the village became the first community to be honored as Righteous Gentiles by the Holocaust Martyrs' and Heroes' Remembrance Authority group in Jerusalem. "We didn't protect the Jews because we were moral or heroic people," recalled one villager. "We helped them because it was the human thing to do."

The Dred Scott Decision

DRED SCOTT was an illiterate black slave bought in the 1830s by army surgeon John Emerson in Missouri. In 1834 and 1836, Emerson took Scott from Missouri, a slave state, into the free states and territories of Illinois and Wisconsin, respectively. After a number of years, Emerson, Scott, and their families returned to Missouri.

After Emerson died in 1843, his widow, Irene Sanford, inherited Scott. Irene was against slavery and considered freeing him, but her abolitionist friends suggested that she use her "property" to seek a legal decision on the rights of slaves who had lived in free territory. In 1846, Irene allowed Scott's lawyers to sue her for his freedom, claiming that by living in a free territory where slavery was illegal, Scott should be a free man.

A St. Louis court heard the case and declared Scott free in 1850, but in 1852 the Missouri Supreme Court intervened and returned him to slavery. Shortly after she lost the *Scott v. Emerson* case, Irene married Massachusetts congressman and abolitionist C. C. Chaffee in 1850, who "sold" Scott to Irene's brother, John Sanford. Scott suddenly had someone new to oppose. *Dred Scott v. Sandford* (the courts misspelled Sanford's name) reached the United States Supreme Court in 1856.

Chief Justice Roger B. Taney was a proslavery man from Maryland. Shortly after James Buchanan was inaugurated president in March 1857, the verdict was announced: The court voted 7–2, denying Scott his freedom. Blacks were "beings of an inferior order," Taney wrote. According to Taney, they were not citizens of the United States and thus had "no rights which any white man was bound to respect," including the right to sue in a court of law. Even if Scott was a citizen, continued Taney, he still could not sue.

The Fifth Amendment to the Constitution ensured that a citizen cannot be deprived of his property without due process, and slaves were considered property. Furthermore, since the Missouri Compromise of 1820 prohibited slavery in the territories north of Missouri—but not Missouri itself—suing for freedom would be unconstitutional. Taney's opinion that Congress could not keep slavery from the territories was a direct attack on the abolition movement and the newly formed Republican Party, which was against the spread of slavery in the territories. Taney's overt defense of slavery was another blow to national unity, eventually leading to the Civil War.

The Crimean War

THE CRIMEAN WAR was the first "modern" war—specifically, in the way it was reported at home. The British public received timely news from the front for the first time, thanks to the unflinching reports of *Times* correspondent William H. Russell.

In July 1853, Russia occupied the Ottoman provinces of Wallachia and Moldavia, pressuring the Sultan in regard to the rights of Orthodox Christians living under Turkish rule. Turkey rejected European efforts to resolve the issue using diplomacy and declared war.

The conflict might have been limited to a shoving match between Russia and Turkey if Russia had not destroyed the Turkish fleet in the Black Sea. Britain and France opposed Russian expansion in the Black Sea area, which threatened their overland trade routes to the East. In response, they declared war against Russia in March 1854.

While the allies enjoyed superior military technology and expected a rapid victory, they were hampered by disease, lack of ground transport, long supply lines, and inept British leadership.

Following their September 20 defeat on the River Alma, the Russians retreated to the strongly armed fort of Sevastopol, which was besieged by British, French, and Turkish troops supplied from the small port of Balaklava. Russian forces moved down to cut the allies' supply line, but a British cavalry brigade intercepted them. Known as the infamous "Charge of the Light Brigade," a third of the brigade was lost in a point-less frontal charge against Russian guns. The charge became emblematic of both British bravery and the incompetence of British command.

Following the Battle of Balaklava, the allies settled into a long winter of siege warfare, in which the besiegers suffered as much as the besieged. Russell and other correspondents reported the British army's lack of fuel, clothing, and supplies; the inadequacy of their medical care; and the inefficiency of Lord Raglan's command. The *Times*'s reports helped raise awareness, which inspired British nurse Florence Nightingale's relief efforts in Crimea.

Sevastopol fell a year later, in 1855. The Congress of Paris of 1856 forced Russia to concede territory to the Ottomans, closed the Black Sea to warships, and allowed free navigation of the Danube. In exchange, the Sultan agreed to recognize the rights of his Christian subjects. Equally important was the reform of the British army, resulting from Russell's and Nightingale's reports to the British public.

England Adopts the Gold Standard

AT THE END OF THE 18TH CENTURY, Western Europe suffered from a scarcity of silver. Increased trade with Asian nations that had little use for European goods drained silver from European economies, and the era's continuous warfare resulted in devalued currencies.

Silver coins were issued in smaller amounts; alternative methods of payment, such as "token" coins, bills of exchange, and banknotes proliferated. The shortage was so pronounced in Britain during the French Revolutionary and Napoleonic Wars that the government ordered the Bank of England to suspend payment of gold or silver for banknotes as a means of maintaining their precious metal reserves for military expenses.

In 1810, the House of Commons established the Currency Commission, also known as the Bullion Committee, to "enquire into the Cause of the High Price of Gold Bullion, and to take into consideration the State of the Circulating Medium, and of the Exchanges between Great Britain and Foreign Parts." The committee found that so many banknotes had been issued that the value of the pound had depreciated. Their recommendation: Allow the Bank of England to once again redeem banknotes with gold. Cash drains related to the wars delayed the implementation of the committee's recommendation, and inflation continued to climb.

In the years following the French Wars, one of the British government's main problems was finding a way to stabilize the currency. In 1819, Parliament passed the long-awaited "Act for the Resumption of Cash Payments," which allowed free trade in bullion and coin. The gold standard, which tied the country's paper currency to the cost of a specific weight of gold, was established on May 1, 1821.

The gold standard improved Britain's foreign exchange position, but caused short-term economic hardship at home. A rapid reduction in the number of banknotes issued brought a fall in commodity prices and widespread unemployment. Many found it difficult to pay rents and repay loans that they had taken during the period of depreciated currency.

By the end of the 19th century, all the major powers used the British gold standard for national and international payments. The system disintegrated during World War I because European governments once again restricted the gold trade for wartime necessities. Following World War II, the International Monetary Fund replaced the gold standard as a mechanism for managing currency exchanges.

The Rosetta Stone

IN 1799, a troop of French soldiers stationed in the Delta Nile during Napoleon's occupation of Egypt found a black basalt slab near the village of Rosetta. On it were three rows of inscriptions, written in hieroglyphics, demotic (a cursive form of hieroglyphics), and classical Greek, which were recognized as a huge coup for historians.

An army of scholars and scientists from the Institute of Egypt had accompanied Napoleon's invasion force to Egypt. They were given the task of recording everything possible about Egypt's past and present. The

Institute recognized the stone could be the key to deciphering ancient hieroglyphics—a problem that had plagued European scholars since the Renaissance.

Following French capitulation in Alexandria, the British seized the stone and other archaeological treasures in 1801 and shipped them to the newly formed British Museum. The French were left with plaster casts and copies.

Scholars in England, Germany, France, and Italy attempted to use the Greek inscription to translate its hieroglyphic counterpart, including young French linguist Jean-François Champollion. Champollion had been obsessed with hieroglyphics since he was ten. Having already mastered Latin, Greek, and Hebrew by age 13, he began to learn Arabic, Syriac, Chaldean, Coptic, and Chinese, and he studied what few excerpts he could find written in Zend and Pahlavi. At 17, he added Sanskrit and Persian. A year later, Champollion made his first attempt to decode the Rosetta Stone inscriptions. In 1822, he published his now-famous *Lettre à M. Dacier,* in which he outlined a decoding methodology.

Unlike his predecessors, Champollion assumed that the hieroglyphs were "phonetic symbols" rather than picture writing. Translation began with the names of the kings. The Greek inscription recorded a decree of the Egyptian priesthood, issued in 196 B.C., praising King Ptolemy Epiphanes. The hieroglyphic section of the text included a group of signs enclosed in an oval ring, which came to be known as a *cartouche.* Champollion deduced correctly that the signs within the cartouche spelled out the king's name in Egyptian, providing a key for decoding the remaining hieroglyphs.

James Watt and the Steam Engine

Born January 19, 1736, in Scotland, James Watt trained as a maker of mathematical instruments. At the time of his birth, steam engines already existed, but they were not efficient. The state-of-the-art device in Watt's day was Thomas Newcomen's 1711 steam-pumping engine, which was used to remove water from English mines.

Watt, who was interested in most things mechanical, was working at the University of Glasgow in 1763 when he had the opportunity to repair a model of Newcomen's engine. He saw that the engine's output was severely limited because the cylinder was alternately heated and cooled. Efficiency would increase dramatically if the cylinder could be kept hot.

The solution to the problem came to him in 1765. He realized that if he could condense the steam in a container separate from the cylinder, it would allow the cylinder to remain hot. Watt built a prototype with this "separate condenser" and discovered that the idea worked. The condenser prevented the loss of steam, increased output, and was far more fuel-efficient that the Newcomen engine.

Watt obtained a patent for his innovations in 1769. Early production efforts ran into problems with the precision manufacturing his engine required. That changed in 1775 when Watt partnered with Matthew Boulton, owner of the Soho Engineering Works in Birmingham. Boulton had the resources Watt needed, and together they managed to solve the production problems. The first Boulton and Watt engine went into use in 1776 at the Bentley Mining Company. It was a resounding success.

The new engines were widely used to drive pumps in mines, but Boulton saw they could also be adapted to more general industrial use. With that in mind, Watt devised a gear system that allowed his engines to be used to power machinery in sawmills, flour mills, textile mills, and other industries. By 1800, nearly 84 cotton mills were using his engines.

Watt went on to patent other important inventions, including a rotary engine, a steam pressure indicator, a double-action engine, and a centrifugal governor to regulate the speed of an engine. He also coined the term *horsepower*. In recognition of his contributions, the unit of power, *watt,* was named after him.

By the time Watt died on August 19, 1819, his steam engine had opened the door to the Industrial Age with all of its implications for the way people live and work. The world would never be the same.

Jawaharlal Nehru (1889–1964)

LIKE MANY LEADERS of the Indian nationalist movement, Jawaharlal Nehru was Western educated. After studying at home under a series of British governesses and tutors, he was sent to England where he earned

a degree in the natural sciences at Cambridge and studied for the bar at the Inns of Court in London. Nehru returned to India in 1912 to practice law with his father, Indian independence proponent Motilal Nehru.

Motilal was already a leader in the Indian National Congress, which was fighting for dominion status within the British Empire at the time. Nehru joined his father as a Congress member in 1918 but did not become deeply involved until Mohandas Gandhi launched his first nonviolent noncooperation movement (*satyagraha*) against the British in 1919. Nehru toured rural India, organized nationalist volunteers, and made public speeches.

The British imprisoned Nehru in 1921 for his nationalist activities. Overall, he spent 9 of the next 25 years in jail for his participation in satyagraha campaigns. He used his time in prison to study and write. The letters that he wrote from prison to his young daughter Indira became the charming and personal book *Glimpses of World History.*

Sponsored by Gandhi, Nehru was elected president of the Indian National Congress in 1928, a position he would hold six times. In the years that followed, Nehru came to be considered Gandhi's successor despite substantial differences in their approaches to India's freedom. When Gandhi was assassinated in 1948, Nehru announced: "The light has gone out of our lives and there is darkness everywhere."

When India achieved independence from Great Britain in 1947, Nehru became its first prime minister and minister for external affairs, a dual position he held until his death in 1964. He developed a policy of "positive neutrality" in regard to the Cold War and served as a key spokesperson for the unaligned countries of Asia and Africa. Nehru committed India to a policy of industrialization, the reorganization of its states on a linguistic basis, and the development of a casteless, secular state.

Nehru's legacy lived on after his death: His daughter Indira and grandson Rajiv held the position of prime minister for a total of 20 years between 1966 and 1989.

The French Wars of Religion

WHEN THE REFORMATION spread across Europe in the 16th century, France was caught in the resulting religious turmoil. Although French theologian John Calvin experienced his great success in the Swiss cantons, his form of Protestantism began in his homeland. French Catholics took exception to the growth of Protestantism—to such an extent that a series of eight wars took place between 1562 and 1598.

Part of France's religious problem was actually political. The French monarchy was very weak at the time, and several large families were vying with each other to influence the court. The primary Catholic family was that of Guise, from the province of Lorraine. The Bourbon family represented the French Protestants, called Huguenots.

After King Henry II died in 1559, he was succeeded by three of his sons, Francis II (1559–1560), Charles IX (1560–1574), and Henry III (1574–1589). Their mother, Catherine de Médicis, used her influence to protect them as well as her own position. She allied with the Guises and then with the Bourbons, depending on the political situation at the moment.

Acting on the advice of his court, 12-year-old King Charles IX issued a 1562 edict that allowed the Huguenots limited religious freedom. The Guises were not happy and instituted a massacre, igniting a brief war in which Protestant and Catholic armies fought each other.

By the early 1570s, both sides had obtained foreign help from England and Spain. Charles was forced to seek an alliance with the Huguenots in order to counter the Spanish aid to the Catholics. Catherine, however, conspired with the Guises and convinced Charles to remain aloof. On August 24, 1572, Catholics attacked Huguenots all over France in what has been called the Massacre of St. Bartholomew.

When Henry III was slain by a deranged friar in 1589, Henry of Navarre, a Protestant, became Henry IV. With help from England, Henry fought against the Catholic League, which controlled Paris. As a stalemate developed, Henry converted to Catholicism in 1593. Most Frenchmen allied with their king, and the Catholic League fell apart.

Henry then fought an inconclusive war with Spain (1595–1598). As this war came to an end, Henry issued the Edict of Nantes in April 1598, which allowed the Huguenots limited religious freedom. Moderate Catholics, called *Politiques,* supported Henry's bold move. The decades of civil war had ruined France, and many people thought it better to allow heretics to live in peace than to fight them.

The Immigration Act of 1924

NATIONAL DEBATE OVER IMMIGRATION is far from new: The 1924 Immigration Act sparked widespread controversy with its restriction on the number of immigrants allowed into the United States.

Also known as the Johnson-Reed Act, the federal law was largely aimed at restricting Southern and Eastern Europeans, who had begun arriving in America in great numbers. The provisions limited the number of immi-

grants to 2 percent of the number of people from that ethnic group who were already residents in the United States, as determined by the 1890 census. For instance, for every 100 Greeks living in the United States, only 2 new Greek immigrants would be allowed.

The exception to the rule was East Asians and Asian Indians—Japanese, Chinese, Koreans, Filipinos, Indians, and others—who were barred entirely because they were nonwhite and therefore not eligible for naturalization. There were no restrictions on immigrants from Latin America.

The act found strong support in the U.S. Congress, with a mere six senators and only a few members of the House of Representatives voting in opposition. The groundswell of support was influenced in part by *The Passing of the Great Race,* published in 1916 by eugenicist Madison Grant. The book purported to offer data demonstrating the superiority of Northern Europeans. Support for the act also came from those who wanted to maintain the ethnic status quo and were concerned about job and wage competition.

The effect of the act was immediately noticeable. According to statistics, about 200,000 Italians entered the United States each year from 1900 to 1910. After the passage of the Immigration Act, the allowable number dropped to a mere 4,000. By contrast, nearly 90 percent of the 165,000 immigrants allowed into the country per year were from Great Britain or Northern European countries.

The quotas imposed by the act remained in effect with a few minor changes until the Immigration and Nationality Act abolished national quotas in 1965. The new act was proposed by U.S. Representative Emanuel Cellar and strongly supported by Senator Edward Kennedy.

Gamal Abdel Nasser (1918–1970)

BORN IN EGYPT IN 1918 to a poor peasant family, Gamal Abdel Nasser went on to become one of modern Egypt's most controversial, yet influential, leaders.

Nasser's rise began when he entered the Egyptian Military Academy in 1937. Through his connections, Nasser became heavily involved in revolutionary activities in Egypt. On July 23, 1952, the military carried out a bloodless coup that deposed King Faruq, who went into exile. The leader of the coup, Major General Muhammad Naguib, announced that he would be president until free elections could be held. However, a year later, Nasser eased Naguib out of his way and took control of Egypt.

Throughout his career as Egypt's president, Nasser stressed his belief in "positive neutralism," which was his attempt to steer a neutral path between the United States and the USSR during the Cold War. In July 1956, British troops left the Suez Canal and five days later, Nasser nationalized the waterway. This, in turn, led to war with France, Britain, and Israel in October of that year. The conflict would have consequences for positive neutralism as well. After the war, the United States convinced Britain, France, and Israel to withdraw from Egypt.

Nasser believed strongly that pan-Arabism could unite the Middle East to fight outside attempts at controlling the region. In 1958, Egypt and Syria formed the United Arab Republic in hope of attracting other Arab states to join them in the pan-Arabian movement. However, other states were wary of Nasser's desire to place Egypt at the forefront of Arab nationalism, and so, in 1961, the republic was disbanded. Nasser also hoped to further Arab socialism, which meant that Arab wealth should be shared among all Arab peoples. He worked to bring socialism to his own country, and in 1961, Egyptian industries were nationalized.

From the time he rose to power, Nasser was also drawn into the Arab dispute with Israel. Wanting Egypt to take the lead in all things Arab, he began a blockade of the Red Sea to keep Israel from using it. In May 1967, Nasser convinced the United Nations to remove its peacekeeping forces from the Sinai, which he proceeded to occupy with Egyptian troops. Worried by this action, as well as an escalation of border incidents with Syria, Israel attacked its neighbors. During the Six-Day War of June 1967, Israeli forces occupied Sinai and gave Nasser a humiliating defeat. Finally, in August 1970, Nasser participated in a 90-day cease-fire with Israel. He died the next month.

The Peloponnesian War

IN 448 B.C., the Greco–Persian War came to an end with a formal peace treaty. Although the Athenians and Spartans had been allies throughout the war, a layer of mistrust existed.

Athens had organized the Delian League, ostensibly an alliance of Greek cities that were really subject states of a growing Athenian empire. Sparta objected to Athens's heavy-handed treatment of other Greeks; in 457 it declared war on Athens. Peace was declared in 446.

Athens continued to grow and prosper under the leadership of Pericles. When Athens intervened in a war between Corinth and Corcyra, and then interfered with the city of Potidea, Sparta again declared war in 431. The result was a decades-long war known as the Peloponnesian War, which left Greece devastated as the various city-states took sides. Pericles's strategy was to snipe at Sparta with his navy while avoiding battle with the superior Spartan army. But when Pericles died during a 429 epidemic, Cleon took over and launched several offensive moves. He rejected a Spartan peace proposal in 425. Spartan general Brasidas then invaded Thrace. During the Battle of Amphipolis in 422, both Cleon and Brasidas were killed, which allowed cooler heads to prevail and come to relative peace in 421.

But the war continued on a smaller scale as both Athens and Sparta sent aid to their allies. In 415, the Athenians sent a small army and fleet to the island of Sicily to attack and capture Syracuse, which was quarreling with an Athenian ally. By capturing Syracuse, Athens hoped to conquer the entire island and expand Athenian territory. Although it was Syracuse that was besieged, the Athenian army was annihilated, since Athenian sailors refused to crew the ships.

Sparta reentered the war in 413 and placed Athens under siege. The Athenians built another fleet, but thanks to a treaty with the Persians, Sparta also had a fleet. Nevertheless, the Spartan ships were destroyed in battle only three years later. The Spartans asked for peace, but Cleophon, the new Athenian leader, rejected their plea. Persia continued to aid Sparta, whose fleets were continuously sunk.

In 404, the Spartans finally destroyed the Athenian navy at Aegospotami. Athens, weakened by a long siege, surrendered in 404, bringing the war to an end. Sparta emerged supreme—an important step in the decline of the great Athenian democracy.

Ivan the Terrible (1530–1584)

K NOWN TO HISTORY as Ivan the Terrible, Ivan IV was the son of the grand prince of Moscow. Ivan was only three years old when his father died in 1533, and a regency was formed to run Moscow until he was older. During that time, the *boyars* (aristocratic families) were actually in control. Ivan was treated well in public but with contempt in private. His mean streak was encouraged; as a result, Ivan grew up to be undisciplined and cruel.

Czar Ivan IV (on horse)

In January 1547, Ivan was crowned as Russia's czar. He married Anastasia Romanovna Zakharina, and soon Ivan set out to reform Russia. He formed an assembly to help govern the country and in 1550 introduced a new law code, the Sudebnik. He brought the Russian Orthodox Church under state control by limiting its land holdings and formed a standing army with the nobility as officers. Ivan also introduced a new monetary system.

Warfare occupied much of his attention. Russian armies moved south to attack what was left of the Golden Horde of Mongols. Russian Cossacks continued to move eastward and eventually reached the Pacific Ocean. But Ivan's armies weren't always successful. In 1571, Tatars from the Crimea raided all the way to Moscow, capturing and sacking the city.

After Anastasia's death in 1560, Ivan began to change for the worse. Although he married several other women, he was never as happy as before. His mind became increasingly unbalanced, and Ivan suspected everyone of conspiring against him. He thought that boyars had poisoned Anastasia and began lashing out against aristocratic families, destroying their power and ensuring that future czars would be free of their control. Ivan's special police arrested, tortured, and executed thousands of people. Some of these enemies were real, others imagined. Ivan's occasional fits of temper harmed his family. In 1581, Ivan struck his eldest son so hard that he died a few days later.

When Ivan passed away on March 18, 1584, Fyodor, his son by Anastasia, was named as his successor.

The Seneca Falls Convention

IN 1840, Elizabeth Cady Stanton traveled with her husband, an abolitionist, to attend a convention in London. While she was there, she and other women were not allowed to participate in the meetings and speeches because of their gender. Ironically, it was the World Anti-Slavery Convention.

It was in London that she met Lucretia Mott, a Quaker and delegate who had also been refused permission to speak at the convention. From their vantage point in the balcony at the convention, and while walking the streets of London, the two women discussed hosting a convention to discuss women's rights. In July 1848, while Mott was visiting a relative in New York, she and some other women, including Stanton, met for a social visit and began discussing the state's Married Woman's Property Rights Act. Before the afternoon was over, the women decided it was time to publicly present the wrongs to women, and they placed an ad in the Seneca County Courier, announcing a convention to be held on July 19 and 20.

Stanton drafted a Declaration of Sentiments, closely paralleling the ideas presented by Thomas Jefferson in the Declaration of Independence. "When in the course of human events, it becomes necessary for one portion of the family of man to assume among the people of the earth a position different from that which they have hitherto occupied, but one to which the laws of nature and of nature's God entitle them, a decent respect to the opinions of mankind, that they should declare the causes that impel them to such a course," she wrote.

She stated there were certain truths that were self evident: that all men and women were created equal, that they were endowed by their Creator with certain inalienable rights, and that the rights included life, liberty, and the pursuit of happiness. Stanton continued, stating, "to secure these rights governments are instituted, deriving their just powers from the consent of the governed." The Declaration of Sentiments listed the repeated injuries and usurpations women had suffered as the result of the acts of man. Stanton also inserted her own beliefs, adding women's right to vote to the list of resolutions. Mott was shocked, but Stanton held firm.

The convention was held in Stanton's community of Seneca Falls, New York, at the local Methodist church. Approximately 300 people attended the meeting; 68 women and 32 men signed Stanton's Declaration of Sentiments. Change was slow to come; in 1920, American women finally were allowed to vote.

José de San Martín (1778–1850)

ALTHOUGH HE WAS BORN in Argentina, José de San Martín moved with his family to Spain when he was eight years old. San Martín attended school in Cádiz and served in the Spanish army against Napoleon. While in Cádiz, he met South American patriots who wanted to be free of Spain's rule.

San Martín resigned his military commission and sailed for Buenos Aires, where he formed a cavalry corps to accomplish independence for the Argentineans. Two years later, in 1816, he sent delegates to a congress that was being held in the city Tucumán and insisted the congress declare its independence from Spain. The congress agreed, and the country of Argentina became independent.

San Martín's "Army of the Andes" continued to liberate other parts of South America. His main objective was to capture Peru and liberate Lima, but he knew his troops could not be successful if they had to cross the Andes to get to Peru. Instead, San Martín and his army moved toward Chile and defeated the army at Maipu and ended Spanish domination there.

Approximately two years later, San Martín transported his soldiers to Peru via sea; in doing so, he created the Chilean navy. San Martín's troops sailed from Valparaiso, landed in Peru, and about nine months later, in 1821, they entered Lima and proclaimed independence for Peru.

While he was in Peru, San Martín met Simón Bolívar, another South American liberator. They shared a similar back story: Bolívar, a member of an influential Basque family living in Caracas, Venezuela, had also returned to Europe when he was a young man. Bolívar returned to Caracas and became an advocate for independence. His military leadership helped establish independence for Venezuela and Ecuador.

San Martín and Bolívar disagreed on the type of government to be formed in Peru, but San Martín remained in command of the military there for a year. He then resigned his command and voluntarily returned to Europe.

Being committed to independence and the cause, San Martín decided to return to South America to see if he could contribute to maintaining peace between the new nations. Once he reached South America, however, he realized his assistance was no longer needed. He returned to France where he retired and lived until his death on August 17, 1850.

Corazon Aquino (1933–present)

CORAZON AQUINO was comfortable with her role as wife and mother of five before her husband, Philippine president Benigno Aquino, was assassinated on August 21, 1983. Two-and-a-half-years later, Aquino was named the first female president of the Republic of the Philippines.

Born in 1933, Aquino received a degree in French and math and then enrolled in law school. She met her future husband while at school, and the two married in 1954. Benigno came from a long line of politicians, and he moved from city mayor to territorial governor and finally to senator in 1967 at the young age of 34. During all of this, Aquino focused on raising their family.

Over the years, Benigno spoke out frequently against then-president Ferdinand Marcos. In 1972, when Marcos instigated martial law, Benigno was one of the first people arrested. While her husband was in prison, Aquino began to get involved in politics.

The Aquinos give Marcos the thumbs-down

After her husband's assassination, Aquino's life turned upside down. Suddenly, she found herself responsible for unifying the anti-Marcos groups. In 1985, a presidential campaign was launched in her name. She agreed to run if one million people wanted her to—and soon more than one million signatures were gathered. After the election, Marcos declared himself the winner. He did not win more votes but instead had used intimidation and violence. People filled the streets in protest, and even the United States complained. In February 1986, Marcos finally fled the Philippines, and Aquino became president.

Some of her first actions were to release 441 political prisoners and force 22 pro-Marcos generals to retire. She promised to bring back the rights to assemble peacefully and to free speech. Not all of Aquino's actions were popular with the people; at least seven coups were directed against her. In 1992, Aquino was succeeded by her former secretary of defense, Fidel Ramos. She will always be remembered, however, for restoring "People Power" to the Filipinos.

The Berlin Conference on Africa

PRIOR TO 1880, Europe's colonial experience in Africa was limited to French Algeria, Cape Colony, the Boer republics in the far south, and a handful of trading posts and refueling stations scattered along the coast. By 1914, with the exception of Ethiopia, Liberia, and a part of Morocco that resisted conquest, the entire continent was under European control. The intervening 30 years are known as the "Scramble for Africa."

The causes of the land grab were nominally economic, but the driving force was rivalry between the European powers. England was the biggest player, expanding its South African colonies into the Boer republics, occupying Egypt, and bringing Nigeria under of its sphere of influence. France, meanwhile, held substantial territory in both northern and western Africa.

Portugal had old colonies on both coasts, dating from its period of maritime dominance in the 15th century. New claimants, including Italy and Germany, challenged the old imperial powers. Even Belgium ended up with vast portions of the Congo basin, held as the private property of King Leopold II. Small clashes between European powers in Africa had the potential to develop into major international incidents.

Germany entered as a serious player in 1884, following Britain's failed attempt to give the mouth of the Congo to Portugal. Chancellor Otto von Bismarck then hosted a conference in Berlin to decide the status of the Niger and Congo river basins. Twenty-four nations were invited, including the United States and the Ottoman Empire; 15 accepted. No African representatives were invited.

Bismarck outlined three topics for the conference: free trade for the Congo, free navigation of the Niger, and rules for future territorial annexations. Although he made it clear that the conference was not meant to negotiate boundaries or sovereignty, informal discussions about sovereignty ran parallel to the formal negotiations throughout the conference.

The General Act of the Berlin Conference, signed in February 1885, addressed all three issues. It established freedom of navigation on African rivers, free trade areas in the Congo Basin, and a deliberately vague definition of "effective occupation." The major accomplishment of the Conference occurred not in the formal negotiations embodied in the General Act, but in the informal negotiations. The British accepted Belgium's control of the Congo in exchange for German support regarding British control of the lower Niger. African desires and rights were not considered.

Henry VIII and the Reformation

HENRY VIII'S BREAK WITH the Roman Catholic Church was not due to religious fervor. More than anything, Henry wanted a son. His wife, Catherine of Aragon, bore five children, but only Princess Mary survived. In 1527, Henry requested an annulment from the pope, arguing that his marriage to Catherine was unlawful because she was his brother's widow. Catherine, meanwhile, argued that her marriage to Henry's brother was invalid, since it was never consummated. Charles V, the Holy Roman emperor and Catherine's nephew, made it clear that he did not wish his aunt to be put aside and his cousin Mary to be made illegitimate. After a formal investigation, the annulment was refused.

Henry was determined to marry Anne Boleyn, with whom he had been involved since 1522. In 1532, he took matters into his own hands, declaring himself the "Protector and Only Supreme Head of the Church and Clergy of England." With this self-appointed power, Henry secretly married Boleyn in 1533. Later that year, Thomas Cranmer, appointed Archbishop of Canterbury by Henry, pronounced the annulment of Henry's marriage to Catherine.

In 1534, Parliament passed two acts that made England's break with the Catholic Church official. The first declared that the pope had no authority in England. The second, known as the Act of Supremacy, established the Church of England as a separate institution with the king at its head. Over the next two years, Henry closed down monasteries and other Catholic religious foundations throughout England, taking their lands and revenues for the crown and its supporters.

Henry's marriage with Anne failed to give him the son he craved, but instead gave him a second daughter, Elizabeth. Jane Seymour, Henry's third wife, died shortly after giving birth to his long-awaited son, Prince Edward. Henry had three more wives but no more children. His son, Edward, ruled for only six years and was succeeded by his sisters, Mary and Elizabeth.

During Mary's reign, England experienced a brief return to Catholicism, but Elizabeth restored Protestantism and established the Anglican Church in 1563. In the end, it was Henry's "Anglican compromise" that determined the shape of Protestantism in England.

The Irish Potato Famine

IN THE 16TH CENTURY, potatoes came across the Atlantic from Peru. They soon became a staple crop throughout Europe. Not only could potatoes produce more food per acre than existing grain crops, but they also could be left in the ground until needed, making them difficult for plundering soldiers to take in times of war.

Ireland was the first European country where potatoes became an important part of the economy. After Cromwell invaded in 1649, the English relocated the native Irish to the western provinces, where it was too wet to grow grain. The Irish developed a subsistence economy that depended heavily on a diet of potatoes, making them particularly vulnerable when a fungus rotted European potato crops in 1845 and 1846.

The blight caused food shortages throughout Europe, but potatoes had never displaced grain and mixed farming on the continent or in England. Since its population was reduced to abject poverty by English laws that limited the right of the Irish to own land, the Irish had to depend on potatoes for survival. In fact, most Irish had no food reserves at all.

By October 1846, 90 percent of the Irish potato crop had been lost. By December, potato prices had doubled. Absentee landlords allowed their agents to evict farmers who could not pay their rent, exacerbating the effects of the blight by further reducing harvests. An epidemic of typhus killed 350,000 of a population already weakened by starvation.

Throughout the five years of famine that followed, Ireland remained a net exporter of food. The potato crop failed, but other crops thrived. In an effort to help the starving Irish peasants, Prime Minister Robert Peel pushed through the repeal of the Corn Laws, which taxed grain imports at a high rate. Lord John Russell, a proponent of laissez-faire economics, eventually replaced him. Russell declared, "We cannot feed the people" and demanded that the starving Irish pay for their own relief.

Committees of volunteers set up relief projects and soup kitchens. Donations came in from places as unlikely as Calcutta, Jamaica, and the Choctaw Indian tribe. By the summer of 1847, more than three million people were being fed in soup kitchens. But it wasn't enough to combat the "Great Hunger"; Ireland lost one-quarter of its population due to the famine and the unwillingness of the British government to provide public relief. About one million Irish died of starvation and disease between 1845 and 1851. Another million left their native land and emigrated to America, Britain, and Australia.

Winston Churchill (1874–1965)

WINSTON CHURCHILL once said that he considered his life prior to 1940 nothing more than preparation for his "walking with destiny."

After a brief army career that included service in India and Sudan and a stint as a war correspondent in the second Boer War, Churchill went into politics as a Conservative member of Parliament in 1900. He changed his allegiance and joined the Liberal Party in 1904. After holding a variety of positions under Liberal governments, he became first lord of the admiralty in 1911. He spent the next three years preparing for a possible war.

In 1915, he was the scapegoat for the failure of the naval expedition to the Dardanelles and joined the army in France. He returned to government in 1917 as Lloyd George's minister of munitions, responsible for the development and subsequent manufacture of thousands of tanks. He returned to the Conservative Party in 1924.

Churchill spent the 1930s out of office. Unpopular because of his opposition to Indian self-rule and his support of Edward VIII in the abdication crisis, he was ignored when he warned the government about the dangers of Nazi Germany and the need for rearmament. When war was declared in 1939, Churchill was called back to the admiralty.

In May 1940, British Prime Minister Neville Chamberlain's government fell. Churchill formed a coalition government in which he served as both prime minister and minister of defense. He traveled 150,000 miles over the course of the war, maintaining morale at home and juggling difficult alliances with the United States and the USSR.

When Churchill's government was defeated in the 1945 elections, halfway through the Potsdam Conference, he became a leader of the opposition and remained a presence in international politics. Popularizing the phrase "the Iron Curtain," he warned about the danger of the Soviet bloc and worked for European and American unity. Churchill again served as prime minister from 1951 to 1955, retiring at age 80. He remained a member of parliament until 1964.

He earned an international reputation not only as a wartime leader but also as an orator, writer, and political tactician, receiving the 1953 Nobel Prize for Literature.

Machiavelli Writes *The Prince*

NICCOLO MACHIAVELLI was a native of the Italian city-state of Florence, who, from 1498 to 1512, worked as a secretary, diplomat, and organizer of the city militia. After a Spanish invasion destroyed the militia and brought the Medici family back to power, Machiavelli was exiled to his family estate outside the city.

Less than a year later, Machiavelli wrote *The Prince.* The book served as a political treatise on how to create and maintain a powerful state. Having lived through an unsettled time, Machiavelli clearly saw the need for a strong ruler to unite the warring city-states and protect Italy from foreign invasion. In *The Prince,* he included studies of ancient strongmen such as Agathocles of Sicily and Alexander the Great.

His prince character had to do whatever was needed to preserve his power; in other words, let the ends justify the means. Machiavelli postulated that a prince could not be morally upright and survive—he had to be cunning, ruthless, cruel at times, and hypocritical if needed. To Machiavelli, the ideal leader was Cesare Borgia, the illegitimate son of Pope Alexander VI. With his father's help, Borgia seized much of the province of Romagna, a part of the rebellious Papal states. He did whatever he had to do to maintain his control, but after the pope died in 1503, his province quickly disappeared.

One of Machiavelli's reasons for writing *The Prince* was to inform his fellow Italians what was needed to unite the fragmented country. "Italy is ready and willing to follow a banner," he wrote, "if only someone will raise it." Machiavelli dedicated his book to Lorenzo de' Medici in hopes that he would read it and follow its suggestions. But his attempt was unsuccessful, and so he continued to write, including *Discourses Upon the First Ten Books of Livy, The Art of War,* two comedies, a biography of Castracani, and *Florentine Histories* (commissioned by Pope Leo X). Machiavelli died in 1527.

After his death, Machiavelli's *The Prince* became an extremely controversial work. His words were often quoted out of context, and Elizabethan-period dramatists damned him for his amoral prose. *The Prince* continues to influence people, counting among its fans leaders such as Napoleon and Mussolini. Even the author himself has become part of the lexicon, as *Machiavellian* now connotes subterfuge and cunning.

The Greek Independence Movement

GREECE HAD BEEN UNDER Ottoman rule since the fall of Constantinople in 1453. In the early 19th century, two European movements fed a growing desire for independence in Greece: the Romantic ideal of Greece as the birthplace of Europe and the rise of nationalism.

Easter Day uprising, 1821

The revolt began with a society of Greek expatriates known as *Philike Hetairia,* led by Alexander Ypsilanti, former Russian general and son of an Ottoman provincial governor. Operating under the impression that he had Russian support for a Greek uprising, in March 1821, Ypsilanti led a band of Greek expatriates on an unsuccessful raid into Moldavia. Two weeks later, an uprising rocked the Peloponnesian peninsula.

The Turks retaliated viciously, hanging the Greek Patriarch in Constantinople on Easter Sunday. In 1822, the Turks, looking for Greek rebels from the neighboring island of Samos, massacred about 20,000 Greeks who lived on the island of Chios. The women and children who survived were sold in Asian slave markets.

European governments condemned the Greek independence movement as another of the nationalist rebellions that had troubled Europe and Latin America after the French Revolution. But as details of the massacre filled Europe's newspapers, the rebels gained increasing support. Whether they were Greek or not, young men across the continent volunteered to serve in the rebel army.

By the end of 1821, the Greeks seemed on the verge of success. In January 1822, the Greek rebels declared independence and drew up a constitution. Four years later, Mehmet Ali of Egypt reconquered the Peloponnesus and threatened to restore Turkish control. Greek rebels retreated to the mountains, hoping for intervention by European powers.

In April 1826, Britain and Russia called for the establishment of Greece as an autonomous vassal state of the Ottoman Empire. Turkey refused. On October 20, 1827, the combined navies of the Triple Alliance defeated the Turkish fleet at Navarino. The Greek war for independence was officially over. It took another three years of fighting to fully drive out the Ottoman army. Finally, in 1832, Otto of Bavaria was crowned King of Greece.

The Mexican Revolution

IN 1910, Porfirio Díaz was elected to his seventh term as president of Mexico. During his long reign in power, Díaz morphed from popular leader into dictator. While Mexico became more industrialized and economically prosperous under his leadership, it came at the expense of the working and peasant classes, who did not own land—foreign investors did.

In an 1908 newspaper interview, Díaz said Mexico was ready for democracy. At the time, a rich businessman named Francisco Madero challenged him in the 1910 election, but Díaz had him jailed and claimed victory. Madero escaped and issued a passionate plea for Mexicans to fight the dictator. Revolutionary leaders such as Pascual Orozco, Pancho Villa, and Emiliano Zapata sprang into action.

By late May 1911, Díaz was gone. But although Madero replaced him, he did not act on land reform, which had been the central issue of the revolution. Zapata issued the *Plan de Ayala*, which demanded the return of ancestral lands and turned the revolution against Madero. Committed to democracy, but lukewarm on land reform, Madero blundered when he put General Victoriano Huerta in charge of fighting the rebels. With the assistance of U.S. Ambassador Henry Lane Wilson, Huerta overthrew Madero on February 18, 1913. Madero and his vice president were assassinated four days later, and Huerta became president.

But Venustiano Carranza, the governor of the Mexican state of Coahuila, rose in rebellion against Huerta because he believed Huerta had violated the Mexican constitution. The Constitutionalists, the name given to the alliance to overthrow Huerta, were joined by Villa, Zapata, and others who pressured Huerta to resign on July 8, 1914.

Then things really unraveled. A convention held in October 1914 to pick a new leader splintered the revolutionary coalition and led to a brutal civil war that ended in 200,000 deaths. Zapata and Villa fought against Carranza and his forces under Alvaro Obregón. Obregón's victories put Carranza in power, and America recognized his government in October 1915. A constitutional convention called by Carranza in late 1916 produced a more radical document than he had envisioned. The constitution, championed by Obregón, committed the government to land reform and restricted the Catholic Church. Carranza ignored much of the document and was ultimately deposed by Obregón in May 1920. Obregón's ascension to the presidency essentially ended the revolution, although violent outbreaks flared up for years to come.

The Development of Hinduism

THE ROOTS OF MODERN HINDUISM can be traced to about 1500 B.C., when Aryans crossed over the Himalayas into India. The Aryans were a branch of the Indo-European tribes that migrated from the Eurasian steppes into Central Asia and Europe. They brought with them the Sanskrit language, a pantheon of gods, and a custom of ritual sacrifice.

Hindus dressed for a religious festival

Over time, Aryan religion combined with the beliefs of the indigenous peoples to create a religion called Brahmanism. The details of this early Indian religious system are recorded in a collection of hymns, ritual texts, and philosophical treatises known as the Veda. The earliest portion of the Veda, the Rigveda, is thought to have taken its final form around 1200 B.C. The shared core of beliefs that make up modern Hinduism appear in Vedic literature: the idea of *karma* and rebirth; the class structure known as the caste system; and the idea of *dharma,* a moral order that shapes the universe and is expressed in a code of duties and obligations.

Between the seventh and fifth centuries B.C., Brahmanism faced a serious challenge. Breakaway sects of ascetics rejected the Veda, as well as the inevitability of rebirth as determined by dharma and karma. Of the sects, the most prominent were Buddhism and Jainism.

Vedic Brahmanism eventually transformed itself into something that could be called Hinduism. Vedic customs were reformulated into a body of religious texts called the *dharmasastras.* Unlike the ritual-based Veda, these new texts were guides for daily life. They divided the life of man into four stages, or *ashramas*: student, married householder, hermit, and *sannyasin* (wandering ascetic). They also codified the idea of the four basic classes, or *varnas,* of the caste system. Hindu social theory now centered on the concept of *varnashrama dharma:* the duties appropriate to an individual's class and stage of life and place.

Hinduism was further transformed by the growth of sects devoted to the worship of a particular god within the Vedic pantheon. Two divisions came to dominate Hindu religious practice: Vaishnavism, or the worship of Vishnu, and Shaivism, or the worship of Shiva. Interwoven with both sects was the worship of the goddess Devi, often as the god's consort.

Canada's Economic Boom

LIKE MANY OTHER INDUSTRIALIZED COUNTRIES, Canada was hit hard by the Great Depression. The country's GNP fell 43 percent between 1929 and 1933, while exports sank 50 percent. Meanwhile, the unemployment rate skyrocketed above 25 percent by 1933. A mild recovery began in 1934, but World War II kicked it into high gear.

William Lyon Mackenzie King served as Canada's prime minister during this time. He served two terms, 1921–1930 and 1935–1948, and is known for being the longest-serving prime minister in the history of the British Commonwealth. In the late 1930s, King attempted to boost the economy through government involvement. He established businesses such as the Canadian Broadcasting Corporation, Trans-Canada Airlines, and the National Film Board. He also introduced social programs such as unemployment insurance in the '40s. During the war, Canada was Great Britain's main supplier of war materiels prior to American involvement. King pushed to create the Department of Munitions and Supply, as well as 28 corporations for large-scale production of manufactured goods. From 1939 to 1941, employment in Canada's manufacturing sector increased by 50 percent. By 1944, Canadian exports had reached $1.2 billion, and total unemployment was less than 1 percent.

After the war, the economy faced the closing of munitions plants and the return of nearly one million Canadian service personnel to the workforce. Embarking on a two-fold strategy, King introduced family allowances to increase consumer demand while also boosting public expenditures to create jobs. Meanwhile, Canadian exports continued to grow, fueling the economy as King committed the country to participation in the European reconstruction effort.

In 1948, King retired and supported Louis Stephen St. Laurent as his successor. St. Laurent continued King's policies and expanded social programs, such as government funding of higher education and a form of Medicare called Hospital Insurance. He also implemented large public works projects such as the Trans-Canada Highway, and the St. Lawrence Seaway. By the mid-'50s, the United States and Canada—both of which saw their infrastructures expand significantly during the war—were enjoying remarkably similar postwar periods of vigorous economic growth.

POSTSCRIPT

■ Mackenzie King believed in spirits and repeatedly held séances.

The Marshall Plan

AT THE END OF WORLD WAR II, Europe struggled with the transition from war to peace. The most immediate problems were severe food shortages and the large numbers of displaced people. Dependent on imports to rebuild shattered economies, Europe had neither the currency reserves nor the export earnings to pay for them. To protect their currency reserves, European governments restricted imports from neighboring countries, further depressing intra-European trade.

In 1947, U.S. Secretary of State George C. Marshall proposed what became the European Recovery Program, commonly known as the Marshall Plan. The purpose of the Marshall Plan was to repair war damage, rehabilitate Europe's economies, and promote political stability.

Marshall claimed in his initial speech, "Our policy is directed not against any country or doctrine, but against hunger, poverty, desperation and chaos." Nevertheless, there was an element of self-interest to the Marshall Plan. A prosperous Europe was seen as the best defense against the spread of communism, especially after the Communist coup in Czechoslovakia in February 1948.

Signed into law on April 3, 1948, the Marshall Plan provided $13.5 billion in aid to Western Europe between 1948 and 1951. The United States invited European nations to outline what they needed for economic recovery so aid could be used effectively. Fearful of American influence, which Stalin described as "dollar enslavement," the Soviet Union rejected the program and put pressure on its Eastern European satellites to do the same. Eighteen nations formed the Organization for European Economic Cooperation (OEEC) that month, which initially reported on the condition of the various European economies and later divided aid among the recipients.

The program included four different kinds of aid: dollar grants that allowed Europe to purchase American goods and services; matching funds set aside by the European governments to rebuild infrastructure; technical assistance; and guaranteed returns to encourage American businesses to invest in modernizing Europe. No distinction was made between ally and enemy. Austria, Belgium, Denmark, France, Greece, Iceland, Ireland, Italy, Luxembourg, the Netherlands, Norway, Portugal, Sweden, Switzerland, Turkey, West Germany, and the United Kingdom all benefited from the program.

Marshall received the 1953 Nobel Peace Prize for his role in Europe's reconstruction.

The Boer War

AFTER THE BRITISH BEGAN to take over South African Dutch settlements in 1795, the descendants of the Dutch settlers, called the Boers, started to leave Cape Colony in 1836. They migrated and established the independent republics of Transvaal and the Orange Free State, or the Boer republics.

By the 1870s, the British had their sights set on the Boer republics. The Boers resisted, and in 1880, Transvaal rebelled against British annexation, winning limited self-rule.

When diamonds and gold were discovered in Transvaal in 1886, foreign prospectors poured in. The Boers slapped the *Uitlanders* (foreigners) with discriminatory taxation and limited political rights. On December 29, 1895, British Dr. Leander Jameson led an Uitlander raid into Transvaal with

Armed Boers

the aim of overthrowing its government. His actions, however, merely increased tension between the colonies.

In 1899, Transvaal declared war on Britain. Boer commandos overran Cape Colony and Natal, besieging British garrisons at three strategic border towns: Mafeking, Kimberley, and Ladysmith. The British sent 21,000 men under the command of General Redvers Buller, Britain's largest overseas force since the Crimean War.

Instead of steamrolling the Boers, the British suffered a trio of humiliating defeats. Canada, Australia, and New Zealand sent reinforcements. Indian army hero Lord Frederick Roberts replaced Buller as commander in chief. Roberts reached Cape Town on January 10, 1900, and the besieged garrisons were relieved by mid-February. By June, the British held the three major Boer cities of Bloemfontein, Johannesburg, and Pretoria. Within two months, the Boer army was in fragments.

For two more years, Boer guerrillas raided isolated British units. The war finally ended when the new commander in chief, Lord Herbert Kitchener, instituted a scorched-earth policy, burning Boer farms and imprisoning women and children in concentration camps. With the 1902 Peace of Vereeniging, the Boer republics, and their substantial mineral resources, joined the British Empire.

Suleyman the Magnificent

THE TENTH OTTOMAN SULTAN, known in Europe as Suleyman the Magnificent, was not one to mince words. In fact, as inscribed on the 16th-century ruler's mosque, he deigned himself "Slave of God, powerful with the power of God, deputy of God on earth, obeying the commands of the Qur'an and enforcing them throughout the world, master of all lands, the shadow of God over all nations, Sultan of Sultans in all the lands of Persians and Arabs."

The Ottoman Empire reached its fullest extent under his rule, from 1520 to 1566. Suleyman personally led 13 major military campaigns. He conquered Belgrade in 1521, using it as a base of operations against Hungary, which remained the last major obstacle to Ottoman expansion in Europe. A year later, he drove the Knights of the Order of St. John from their stronghold in Rhodes, where they had harassed Muslim shipping and pilgrims for 200 years. He took Iraq from the Safavids in 1534, conquered much of Hungary, and spread Ottoman control into North Africa as far west as Algeria. His fleets dominated the Mediterranean, though he failed to capture Malta.

Known to his subjects as "Suleyman the Lawgiver," the sultan created a single code of law combining the Islamic law known as shari'ah and the customary law of the previous nine Ottoman sultans. Suleyman's legal code detailed the duties of his subjects, down to the clothing worn by different classes of people, and outlined the relationship between Muslim and non-Muslim peoples within the empire. It would remain in effect for 300 years.

The geographical and political power of the Ottomans under Suleyman was reflected in the empire's economic growth and artistic achievement; Suleyman, trained as both a goldsmith and a poet, was an enthusiastic patron of the arts.

Suleyman died during the siege of Szigeth, Hungary. His grand vizier concealed his death from the army until the successful conclusion of the siege. His body was embalmed and carried in the sultan's litter as if he were still alive until the army neared home.

POSTSCRIPT

▦ Suleyman amazed Ottoman society and Western observers by falling in love with and marrying a harem slave named Hurrem Sultan.

The First Crusade

IN 1071, an invading group of Seljuk Turks destroyed a major Byzantine army in what is now Turkey. The result was a dynastic struggle in Constantinople that shook the empire's foundations and led to the loss of much of Anatolia. Ten years later, General Alexius Comnenus seized the throne and established a new dynasty. Alexius was an able emperor, but the loss of so much territory meant that his army was unable to recruit enough men to launch a concerted effort to drive the Turks away.

To help obtain soldiers, Alexius sent envoys to Pope Urban II in March 1095.

Pope Urban II (on horse, left) in France

Urban received the Greek ambassadors with an open mind. The Byzantines were Orthodox Christians and did not recognize the primacy of the pope; in fact, there had been a schism between the eastern and western churches for the past 40 years. However, Urban reasoned, that by helping Alexius, he might be able to heal the rift between the churches and gain more power for the papacy.

On November 27, 1095, Urban preached to an audience of French nobles and clergy at Clermont, France: Jerusalem must be taken back from the Muslims. France was overcrowded, he said, but Palestine was overflowing with milk and honey. All Christians should help their oppressed brothers. Any who died during this undertaking would be cleansed of their sins.

Urban's plea was received with great enthusiasm, resulting in what is now called the First Crusade. In 1096, a procession of nobles and their followers left Europe and assembled near Constantinople. From there they fought their way across Anatolia to Antioch, which was captured after a lengthy siege. The Crusaders appeared before Jerusalem in June 1099. After a month's siege, they broke into the city and slaughtered everyone.

Over the next two centuries, there would be seven more crusades, though none as successful as the first. Instead of healing the rift between East and West, the Crusades resulted in more intense suspicion between Byzantium and Catholic Europe. However, the Crusades also brought Islam and Christianity into closer contact and led to increased commercial, cultural, and philosophical exchanges.

Hannah Arendt (1906–1975)

HANNAH ARENDT was one of the most influential political philosophers of the 20th century. She described herself as a "political theorist," rejecting the term "philosopher" on the grounds that philosophy dealt with "man in the singular," and that "men, not Man, live on the earth and inhabit the world."

Born into a secular German-Jewish family in 1906, Arendt completed her doctorate in philosophy at Heidelberg University in 1929 under the direction of existentialist philosopher Karl Jaspers. She fled Germany in 1933 after being arrested by the Gestapo about her research into anti-Semitism. Following brief stays in Prague and Geneva, she settled in Paris, where she spent the next six years working for Jewish refugee organizations.

With the German occupation of France in 1940, Arendt was held briefly in the Gurs internment camp. She managed to escape and once again fled abroad, this time to the United States via Lisbon. She traveled with her husband and mother, using illegal visas issued by American diplomat Hiram Bingham. They settled in New York, where Arendt wrote for the German-language newspaper *Der Aufbau.* Following the war, she taught at several major American universities but was most closely associated with the New School for Social Research in New York, where she was a professor of political philosophy until her death in 1975.

Arendt is best known for two works, *The Origins of Totalitarianism* (1951) and *The Human Condition* (1958). *Origins* attempted to provide a framework for understanding the rise of the Nazi and Stalinist regimes, tracing the roots of 20th-century totalitarianism in 19th-century imperialism and anti-Semitism. "Equality... is the result of human organization. We are not born equal," she noted. *The Human Condition* examined the fundamental categories of the *vita activa,* the active life, which Arendt defined as labor, work, and action. She also wrote important works on the nature of revolution, freedom, authority, tradition, and the modern age.

In 1961, Arendt reported on the trial of Adolf Eichmann in Jerusalem for *The New Yorker.* She expanded her *New Yorker* articles into what became her most controversial work, *Eichmann in Jerusalem,* in which she used the phrase "banality of evil" to describe the fervor sweeping Europe. Although she ultimately supported the decision to execute Eichmann, she criticized both Israel's handling of the trial and the behavior of many Jewish leaders during the Holocaust.

The Spartacus Slave Revolt

BORN IN THRACE, Spartacus served as an auxiliary in the Roman army. He later became the leader of a bandit group but was captured and sold into slavery. Perhaps because of his military background, Spartacus was designated to receive gladiatorial training. By the year 73 B.C., he was among approximately 200 slaves held at a gladiatorial school in Capua, about 20 miles from Mount Vesuvius.

Spartacus showing his determination by killing his own horse

While at the school, Spartacus and two comrades incited a riot. Armed with weapons from a kitchen, about 80 gladiators escaped into the streets. They fled south to Vesuvius. Spartacus's defiance heartened slaves throughout the region. Reinforcements streamed into his encampment by the thousands. Alarmed, the Romans sent 3,000 militiamen to eradicate the rebels. Using vines as ropes, Spartacus's men clambered down the side of Mount Vesuvius. The Roman force was caught by surprise and fled.

The defeat was the first of many that the Romans would suffer at Spartacus's hands over the years. Upward of 120,000 slaves flocked to join his "servile army." Despite their successes, the rebel army was not able to defy the mighty Roman Empire indefinitely. In 71, Spartacus was finally cornered near the Silarus River by Roman forces under the command of Crassus.

By the end of the battle, somewhere between 12,500 and 60,000 slaves were dead. Although the body of Spartacus was never found, it is assumed that he died at Silarus.

The Romans crucified more than 6,000 captured slaves along 150 miles of the Appian Way as a lesson to any future malcontents. But they could not kill the ideas Spartacus represented. The rebel gladiator became a symbol of freedom; even centuries after Spartacus's death, he inspired revolutionaries such as Karl Marx and Che Guevara and influenced their belief in the rights of the proletariat.

The 1973 Oil Crisis

EARLY OIL EXPLORATION IN the Middle East was done by Western companies that received much of the profit. To counter Western influence and place more wealth in their own hands, several Middle Eastern oil-producing countries formed the Organization of Petroleum Exporting Countries (OPEC) in 1960.

In its early years, OPEC was an informal cartel to control the sale of oil by Third World nations. By 1973, members included Venezuela, Saudi Arabia, Iran, Iraq, Kuwait, Qatar, Indonesia, Libya, Gabon, Algeria, Nigeria, Ecuador, and the United Arab Emirates.

Angry over Western support of the Israeli military during the Yom Kippur War, Arab members of OPEC unilaterally raised oil prices 17 percent on October 16, 1973. They also announced production cuts in order to force oil prices higher. On October 19, OPEC ministers began a boycott of oil shipments to the United States as further punishment. OPEC later extended the boycott to the Netherlands, Portugal, Rhodesia, and South Africa, as it continued to slash production quotas for member states.

The embargo was lifted in March 1974; that year oil prices worldwide quadrupled. Although some of the wealth coming into the Middle East went to help other underdeveloped countries, most of it was hoarded by the elite who reinvested in the West or simply indulged themselves. Arms purchases rose sharply.

In the United States, the price of gas rose, and fuel shortages developed nationwide as long lines of automobiles formed at gas stations. Factories cut production, and workers were laid off; even daylight saving time was extended to save energy. Gas was rationed, and price controls were established. A nationwide speed limit of 55 mph was imposed. In 1977, the Department of Energy was created to coordinate national energy policy and establish a Strategic Petroleum Reserve.

Worldwide, other countries also suffered economic declines in the short run. Japan, dependent on oil imports, began to design smaller, more fuel-efficient cars. Heavily dependent on oil-intensive industries, the Japanese economy began to turn to investments in other industries such as electronics as a way to ensure economic stability. Intensive research on alternative forms of energy, such as solar and wind power, developed.

In the long run, however, OPEC lost much of its influence as the Soviet Union and other countries increased their oil production to counter the cuts by OPEC.

The *Communist Manifesto*

FRIEDRICH ENGELS had been sent to Manchester, England, to work in his father's textile business. Outraged by the conditions of Manchester's slums, he began to write about the industrial poor. His writings caught the attention of philosopher and revolutionary Karl Marx. In Paris, Marx was editing a short-lived radical magazine when he and Engels met in 1844. The social visit turned into a lifelong collaboration.

Marx was expelled from Paris in 1846, so he took his family to Brussels, where he and Engels organized the Communist League. Together they wrote the *Communist Manifesto,* both as a statement of the league's platform and as a means of outlining tactics for a working class movement. Ending with the famous exhortation, "Workers of all countries, unite! You have nothing to lose but your chains," the *Manifesto* linked the new ideas of socialism with the much older ideas of communism.

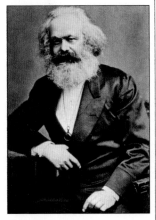

Karl Marx

Marx and Engels described human history as a series of class struggles between oppressors and the oppressed. In capitalism, Marx defined the oppressors as those who own the "means of production." These means, such as factories, land, and capital, are essential to produce the goods and services that sustain a society. As these owners profit off the work of laborers, the invariable conflict between the groups leads to the next stage of social evolution. Because capitalism fundamentally relied on this model of labor exploitation, it could not be reformed. Marx theorized that, just as feudalism evolved into capitalism, the unification and rebellion of these industrial workers would lead to a classless society marked by a communal ownership of the means of production. The only immediate effect of the *Manifesto* was Marx's expulsion from Cologne for a second time. Once settled in London with his family, Marx produced his most important work, *Das Kapital,* which furthered his philosophies first outlined in the *Communist Manifesto.* Engels completed *Das Kapital* after Marx's death in 1883.

Marx demonstrated what he believed would be the inevitable collapse of capitalism, but he had little to say about what a communist state would actually look like. The architect who showed the world what 20th-century communism resembled was Vladimir Lenin.

The Incan Empire

THE INCAN EMPIRE, which ran from the 13th through 16th centuries, was the largest of the pre-Columbian empires, with nearly 20 million people. Its territory included most of modern-day Peru; it encompassed mountain and valley areas and included many different peoples. The Incas left a legacy for future generations in many areas, including architecture, agriculture, infrastructure, and written language.

Incan society was based on a hierarchy, whose leader was purported to be the son of the sun god Inti. Beneath this ruler were priests, nobles, and others in descending order of importance until the peasant level was reached. Their religion used divination, fasting, feasts, and other means of communicating with the gods. They had occasional human sacrifices, but far less often than the Aztecs.

The Incas built some of South America's most significant early architecture. Machu Picchu, a site northwest of the central city Cuzco, is one excellent example. Large stones were hand cut with precision and fitted without the use of mortar. These mortarless foundations were the key to the structures' survival. Incan builders rounded corners of buildings and constructed interior walls that were slightly inclined. As a result, the buildings were more flexible during earthquakes. Many of the buildings and temples still exist.

Mountain terracing was another Incan architectural achievement, which not only increased the amount of land available for farming but also served as a barrier for cities in danger of landslides. They also built a road system that linked mountains and valleys, much of which survives today. The roads cut through rocky terrain and followed turbulent rivers for thousands of miles, providing a communications link for remote settlements.

The Incas also created a notation system with knotted strings that functioned like an abacus. The system, called *quipu,* included strings of various colors that were arranged in sequence. With this system, the Incas kept census, work, and financial records. Many scholars believe the quipu was only for record keeping, but others believe it to be an early form of writing as well.

The beginning of the end came in 1526, when Spanish conquistadors, led by Francisco Pizarro, arrived. They saw the wealth and abundance the Incas had to offer and decided to conquer the region. After years of civil war, Spanish rule, and diseases including smallpox and measles, the Incan Empire was demolished by the early 1600s.

The First President of the United States

GEORGE WASHINGTON was once described as "First in war, first in peace, and first in the hearts of his countrymen," by Colonel Henry Lee. And Washington truly was one of America's greatest leaders. In the 1750s, he served in the French and Indian War. He lost more battles than he won, yet as commander in chief, he held the main Continental army together during the American Revolution against the British. As presiding officer of the 1787 Constitutional Convention, he helped save the convention from breaking up as delegates argued about the document that would define America.

Washington was the first president of the United States, winning rather easily in both the 1789 and 1792 elections. As the nation's first chief executive, Washington was keenly aware that his every move was scrutinized. "I walk on untrodden ground," he wrote. The new Congress and government sought his advice on everything concerning the new nation, and Washington had to steer a neutral course on varied topics, from finance to foreign relations. The United States was still young and had to toe the line with France, Britain, and Spain, whose territories bordered the new nation.

When he stepped aside as president, Washington composed a farewell address with help from Alexander Hamilton and John Jay. It is thought of as one of the most insightful documents in American history. In it, Washington stressed that the nation must remain unified: The North, South, and West needed each other to survive.

He also wrote that partisan politics were bad and should be avoided. The Constitution is sacrosanct, he wrote: Its principles should remain intact; should it need to be changed, it should be done peacefully. Cherish the public credit, he continued, and avoid national debt. Practice good faith and justice toward all other nations. Treat all equally. Be wary of foreign political intrusions and avoid entangling foreign alliances. Stay out of European politics, and keep America focused on its own growth.

POSTSCRIPT

In *The Life of Washington* (1800), Mason Locke Weems, better known as Parson Weems, wrote stories about the first president that have now become legend, including the infamous cherry tree incident in which a young George uttered, "I cannot tell a lie."

The Russo–Japanese War

IN THE MID-1870S, Japan began to take an interest in neighboring Korea. When the Russians occupied Port Arthur in southern Manchuria in 1898, they effectively blocked the Japanese from occupying Korea. Tensions between the two countries began to rise.

In retaliation, Japan decided to drive the Russians from Korea and Manchuria. On February 8, 1904, Japanese torpedo boats attacked the Russian fleet in the Port Arthur harbor, causing severe damage to several ships. A formal declaration of war by Japan followed two days later. Initially, Russian ships were active in countering Japanese naval movements, but the death of Admiral Makaroff, one of the few aggressive Russian naval leaders, spelled doom for the Russian fleet.

By May 25, 1904, the Japanese were positioned to besiege Port Arthur. Japanese army units landed close to Port Arthur and began to advance on the city, which was defended by 40,000 soldiers. Although the Japanese suffered more than 59,000 casualties, the Russians weren't able to delay the relentless advance of the Japanese infantry. The siege lasted until January 2, 1905, when the surviving 10,000 Russians surrendered. Meanwhile, the Russian Baltic Fleet had left its home port in October 1904 to steam around South Africa all the way to the Far East. On May 27–29, 1905, the Russian fleet was destroyed during the naval battle of Tsushima. Japan then had complete command of the sea.

Other Japanese units moved to block the major Russian land armies, which began to concentrate around the Chinese city of Mukden. Though the estimates vary widely, it is thought that during the Battle of Mukden (from February to March 1905), more than 70,000 Japanese fell in combat, as well as approximately 89,000 Russians.

As the war stagnated, U.S. President Theodore Roosevelt acted as mediator at a peace conference held in Portsmouth, New Hampshire. A treaty was signed there on September 5, 1905. Russia surrendered Port Arthur and half of the island of Sakhalin and withdrew its troops from Manchuria. The Japanese remained in control of Korea, and Japan was now recognized as an emerging international power.

Edmund Burke Formulates Conservative Philosophy

ENGLISH STATESMAN EDMUND BURKE was noted for his consistent rejection of abuse, misgovernment, and excess.

Burke was born in Dublin, Ireland, in 1729. At first, Burke seemed bound to follow in his father's footsteps as a solicitor, but eventually his interest turned from law to literature and politics. He began to publish political and social essays in 1756, some of which gained attention from politicians and philosophers such as Emmanuel Kant, Denis Diderot, and William Godwin. In 1765, Burke became a member of Parliament representing Wendover, a pocket borough.

He soon became a rising star in the Whig party as an ally of the Marquis of Rockingham. He was known as a voice of protest against the corruption and extravagance that marked Lord North's Tory governments from 1770 to 1783. He was sympathetic toward the American colonies and Irish Catholics, as well as a strong opponent of the French Revolution. He campaigned in Parliament for economic reform in government, abolition of the slave trade, and Catholic emancipation.

Burke's political essays still captivate the modern reader. In *On American Taxation* (1774), he argued unsuccessfully for the repeal of the tax on tea imported into the colonies. In *On Conciliation with the Colonies* (1775), he described a system of American autonomy that would preserve English superiority and colonial liberty. In *On the Nawab of Arcot's Private Debts* (1785), Burke attacked abuses related to the East India Company's rule of Bengal.

Burke's best-known work is *Reflections on the Revolution in France* (1790). Written as a letter to a Frenchman, the work attacks the leaders and principles of the French Revolution for their violence and excesses, urging reform rather than rebellion as a means of correcting social and political abuses. Burke continued, recommending that leaders respect their nation's customs and traditions. In later publications, he went even further, urging the government to suppress free opinions at home. Although it was extremely controversial at the time, when many of Burke's predictions regarding the revolution came true, the work found its supporters.

Burke never systematized his political philosophy. Although himself a Whig, his emphasis on freedom within tradition and constitutionally imposed limits became a major element in forming British Conservatism.

The Justinian Code

Roman Emperor Justinian (ruled A.D. 527–565) presided over a territory that was changing into what many historians call the Eastern Roman Empire. The western provinces had been occupied by several different foreign peoples, such as the Franks, Visigoths, Ostrogoths, and Vandals, and the eastern part of the empire shifted toward Greece. The eastern empire's primary language was Greek instead of Latin, and most Christians there professed loyalty to the Patriarch of Constantinople rather than the pope in Rome.

One of Justinian's best-remembered accomplishments was his order to update and streamline centuries of Roman law. At the time, the Roman legal system was in disarray, primarily as the result of its sheer size and age. Justinian understood the need for a contemporary legal doctrine that was more in line with Christian society than with the old pagan ways. He chose a man named Tribonian to supervise the project. Tribonian was himself a pagan, but he was also a man of great legal expertise. Assisted by nine others, Tribonian and the commission worked from February 528 until April 529, when the new Justinian Code was officially put into effect. The code was a compilation of imperial decrees that had been updated by excising obsolete acts, merging repetitious decrees together, and changing words to remove contradictions.

In December 530, Tribonian launched the next phase of the project when he and 16 colleagues began work overhauling Roman jurisprudence. The commission faced a daunting task as they worked through all writings of men to whom previous emperors had granted the right to interpret the law. They arranged them by subject and then, as they had with the Code, removed contradictions, repetitions, and obsolete remarks. Three years later, the Digest was presented to the empire. A year later, Tribonian completed a second edition of the Code that brought it in line with the new Digest.

Concurrent with the work on the Digest, Tribonian's commission edited a new legal textbook called the *Institutes,* which became the official—and only—text used by lawyers and students throughout the empire. Other commentaries on the rewritten code of law were forbidden since they would only lead to ambiguity and uncertainty. Justinian also reduced the number of sanctioned law schools in the empire to two, in Constantinople and Berytus, and increased the course of study by a year.

Justinian's overhaul of the Roman legal system later became the foundation for much of Western Europe's legal system.

Japanese American Internment Camps

IN FEBRUARY 1942, President Franklin Roosevelt signed Executive Order 9066, which designated military areas "from which any and all persons may be excluded." Though broadly written, the order was specifically used to authorize the removal of Japanese Americans from the West Coast. The "evacuations" were prompted by widespread anger against the Japanese, deep-seated racism, and fear of sabotage.

Not everyone approved of the displacement of Japanese Americans. Among the opponents was FBI Director J. Edgar Hoover. Not only did the action appear unconstitutional, the FBI saw little cause for concern about the general Japanese American population. But Hoover was in the minority. The majority sided with General John L. DeWitt, who declared,

"A Jap's a Jap. It makes no difference whether the Jap is a citizen or not." As military commander of the Western Defense Command, DeWitt issued more than 100 military "Exclusion Orders" directed at Japanese Americans living in the area.

Approximately 110,000 people were moved to War Relocation Camps where they were held under armed guard behind barbed wire. More than 60 percent of the internees were American citizens. Allowed to take only what they could carry, they lost homes, businesses, and personal possessions. In 1943 and 1944, four major court cases contesting the constitutionality of the action reached the Supreme Court, but they were not successful.

As fears subsided, the government began allowing internees to return home on a case-by-case basis in 1944. In 1945, the order was lifted entirely, and the internees returned home to try to resume their lives.

In 1988, President Ronald Reagan signed the Civil Liberties Act of 1988, which granted reparations to each surviving Japanese American internee. The act admitted that the internments had been based on "race prejudice, war hysteria, and a failure of political leadership."

Sigmund Freud Visits America

TO HONOR THE COLLEGE'S 20TH ANNIVERSARY, G. Stanley Hall, president of Clark University in Worcester, Massachusetts, invited two guest speakers from across the Atlantic, both of whom had begun to make headlines on a regular basis: Swiss psychiatrist Carl Jung and Austrian neuropsychologist Sigmund Freud.

The September 1909 lecture series Freud gave at the university, titled "The Origin and Development of Psychoanalysis," would be the only one he ever gave in the Western Hemisphere. In return for his speeches, the university gave him an honorary degree, which meant a great deal to him. Although today Freud is regarded as the father of psychoanalysis and one of the great intellectuals of the 20th century, that wasn't always the case. In Europe, he often felt as if his theories were not only dismissed but also ridiculed; it felt wonderful to be appreciated as a scholar and expert. He was intensely gratified when he found that colleges studied his writings and honored his theories. In his autobiography, Freud wrote, "As I stepped onto the platform at Worcester to deliver my Five Lectures upon Psychoanalysis it seemed like the realization of some incredible day-dream: psychoanalysis was no longer a product of delusion, it had become a valuable part of reality."

The subject matter of Freud's lectures was quite scandalous for the time period. In 1905, he had published *Three Essays on the Theory of Sexuality,* which introduced his theory of the Oedipus complex and outlined psycho-sexual development. Freud believed that the mind is divided up into three parts: the *id* (instincts), the *ego* (mediator between instincts and reality), and the *superego* (conscience). His theories of psychoanalysis stated that if the parts of the mind are not in harmony, a mental or emotional disorder, called a *neurosis,* occurs. Many of his ideas also focused on sexual elements in a time when such topics were rarely mentioned aloud.

Despite the warm reception Freud was given, his stay in America was less than pleasurable. He disapproved of America's supposed inability to drop its inhibitions and be more sexually liberated. Freud criticized what he saw as Americans' rampant materialism, dubbing the United States "Dollaria." To make matters worse, while in the United States, he developed intestinal problems. "America is a mistake, a gigantic mistake," remarked the famed psychoanalyst. "America is the most grandiose experiment the world has seen, but, I am afraid, it is not going to be a success."

Churchill's Iron Curtain Speech

O N MARCH 5, 1946, former British Prime Minister Winston Churchill was at Westminster College in Fulton, Missouri, to receive an honorary degree. During his oration, Churchill described the current European situation: "From Stettin in the Baltic to Trieste in the Adriatic, an iron curtain has descended across the Continent."

Churchill was very concerned about the future of Europe. The victorious Allies of World War II had already drifted apart. The Soviet Union, under the iron hand of Joseph Stalin, mistrusted Western powers. As American foreign policy expert George F. Kennan noted in his "Long Telegram," the Soviet view of the world was skewed since every country bordering the USSR had attacked it at one time or another. Thus, the Soviets mistrusted their erstwhile allies.

Churchill was correct in the term "iron curtain," as the Soviets decided to create a buffer zone to prevent future attacks from Europe. Eastern Europe became communist controlled, subject to orders from Moscow. Communist guerrillas began activity in several Non-Aligned countries—most notably Greece—in attempts to subvert the government. The result was an undeclared war between capitalism and freedom on one side and communism and state control on the other. Analysts coined the term "the Cold War" to describe the tense situation.

President Harry Truman decided that Europe needed American protection. In March 1947, the Truman Doctrine was announced: America would assist Greece and Turkey against the communist threat. In April 1948, the Marshall Plan went into action as the European Recovery Program, bringing economic aid to help rebuild Western Europe.

The Cold War heated up in 1948 when the USSR cut mandated supply routes to Berlin, located deep inside Soviet-occupied East Germany. The United States responded with a massive airlift to Berlin that kept the city supplied. A year later, the United States and Western European nations formed the North Atlantic Treaty Organization (NATO), an alliance designed to neutralize the Soviets. When West Germany joined NATO in 1955, the USSR responded with the Warsaw Pact.

In August 1949, the Soviet Union exploded its first atomic bomb, spurring America to develop the hydrogen bomb, a far more powerful nuclear weapon. With both sides building large quantities of such weapons, many people across the world began to fear nuclear war. The Cold War continued until the USSR broke apart in 1991.

Vasco da Gama (1460–1524)

WHEN VASCO DA GAMA sailed into the Indian port of Calicut in May 1498, it was the culmination of more than a half-century of Portuguese nautical exploration. From the time of Prince Henry the Navigator, Portuguese ships had explored the African shoreline, first rounding the treacherous Cape of Good Hope a decade earlier.

Sponsored by King Manuel I, da Gama left Lisbon in July 1497 to discover a sea route to the East. Using the findings of earlier Portuguese explorers, da Gama sailed south down the coast of Africa, taking advantage of the prevailing winds. He successfully rounded the Cape of Good Hope by sailing out into the Atlantic and then veering back on a long arc that brought him to the east coast of Africa. At the port of Melinda, he hired an experienced Arab pilot who navigated the expedition across the Indian Ocean and into the port of Calicut. Da Gama returned to Lisbon in September 1499 with a load of spices worth 60 times the cost of his two-year voyage.

Encouraged by the enormous profit, Manuel immediately sent a second expedition to India under the command of Pedro Alvarez Cabral. Cabral acquired limited trading privileges from the ruler of Calicut and founded the first European trading post in India. He departed for home, leaving behind 40 Portuguese merchants to buy spices when prices were low and store them until the next fleet returned to Calicut. Soon after Cabral left Calicut, Muslims attacked the Portuguese warehouse and killed most of the merchants. Manuel then sent da Gama to avenge them with a squadron of heavily armed ships. Da Gama arrived in 1502, bombarding Calicut and attacking an Arab trading vessel. He also established trading posts along the eastern coast of Africa in what is now Mozambique. In December 1503, he returned to Portugal with 13 ships laden with riches.

Da Gama lived quietly for the next 20 years. In 1524, in response to reports of corruption among Portuguese officials in India, King John III sent da Gama back to India as the new viceroy. Da Gama died of malaria on December 24, 1525, only three months after his arrival. But the Portuguese trading empire did not die with him—Portugal had a virtual monopoly on Europe's spice trade with Asia for the next 100 years.

The English Civil War

THE DEATH OF ELIZABETH I in 1603 not only brought a new ruling family to power in England—the Stuarts of Scotland—but also a belief in divine rights and absolute power. Elizabeth's successor James I believed he was answerable only to God and began to collect taxes without Parliamentary authorization.

After James's death in 1625, his son Charles I was crowned king. He shared his father's beliefs, and like his father before him, he clashed with Parliament. He dissolved Parliament for 11 years but needed them to provide funds to squelch a Scottish rebellion. Parliament reconvened in 1640. Two years later, Charles sensed the start of a rebellion and led troops into the House of Commons to arrest radical leaders. The leaders escaped through a back door and raised an army, starting the English Civil War, which had three phases: 1642–1645, 1648, and 1650–1651.

The Cavaliers, who supported the monarch, were made up of aristocrats, landholders, Anglicans, and Catholics. They were generally trained in warfare, and they expected a quick victory. The Roundheads, forces supporting Parliament and comprised of the middle class, merchants, and Puritans, were bolstered by their convictions. Led by Oliver Cromwell, the Roundheads marched into battle singing hymns.

In 1647, Charles was turned over to Parliamentary forces, and in 1649, he was tried and executed. The House of Commons abolished the House of Lords, the monarchy, and the official Church of England. The nation was declared a republic, known as the Commonwealth, with Cromwell as its leader.

Once the Commonwealth was established, some of Cromwell's supporters found themselves disagreeing with their leader. In addition to advocating the abolition of the monarchy and the House of Lords, the Levellers, who wanted to diminish government power, believed all adult males, even ones without property, should be able to vote. The group called the Diggers went even further, wanting to eliminate the concept of private property. Cromwell remarked that universal suffrage tended "very much to anarchy." Finding himself at odds with a coalition of Levellers, Royalists, and religious extremists, Cromwell dismissed Parliament in 1653. Under Cromwell's leadership, England found itself guided by military rule and Puritan ethics.

Within two years of Cromwell's death in 1658, England, longing for a change, invited Charles II to return from exile and become king.

The Welfare State in Europe

THE MODERN WELFARE STATE, with its comprehensive system of social services funded by taxation and national insurance, has its roots in the 19th century.

The emergence of the strong secular state in 19th-century Europe was characterized by state involvement in education, public health, and housing. Public education systems were first introduced in France and Prussia early in the 19th century. A system of social insurance regarding workmen's compensation, sickness, and old age for wage earners was pioneered in the 1880s in Germany, and other European states soon followed. In 1911, Britain's Liberal government introduced unemployment assistance and health benefits based on worker contributions to a national insurance system. All of these systems differed from earlier forms of "poor relief" in that they offered nearly universal coverage to the working classes.

The hardships of the Great Depression in the 1920s and '30s changed popular attitudes regarding government assistance and accelerated the development of the welfare state, which was seen as an alternative "middle way" between capitalism and communism.

The move to a true modern welfare state came to Great Britain after World War II. Despite the hardships brought about by the war, it had also brought full employment and a new experience of social equality. Widespread rationing actually raised food consumption for the poor and gave them access to institutions such as hospitals.

Over time, people began to ask why the type of planning that supported the war could not be applied to peacetime as well. In 1942, a report by economist William Beveridge proposed a comprehensive British system of national social insurance that would cover citizens "from the cradle to the grave," tackling what Beveridge called the "five giants": want, disease, idleness, squalor, and ignorance. Clement Attlee's Labour government began implementing the Beveridge Report proposals in 1946. Many European countries followed Britain's lead, moving from a partial provision of social services to comprehensive coverage.

With the financial crises of the 1970s, the concept of the welfare state came under attack. In Britain, Prime Minister Margaret Thatcher rose to power by criticizing the heavy public expenditure required to distribute social benefits as the "nanny state." Although Thatcher's Conservative government undertook a revision of the National Health Service and social security system in the 1980s, welfare costs continued to rise.

The Assassination of JFK

THE BLACK-AND-WHITE PHOTOS from November 22, 1963, are stark. In one, President John F. Kennedy sits in the backseat of the convertible presidential limousine while on a political trip in Dallas, Texas. Seconds later, he is felled by lethal gunshots; his wife, Jacqueline, clutches him. In a later photo, young John Kennedy, Jr., salutes his father's coffin.

The assassination of the president was a painful shock to the country. Kennedy was handsome, charming, and young. All of that ended at 12:30 P.M., when he was shot three times in the head and throat. Although the president was still alive when he reached Parkland Memorial Hospital, he died 35 minutes after being shot.

Witnesses stated that they saw where the shots had been fired from; police immediately went to the scene. They found three empty cartridge cases on the floor of the Texas School Book Depository, as well as a Mannlicher-Carcano rifle stuck beneath some boxes. That afternoon, Officer J. D. Tippit encountered a man walking down the street; during their conversation, the man pulled out a gun and murdered the policeman. When a witness saw the man duck into a movie theatre, he called the police. They arrested the man—Lee Harvey Oswald.

In the following days, the police were able to tie Oswald to the president's murder through a variety of evidence, including palm prints and eyewitness testimony. On November 24, only two days after Kennedy's death, Oswald was being transferred to county jail. As he was guided through the basement of police headquarters, a man named Jack Ruby suddenly rushed forward and fatally shot him in the abdomen.

Ruby was convicted of murder and given the death sentence; he appealed and his sentence was overturned. Just before his new trial, however, he was hospitalized with pneumonia. He died soon after from cancer of the liver, lungs, and brain.

Thanks to a plethora of conspiracy theories, newly inaugurated President Lyndon B. Johnson set up a commission to investigate who did—and did not—kill Kennedy. Known as the Warren Commission, it decided that Oswald acted alone and fired all the shots. Yet, to this day, conspiracy theories abound regarding the case.

The Globe Theatre

In 1597, the Lord Chamberlain's Men, a theater troupe made up of William Shakespeare, James and Richard Burbage, John Hemmings, Augustine Phillips, Thomas Pope, Will Sly, and G. Bryan, found themselves at a loss. They had always acted at The Theatre, but landlord Giles Allen had informed them that their lease was up. The landlord strongly disapproved of fancy theatrical productions and saw this as a chance to finally kick out the troupe. Allen raised the rent exorbitantly, knowing that these men would never be able to afford it. Shakespeare and his fellow actors were out of ideas, and their rivals, the Admiral's Men, had already grabbed the Rose Playhouse.

The troupe decided to build their own theatre but realized they lacked the funding. Eventually, the Burbages each bought 25 percent of the theatre, and the other actors put in enough to purchase the other 50 percent. Construction on the new building, christened the Globe Theatre, began in 1599 with wooden beams the men pilfered from the demolition of The Theatre. The beams were transported across the River Thames to the Globe's location in the Southwark district.

The Globe Theatre opened that year with a performance of *Julius Caesar,* written by Shakespeare. From the beginning, the Globe was a success.

The Globe was circular with rows of seats, three balconies, and a stage in front. The stage stood five feet off the ground and was 44 feet wide and 26 feet long. Over the entrance of the theater were the words *"Totus mundus agit histrionem,"* or "The whole world is a playhouse." Since there was no lighting, most plays were performed in the afternoon. The acoustics were atrocious; the actors had to practically scream to be heard.

The first roof of the theatre was made out of thatch and only covered a portion of the theatre. On June 29, 1613, the roof caught fire when a cannon fired during a performance of *King Henry VIII.* The Globe burned to the ground. When the theatre was rebuilt in 1614, it had a tile roof.

In 1644, the famous Globe Theatre was taken down. All other London playhouses were closed as well, victims of their time. Oliver Cromwell's Puritan influence was at the forefront now—and it, like the former landlord Allen, disapproved heartily of theatrical performances, regarding them as sinful.

Genocide in Rwanda

THE HUTU AND TUTSI TRIBES, who share the same culture and language and frequently intermarry, inhabit the small, landlocked country of Rwanda. The Hutu, primarily farmers, make up the majority, and the Tutsi, originally herdsmen from northern Africa, are the minority.

When Belgium took control of Rwanda in 1916, it introduced racial classification and issued identity cards for both groups. The Belgians considered the Tutsi superior and provided them with better jobs and educational opportunities. Hutu resentment resulted in the 1959 overthrow of the Tutsi government. Finally, Rwandan independence in 1962 forced hundreds of thousands of Tutsi and moderate Hutu into exile in neighboring countries.

In 1990, the Rwandan Patriotic Front (RPF) made up of Rwandan refugees, launched an offensive against the Hutu government. In 1993, the UN negotiated the Arusha Peace Accord between Rwandan President Habyarimana and the RPF. Hutu extremists regarded this as unacceptable, and unrest continued. On April 6, 1994, Habyarimana and the president of Burundi were killed by a missile attack of unknown origin while they were on Habyarimana's plane.

Blame was laid on the Tutsi. Immediately, the Rwandan Armed Forces and Hutu militia, known as the Interahamwe, put up roadblocks and went house to house, killing Tutsi men, women, and children, as well as moderate Hutu. By the end of the first day, 8,000 people had died. The United Nations Assistance Mission in Rwanda (UNAMIR) Peace Keeping Forces were forbidden to intervene. Despite this, ten Belgian soldiers assigned to guard the moderate Hutu prime minister were tortured and killed. Urged on by radio propaganda, forced by the military, or bribed with food, money, and Tutsi land, ordinary people used machetes and clubs to slaughter their neighbors and relatives. The massacre took place in schools, churches, and in the streets. By the third day, 30,000 people were dead.

Belgium withdrew from UNAMIR. On April 21, the UN Security Council voted unanimously to cut UNAMIR troops from 2,500 to 270. The troops that remained were without equipment or medical supplies. By mid-May, an estimated 500,000 in Rwanda had died.

By mid-July, the Tutsi-led RPF captured the capital city, Kigali. Two million Hutu fled to Zaire (now the Democratic Republic of Congo), where a multi-ethnic government was formed.

Jane Addams and Hull House

JANE ADDAMS was raised to believe that being a woman meant more than marriage and family; it also meant developing a strong work ethic and solid leadership qualities. After graduating, she wanted to further her studies, but her family discouraged her: Being a strong and confident woman was one thing; ignoring marriage and motherhood was another. While travelling in London in 1887, she visited Toynbee House, a settlement home in London's East End that functioned as a neighborhood social works project.

She decided to imitate the Toynbee House project in the slums of Chicago. In 1889, she cofounded Hull House with Ellen Gates Starr. Money poured in, allowing her to offer medical services, childcare, legal aid, and classes for immigrants.

Soon Hull House supported more than 2,000 people a week. Addams realized, however, that poverty would never end if laws were not changed. She began lobbying the state, forcing the examination of child labor, factory inspection, and juvenile justice systems. Addams worked hard to stop the exploitation of immigrants and limit working hours for women. She advocated mandating school for children and implementing industrial safety. She also threw herself into the women's suffrage movement.

Not everything Addams did was popular with the public. When horrible working conditions resulted in the 1886 Haymarket Riot, Addams was attacked for supporting the workers. When donors pulled their money from Hull House, she used her own funds to support it. Addams also worked with the Women's Peace Party, the American Civil Liberties Union, and the National Association for the Advancement of Colored People. She received the 1931 Nobel Peace Prize for her work.

During her lifetime, Addams was called everything from a socialist to an anarchist. But mostly, she's remembered as an inspiration. "[Women] have not wrecked railroads, not corrupted legislatures, nor done many unholy things that men have done," she said, "but then we must remember that we have not had the chance."

The Congress of Vienna

AFTER NAPOLEON'S DEFEAT in April 1814, European nations met in Vienna from November 1, 1814, to June 8, 1815, to redraw boundaries and reestablish a balance of power among the nations. The four main powers in attendance were Austria, Russia, Great Britain, and Prussia. In addition to Spain and France, smaller and less important nations also attended the congress.

Prince Klemens von Metternich represented the Austrians. He was conceited, conservative, and was not an advocate of equality. According to Metternich, men were only equal in the eyes of God and the law. Metternich became the Austrian foreign minister before Napoleon's defeat, and he played a prominent role in the congress as an advocate for the reconstruction of Europe.

Charles de Talleyrand represented the French and served as their protector, opposing delegates who wanted to deprive France of all of its conquered territories. Talleyrand, like Metternich, was unique. He was known to be so self-confident as to be arrogant. When the major powers decided that France, Spain, and the lesser powers would have no voice in making important decisions, Talleyrand convinced the delegates to permit France to have a voice in matters. By having a voice at the congress, Talleyrand influenced many of the decisions and often cast the deciding vote, helping to reestablish France as a major power.

The congress began with the redrawing of European boundaries, an important step in preventing another Napoleonesque state of affairs. France was deprived of all the territory Napoleon had conquered, and Russia was awarded land in Poland. Norway and Sweden were joined, and Swiss neutrality was guaranteed. Some territory was returned to Austria, and Austrians were established as the new rulers of the Germanic Confederation, comprised of 39 nations and four independent city-states.

It was also decided that serfdom would be abolished and municipal self-governments would be established. The most significant accomplishment of the Congress, however, was its ability to negotiate a peace in Europe that lasted 40 years.

POSTSCRIPT

▦ Talleyrand was excommunicated by the pope in 1791, in part for taking an oath to the French Constitution.

Nelson Mandela Freed from Prison

Nelson Mandela was born Rolihlahla Mandela on July 18, 1918, in the village of Mvezo in South Africa. His great-grandfather was a king of the Thembu people, who were later conquered by the British.

In school he was given the Anglo name "Nelson," possibly after British admiral and war hero Horatio Nelson. After all, Rolihlahla means "to pull a branch of a tree" or more loosely, "troublemaker."

And make trouble he did. As a leader of the antiapartheid African National Congress (ANC), Mandela and 150 other activists were arrested in 1956 as part of a series of marathon treason trials that lasted until 1961. That year, Mandela abandoned his commitment to nonviolence and became the leader of Umkhonto we Sizwe, the ANC's armed wing, where he coordinated a campaign of sabotage against military and government installations. After living on the run for more than a year, Mandela was arrested on August 5, 1962, and later sentenced to prison. He would spend most of his 27 years in prison on Robben Island, doing hard labor. While in prison, Mandela took a correspondence course with the University of London External Programme and received a law degree.

Robben Island soon became known as Mandela University. Mandela's influence was so vast that the South African intelligence service hatched a plan to aid him in escaping, only so they could shoot him during recapture. All efforts at diminishing his influence failed, however, and in 1985, South African President Pieter Willem Botha offered Mandela his freedom on the condition that the ANC renounce armed struggle. Mandela spurned the offer: "What freedom am I being offered while the organization of the people remains banned... Only free men can negotiate. A prisoner cannot enter into contracts."

Over the next four years, a series of meetings took place amid growing international opposition to South Africa's racial policies. On February 2, 1990, President Frederik de Klerk legalized the ANC, and shortly thereafter Mandela was released from prison. For the next four years, he led the ANC though multiparty negotiations that resulted in the nation's first multiracial election. In April 1994, the ANC won more than 60 percent of the vote, and Nelson Mandela became the country's first black president.

Johannes Kepler (1571–1630)

JOHANNES KEPLER, who would one day define some of the important scientific laws in the universe, was not sure he would see adulthood. He had terrible eyesight and was so frail that while he was growing up, many believed the only possible occupation for him was in the ministry.

Born in 1571 in Weil der Stadt, Germany, Kepler was six years old when his mother took him outside to show him the Great Comet of 1577. Kepler was fascinated, and he wanted to know more about the universe. After getting degrees in philosophy, mathematics, and astronomy by age 22, he took a job teaching at a Protestant school in Graz. Since the pay was minimal, Kepler supplemented his income by publishing calendars and horoscopes.

In 1596, Kepler wrote his first book, *Mysterium Cosmographicum* (*The Cosmographic Mystery*), which debated the accuracy of the Copernican system. Four years later, Kepler and his family were banished from Graz for refusing to convert to Catholicism. Luckily, Kepler was asked to work in Prague with Danish astronomer Tycho Brahe. When Brahe died a year later, Kepler assumed the position of imperial mathematician and published works on everything from the workings of the eye to why new stars appear. In 1609, his book *Astronomia Nova* (*New Astronomy*) was published, introducing the first of Kepler's two laws about planetary motion. These laws stated that planets move around the sun in an elliptical orbit and that the planets move fastest when closest to the sun.

Kepler was a strong supporter of Galileo's discoveries and published several papers that helped prove the astronomer's theories. In 1613, Kepler wrote about the year Jesus was born, pointing out that Christian calendars were off by five years. His theory that Jesus was actually born in 4 B.C. still stands today.

In 1619, Kepler created a third law that described the connection between the distances of the planets from the sun and their velocities. In 1623, he created the *Rudolphine Tables,* which allowed astronomers to calculate the positions of the planets. Soon after, soldiers attacked his home in Linz, Austria, during the Thirty Years' War. Suddenly, Kepler had neither home nor job; before he could find either, he died at age 59.

POSTSCRIPT

▪ The last book Kepler wrote before dying was *Somnium,* a science fiction novel about a man who traveled to the moon.

World War I and Trench Warfare

Since artillery became an important element in warfare, soldiers have retreated to entrenched positions, but never on a scale to match the dogged trench warfare of World War I.

The war began with sweeping German advances across Belgium and France, but it almost immediately degenerated into gridlock. Following the Battle of the Marne in September 1914, the German army was forced to retreat. Rather than give up the territory they already held, the Germans dug in along the Lower Aisne River, where they deployed machine guns and heavy artillery to defend their position. Unable to break the German trench lines, the Allies followed their example. Soon it was clear that neither side could successfully assault the entrenched position of the other.

Both sides attempted to circumvent the trenches by moving north into Flanders toward the English Channel, the so-called "Race to the Sea." Each continued to dig in and build defensive trenches. By November, 475 miles of continuous trenches stretched from the North Sea to the Swiss border.

The deadlock held until the last few months of the war. Advances were measured in terms of a few miles gained over several months. Every push forward left hundreds of thousands dead and wounded. The 1916 Battle of the Somme cost the Allies more than half a million casualties and pushed the German line back only five miles.

The trenches, generally seven feet deep and six feet wide, were protected on both sides by lines of barbed wire and sandbags. Between them stood no-man's-land, a disputed strip of craters and burned-out buildings, with a width averaging 250 yards. In some places, it was narrow enough that a soldier with a good arm could throw a grenade into the enemy trenches.

Life in the trenches was a mixture of boredom and terror. Neither barbed wire nor sandbags protected those on the line. Approximately one third of the war's casualties occurred in the trenches as a result of constant shell fire and enemy snipers. Many soldiers were killed on their first day as they peered over the parapet of sandbags into no-man's-land.

Disease was a constant problem, carried by the rats and lice that infested the trenches. Poor drainage resulted in the dreaded "trench foot," which could actually rot feet. Battlefields were rancid with the fumes from rotting carcasses in no-man's-land, overflowing latrines, and the remains of poison gas.

The Rosenberg Trial

AMERICAN COMMUNISTS Julius and Ethel Rosenberg gained international notoriety when they were prosecuted for passing atomic weapons secrets to the Soviet Union during World War II.

In 1939, Julius Rosenberg graduated from the City College of New York with a degree in electrical engineering. A year later, he enlisted in the army and was assigned to work with radar equipment. Later, KGB agent Alexandre Feklisov revealed that Julius was recruited by Soviet intelligence in 1943 through his contacts with the Communist Party USA. According to the agent, Julius provided classified reports to the Soviets, including information on the top-secret artillery proximity fuse. He recruited others to work for the Soviets, including his wife Ethel's brother, David Greenglass, who was a machinist at Los Alamos, where the atomic bomb project was underway.

Their hidden life unraveled in 1950, after the arrest of theoretical physicist Klaus Fuchs for passing atomic bomb information to the Soviets during the war. Fuchs pointed to a chain of conspirators that included David Greenglass, who then turned in his sister and brother-in-law. The Rosenbergs were immediately arrested.

Their trial began on March 6, 1951, during which Greenglass testified that in September 1945, Ethel had typed up notes about U.S. nuclear secrets in the family apartment. He also claimed to have given Julius a cross-section drawing of the plutonium bomb. The Rosenbergs denied the charges, but when asked about their Communist activities they invoked their Fifth Amendment right against self-incrimination. On March 29, 1951, they were convicted under the Espionage Act. They were executed by electric chair on June 19, 1953, at the Sing Sing Correctional Facility.

The Rosenbergs' guilt was hotly debated, particularly by the left, but intelligence gathered later confirmed Julius's treachery; Ethel's role is less clear. The imposition of the death penalty also remains controversial. The Rosenbergs were the only two American civilians executed for espionage during the Cold War. Tried amid the anti-Communist hysteria of the Korean War, their sentence has been criticized as overly severe compared to the prison terms given to other offenders.

Austria: A Multinational Empire

IN THE EARLY 19TH CENTURY, the Austrian empire included 11 nationalities: Croats, Czechs, Germans, Italians, Hungarians, Poles, Romanians, Ruthenians, Serbs, Slovaks, and Slovenes. By the 1840s, these minority groups began to aspire to national autonomy.

In March 1848, uprisings in Vienna spread to Prague, Venice, Milan, and Budapest. By October, only the Hungarian revolt remained alive. Austria finally defeated the Hungarian rebels in August 1849 with help from Czar Nicholas, who feared that Hungarian success might set off a similar revolt in Poland, and by minority groups who feared Hungarian domination.

The 1848 defeat of the revolutionaries did not end Austria's problems. In 1860, Emperor Francis Joseph enacted a new constitution, the so-called October Diploma, which ended the policy of centralization that had favored Austria's German population and gave local control to the provincial assemblies. The Hungarians, still the most determined of the nationalist groups, objected because the new policy did not give them enough independence. The Germans, meanwhile, resented their loss of power. Their combined opposition guaranteed the failure of the new constitution.

Alarmed at the efforts of the German population to increase the power of parliament at the expense of the crown and their willingness to use Hungarian disaffection as a political tool, the emperor made concessions to Hungarian nationalists in 1867. The Dual Monarchy of Austria–Hungary established Austria and Hungary as autonomous nations under a common Hapsburg monarch, now emperor of Austria and king of Hungary.

However, the dualist system came under pressure from Austria–Hungary's other ethnic minorities. Attempts to conciliate these groups resulted in renewed German nationalism. Ethnic minorities in Hungary were suppressed under the policy known as "Magyarization." The situation became more volatile following the 1878 Congress of Berlin, during which Serbia, Romania, and Montenegro gained their independence from Turkey but were not granted all the territory they claimed. Austria was given the right to occupy Bosnia–Herzegovina, a decision that Serbian nationalists bitterly opposed.

On June 28, 1914, a Bosnian Serb nationalist assassinated Archduke Franz Ferdinand, heir to the Austro–Hungarian Empire. The archduke's death triggered the tangled alliances that ultimately threw Europe into World War I.

The Parthenon

THE PARTHENON WAS BUILT in the mid-fifth century B.C. as a temple to the goddess Athena. It was built on the Acropolis of Athens under the supervision of the sculptor Phidias. The Parthenon was part of an ambitious building program, which also included the Propylaia, the Erechtheion, and the temple of Athena Nike. The origin of the name *Parthenon* remains unclear. Some scholars believe the term translates roughly to "of the virgins," perhaps referring to the girls chosen to serve the goddess Athena. It may also refer to a cult associated with the temple or possibly to Athena herself.

Called the most perfect Doric temple ever built, the Parthenon is not large by modern standards. Its base measures approximately 225 feet by 100 feet. The Doric columns on the exterior are 34 feet tall. It has 17 columns along the length and 8 along the width, all carefully tapered in order to preserve their graceful appearance.

The Parthenon had a varied history. Although it was originally built as a temple, it was also used as a treasury. In the sixth century A.D., it was used as a Christian church. More than 900 years later, the occupying Ottomans converted it to use as a mosque. The building was severely damaged in 1687 when a bombardment by Venetian forces set off ammunition stored inside. By the early 19th century, it was in ruins.

The Parthenon was decorated with some of the finest ancient sculptures known, including a series of magnificent figures carved into the pediment. Many of these carvings were removed from the ruins of the Parthenon at the beginning of the 19th century by British diplomat Lord Elgin.

The Parthenon Frieze also survived over the years, depicting a procession of 360 nobles accompanied by various animals and gods. Standing only one meter tall, it originally circled the upper walls of the temple for a total length of 160 meters.

Today this national treasure is a major tourist attraction. Its importance in Western civilization is reflected in international efforts to preserve and restore the structure.

The Six-Day War

THE 1948 CREATION OF ISRAEL didn't sit well with the Arab nations of the Middle East, who felt the move had taken over the Palestinian homeland. In retaliation, Arab groups refused to sign peace treaties and continued to sponsor terrorist attacks on the Jewish state.

Israel became a militarized state, mandating that all adults serve in the military, primarily as reservists; women were given noncombat roles. It soon became an international affair: Israel's army was armed with British, French, and American equipment, while Israel's Arab neighbors used Soviet equipment and U.S. tanks.

In mid-May 1967, President Nasser of Egypt demanded that United Nations peacekeeping forces patrolling the Sinai peninsula border with Israel withdraw. He then moved troops into the Sinai, close to the Israeli border. During this time, Israeli intelligence also noticed Syrian activity on the Golan Heights overlooking northern Israel. By May 20, Israel had mobilized its army and was ready for a defensive war. But the Arabs did not attack and Israeli leaders had a tough choice to make: keep its own army of reservists on alert and endanger its economy or stand down and hope that the enemy did not attack.

Then the Egyptians and Jordanians jointly closed the Strait of Tiran to Israeli shipping and demanded that Israel give up its Red Sea port of Eilat. Israeli leaders answered with a preemptive strike to ensure Israeli safety. On the morning of June 5, the Israeli air force hit every major Egyptian airbase within range, wiping out most of Egypt's grounded warplanes. This was followed by a large armored strike across the border into Sinai and the Gaza strip. Three days later, Israel had pushed to the Suez Canal and occupied the entire Sinai Peninsula. Israeli forces also hit Jordanian positions along the West Bank and in Jerusalem. Jordanian troops were pushed back across the Jordan River, and Israel controlled Jerusalem. In all, they inflicted tens of thousands of casualties and destroyed more than 800 Soviet-made tanks.

The fighting continued for the next couple of days. On June 9 and 10, Israeli troops moved onto the Golan Heights, pushing back Syrian troops in entrenched positions and occupying the heights. With these tactics, Israel more than tripled its territory that year, but the cost for doing so was high. Israel's neighbors still refused to sign peace treaties, and the war exacerbated the Palestinian refugee problem. The cycle of Arab–Israeli violence in the Middle East continued.

Czar Nicholas I

NICHOLAS I was never meant to be the czar of Russia. When his brother Alexander I died in 1825, the throne logically would have gone to the next oldest brother, Constantine, but Constantine had renounced the throne to marry a Polish woman. Alexander had indicated in an unpublished document that Nicholas would succeed him as czar, but there was still some confusion.

Taking advantage of this lull in leadership, a group known as the Decembrists staged a mutiny among some of the army units stationed in St. Petersburg. The revolt was put down, though not without incurring loss of life. This shaky start to his reign hardened Nicholas against any changes in his empire, and he effectively halted any progress in Russia for 30 years.

Nicholas was also determined to prevent revolution. In 1833, he declared the policy of "Official Nationalism," composed of Orthodoxy (Russian Orthodox Church supremacy), Autocracy (absolute power of the czar), and Nationality (dedication of the people to the state). Nicholas appointed his most trusted advisors to a series of committees that controlled the vast expanse of Russia. He also controlled the secret police, which investigated every possible hint of revolt. Literature was strictly censured, and travel was restricted. As a result, the country turned inward. Although Nicholas abhorred serfdom, he was afraid to change social structures because he feared revolt by either the peasants or the aristocracy.

Nicholas was constantly on his guard and tried hard to maintain the status quo in Europe. Revolutions in France in 1830 and 1848 worried him. In 1849, Nicholas sent troops to help suppress the rebellion in Hungary and harshly dealt with Polish insurrection in his own empire.

In 1828, the Russians had fought a brief war with Turkey; a second war followed in 1853 when the Turks refused Russian demands to ease restrictions on Orthodox Christians living in their empire, especially in Palestine. The situation escaped Nicholas's control quickly, and it became a war of European proportions when England and France came to the aid of the Ottomans. The conflict, dubbed the Crimean War, was still in progress when Nicholas died in 1855.

Isaac Newton (1642–1727)

AS THE STORY GOES, Sir Isaac Newton discovered the law of gravity by watching an apple fall off a tree. This event occurred in approximately 1666. Yet, it took Newton almost 20 years to interpret the results of that one moment of inspiration. In his first attempt, he tried to demonstrate his theory that the force that keeps the Moon in orbit around Earth is the same force that makes an apple fall from a tree; he failed because he used an inaccurate estimate of the radius of Earth. Frustrated, he dropped the investigation and moved on to the study of light and the construction of telescopes.

Working with sunlight refracted through a prism, Newton determined that white light is made up of rays of different colors and rates of refraction, which led him to construct the first functioning reflecting telescope in 1668.

During this same period, Newton began work on what he called "the method of series and fluxions," now known as calculus, setting out the basic rules of differentiation and integration in a paper published in 1666. Newton developed the method of differential calculus at roughly the same time as Gottfried Leibniz, who was working on the problem in Germany. The competing claims of the two scientists as to which one was the "inventor" of calculus accelerated into a bitter personal dispute; the final verdict was that Newton was the inventor.

In the 1670s, Newton returned to his apple and resumed work on the question of gravity. His 1687 *Philosophia naturalis principia mathematica* (*Mathematical Principles of Natural Philosophy*) demonstrated that gravity is a universal force, applicable to all objects in the universe.

Newton's interests were not limited to optics, mathematics, and physics. He was a student of alchemy, and he believed that hieroglyphics were a magical symbology disguising the lost knowledge of ancient Egypt. Newton also wrote a textual history of the Bible and the writings of the early church fathers demonstrating that the Trinity was a heretical error.

Newton also helped defend the rights of the university against the illegal encroachments of James II in 1687, and he represented Cambridge University in the House of Commons for two terms. He served first as warden and later as master of the Royal Mint from 1696 to 1722. The position of master was traditionally a lackadaisical one; to the annoyance of officials at the mint, Newton took the position seriously and campaigned against corruption and inefficiency.

The Conquest of New Spain

B Y THE REIGN of the emperor Montezuma II in 1502, the Aztecs ruled most of Mexico and were spreading into the Yucatán, demanding tributes from their vassal states including food, textiles, pottery, and, increasingly, humans for sacrifice to the Aztec gods.

In 1518, the governor of Cuba sent Spanish explorer Hernán Cortés on an expedition to the Yucatán peninsula, supported by 600 men. Once they had landed, Cortés declared himself independent of the governor. He founded the city of Veracruz and symbolically scuttled his own boats, before fighting his way inland toward the Aztec capital, gathering allies among the Aztecs' oppressed subjects.

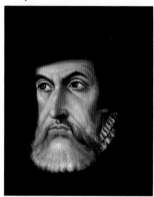

Cortés and his allies reached Tenochtitlán in November 1519. Montezuma, believing Cortés to be an incarnation of the god Quetzacoatl, welcomed the conquistador. In turn, the Spanish captured Montezuma and forced him to make a public declaration of submission to Spain.

Early in 1520, Cortés left to defend Veracruz against a Spanish force sent to relieve him of his command. He returned to Tenochtitlán to find that the Spanish

Hernán Cortés

garrison had massacred Aztec chiefs during a festival and the enraged Aztecs had risen against them. Confronted by the Aztec army under the leadership of Montezuma's brother, the Spanish escaped on the night of June 30, 1520, known in Mexican history as the *Noche Triste,* or Night of Sorrows. The Spanish suffered heavy losses, and Montezuma was killed in the fighting.

Cortés returned the next year with support from his Tlaxcalan allies. After three months of fighting and a devastating plague to which the Aztecs had no resistance, Tenochtitlán fell.

Cortés razed the city, building Mexico City in its place as the capital of the colony of New Spain. Appointed governor and captain-general of the new colony, Cortés brought the Aztec lands, Honduras, and much of El Salvador and Guatemala under Spanish control over the next five years. Political rivals feared Cortés would establish an independent kingdom in Mexico, and so the Spanish crown gradually eroded his title and estates. Cortés returned to Spain in 1540, where he died poor.

Lyndon Johnson's Great Society

IN THE 1964 PRESIDENTIAL ELECTION, Lyndon Johnson beat Republican Senator Barry Goldwater, carrying 44 of 50 states. That overwhelming voter mandate, and the fact that he had been in Congress since 1937 and knew how to play the legislative game, gave Johnson the confidence to launch the most ambitious domestic agenda since Franklin Roosevelt's New Deal: The Great Society. But whereas the New Deal was born during the Depression, Johnson's Great Society was put forth at a time of domestic prosperity. "The Great Society," he said, "rests on abundance and liberty for all."

In 1965, Johnson submitted 87 bills to the first session of the 89th Congress. Since many of its members had ridden into office on his coattails, Congress passed 84 of the bills. His plan for reform was underway. From Johnson's group of 14 task forces came a blizzard of new programs designed to transform American society: federal scholarships for college students, funding for schools serving needy children, programs for research into life-threatening diseases, Medicare, and Medicaid.

New federal agencies also emerged, such as the departments of Housing and Urban Development and Transportation, the National Foundation of the Arts and Humanities, and the Administration on Aging. The 1964 Economic Opportunity Act was his "war on poverty." It created antipoverty programs including the Office of Economic Opportunity to oversee VISTA (a domestic Peace Corps) and a Job Corps for school dropouts. Johnson's emphasis on civil rights resulted in the landmark 1964 Civil Rights Act, which banned discrimination against minorities in employment and in places of public accommodation. The War on Poverty also produced other antidiscrimination safeguards, the Voting Rights Act of 1965, the 1968 Civil Rights Act, and other legislative efforts. To help the environment, the Endangered Species Act and numerous other laws were passed.

Federal spending on health, education, welfare, and Social Security more than doubled between 1965 and 1970. Unfortunately, while Johnson was presiding over this massive domestic initiative, he was also steadily expanding the Vietnam War. Ultimately, the Great Society became tangled up in the furor over the war.

POSTSCRIPT

■ Johnson first formally used the term *Great Society* in a May 1964 speech at the University of Michigan when he said, "We will begin to set our course toward the Great Society."

Ali Shari'ati (1933–1977)

NOT MANY PEOPLE outside of Iran have heard of Ali Shari'ati. Still, he is considered the "ideological father" of the 1979 Iranian Islamic Revolution.

Shari'ati was born on November 24, 1933, in the village of Kahak in eastern Iran. His mother was such a devout Muslim that one of his childhood friends said he could never remember seeing her face. Shari'ati was first exposed to political events while he attended Teachers' Training College. He also attended lectures at the Centre for the Propagation of Islamic Truths. It was here that speakers, including his father, nationalist leader Aqa Muhammad Taqi Shari'ati, demonstrated that Islam offered solutions to modern political, economic, and social problems.

By 1962, Shari'ati was advocating overthrowing the Iranian regime. After he received his doctorate in sociology from Sorbonne University in Paris in 1963, he returned to Iran. He was working as a teacher when he was imprisoned for being involved in political activities in Paris. After his release in 1965, he taught at the University of Mashhad, where his extremely popular courses reinterpreted Islam for a generation that had considered the ideology irrelevant. Using a sociological framework, he showed how Islamic thought could be applied in contemporary society.

He was fond of making sweeping judgments, and his view of Western society was typical of his condemnation of modern Europe. "Come friends, let us abandon Europe," he said. "Let us cease this nauseating, apish imitation of Europe. Let us leave behind this Europe that always speaks of humanity but destroys human beings wherever it finds them."

The government, threatened by the burgeoning popularity of his courses, shut them down. Shari'ati soon became the principal speaker at the Houssein-e Ershad Religious Institute in northern Tehran, which had been established in order to reverse the Westernization of Iranian youths and return them to Islam.

In 1973, Iranian police surrounded the institute and arrested many of its participants, including Shari'ati. An 18-month stint in prison ended in March 1975 due to international pressure. Under strict surveillance and unable to publish his writings, he moved to England in mid-1977. Shari'ati was found dead in his London apartment three weeks later. It has been speculated that he was killed by SAVAK, the Iranian secret police.

Shari'ati's revolutionary theories are considered the impetus for the Ayatollah Khomeini's 1979 overthrow of the Shah's government.

Picasso Paints *Guernica*

A ROUND 1901, Spanish-born painter Pablo Picasso set up his studio in the Montmartre district of Paris. Already a master of traditional form, he quickly absorbed the Impressionist influences of Toulouse-Lautrec, Degas, and Vuillard before moving on to develop his own idiom.

In 1907, Picasso broke with tradition with *Les Demoiselles d'Avignon,* a painting that combined angular forms inspired by African sculpture with the beginnings of what would become Cubism. The study features figures and surface alike that are broken into angular facets, creating a three-dimensional effect without the use of perspective.

A study for Guernica

Picasso joined forces with Georges Braque in 1909; together the two painters explored the implications of Cubism through its various phases, using the innovative technique of collage to move beyond the limitations of paint. Their collaboration ended in 1914 when Braque was drafted to serve in the First World War.

Possibly the most important of Picasso's paintings was the immense mural *Guernica* (1937). Painted for the Pavilion of the Spanish Republic at the 1937 Paris International Exposition, the painting was inspired by the bombing of the Basque city of Guernica. Picasso did not illustrate the event; instead he evoked the horror of war using a series of images heavy with cultural resonance: the Pietà, the Statue of Liberty's lamp, a broken sword. In *Guernica,* the anatomical distortions and fragmentations of Cubism move beyond technical virtuosity to a powerful metaphor for the confusion and pain of war.

Picasso supported the Republicans in the Spanish Civil War and he left Spain following Franco's victory. Although he was condemned by the Nazis as one of the reviled "degenerate artists," Picasso remained in Paris throughout World War II. In 1944, after the liberation of Paris, he joined the Communist Party and became active in the Peace Movement.

More famous during his lifetime than any artist before or since, Picasso remained productive and creative in the years after the war. During his lifetime, he produced an estimated 20,000 paintings, sculptures, etchings, and ceramics, irrevocably changing the face of 20th-century art.

The Americans with Disabilities Act

Duringing the 1960s, many different issues regarding race, religion, and sex were debated and discussed; the result was the Civil Rights Act of 1964. The law made discrimination based on race, religion, gender, national origin, and other characteristics illegal.

A little more than 25 years later, President George H. W. Bush signed another act to expand protections against discrimination. This act, the 1990 Americans with Disabilities Act (ADA), was written to help those who are officially defined as having "a physical or mental impairment that substantially limits one or more major life activities." In effect, the act aims to make certain that those with disabilities are not denied any opportunities or basic rights. The determination of disability is made on a case-by-case basis.

The ADA is divided into three introductory sections and five titles. The first title deals with employment and outlines how people, employment agencies, or labor organizations cannot discriminate against any qualified person just because he or she has a disability. This applies to everything from job application procedures and hiring to worker's compensation and job training.

The second title deals with public services providing access to the disabled, including public transportation. As it states, "no qualified individual with a disability shall, by reason of such disability, be excluded from participation in or be denied the benefits of services, programs, or activities of a public entity, or be subjected to discrimination by any such entity."

The third title of the act focuses on public accommodations, stating that a person cannot be discriminated against in public places such as hotels, stores, schools, and restaurants. The fourth act deals with telecommunications and ensures that equal services are provided to people who are deaf, hard of hearing, or have speech impairments. This part of the law led to the development of Video Relay Service (VRS) calls and Telecommunication Relay Services (TRS), which gives disabled people the ability to use the telephone to communicate with others. According to one statistic, in 2006, the Federal Communications Commission (FCC) estimated that VRS calls receive an average of two million minutes per month. The fifth title, meanwhile, deals with several miscellaneous provisions and technical issues.

Together, the titles serve to show a growing sensitivity in American society to a wide variety of minorities and challenged persons.

John Stuart Mill Publishes *On Liberty*

BORN IN 1806, John Stuart Mill was educated primarily by his father, James, who saw his son as a sort of heir to his philosophical throne. James and his friend Jeremy Bentham led a group known as Philosophical Radicals, or Utilitarians, who expounded many of the ideas that Mill would later articulate. They particularly discussed the notion that the greatest happiness of the greatest number of people should be the central goal of any system of government. As an adult, Mill worked as an examiner at the British East India Company. Fortunately, the demands of his position were such that he had enough spare time to devote to his first love—political philosophy.

On Liberty is arguably Mill's most important and influential work. In it, he attacks "the tyranny of the majority," an expression he borrowed from French thinker Alexis de Tocqueville. For Mill, mindless commitment to majority rule that fails to protect minority rights is a form of tyranny no less oppressive than absolute monarchy. Indeed, he argues, it can lead to a bleak conformity.

For Mill, the basic principle that societal and governmental relationships to individuals should be based on is the "harm principle." Stated simply, every person (except for children or those living in primitive cultures) has the right to act as he or she wants, so long as the action harms no one else. As Mill put it, in a ringing endorsement of individual rights, "In the part [of human conduct] which merely concerns himself, his independence is, of right, absolute. Over himself, over his own body and mind, the individual is sovereign."

A powerful corollary to Mill's concept of individual sovereignty is his impassioned defense of freedom of expression. He was convinced that without freedom of expression there could be no human progress; even ideas considered wrong by a majority might have a grain of truth in them. Above all, free discussion allows people to examine their beliefs through debate, thus avoiding mindless dogma. As he notes in *On Liberty,* "We...recognize the necessity to the mental well-being of mankind (on which all their other well-being depends) of freedom of opinion, and freedom of the expression of opinion."

POSTSCRIPT

■ Mill's father taught him Greek at age three and Latin at age eight.

Augustus Reigns Supreme

AUGUSTUS WAS BORN GAIUS OCTAVIUS, or Octavian, in 63 B.C. Julius Caesar, who did not have a son of his own, adopted Octavian (whose mother was Caesar's niece) and prepared him for a career in politics. When Caesar was assassinated in 44 B.C., Octavian allied with Mark Antony and Marcus Aemilius Lepidus in a bloody civil war. Antony was married to Octavian's sister but had an affair with Cleopatra, queen of Egypt. This led to another civil war that left Octavian in control of Rome.

Octavian was determined not to repeat the mistakes that led to the civil wars. He decided to retain the republican institutions of Rome; in 27 B.C. he announced that he would restore the republic and give up all of his power. However, the Senate wished that he still serve as Rome's *princeps*, or first citizen, and conferred upon him several titles and positions, including commander of the army. Octavian was now called Augustus, which means "revered," and he effectively controlled the three provinces where most of the army was stationed. In effect, Augustus had become de facto emperor with the final word in any major legislation.

His generals extended the empire's boundaries to the Danube River and consolidated Asia Minor. Historians have labeled the period of relative peace and prosperity during Augustus's reign the *Pax Romana,* or Roman Peace. During this time, Augustus initiated a massive road-building program, revised the Roman tax structure, built several new public buildings in Rome, and refurbished many temples. He also created the Praetorian Guard to ensure his personal safety. Between 19 and 16 B.C., he championed the Julian Laws to help strengthen Roman family life. A census taken in A.D. 14, the year of Augustus's death, counted nearly five million Romans, an increase of more than 800,000 from the 28 B.C. census.

In theory, it was up to the Senate and the people to choose a successor after Augustus died. However, he realized that if this were to occur, there would likely be another civil war. So, to ensure a smooth transition of leadership, Augustus designated his stepson Tiberius to succeed him upon his death.

Claude Lévi-Strauss (1908–present)

A FTER SPENDING YEARS AMONG the various indigenous peoples of Brazil, anthropologist Claude Gustave Lévi-Strauss (not to be confused with the Levi-Strauss of blue jeans fame) came to an important conclusion: All of mankind was essentially created equal. According to Lévi-Strauss, a scholar of Western civilization was no more important or brilliant than a tribal leader in the rainforest. Just because a society was primitive, he believed, did not make it any less valuable. As he wrote in *The Savage Mind,* "A primitive people is not a backward or retarded people; indeed it may possess a genius for invention or action that leaves the achievements of civilized peoples far behind."

Lévi-Strauss was born in Brussels on November 28, 1908, but he grew up primarily in France. After getting a degree in sociology, he taught at Brazil's Sao Paula University from 1935 to 1939. There, he began spending time with native peoples, studying their culture, behavior, and traditions. From 1939 to 1941, Lévi-Strauss found himself in an entirely different environment: the French army. Soon after his service ended, he fled Europe to escape the Nazi invasion. He spent most of the years during World War II in New York City, at first teaching at the New School for Social Research and later becoming the French embassy's cultural attaché.

In 1955, Lévi-Strauss garnered critical praise for his travelogue-meets-philosophy, *Tristes Tropiques,* which detailed his travels abroad in the '30s. Based on what he learned during his time in Brazil, he published *The Savage Mind* in 1962. The book featured a blend of autobiography and philosophy, and it further established his Structuralism theory about the similarity and equality of mankind, or, as he called it, "the search for unsuspected harmonies." He showed how all minds, regardless of culture, education, or societal structure, are just as rich, complex, and scientific as all other minds. This was a rather radical idea for the time, as Western culture prided itself on being superior to others, especially to those such as Brazil's indigenous peoples. "No contact with savage Indian tribes has ever daunted me more than the morning I spent with an old lady swathed in woolies who compared herself to a rotting herring encased in a block of ice," he wrote.

Lévi-Strauss's writings resulted in a number of awards as well as honorary doctoral degrees from Oxford, Yale, Harvard, and Columbia. As he said, "The scientist is not a person who gives the right answers; he is one who asks the right questions."

Filippo Brunelleschi (1377–1446)

B Y THE EARLY 1400s, Filippo Brunelleschi was already a master goldsmith. While teaching at a local art school in 1401, Brunelleschi entered a competition to design bronze doors for the Florence Baptistery. Unfortunately, he lost to famed sculptor Lorenzo Ghiberti.

Disappointed, Brunelleschi turned to architecture. He went to Rome to study the architecture of the ancient Romans, accompanied by his close friend Donatello. There Brunelleschi found inspiration.

Brunelleschi was also interested in mathematics: In 1415, he redis-covered the principles of linear perspective using mirrors. He understood that all parallel lines in a plane should converge on a single vanishing point on a canvas. In fact, Brunelleschi's principles on perspective still continue to inspire others.

The dome at Santa Maria del Fiore

Brunelleschi's greatest fame, how-ever, came from his construction work in Florence. His first com-mission was the Ospedale degli Innocenti, the city's Foundling Hospital. With its columns and capitals, it was the first building in Florence obvi-ously based on classical antiquity. In 1418, he entered another competi-tion: the daunting task of constructing the dome on the nearly finished Santa Maria del Fiore, Florence's great cathedral. This building had been under construction for more than a century, and its builders were stymied by how to add a dome over the octagonal baptistery. Again, the competitors were Brunelleschi and Ghiberti. This time, Brunelleschi won.

To support the dome's weight, Brunelleschi designed a double self-supporting shell and rib structure. Brick was laid in a rotating herringbone pattern. To lift materials to the dome, Brunelleschi designed a counter-weight device that enabled a single ox to lift a load where previously six would have been required. By the time he died in 1446, the dome was almost finished.

Brunelleschi also designed other churches and buildings in Florence, including the Basilica di San Lorenzo di Firenze and Santo Spirito di Firenze. His classical architecture was widely copied by other great archi-tects such as Palladio and Alberti.

The North Atlantic Treaty Organization

Ever since George Washington's farewell address warning against "entangling alliances," America had a history of wariness of excessive involvement in European affairs—unless it was in self-defense.

After World War II, tensions between the Communist world headed by the Soviet Union and non-Communist nations led by the United States became increasingly strained. In 1947, after the USSR made threatening moves toward Turkey and Communist rebels posed a threat to Greece, President Harry S. Truman pushed a substantial military and economic aid bill for the two countries through Congress. In 1948, the creation of West Germany out of the American, British, and French occupation zones led the Soviet Union to blockade West Berlin, which was in the Soviet occupation zone. The United States responded with a successful airlift of supplies to the non-Communist zones in Berlin. That year, a Communist government also took power in Czechoslovakia.

The threat of continued Communist expansion in Europe posed a real quandary for the United States. Because the United States demobilized the vast majority of its military forces after World War II—and the USSR did not—the Soviets held a huge advantage in ground forces. The United States was reluctant to rely solely on its nuclear weapons to defend Europe. Truman saw the need for some kind of military alliance among Atlantic nations to deter potential Communist aggression—a view shared by most non-Communist nations.

Twelve nations formed the North Atlantic Treaty Organization: the United States, Canada, the United Kingdom, Belgium, Denmark, France, Iceland, Italy, Luxembourg, the Netherlands, Norway, and Portugal. Greece and Turkey became members in 1952, while West Germany joined in 1955. In a none-too-subtle message to the USSR, Article V of the North Atlantic Treaty, signed April 4, 1949, states, "An armed attack against one or more members . . . shall be considered an attack against them all." In response, the Soviet Union and its eastern European client states established the Warsaw Pact, a kind of mirror image of NATO.

While many factors, including a nuclear stalemate between the United States and the USSR, prevented a Communist attack on Western Europe, NATO was undoubtedly an important one. In fact, until the USSR collapsed in the early '90s, NATO's primary focus was the containment of communism.

The Assassination of Caesar

DURING HIS RISE TO POLITICAL POWER, Gaius Julius Caesar played to the citizens of Rome. Although he was aristocratic, Caesar readily identified with the masses and won their approval. During the reign of the dictator Sulla, one of Caesar's supporters brought a law before the People's Assembly that returned the right to elect the *pontifex maximus,* or high priest to the assembly, taking the power from the Senate, which had been abolished by Sulla. When this law was passed and Caesar won the election, it meant that the people had elected him—and not the Senate. In fact, most of the Senate abhorred Caesar and mistrusted his motives.

The murder of Caesar (center)

Caesar became governor of three provinces in southern Gaul and northern Italy. For eight years (58–51 B.C.), Caesar campaigned in Gaul and Britain, annexing most of modern-day France and Belgium. Following his victories there, the Senate ordered him back to Rome without his troops. Caesar feared that his life was in danger, and so he crossed into Italy with his troops. Caesar occupied the city with relative ease in 49. It wasn't until the great Roman Civil War was over in 45 that Caesar was left in firm control of the Republic.

Caesar worked to eliminate injustices perpetrated on the common people, created jobs for his veterans, reformed the calendar, made plans to drain marshes and build new roads, and created other public works. The Senate nominated him to be dictator for ten years in order to allow him to carry out his plans for reform. To further honor Caesar, the month of Quintilis was renamed Julius.

But much of the Senate was angry that one man had so much power. Hoping to save the Republic, they hatched a plan to kill Caesar. On March 15, 44 B.C., the infamous "Ides of March," a group of senators duped Caesar into accompanying them to view a document. When he was alone with them, they stabbed him multiple times. His death ignited a civil war that left Caesar's adopted son Octavian (later known as Augustus) in control of the Roman Empire.

Giussepe Mazzini
and Italian Nationalism

IN THE EARLY 1800s, Italy was a series of patchwork states primarily under Austrian control. Giussepe Mazzini, however, believed in a unified Italy. In 1830, he joined the *Carbonari* (charcoal burners), a secret Italian political society. Mazzini was arrested and spent six months in prison, which only strengthened his nationalistic feelings. On his release, he went to exile in France, quit the Carbonari, and founded *La giovine Italia* (Young Italy), a new political society dedicated to unifying Italy as a republic. Mazzini had become one of the founders of the *Risorgimento*— the Italian resurgence.

Mazzini fled after the failure of a series of revolts he orchestrated. He wound up nearly destitute in London in 1837. In 1844, after another failed attempt at revolution, it was revealed in the British House of Commons that Mazzini's private correspondence had been opened by authorities. Mazzini received sympathy and support from British liberals.

In 1848, the German states, Poland, France, Italy, and the Hapsburg Empire were all engulfed in nationalistic revolts. The year began with the people of Milan rebelling against Austrian rule. This seemed the beginning of an Italian uprising, and Mazzini hurried to Milan, but Austrian troops eventually restored order. Meanwhile, nationalistic revolutions were burning like brush fires all over the Italian peninsula in cities including Venice, Sicily, and Bologna.

In November 1848, the papal minister was assassinated in Rome, causing Pope Pius IX to flee the city. A republic was declared in Rome in January 1849. Mazzini went there, and by the end of March, he had become a government leader. He donated part of his salary to hospitals, ate in secondrate restaurants, gave some of the Catholic Church's lands to peasants, and introduced prison and insane asylum reforms, freedom of the press, and secular education. But French President Louis Napoleon wanted the support of Catholics and sent troops to restore the pope. By July, Rome had fallen; Mazzini once more went into exile. Though he continued to call for revolution, his moment had passed. Italy was unified as a kingdom in 1861, but it was a far cry from Mazzini's republican government.

POSTSCRIPT

Mazzini refused a seat in the Turin parliament in 1865 because it required an oath of allegiance to the monarchy.

Sun Yat-sen (1866–1925)

Born in 1866 to a Chinese peasant family, Sun Yat-sen was a precocious student and joined his brother in Hawaii to study. He later moved to Hong Kong to study medicine, graduating in 1892. During the 1880s, he also converted to Christianity.

Troubled by China's backwardness and the policies of its conservative Qing government, Sun turned from medicine to political activism. He originally backed the institution of a Western-style constitutional monarchy, but soon he turned to advocating the establishment of a republic. In 1894, he founded the Revive China Society as an instrument for reform.

His philosophy centered on the "Three People's Principles": The Chinese government should be run by Chinese (nationalism); the government should be democratically elected (democracy); and the government should correct inequities in wealth and land ownership (equalization).

In 1895, Sun fled China after a failed coup against the government. He spent the next 16 years in exile in Europe, the United States, Canada, and Japan. During that time, he worked to unite dissident groups and raised money to fund revolutionary activities in China.

His moment arrived on October 10, 1911, when a military uprising at Wuchang precipitated the downfall of imperial rule in China. Sun finally returned home. On December 29, representatives from the provinces elected him provisional president of the Republic of China.

Sun believed in "rule by the people" based on "the four powers of the people." These powers included the right to vote, the right to recall, the power to initiate legislation, and the power to amend laws. However, he felt these powers should be initiated gradually as the Chinese progressed toward democratic self-rule. Democracy would be preceded by the "Three Stages of Revolution": military dictatorship while the old rule was dismantled; "political tutelage" while the people learned about the workings of democracy and gained experience; and finally, full democracy.

Despite Sun's hopes, China remained in turmoil, torn between warlords, the army, and divided loyalties. Sun fell out of power as the dictatorial Yuan Shikai seized control. Over the next decade, Sun cofounded the Kuomintang, or National People's Party, and served as its first leader.

Although Sun did not realize his political dream, his contributions were immense. Today, he is revered by both the People's Republic of China and Taiwan as the "Father of the Nation."

The Great Indian Mutiny

IN THE MID-19TH CENTURY, British officers in northern India began to notice unrest among the Indian soldiers known as *sepoys,* who dominated the enlisted ranks of the East India Company's army.

Many of the requirements for British soldiers meant those sepoys, if they were Hindu, would lose caste. For example, their new Enfield rifles used cartridges that had to be opened by biting the end. Rumors circulated that the cartridges were greased with cow and pig fat, which made them a religious abomination to both Hindu and Muslim sepoys. They were reassured that the cartridges were greased with beeswax and vegetable oil, but it made no difference. Rumors continued to spread that the British wanted to destroy the sepoys' caste, making it easier to convert them to Christianity.

Groups outside the army had their own reasons for discontent. Reforms that outlawed traditions including suttee and child marriage and that allowed converts from Hinduism to inherit family property were seen as attacks on traditional law. An aggressive policy of annexing Indian states created resentment among the nobility who had traditionally supported the British. Land reform in Bengal displaced landholders.

On May 9, 1857, the discontent boiled over in Meerut. Eighty-five sepoys who refused to use the Enfield cartridges were tried, stripped of their uniforms, and put in irons. The next day, three regiments stormed the jail, killed the British officers and their families, and marched toward Delhi, where the last Mughal emperor, Bahadur Shah II, held his title as a British pensioner. Two days later, the mutineers entered Delhi, demanding an audience with the emperor. Once in the palace, they killed all the Englishmen. At first, Indian regiments in Delhi continued to take orders from their British officers, but they soon joined the mutineers in occupying the old Mughal capital. Bahadur Shah was named as their leader.

The violence spread through northern India as leaders whose power had been threatened by British policies transformed a local mutiny into organized resistance. With only 40,000 European troops in India, the British held the subcontinent largely because the Punjab remained loyal. By December 1858, the mutiny was over, though bands of mutineers continued guerrilla actions well into the following year. The mutiny led to the passage of the India Act of 1858, which transferred the possessions of the East India Company to the British Crown.

The Rise of Skyscrapers

THE WORD *skyscraper* was coined in the 1880s to describe the tall office buildings created in Chicago in the last two decades of the 19th century. Rapidly adopted by other cities, the skyscraper defined the 20th century as clearly as the cathedral defined the medieval world.

Previously, the height of buildings was limited by the ability of masonry walls to support not only their own weight, but also that of the floors above. Early tall buildings, such as the 16-story Monadnock Block designed by Chicago architects Burnham and Root, used masonry load-bearing walls that needed dramatically thickened bases to support the weight of the floors.

The development of skeleton framing and curtain walls, in which a metal frame supports a strong but thin outer wall, ended the structural limitation on building heights. Lighter frames meant the doors and windows no longer had to be minimized to maintain the strength of the wall, allowing for larger expanses of glass. Improvements in foundations, plumbing, lighting, and ventilation all made increases in building height possible. Elisha Otis's invention of the safety elevator in 1853 made higher buildings practical as well as possible. The Home Insurance Building, constructed in Chicago in 1884–1885, was the first building to use true skyscraper construction.

The earliest skyscrapers were 10 or 12 stories tall and built with an eye to efficient use that created handsome structures almost by accident. The iconic "Chicago window," the three-part projecting window responsible for the lively facade of many of the early buildings, was designed to capture as much light and air as possible.

Architect Louis Sullivan was the first to grasp the aesthetic possibilities of the new technology. Coining the phrase "form follows function," Sullivan abandoned classical principles of composition and expressed the framework of the skyscraper in the facades of his buildings. His buildings emphasized the "loftiness" of the skyscraper, which he felt should be "a proud and soaring thing."

The second generation of tall buildings returned to the architectural vocabulary of historical styles, encasing the steel frame in a Gothic or classical stone facade. The results were often spectacular: the Gothic style of the Woolworth Building in New York, the Art Deco splendor of the Chrysler Building, and the massive Empire State Building. This golden age of skyscrapers continued until the Great Depression curtailed construction.

The Transcontinental Railroad

On July 1, 1862, President Abraham Lincoln signed the Pacific Railway Act. This piece of legislation authorized the construction of a transcontinental railroad that would stretch from Nebraska to California.

The United States had embraced railroad building in the 1830s; by 1850, the call went out for a railroad to link the east and west coasts.

Under the Pacific Railway Act, two new rail companies were created to undertake the daunting task of planning and construction. The Central Pacific would start in Sacramento, while the Union Pacific would build west from Omaha. The rail companies would also receive government subsidies to help with the construction.

The two rail companies meet in Utah

The Central Pacific had the hardest job—the construction gangs, which included thousands of Irish and Chinese immigrants, had to tackle the Sierra Nevada Mountains. Using picks and shovels, mule-drawn carts, and black gunpowder, construction inched slowly forward but was hampered by heavy snows in the mountains. The men dug 14 tunnels and constructed 40 miles of wooden sheds to protect stretches of track from snowfall.

Out on the Great Plains, the gangs working for the Union Pacific made rapid progress over the level terrain, but they had to contend with hostile Native Americans who did not take kindly to the "iron horses" coming through their territory. By November 1867, the Union tracks approached the Black Hills in the Wyoming Territory, where a route was finally located through the granite hills to the flat land beyond. A year later, track had been laid through the Rocky Mountains and into Utah.

By the spring of 1869, both companies had entered Utah and were actually laying track parallel to each other. The rivalry had become bitter. Congress intervened and stipulated that the two companies would unite their track at Promontory Point, just north of the Great Salt Lake. The official ceremony took place on May 10, when a golden spike was hammered into place.

The Glorious Revolution

THE GLORIOUS REVOLUTION, also known as the English Revolution of 1688, ended the struggle between Catholics and Protestants for control of the English throne. The event marked the end of Stuart attempts at despotism and confirmed the constitutional importance of Parliament.

It all began when Oliver Cromwell's Roundheads executed Charles I, the second Stuart ruler of England, in 1649. James II was the second son of Charles I. In the late 1660s, he became a Catholic like his father. Between 1679 and 1681, Parliament made three attempts to exclude him from the succession, but he succeeded to the throne without opposition when his brother, Charles II, died in 1685.

Within three years, James had alienated every important segment of England's political arena. In defiance of the law, he appointed Roman Catholics to important positions in the army, universities, church, and government. His two Declarations of Indulgence, issued in 1687 and 1688, suspended penal laws against Roman Catholics and dissenters and led to widespread protest and defiance.

Anxiety about the future of English Protestantism intensified with the birth of James's son James Stuart, later known as the "Old Pretender." Confronted with a Catholic heir to the throne, Whigs and Tories united to invite the king's son-in-law, the Protestant William of Orange, to invade England. William landed with a Dutch army in November; deserted by most of his officers, James fled to France.

Parliament offered the vacant throne to William and his wife (James's daughter Mary). The offer, however, was dependent on their acceptance of a Declaration of Rights. Incorporated into a subsequent Bill of Rights, the Declaration established principles of parliamentary supremacy and denounced James II for attempting to subvert the Protestant religion and the fundamental laws of the realm. The couple became joint sovereigns as William III and Mary II in February 1689.

In an attempt to regain his throne, James landed in Ireland with French troops in March 1690. He was defeated at the Battle of the Boyne in July and returned to France, where he remained in exile until his death in 1701. His grandson, known as Bonnie Prince Charlie, would later lead an unsuccessful uprising in the Scottish highlands from 1745 to 1746.

The Vietnam War

SINCE THE 1880s, France had ruled French Indochina, including Vietnam, Laos, and Cambodia. When Ho Chi Minh and his Viet Minh fighters (who had been battling France for Vietnam's indepen-

dence) appeared to be Communist, the United States decided to support the French. Their 1954 defeat at Dien Bien Phu ended France's Indochina Empire; the United States was afraid that all Southeast Asian countries would fall to Communism.

Vietnam was divided: North Vietnam became Communist under Ho, and South Vietnam anti-Communist under Ngo Dinh Diem. Under presidents Eisenhower and Kennedy, America poured economic and military aid into South Vietnam. The combination of Diem's overthrow and death in a 1963 coup and Kennedy's assassination dropped the Vietnam problem in President Lyndon B. Johnson's lap. Johnson ratcheted the number of American troops in Vietnam up to 70,000 and conducted a bombing campaign. In 1965, he sent 175,000 more troops to Vietnam.

The war's escalation jump-started U.S. antiwar protests. Still, by early 1967, America had 400,000 troops in Vietnam. U.S. troops were finding it difficult to fight a guerrilla war in a jungle terrain; America had the technological edge, but the enemy was resourceful and resilient.

More troops were needed, but the request caused public support for the war to wane. In January 1968, the Communists launched the Tet Offensive. Although not a military success, it showed that the Communists were ready and strong enough to fight indefinitely against America. After Richard Nixon became president in 1968, he shifted more responsibility for fighting to the South Vietnamese (a process called *Vietnamization*) and escalated the war into neighboring Cambodia. The escalation caused massive protests on college campuses in 1970.

Finally, in January 1973, U.S. Secretary of State Henry Kissinger negotiated the Paris Peace Accords, ending a war in which more than 58,000 American troops had died. In 1975, the North invaded South Vietnam. The next year, the two halves united as the Socialist Republic of Vietnam.

Vatican II

CHANGE SOMETIMES COMES SLOWLY, but when it does come it can be substantial. When the Second Ecumenical Council of the Vatican, or Vatican II, met more than 40 years ago, the resulting modernizations rocked the church and its believers.

Only three months after Pope John XXIII was elected in 1958, he announced his intention for the Church Council to gather because he wanted, as he phrased it, to "throw open the windows of the Church so that we can see out and the people can see in." Pope John wanted to modernize the church and reach out to become more relevant to younger generations.

It took almost three years for the meeting preparations to be made. When the Council finally met on October 11, 1962, it had almost 1,000 proposed constitutions and decrees submitted for consideration. The general sessions took place over four successive years in St. Peter's Basilica. Attendees included 2,908 Council Fathers. An invitation was also issued to Protestant, Orthodox, and other non-Catholic leaders to be part of this event—a first in Vatican history. The decisions made during this time modernized the Catholic Church and identified the church as "people of God" whose mission was to address the problems and hopes of the world as a whole. Upon the death of John XXIII in 1963, Pope Paul VI was elected and continued the Council.

The changes incurred by Vatican II made Catholicism more approachable. Altars were turned around to allow priests to face their congregations, and Masses were given in a region's common language rather than in Latin. Sacraments were updated or simplified, and an emphasis was placed on making connections and establishing relationships within the community, regardless of religious beliefs.

When Vatican II finally came to an end, a total of 16 documents were approved, including the Constitution of the Sacred Liturgy, the Declaration on Religious Freedom, and the Decree on the Ministry and Life of Priests. *Nostra Aetate,* or Declaration on the Relationship of the Church to Non-Christian Religions, was particularly controversial for its statement that, as a people, the Jews at the time of Christ—and today—weren't to blame for the death of Jesus. Meanwhile, the Pastoral Constitution on the Church in the Modern World was noted for its efforts in regards to campaigning for peace, avoiding nuclear war, helping underdeveloped nations, and finding an acceptable means of birth control.

The Enlightenment

THE 18TH-CENTURY philosophical and scientific movement known as the Enlightenment challenged traditional assumptions about the church, state, monarchy, education, and social institutions.

Rooted in the Scientific Revolution of the 17th century, the Enlightenment began in France with the *philosophes.* This diverse group of writers, scientists, and philosophers shared a belief in the supremacy of reason and the perfectibility of humanity. The ability to apply reason to human concerns was the common thread of the most important themes of the Enlightenment: the ideals of progress, deism, and religious tolerance.

The Enlightenment's emphasis on reason contained an inherent challenge to the status quo. Deists argued that the creator of the universe, seen through the lens of Newton's theory of gravitation, was a master mathematician who set the stars in place but did not interfere in human affairs. According to this belief, if God did not interfere, then the church was based on superstition and the credulity of individuals. If God did interfere, however, then the divine right of kings was fiction. Political theorists subsequently looked for a new basis for political authority, developing variations on the ideas of the social contract and natural rights.

Individually, the philosophes produced important works that ranged from Locke's work on the nature of human reason and Montesquieu's *The Spirit of Laws* (1748) to Rousseau's novel *Émile* (1762). Their great collective work was the *Encyclopédie,* published between 1751 and 1772. Edited by philosopher Denis Diderot and mathematician Jean le Rond d'Alembert, with contributions by French thinkers such as Voltaire, Rousseau, and Montesquieu, the *Encyclopédie* summarized not only the natural and social science of the period, but also the mechanical arts. The *Encyclopédie,* with its skepticism, emphasis on scientific determinism, and criticism of abuses by government and church, enraged both civil and religious authorities, who suppressed and stopped its publication at various times.

The Enlightenment soon spread to other European countries, most notably Britain, where a parallel movement flourished in Scotland around 1740. The Scottish Enlightenment's most prominent members were skeptical philosopher David Hume and political economist Adam Smith. The first edition of the *Encyclopedia Britannica* was issued in 1768 by a "Society of gentlemen in Scotland," in imitation of the French model. The political and social theories of the Enlightenment provided the intellectual basis for the American and French revolutions.

June 6, 1944: D-Day

JUST WHAT THE *D* IN D-DAY stands for has been a mystery for some people for more than six decades. Speculation has included deliver, depart, decision, deploy—but according to the U.S. Army's manual from World War II, the D simply stood for "day," as in the "day of the invasion."

D-Day had been planned for almost a year. Known as Operation Overlord, it was a chance for the Allies to face up to Hitler's regime and make a powerful statement. For more than two-and-a-half centuries, not a single invading army had crossed the English Channel, but in June 1944 a 5,000-vessel armada making its way through the notoriously choppy and dangerous waters to Nazi-controlled France. Inside the ships were more than 150,000 men and 30,000 vehicles. Eight hundred airplanes flew overhead carrying six parachute regiments with 13,000 men. Another 300 planes carried bombs. The Battle of Normandy had begun.

By the time the sun went down in Normandy on the night of June 6, about 10,000 Allied soldiers were either dead or wounded. Still, more than 140,000 men had successfully landed on the beaches and were wresting control of French coastal villages away from the Germans. The fight went on for weeks. Thirty thousand captured German prisoners of war were sent to U.S. detention camps every month.

Today it can be difficult to imagine a time where every second of battle was not reported in full color on multiple television channels, but in the 1940s, most Americans heard their news on radios. American reporter George Hicks gained instant fame when he broadcast from the deck of one of the warships on D-Day. "You see the ships lying in all directions, just like black shadows on the grey sky," he described. Every word was accompanied by the sounds of bombs, sirens, low-flying airplanes, and the voices of thousands of men yelling directions and shouting orders.

D-Day was a major Allied victory in the war. It required a large sacrifice, but the reward was a liberated France.

The New Deal
and the Supreme Court

President Franklin D. Roosevelt's New Deal, designed to put Americans back to work and end the Great Depression's stranglehold on the nation's economy, was buffeted by a string of negative Supreme Court rulings. In short, by 1937 it was in trouble. Roosevelt had a solution, but his methods were controversial.

By 1932, the Great Depression was in full swing. The 4 million unemployed in 1930 had ballooned to 16 million. Despair and hunger were everywhere. Newly elected Roosevelt promised "a new deal" for everyone. His first 100 days in office resulted in 15 major pieces of legislation, as out of Washington poured an alphabet soup of programs designed to get America working again. The Civilian Conservation Corps (CCC) planted trees, the Civil Works Administration (CWA) built schools and paved roads, the Agricultural Adjustment Administration (AAA) assisted farmers, and the Works Progress Administration (WPA) put unemployed people back on the job. The National Recovery Administration (NRA) was established to enforce fair practice codes for business and industry.

But by 1935, the New Deal was facing difficulties. Although the blizzard of programs had helped some, 11 million Americans were still unemployed. That year the United States Supreme Court declared the NRA and AAA unconstitutional. In 1936, the court struck down the price provision of the Bituminous Coal Conservation Act. Roosevelt was furious; the court's "nine old men" (only three members were under 70) and their old-fashioned thinking curbed his attempts to get America moving.

Roosevelt's 1936 landslide victory for reelection convinced him that public support was on his side. On February 5, 1937, he proposed a new law that required all Supreme Court justices to retire at age 70. If they didn't, younger judges would be put on the court to assist them. Under the plan, the court could consist of up to 15 members. Amid criticism, Roosevelt tried to sell the plan as helping the court by lightening the workload. His opponents called it "packing" the court with justices he favored.

Chief Justice Charles Evans Hughes fired back that the court was quite capable of keeping up with its workload. Senate Democrats had difficulty finding supporters for the bill. In July, the Senate voted the bill be rewritten to strip it of controversial language. The revised bill was passed a week later, but it did not aid the president's court-packing proclivities.

Václav Havel
and the Velvet Revolution

SINCE 1948, Czechoslovakia had been ruled by a Communist regime. During the country's famous "Prague Spring" of 1968, reformers tried, and failed, to liberalize their government.

The Velvet Revolution in Czechoslovakia began on November 17, 1989, at a legal rally. After the demonstration was over, 15,000 protestors marched into downtown Prague, chanting anti-Communist slogans. They were met by riot police. After a standoff in which the protestors gave the police flowers, police began beating the students. Students called a strike and were joined by the actors' and workers' unions. On November 19, as strikes spread throughout Czechoslovakia, the Civic Forum, led by writer Václav Havel, was formed.

Havel, born on October 5, 1936, was a politically prominent playwright and espouser of nonviolent protest. His early plays *The Garden Party* and *Memorandum* earned him acclaim, but his work was banned after the Prague Spring. Havel became more politically active and wrote *Charter 77* manifesto in response to the imprisonment of members of a Czech psychedelic band. Government harassment and prison terms followed; in response he wrote *Largo Desolato,* a play about a writer scared of returning to prison. His famous essay on "post-totalitarianism" explained how people could function in a society of lies.

Havel's Civic Forum demanded the resignation of the Communist government, the release of political prisoners, and investigations into the November 17 police actions. By November 21, there were peaceful, but paralyzing, strikes in most major Czechoslovakian cities. The government tried sticking to a hard line, but to no avail. Mass demonstrations of 750,000 people in Prague forced the Communists to hold talks with the Civic Forum. The Communists tried shuffling the government, opening up restricted travel, and other concessions, but on December 10 a new government was named—the first since 1948 in which the Communists did not have the majority. On December 28, Alexander Dubcek, one of the leaders of the Prague Spring, was elected speaker of the Federal Assembly. The following day, Havel was elected president of Czechoslovakia.

POSTSCRIPT

■ Havel was the last president of Czechoslovakia and the first president of the Czech Republic.

September 11, 2001

JUST AS PEARL HARBOR was the defining moment for America in the 1940s, after September 11, 2001, nothing in the United States was quite the same. Ever since, events have been measured as *before* 9/11 or *after* 9/11.

Peace in the U.S. had reached a point where it was often taken for granted. Suddenly, Americans found themselves entering a long-term war against terrorism that they could not have even imagined 24 hours earlier.

On a sunny autumn morning, terrorists did the unthinkable. They placed men on four different airplanes; each took over the plane's controls, effectively turning them into massive bombs as they crashed into specific buildings. The Afghanistan-

Planes hit the World Trade Center

based al Qaeda terrorist group, commanded by Osama bin Laden, claimed responsibility for the attacks in a video later released to the public.

One plane hit the first World Trade Center tower; the other tower was demolished by a second plane. These acts killed thousands of people, including everyone on the airplanes. The towers collapsed within a matter of hours. The ensuing fires burned for almost 100 days afterward.

The third plane hit the Pentagon; the fourth may have been aimed at the White House, but passengers fought back and it did not reach its target. The death toll for the day was staggering: 2,976 innocent people lost their lives, including 403 New York police officers, firefighters, paramedics, and Port Authority officials.

President George W. Bush and his cabinet quickly responded. Twenty-six days after the attacks, the United States began bombing Afghanistan.

In reaction to future threats of terrorist attacks, the USA Patriot Act (aka Uniting and Strengthening America by Providing Appropriate Tools Required to Intercept and Obstruct Terrorism Act of 2001) was enacted on October 26, 2001. It gave federal officials greater authority to track and intercept communications, close the nation's borders to foreign terrorists, and detain or remove suspected terrorists from within the country's borders. It also created new crimes, penalties, and procedures for use against terrorists.

The 1919 Treaty of Versailles

FOLLOWING "THE GREAT WAR," the Treaty of Versailles was signed on June 28, 1919, formalizing the peace between Germany and the Allies. However, the document also sowed the seeds of future war.

As the victors in World War I, Britain, France, and Italy were not inclined to be charitable to the losers. They had lost millions of men and emptied their treasuries over four years of conflict.

Only U.S. President Woodrow Wilson expressed any desire for leniency. His views, as expressed in his Fourteen Points, emphasized the need to bring Germany back into the community of nations. This would not be possible if the imposed peace were too harsh. With the exception of the United States, all of the victorious countries wanted something: territory, reparations, and punishment—a Germany left impotent, stripped of power and influence. The best Germany could hope for was fair and respectful treatment according to Wilson's Fourteen Points in a negotiated peace.

Months of squabbling ended with resigned agreement among the victors. Wilson traded many of his idealistic goals in order to secure a League of Nations. France got a Germany that presumably would never again present a military or economic threat. Britain got a Germany with an insignificant navy. All but the United States received valuable territory and massive reparations.

The treaty stripped Germany of Alsace-Lorraine, Northern Schleswig, West Prussia, the coal-rich Saar, Upper Silesia, and other lands, as well as its overseas colonies. The German army was limited to 100,000 men with no tanks and no aircraft. A demilitarized zone was created along the Rhine. Billions of dollars of reparations—far beyond Germany's ability to pay—were levied. Germany was also forbidden to unite with Austria. Finally, there was Clause 231, the notorious "War Guilt Clause." Germany was forced to admit responsibility for the war, making it liable for all war damage.

This was not a negotiated peace as the Germans had anticipated. It was an imposed settlement, a dictate, that bore no resemblance to Wilson's promises of economic and political equality. The severe terms aggravated Germany's postwar economic distress and undermined the fledgling democratic Weimar Republic. Widespread public anger and humiliation created a sense of victimization among Germans. Within a few years, Adolf Hitler would put this resentment to his own use, with horrific results.

Simone de Beauvoir (1908–1986)

FRENCH FEMINIST AND WRITER Simone de Beauvoir wasn't the typical rebellious teenager. Born in Paris in 1908, she was raised by a strict Roman Catholic mother and an atheist father. Beauvoir was torn between the two ideologies until she decided at age 14 that there was no god.

As an adult, she left home to live with her grandmother and study philosophy at Sorbonne University. It was there that she fell in with a group that her mother certainly would have warned her to avoid. One of those new friends was philosopher and writer Jean-Paul Sartre.

After graduating, Beauvoir turned to teaching philosophy; at age 21, she was the youngest philosophy teacher in France. Over the years, she and Sartre vacillated between friends and lovers. Beauvoir was intimate with both men and women, which often sullied her reputation as an intellectual. In 1933, she transferred to the Joan of Arc School in Rouen. When Germany gained control of France in 1940, she was fired from her job by the Nazi government. The next year she was fired again from Lycée Camille-Sée in Paris. She never taught again.

Instead, she turned to another passion: writing. Beauvoir's first book of short stories initially was rejected, but in 1943 *She Came to Stay,* her autobiographical novel about her life with Sartre and one of her students, was published. It was a success and was followed by *The Blood of Others,* a book considered to be one of the most important existential novels of the French Resistance.

In 1945, Beauvoir and a group of other intellectuals founded a journal called *Les Temps Modernes* (*Modern Times*). She continued to write; as time passed her focus turned more often to the domination of women, stating, "All oppression creates a state of war." In 1949, she published the two-volume treatise *The Second Sex,* confirming her role in the history of feminism.

In the '70s, Beauvoir helped launch the French Women's Liberation Movement, and she continued to share her life with Sartre, who died in 1980. Her book about their life together, *Adieux: A Farewell to Sartre,* was published the following year.

The Medieval Manor

THE MEDIEVAL PERIOD extended roughly from the 5th century through the 15th century. During that time, feudalism came into play, brought from Normandy when William conquered England in 1066.

Feudalism was a class system in which the nobility was given land in return for military protection. A manor contained many different social classes. The king distributed parcels of land, called manors, to the nobles. In exchange for this land, the lord or baron—the man to whom the king had given the land—owed him allegiance.

In turn, the lord of the manor often granted a smaller portion of the land, called a fiefdom, to a vassal in exchange for military service. The vassal was then duty bound to serve and protect his lord. In return for the vassal's service, the lord was obligated to protect the vassal's family and provide any military support the vassal needed.

The vassal not only provided men for battle, but he also helped administer justice and collect monies owed to the lord. He also agreed to provide accommodations and meals for the lord or monarch whenever they were in his domain. Depending upon the number of people in the entourage, this could be quite costly.

At death, a vassal was permitted to transfer his land to an heir, as long as the heir swore an oath of fealty to the lord. If the vassal died without an heir, the land reverted back to the lord and could be transferred to the person of the lord's choice.

Serfs were also an integral part of feudal society. They worked as laborers and were vital to the success of the manor. Serfs were not slaves, but their lives were committed to the lord of the manor. Serfs worked the lord's fields and lands but could never own their own property. They also had to pay fees for the use of the lord's farming implements. The lord even had to give his permission for serfs to marry. According to law, if a serf escaped and managed to live in a town for a year and a day, he was considered a free man.

Despite their harsh life, serfs were always protected by their lords, were not required to fight or serve in the lord's military, and were bound to the land—they could not be forced to leave the manor if its ownership changed.

Desmond Tutu (1931–present)

ARCHBISHOP DESMOND TUTU was born October 7, 1931, near Klerksdorp, Transvaal. At age 12, he met Father Trevor Huddleston, the Anglican cleric of the Johannesburg Township and an outspoken opponent of apartheid. At first, Tutu resisted a religious calling, but in 1958, he began his theological study and became an ordained priest. For six years, he lived and studied in London, where he earned advanced theology degrees. In 1967, he returned to South Africa, where he began teaching at the World Council of Churches and the University of Botswana, Lesotho and Swaziland. He first gained broader notice when, in 1975, he was the first black person to hold the position of Dean of St. Mary's Cathedral in Johannesburg. In 1978, he scored another coup as the first black General Secretary of the South African Council of Churches.

Desmond Tutu (left) *receiving the 1984 Nobel Peace Prize*

Tutu worked easily with established institutional leaders, gliding between American, European, and African interest groups. He also spoke out passionately against apartheid.

In June 1976, an uprising on the southwestern outskirts of Johannesburg began when high school students protested curriculum that forced them to speak and write in Afrikaans, the language of their oppressors. Police responded with tear gas and force, which set off a chain of violence. Weeks of marches, boycotts, and demonstrations swept South Africa. Ten months later, around 660 people lay dead, and thousands of others had been arrested. Thousands more had escaped the country with the Afrikaans police and military in hot pursuit.

As the newly installed Bishop of Lesotho, Tutu challenged apartheid as "evil and unchristian" and advocated nonviolent resistance, economic sanctions, and civil protest. He also helped organize a coalition of almost 600 organizations named the United Democratic Front (UDF). By 1984, the UDF had a total membership of more than three million people.

After the fall of apartheid, Tutu won high marks as head of South Africa's Truth and Reconciliation Commission and, more recently, he has emerged as one of the most eloquent spokespersons in the global campaign against AIDS.

The Mayan Empire

THE MAYAN EMPIRE was a Mesoamerican civilization that lasted from about 300 B.C. until the Spanish arrived around A.D. 1500. Their kingdom encompassed much of modern Central Mexico, Guatemala, Belize, and Honduras. Tikal, located in the jungles of Guatemala, and Chichén Itzá, in Mexico's Yucatán peninsula, are two of the best-known Mayan cities.

Religion was the keystone of Mayan society, and they practiced an intricate series of rituals, including festivals and sacrifices. The Mayans were also skilled architects and mathematicians, improving on the inventions of earlier peoples as they developed their own society. They had a highly developed calendar system, which was extremely accurate. It consisted of two calendar years that coincided every 52 years. One calendar had a 260-day cycle and the other had a 365-day cycle. Each Mayan month had 20 days that were named for things in nature.

They also developed a sophisticated mathematics system, using only three symbols. A dot had a value of one, a bar represented the number five, and a shell symbol represented zero. By using these in various combinations, the people could conduct trade and commerce—and understand their complex calendar system. Mayan numbers were based on groups of 20, rather than ten, as modern mathematics is. The Mayans were also astronomers and followed the phases of the moon, the planets, and other celestial objects.

Most Mayans lived in hay or stone huts, but they constructed pyramids and intricate, beautiful temples for worshipping their gods. The religious structures were constructed of polished stone; both interior and exterior walls were sometimes covered with a stucco made of concrete. Murals and sculptures often were used to decorate the buildings. They also constructed ball courts, plazas, and palaces.

The Mayans were the only pre-Columbian culture to use a fully developed written language. They used a form of hieroglyphic writing based on nearly 800 phonetic signs. Each sign could represent a word or a symbol, or both. Some of the glyphs represented the same sound. Signs were often combined to form words, and the glyphs were arranged top to bottom in multiple-width blocks. The words were read left to right as in English.

No one is entirely sure why the Mayan Empire died out, but Mayan descendants can still be found in Mexico and Guatemala.

France's Reign of Terror

THE FRENCH REVOLUTION began innocently enough, as King Louis XVI called an Estates General gathering to find ways to deal with the repressive and ineffectual tax system that was bankrupting the country. The three estates were first, the clergy; second, the aristocracy; and third, the general populace. Events quickly spiraled out of control as the meeting became a battle pitting the Third Estate against the other two. Armed mobs began attacking royal symbols, including the Bastille in July 1789. By the time the king was convicted of treason and sent to the guillotine in January 1793, the revolution had taken a bloodthirsty turn.

The execution of Robespierre

With civil war broiling at home and foreign enemies threatening France, the governing 12-member Committee of Public Safety was unable to deal with the twin crises. The death of politician Jean-Paul Marat in July left Maximilien Robespierre as the committee leader and most powerful revolutionary figure.

The Law of Suspects was passed in September, allowing anyone found guilty of being an enemy of the revolution to be punished. People could be convicted for virtually any reason, from speaking against the revolution to showing sympathy for a guillotine victim—even if they were related to the victim. Every day scores of people were brought to the guillotine and executed. Robespierre felt virtue was necessary for a nation's people, and it could only be maintained by punishing anyone who questioned the revolution: "Virtue, without which terror is fatal and terror, without which virtue is powerless," was his motto. When the guillotine was not quick enough, "convicted" people were herded onto barges that were sunk, or grouped together and killed en masse by cannon fire.

Robespierre went too far when he executed popular leader and former ally Georges Danton. The people turned against him. Robespierre and his followers were arrested on July 28, 1794, and sent to the guillotine. The Reign of Terror was over, but France's reputation was tarnished.

The Golden Age of the Dutch Republic

THERE WAS A TIME when the Dutch were masters of the world. In the 16th century, the Netherlands were part of the Spanish, or Hapsburg, empire. In 1568, some provinces started a rebellion against Spanish rule. But whereas the southern Netherlands fell back into line, by 1572 the northern provinces had gained their independence. This area became known as the Dutch Republic or the United Provinces. It was the modern world's first republic.

With the loss of the south, many rich merchants and businessmen fled north, settling in Amsterdam, which turned from an insignificant port into a major city. Cheap energy generated by windmills, ease of transportation via canals, and the construction of a massive sea-going fleet introduced the beginning of the Dutch Golden Age in the 17th century.

In 1602, the Dutch East India Company was founded. As the first multinational corporation, it established a monopoly on Asian trade that lasted two centuries. Huge profits and customers' insatiable appetite for spices made it the largest commercial venture of the 17th century. As a result, Amsterdam became one of the wealthiest European cities. It even held the first full-time stock exchange in Europe. In the first half of the 17th century, the average income was the highest in Europe. Attracted by Amsterdam's prosperity and religious tolerance, people flocked to the city; its population soared from 30,000 in 1565 to 115,000 by 1630.

The Dutch also dominated trade between other European countries. The provinces were ideally located to provide a gateway into Germany as well as a connection between virtually all other European countries. Half of Europe's trade was carried in Dutch ships. The New World-oriented Dutch West India Company prospered via mahogany and sugar from Brazil and the Caribbean Islands. In North America, the Dutch established a colony that extended from New Amsterdam (now New York City) through Connecticut and inland to present-day Albany.

The prosperity of the Dutch gave rise to the lucrative business of portrait painting, featuring such artists as Rembrandt van Rijn. The Dutch upper-class were wealthy and showed it off by having portraits painted—so much so that there is probably more known about their appearance than any other society in history.

But it was not to last; in the second part of the 17th century, England's naval might eclipsed that of the Dutch.

The Standard Oil Bust

P RIOR TO THE CIVIL WAR, most American businesses were small and
locally owned; during the war, many individuals made fortunes in
business pursuits. It was in the postwar Reconstruction period and into
the 1890s that many of the country's new millionaires consolidated their
holdings and established businesses that extended their pursuits both
nationally and worldwide.

John D. Rockefeller was one such entrepreneur. Through his company,
Standard Oil of Ohio, he purchased oil refineries, streamlined production, bought out competitors, negotiated with the railroads for preferen-
tial rates, and obtained rebates from railroads for transporting petroleum
with certain companies.

Business was becoming "big business," and businessmen were creating
methods to maintain their position of advantage in the economic world.
As companies eliminated competition, they became monopolies. Monopolies restrained trade and were identified by certain characteristics. One
type of monopoly was a "trust" created by stockholders in competing
corporations, who in turn gave their certificates of stock ownership to
a "trustee" in exchange for a trust certificate. The trustee then served
as manager for the combined corporations. The resulting trusts had a
monopoly over pricing and markets, and they could eliminate smaller
businesses and other less-organized competition through unethical
business practices. Railroads, steel, and petroleum were just a few of the
industries targeted by reformists during the late 1800s and early 1900s as
being anticompetitive.

The dual issue of trusts and monopolies was highlighted in the 1896 presidential election. To the public, the new "captains of industry" were now
"robber barons." The public demanded measures be taken to curb the
abuses of industrialization. In 1890, Congress passed the Sherman Antitrust Act, which provided that "every contract, combination in the form
of trust or otherwise, or conspiracy, in restraint of trade or commerce"
in interstate or international commerce was illegal. The federal act made
monopolizing and attempts at monopolizing a criminal offense.

"Trust-busting" became an important way for courts to eliminate
restraints on competition and trade. In 1911, the U.S. Supreme Court
applied the Sherman Act to the Standard Oil trust, which controlled
about two-thirds of the market. It also found that the company's monop-
olistic practices required Standard Oil to be broken up into smaller
companies.

The Ming Dynasty

OVER A PERIOD of nearly 300 years (1368–1644), the Ming dynasty brought prosperity and advances in the arts and sciences to China.

The *Ming,* or brilliant, dynasty followed the collapse of the Mongol-led Yuan dynasty. The Yuan dynasty was already weakened when a peasant uprising toppled it and drove the Mongols back into the steppes. This victory reunited China and brought stability after 400 years of foreign occupation.

A rebel group led by Zhu Yuanzhang gained dominance during the uprising and subsequently established the Ming dynasty in Nanjing in 1368. Zhu adopted the title "Hongwu" but historically is known as Emperor Taizu. Succeeding Ming emperors were all members of the Zhu family.

Ming rule was overseen by a strong central government that reinforced stability. The Ming believed they enjoyed the "perfect civilization." New crops were introduced,

Emperor Taizu

including cotton, corn, and sweet potatoes. Industry flourished with the production of textiles and exquisite porcelains, and books were printed using movable type. Great private land estates were confiscated by the government, divided up, and rented out to the peasantry. Private slavery was outlawed.

One of the most visible achievements of the Ming was the Great Wall. Although the wall dated back to earlier times, the Ming repaired large sections and built new ones. Watchtowers were redesigned, sections of the wall were enlarged, and cannons were put in place.

Ming power at its height included a vast army and navy, but as conflicts with the Mongols and the Japanese took their toll, the dynasty eventually began to decline. High taxes toward the end of the Ming era prompted many peasants to abandon their land, which ushered in an economic crisis and a 1627 peasant uprising.

The Ming was the last native Chinese dynasty to rule the empire. Seventeen years after the 1627 uprising, the Manchu took advantage of a rebellion against the Ming and seized control of China, instituting the Qing dynasty, which ruled from 1644–1911.

The League of Nations Mandates

THE YEARS FOLLOWING WORLD WAR I were a time of chaos in the Middle East. During the war, the British, who occupied Egypt, had persuaded Husayn, the sharif of Mecca, to side with them against the Ottomans by promising to create independent Arab nations as a reward. Starting in 1916, Husayn led an Arab revolt against the Turks. After the war ended, the Ottoman Empire collapsed, creating a power vacuum that England and France rushed to fill.

Despite their promises to Husayn, the British had made secret agreements with France to divide up the region into two spheres of influence. The British also supported the Balfour Declaration, which endorsed the creation of a Jewish homeland in Palestine. In 1920, the newly formed League of Nations implemented a mandate system, under which the territories taken from defeated powers, including the Ottoman Empire, were placed under Allied control until they were ready for nationhood. England received control of Iraq and Palestine, while France was given Syria and Lebanon. Husayn received an independent state called Hijaz, which was located on the western coast of Arabia and included the holy cities of Mecca and Medina.

France immediately occupied Syria, driving out Faysal, one of Husayn's sons, who had already set up an Arab government in Damascus. The French occupation of Syria was harsh and subject to constant Arab revolt. However, France would eventually grant independence to its mandates: Lebanon in 1943 and Syria in 1946.

The British faced similar Arab unrest in their mandates. To help pacify the people of Iraq, the British rigged an election that declared Faysal the leader of that mandate. Eventually, the British granted Iraq independence in 1932. To placate another of Husayn's sons, Abdullah, the British took a portion of Palestine, creating Transjordan (present-day Jordan) for him to control in 1921. Abdullah's rule lasted until his death in 1951.

Husayn was not as fortunate as his sons and was driven out of Hijaz in 1924 by Ibn Saud, whose family had begun its rise to power in the region a hundred years before. As Saud's small army attacked Hijaz, the British simply stood by, since Husayn had refused to sign peace treaties and referred to himself the "king of the Arabs." In 1932, Ibn Saud officially declared the kingdom of Saudi Arabia.

Great Britain remained in control of Palestine until 1948, when it abandoned the mandate in favor of the United Nations partition plan that officially created the Jewish state of Israel.

Luther Posts 95 Theses

Martin Luther was born in 1483 in Eisleben, Saxony. His father wanted him to be a lawyer, but following a near-death experience, Luther chose to enter an Augustinian monastery in 1505 and later became a respected teacher at the University of Wittenberg.

Luther was troubled over the issue of humanity's salvation. His search for answers led him to St. Paul's Epistle to the Romans, which Luther interpreted differently than the traditional Catholic teaching. He believed that Paul intended to say that people could be saved simply by having faith in the merits of Christ's sacrifice rather than through any deed.

In 1515, the Catholic Church announced the sale of indulgences in two German provinces to help fund the building of St. Peter's Basilica in Rome. Indulgences were sold to people as a way to reduce their time in purgatory. When used properly, indulgences were effective in raising money to build hospitals, almshouses, and other philanthropic institutions. However, the papacy failed to make public that half of the income from the sale of indulgences would go to Albert of Mainz, the ruler of the two provinces, to help him repay a debt.

Luther was horrified by the church's corruption, and he decided to respond to Wittenberg's latest round of indulgences. On October 31, 1517, Luther posted a series of 95 theses on the door of the church, a common practice that would often spark a debate over the posted document. His theory was that good works had no merit in regard to salvation and thus indulgences were unnecessary. Thanks to the relatively recent innovation of the printing press, the theses soon spread to the public. Someone obtained a copy of Luther's document, and it was quickly translated from its original Latin into German, reproduced, and distributed across Germany.

The Vatican investigated the document, and Luther was accused of heresy. He was brought before a tribunal and given the opportunity to recant his position, but he refused. Many German princes sided with Luther, and because of the widespread printing of the document, Luther's ideas proved impossible to repress. Ultimately, Luther's theses would result in the Protestant Reformation and the splintering of the Catholic Church.

The Dust Bowl

THE GREAT DEPRESSION, combined with the effects of a massive drought, created the Dust Bowl of the 1930s, affecting some 100 million acres in the American Great Plains and the Southwest, including parts of Texas, New Mexico, Colorado, Kansas, and Oklahoma.

The roots of the Dust Bowl disaster lay in World War I, when farmers plowed land they had previously thought too poor to farm in order to meet the increased demand for wheat. Farmers also took out loans to buy the equipment necessary to farm on a larger scale. But when wheat prices dropped after the war, the debts remained. Despite the condition of the soil, farmers planted on more land so they could make their payments.

Rainfall was irregular throughout the '20s; in 1932, it stopped altogether. Native ground cover had been ploughed under and stripped by overgrazing. Wheat had exhausted the topsoil. With nothing to protect the land against wind, the soil began to drift. The first great dust storm came in mid-April 1934 and the second in May, each blowing great curtains of dust to the Atlantic Coast and into the Gulf of Mexico. "Black blizzards" rained dirt, and farmhouses were hidden behind drifts of dust.

Ecological disaster was accompanied by economic disaster. With no crops or land for grazing, tenant farmers and sharecroppers were evicted when they could not pay the rent. When landowners could not make mortgage payments, banks foreclosed. Land rich and cash poor, many banks failed. As many as 2.5 million people—about a quarter of the population of the Dust Bowl region—were forced to abandon their ruined farms. Many moved to the nearest city, while others joined the army of migrant agricultural workers that followed the harvest from Florida to Montana and squatted in shantytowns outside of California's cities.

The Great Plains did not begin to recover until regular rainfall came again in 1939 and World War II created a renewed demand for wheat. The struggles of the Dust Bowl migrants live on in Woody Guthrie's ballads, John Steinbeck's 1939 novel *The Grapes of Wrath,* and the WPA photographs of Dorothea Lange and others.

Peter the Great
Founds St. Petersburg

Czar Peter the Great is considered the modernizer of Russia. Peter understood that his country lagged behind much of Western Europe, and so, shortly after he came to the throne in 1682, he set out to update his country's ways, including the government, military, and technology. In doing so, he transformed Russia into a major European empire.

Peter had his eye on increasing Russia's territory, and he wanted to move Russia's borders westward to the Baltic Sea. Sweden held land in the region and stood in the way of Peter's conquest. From 1700 to 1721, Peter's troops fought in the Great Northern War against Sweden, which at the time was one of Europe's strongest powers.

In 1703, Peter's troops succeeded in capturing territory at the mouth of the Neva River. On May 27, in the midst of the scores of islands that formed the river's delta, Peter formally dedicated a new city, named St. Petersburg after his patron saint. The site chosen for the city was marshy and at sea level, making construction extremely difficult. Stone for building had to be transported to the site. To obtain laborers, Peter levied a conscription of one laborer for every 9 to 16 households in Russia. Most were peasants, and many were forcibly removed to St. Petersburg. Tens of thousands died from exposure to weather, disease, and malnutrition. But Peter's iron will drove the construction forward. He and his family moved to the new city in 1710, and two years later he made it the new capital of Russia. By the time of Peter's death in 1725, 40,000 people called St. Petersburg home.

St. Petersburg steadily grew in size as succeeding czars added to the city's splendor. Magnificent churches and schools were built, and the city eventually became the third-largest city in Europe, after London and Moscow. It remained the capital of Russia until 1918 (with the exception of 1728–1732), when Lenin moved the capital back to Moscow.

In 1914, at the beginning of World War I, the city's name was changed to Petrograd because many Russians thought St. Petersburg sounded too German. In January 1924, days after Lenin's death, the city was renamed Leningrad. In 1991, with the collapse of the Soviet Union, residents voted to change the name back to St. Petersburg.

Mary Wollstonecraft (1759–1797)

MARY WOLLSTONECRAFT was born in London on April 27, 1759. As an adult, she worked as a teacher, lady's companion, and governess. Her passion lay in her writing, however, and she became known for her essays on the importance of education for both genders. She traveled to France in 1792; there she met an American adventurer named Gilbert Imlay. The two became lovers, and Wollstonecraft soon became pregnant. After she gave birth to daughter Fanny, Imlay left her. Devastated, she attempted suicide but was rescued. Imlay sent her to Scandinavia, where she wrote popular letters, later collected as a book, about the culture there.

Eventually, Wollstonecraft met and married William Godwin. She began to write about the concept of women's rights—an issue that was unheard of at the time. She felt that too often women were measured against standards for men instead of being appreciated for their own natural, but different, talents.

In response to Edmund Burke's *Reflections on the Revolution in France,* Wollstonecraft set out to explain her philosophy with *A Vindication of the Rights of Men* (1790). A year later, she published *A Vindication of the Rights of Woman*. In it, she advocated emancipation for women through education. Eighteenth-century society was going through a period of Enlightenment, and skepticism about established institutions, including gender roles, was common. While controversial, her commentary received many positive reviews and was widely read.

On September 10, 1797, Wollstonecraft died of "childbed fever," or septicemia, after the birth of her daughter Mary. Soon after, Godwin published his wife's semiautobiographical book *Maria, or the Wrongs of Woman,* as well as a memoir of his life as her husband. Unfortunately, the honesty in those books—tales of her depression and financial woes—opened the door for critics to focus on her personal life rather than her work and ideas. It took years before the wisdom and elegance of Wollstonecraft's words were read again. In the 1960s and '70s, the feminist movement picked up on Wollstonecraft's proto-feminist writings. Once again, her words were back in the spotlight.

POSTSCRIPT

■ Wollstonecraft's daughter Mary eloped with poet Percy Bysshe Shelley. Mary later went on to write the classic novel *Frankenstein*.

The Panama Canal

PRIOR TO THE COMPLETION of the Panama Canal in 1914, a ship sailing from New York to San Francisco was forced to make a treacherous, 14,000-mile voyage around Cape Horn at the southern tip of South America. The canal cut that journey to 6,000 miles.

The idea of constructing a 48-mile canal connecting the Atlantic and Pacific oceans through the Isthmus of Panama dated back as far as the 16th century, but it was not until 1881 that the first attempt to actually build one took place, under French supervision. That effort failed due to poor planning and disease, as more than 22,000 workers perished.

The canal was resumed by the United States in 1904. Possible routes through Nicaragua were rejected in favor of a system of locks across the Isthmus of Panama. The project began after the United States helped Panama gain independence from Columbia. In exchange, Panama turned over control of the Panama Canal Zone to the United States.

U.S. scientists and engineers prepared carefully for the enormous undertaking under chief engineer George Washington Goethals. Equipment designed for

President Theodore Roosevelt (center) on a steam shovel

such a large-scale project was brought in, which helped speed up construction. Still, the key to success was the use of superior disease control. Health measures and a greater understanding of mosquito-borne diseases greatly reduced the mortality rate. However, even with greater health measures, about 5,609 workers died, bringing the total death toll for the Panama Canal to about 27,500.

The canal formally opened on August 15, 1914. An economic and strategic jewel, it remained to some extent under U.S. control until 1999, when authority was handed over to Panama under the Torrijos-Carter Treaties.

The average passage through the canal takes nine hours, and the average toll is $54,000. As many as 14,000 vessels pass through the canal in any given year. Efforts are currently under way to expand the canal as ships increase in size. The project, which began in 2007, will include new sets of improved locks and the widening of the channel.

The Great Schism

THE ROMAN CATHOLIC CHURCH once had two popes—a situation that left no one very happy. "The Great Schism" lasted about 70 years, from 1378 until 1417, with one pope seated in Rome and another ruling from Avignon, France.

The origin of the Great Schism dates back to 1309, when Pope Clement V moved the papacy to Avignon. The arrangement, known as the "Babylonian Captivity," allowed the king of France to exert considerable political influence over the pope. When Pope Gregory XI returned the papacy to Rome in 1377, the king was less than delighted.

Following the death of Gregory XI, a new pope was elected. The French took the opportunity to elect a pope of their own to rule from Avignon. The result was the division of Western Christendom, with the papal authorities in competition. The division, however, was more political than religious: France, Sicily, Scotland, Castile, and Aragon lined up with the Avignon pope. Rome, Flanders, Poland, Hungary, and the majority of the German states supported the pope in Rome. Portugal first sided with the Avignon pope, and then, under pressure from England, switched to the Roman pope.

The general population became more cynical as the conflict dragged on, each side jockeying for power and referring to the other as the antipope. Pious Christians were left bewildered and alienated by the bickering, and the papal offices lost influence.

The cardinals of both popes tried to resolve the split in 1409 when they asked the Church Council in Pisa to elect a new pope that could bring both sides together. They did, only to find that neither pope was willing to relinquish his authority. As a result, there were now three popes.

Finally, in 1414, the Council of Constance was gathered to resolve unfinished business from Pisa regarding internal reform of the church. They also began drastic measures to resolve the split. In order to start again, tabula rasa, the council deposed both the third pope and the Avignon pope, and they arranged the resignation of the Roman pope. The Council of Constance then elected Pope Martin V, who ruled for almost 14 years. The schism had ended, and papal authority was permanently placed in Rome, where it remains today.

Cesar Chavez and the United Farm Workers of America

MIGRANT WORK was especially rough in the United States during the 1960s, where "top wages" were 90 cents per hour. Without any state laws to govern working standards, farmers often treated their workers like slaves.

On many farms, migrant workers had to pay a quarter for each drink they took. The temporary housing provided for them often consisted of little more than an unheated metal shack without a kitchen or any indoor plumbing. Young children were put to work, and many pickers were injured or died in work-related accidents. The average life expectancy for someone in this demanding occupation was only 49 years.

Something had to be done to protect migrant workers. In 1959, the Agricultural Workers Organizing Committee was formed, led by Larry Itliong and Dolores Huerta. In 1962, a Mexican American named Cesar Chavez stepped in. The son of a poor farm-working family, he personally knew about the hardships of migrants. That year he founded the National Farm Workers Association and traveled throughout California meeting with farmworkers to tell them about NFWA.

Chavez showed his passion for his mission in other nonviolent ways, including leading worker strikes, boycotts, and pickets. He even fasted to bring national attention to the plight of the farmworkers, drinking only water for up to 36 days. "It is a fast for the purification of my own body, mind, and soul," he said. "The fast is also a heartfelt prayer for purification and strengthening for all those who work beside me in the farmworker movement. The fast is also an act of penance for those in positions of moral authority... who know that they could and should do more."

Chavez pushed to help farmworkers organize a union and get better pay and safer working conditions. In 1971, the NFWA became the United Farm Workers of America. Chavez died on April 23, 1993. The following year, he was posthumously awarded the Presidential Medal of Freedom.

Sparta

SPARTA was one of the most important city-states during Greece's classic age from about 700 to 400 B.C.

According to tradition, Dorian Greek invaders settled the fertile valley of the Eurotas River on the Peloponnesus. Spartans claimed their ancient ancestors lived in equality with these invaders. They operated under a dual kingship, which had its origins in two reputed descendants of Hercules ruling the region. Sparta's two kings were aided by the *rhetra,* an assembly of men over the age of 30. The assembly in turn elected the *gerusia,* a council of 28 elders (men older than 60) who worked with the kings. Further, five *ephors* were elected to supervise Spartan society; these men also were able to check the kings from exercising too much power.

In the seventh century B.C., there was enough social unrest to culminate in the three Messenian Wars, which resulted in Spartan control over much of the Peloponnesus. After the revolts were subdued, Sparta became a militarized society to prevent future rebellions. Spartan society was organized in three layers. At the top were the *Spartiates,* the free Spartan citizens whose males all had the right to vote. Next came the *perioikoi,* or "dwellers-about," who were nonvoting citizens. At the bottom were the *helots,* peasants who formed the largest class and who were not eligible for voting rights or military service.

Upon birth, Spartan males were checked to see if they were physically fit to be raised. At age seven, they left their homes and were trained in groups by teenage leaders. At age 20, they were placed into 15-man squads, where they ate a common meal each day and practiced their military duties. They could marry but were not allowed to be at home with their wives until age 30. Meanwhile, the helots lived as serfs who farmed the land, while the perioikoi conducted trade and developed industry.

This militarized society produced the finest fighting men in Greece. The brave Spartans were lionized at the Battle of Thermopylae, where King Leonidas, his 300 Spartans, and others died fighting the Persians, delaying the enemy long enough for Athens to organize a defense against the attack. Later, Athens and Sparta came to blows in the Peloponnesian War in 431 B.C. Sparta eventually won the war and tried to impose peace among the warring Greek states. However, eventually, Thebes defeated Sparta in 371 B.C., shattering the myth of Spartan invincibility.

Hiroshima

O N AUGUST 6, 1945, at 8:15 A.M., a B-29 Superfortress named *Enola Gay* opened its bomb bay doors 31,000 feet over the Japanese city of Hiroshima. Seconds later, the world changed forever as an atomic bomb exploded in a massive fireball over the Aioi Bridge.

A pillar of smoke and debris as high as Mount Everest mushroomed into the sky. The fireball was so intense, it melted granite. An estimated 70,000–80,000 people were killed instantly by the blast and 90 percent of the city's buildings were damaged or destroyed. Many of the victims caught near the epicenter of the explosion were simply vaporized, some leaving only their silhouettes imprinted on walls or pavement. Others died of burns, from flying debris, in collapsed buildings, or in the fires that followed.

The bomb, dubbed "Little Boy," was the culmination of the Manhattan Project, a top-secret effort. The multibillion-dollar project was overseen by General Leslie Groves. The scientific team located at Los Alamos, New Mexico, was headed by American physicist Robert Oppenheimer.

President Truman decided to use the bomb after Japan's leaders rejected surrender demands in July 1945. Hiroshima was chosen due to its importance as a military headquarters and logistics base. There were few qualms about civilian casualties in this new era of total war, as hundreds of thousands of civilians had already been killed in firebombings of Japanese cities.

The Japanese did not immediately capitulate following the Hiroshima bombing. Three days later, the B-29 *Bock's Car* dropped a plutonium bomb on Nagasaki, killing about 70,000 people. Japan finally capitulated on August 15.

The morality of the bombings has been hotly debated. Critics insist that Japan was already near surrender. They maintain the bombings were motivated by racism and a desire to frighten the Soviet Union. Proponents point out that casualties from the bombs were actually fewer than those caused by the incendiary attacks. Oppenheimer was particularly appalled by the civilian deaths his creation had brought. After the war, he actively lobbied for international control of atomic energy.

The Suez Canal

FERDINAND DE LESSEPS was the mastermind behind the construction of the Suez Canal, linking the Red Sea with the Mediterranean. A French diplomat stationed in Egypt during the 1830s, de Lesseps quit his diplomatic career in 1854 and obtained permission from Said Pasha, the viceroy of Egypt, to construct a canal.

De Lesseps faced an uphill battle. The British did everything in their power to disrupt and discourage the Frenchman, as the canal would give France the shortest route to India—the reduced shipping route would cut the trip by about half.

By 1858, about $40 million in capital had been raised for the project. More than half of the stocks were bought by de Lesseps's countrymen— over 20,000 Frenchmen purchased 207,111 shares, the proceeds of which allowed him to start construction. Emperor Napoleon III also threw his support behind the project; but then again, the emperor's wife, Eugenie, was de Lesseps's cousin.

The Suez Canal Company was formed in December 1858, and work started the next year. Egyptian laborers supplied the initial work, constructing a small service canal to allow easy access along the intended route. It was difficult work, and many laborers died along the way. Eventually, European engineers with heavy machinery finished the canal, which measured 101 miles long.

The canal proved to be Egypt's financial ruin. When Ismail Pasha took over the Egyptian government in 1863, he lavished money on the project. The initial estimate of the canal's cost was $40 million, but in the end the cost was greater than $100 million. Although Pasha's actions were progressive for Egypt, the debts incurred later proved his country's undoing.

The Suez Canal was dedicated on November 17, 1869, with much pomp and ceremony. The canal proved an immediate success. The British purchased a large share of canal stock from Egypt and in 1882 occupied the country. Six years later, an international convention guaranteed that the canal would be open to ships of all nations. When the British left in 1956, Egyptian President Gamel Abdel Nasser nationalized the canal, closing it entirely after the 1967 war with Israel. The canal reopened in 1975. Today, about 8 percent of international shipping passes through the canal, which has been widened and deepened over the years to accommodate larger vessels. Today the canal is 120 miles long and 741 feet wide at its narrowest section.

The Lowell Girls

BETWEEN 1823 AND 1841, the town of Lowell, Massachusetts, experienced a textile mill boom. The mills needed dependable labor, and they found it in New England's farm girls and young women. The recruiters promised two dollars a week beyond board—high wages at the time—and a chance for independence during an era in which a woman's opportunities were severely limited.

Lowell Girls

In 1840, the factories employed nearly 8,000 female workers. Some of these "Lowell Girls" were as young as ten, with most between the ages of 16 and 25. The average girl stayed for about four years and lived year-round in company-supervised boarding houses. Each house had 25 girls, with as many as eight girls sharing a bedroom. The girls were expected to attend church and behave in a moral fashion. They ate, lived, and worked as a community. At one point, they even had their own monthly magazine.

By modern standards, factory conditions were poor. The girls worked an average of 73 hours a week. As many as 80 women operated the machines in one room. The noise, recalled one worker, was "something frightful and infernal." Particles of thread and cloth filled the air, choking workers.

In 1834 and 1836, the Lowell Girls launched two of the earliest strikes in the United States after it was announced that wages would be cut. The mills were briefly shut down, and the girls marched out to listen to "incendiary speeches" from labor activists. Both efforts failed, but they left the male-dominated management with a different perspective on women. Labor concerns also led to the formation of the Factory Girls Association, which eventually boasted more than 2,500 members and succeeded in making organized action more effective.

The Lowell Girl phenomenon eventually waned, a victim of lower wages and a greater number of job and educational opportunities for women. But in their day, they had served the capitalist need for dependable labor. They also impacted society in unexpected ways, advancing women's rights and labor reform.

Khrushchev Denounces Stalinism

WHEN SOVIET LEADER Nikita Khrushchev denounced Joseph Stalin in 1956, the foundations of Communism were shaken to the core.

Stalin, who died three years earlier, had led the Soviet Union for many years, and his political purges and repressions had cost the lives of millions of people. Yet in the closed, never-admit-a-mistake society of the USSR, it seemed Stalin's bloody regime would be explained away as necessary to preserve the Soviet state, and Stalin would remain a hero.

That's why it was so shocking when, in February 1956, Khrushchev condemned Stalin during a speech before the 20th Congress of the Communist Party in Moscow. Accusing Stalin of creating a regime based on "suspicion, fear and terror," Khrushchev laid bare the political purges of 1936–1938. He also derided Stalin's foreign policy during World War II, saying that he had repeatedly ignored warnings that the Germans were going to invade Russia. Khrushchev explained the reason he was speaking out was to break the cult of Stalin, which still gripped Soviet citizens.

Khrushchev himself was no stranger to Soviet political intrigues. He became a Bolshevik party member in 1918 and steadily rose through the ranks as the Communists solidified their hold on Russia in the years following World War I. In 1938, he became the First Secretary of the Central Committee of the Communist Party of Ukraine, a top-level regional position. Ironically, in the years leading up to Stalin's death, Khrushchev had carried out his orders without hesitation. After Stalin's death, Khrushchev emerged as one of the key players in the drama to see who would succeed him. In 1958, Khrushchev became premier of the Soviet Union, the most powerful man in the country and the party.

Khrushchev's denunciation of Stalin ushered in a brief period of hope that the Soviet Iron Curtain in Eastern Europe was ending. But the use of tanks to crush the Hungarian Revolution in October 1956 ended that dream. Domestically, he did attempt reforms of the Soviet economy. Khrushchev was removed from power in 1964.

POSTSCRIPT

▩ Khrushchev's anti-Stalin speech was not printed in Russia until 1988.

▩ The speech reportedly caused many delegates to cry, and several delegates had heart attacks.

The Korean War

S OMETIMES CALLED "THE FORGOTTEN WAR" because it occurred directly after World War II, the Korean War was the first of the limited wars fought by the superpowers.

Following World War II, Korea was divided along the 38th parallel into a Russia-dominated north and a U.S.-dominated south. On June 25, 1950, the armies of Communist North Korea poured over the border, intent on reuniting the country under dictator Kim Il Sung.

UN forces withdrawing from North Korea

The United Nations leapt to South Korea's aid. In September, the U.S. Marines, under command of General Douglas MacArthur, landed at the South Korean port of Inchon, throwing the Russian-backed North Koreans into disarray. UN forces pursued the fleeing enemy nearly to the Chinese border, despite warnings from China. In late November, hundreds of thousands of Chinese troops entered the war, forcing a UN retreat.

Concerned that the war would expand into a global armed conflict, President Harry S. Truman placed severe strictures on U.S. commanders. Fighter planes were forbidden to pursue enemy jets back over the Yalu River into Chinese airspace. U.S. bombers were forbidden to hit assembly points, bases, and airfields in Chinese territory even if they were directly assisting the enemy. An offer by the Chinese Nationalists to participate on the UN side was rejected for fear it might expand the war to Taiwan.

MacArthur urged Truman to let him take the war into China itself. He also advocated the possible use of nuclear weapons. Annoyed by the general's outspokenness and apparent lack of concern for a potential Third World War, Truman relieved MacArthur of command in April 1951. Negotiations ended the conflict with a cease-fire on July 27, 1953.

Nearly 37,000 U.S. soldiers were killed in Korea. More than 400,000 South Korean, 520,000 North Korean, and an estimated 900,000 Chinese troops also died. Although neither side gained much, China showed it was a power to be reckoned with, and the U.S. managed to contain communism on the peninsula. Korea, however, remains divided along the 38th parallel.

The Hammurabi Code

NEARLY FOUR THOUSAND YEARS have passed since he ruled Babylon, but King Hammurabi is still remembered for his early set of laws written in the 18th century B.C., known as the Code of Hammurabi.

Modern-day scholars are familiar with the code thanks to the early 20th-century discovery of a roughly 7½-foot black stone slab, or *stele,* inscribed in cuneiform with the king's dictums. In ancient times, steles were erected throughout the kingdom so that all subjects could read the laws and know their rights. This particular stele, now housed in the Louvre in Paris, also featured a depiction of the sun god Shamash passing a scepter and ring to Hammurabi, symbolizing the divine origin of the code of laws.

Many scholars consider the Code of Hammurabi to be a testament to Hammurabi's commendable sense of justice. It contains 300 laws dealing with a wide range of social, moral, religious, commercial, and civil issues. The code placed strong emphasis on the family and morals and generally reflected the principle of "an eye for an eye." As described, the penalty for stealing a loaf of bread was loss of a hand; someone who blinded a man's eye would forfeit his own eye.

There was no provision for prison terms or forced labor, but the death penalty could be imposed in a variety of macabre ways: burning, impalement, drowning, gibbeting, or being buried alive. Death was the penalty for a wide variety of crimes, including sheltering a runaway slave, incest, adultery, stealing from the temple or the court, burglary, robbery, looting, and the inability to pay certain fines.

The code did not treat all subjects equally but defined how each class system interacted with one another. The classes included *amelu,* the upper class; *mushkinu,* the middle class; and, at the bottom of the social scale, *wardi,* the slaves. While there was no distinction in matters of property, the criminal code did make distinctions in an individual's value depending on his social class.

Women also lacked equal status under the law, though they were not entirely without protection. One tenet concerned a wife who "lives in his house, wishes to leave it, plunges into debt, tries to ruin her house, neglects her husband, and is judicially convicted." If her husband released her, she was free to go on her way. But, as the code dictated, "If her husband does not wish to release her, and if he take another wife, she shall remain as servant in her husband's house."

The Watergate Scandal

Pʀᴇꜱɪᴅᴇɴᴛ Rɪᴄʜᴀʀᴅ M. Nɪxᴏɴ had seen some policy successes during his first term in office, including a diplomatic opening toward China and détente with the Soviet Union. But his presidency was undone by his use of dirty tricks in the Oval Office.

"Tricky Dick" had a history of illegal shenanigans against political enemies. In 1971, he ordered White House operatives E. Howard Hunt and G. Gordon Liddy to break into a psychiatrist's office. The objective of this felony was to discredit Daniel Ellsberg, the former Pentagon analyst who had exposed the government's Vietnam decision-making to the press. On June 17, 1972, Nixon's "plumbers" (who fixed White House leaks) went to work breaking and entering Democratic national headquarters in the Watergate apartment complex during the presidential campaign. Five men were caught and arrested.

Two *Washington Post* reporters, Bob Woodward and Carl Bernstein, pursued the story tenaciously. By October, the break-in was linked to Attorney General John Mitchell, head of the president's 1972 reelection committee. The burglars, along with Hunt and Liddy, were convicted in January 1973. Two months later, District Court Judge John Sirica revealed a letter from one of the conspirators alleging White House involvement in the burglary. By then, the Senate was investigating.

The matter might have remained unresolved but for the discovery of the White House audiotapes in July, in which taped conversations flatly incriminated Nixon as part of an illegal cover-up conducted by the CIA. The scandal dragged on as Nixon battled to keep the tapes secret. Finally, in July 1974, the Supreme Court forced Nixon to release the tapes to the special prosecutor. Under imminent threat of impeachment, on August 9, 1974, he became the first U.S. president to resign from office.

The Watergate scandal was certainly a low point for the presidency, but it was a success for the constitutional system as a whole. The legislative and judicial branches successfully checked the abuse of executive power, and the press played the crucial role Thomas Jefferson had envisioned for it. Nevertheless, Americans have been even more ardently cynical about politicians ever since.

The Crystal Palace

ONE OF THE ARCHITECTURAL WONDERS of the 19th century, the Crystal Palace was the centerpiece of the 1851 Great Exhibition in London's Hyde Park. This early version of a world's fair was the brainchild of Queen Victoria's husband, Prince Albert, who wanted to showcase the industrial, scientific, and economic predominance of Great Britain.

Architect Sir Joseph Paxton designed the exhibition hall in only ten days. It was a mammoth structure at 1,851 feet long and using 9,642 tons of iron and more than 25 acres of glass. It contained 990,000 square feet of exhibition space. Some 5,000 laborers worked on the structure, with some 2,000 actually on site at the same time. As its name suggests, the Palace's most prominent feature was its glass roof and sides, providing a sense of openness for visitors.

And the Crystal Palace enjoyed plenty of visitors. Indeed, during the exhibition's six-month run, more than six million paying customers flocked to gawk at nearly 13,000 exhibits from all over the world, including pottery and steam hammers from Great Britain, a reaper from the United States, and a Jacquard loom from France. One of the biggest hits was the world's first dinosaur display, featuring several life-size models placed near the park's lower lakes.

The exhibition proved to be a great financial success, as well. Profits made from ticket sales helped finance such major London cultural landmarks as Albert Hall and the Victoria and Albert Museum.

Although the Crystal Palace was supposed to be torn down at the end of the exhibition, it was so popular that the government decided to dismantle and move it to Sydenham Hill in South London. In 1911, the Palace housed the Festival of Empire, which featured models of the parliament buildings of Empire and British Commonwealth countries, as well as exhibits of their products. It later served as a venue for naval training during World War I. It was also the original site of the Imperial War Museum and played home to a pioneering television company in the '30s.

Alas, this symbol of British power at the height of the Victorian age was destroyed by fire in 1936, three years before World War II broke out and Britain's role in the world was forever altered.

POSTSCRIPT

■ Benjamin Hawkins, designer of the dinosaur exhibit, hosted a dinner for 22 inside the body of the *Iguanodon*.

Leaves of Grass

CELEBRATING HIS OWN personal independence, Walt Whitman published the first edition of *Leaves of Grass* on July 4, 1855.

Whitman was born in New York in 1819. From an early age, his life revolved around words. He was a voracious reader, an intense journalist, a passionate teacher, and a dedicated publisher. Words were his playthings, and he wanted to bring the art of poetry to the common people. Whitman used unusual writing patterns, including free verse and anaphora, the repetition of the first word in successive phrases. His writings came as America was creating a culture of literature; contemporary readers were eating up the works of Edgar Allan Poe, Nathaniel Hawthorne, Herman Melville, and Henry David Thoreau.

Before publishing *Leaves of Grass,* Whitman had only had a handful of poems published. He designed the cover himself and paid for the book to be printed. The first edition of the book was far different than what it is today. Each time *Leaves of Grass* was printed, it got bigger; the first one had 12 poems, and by the final edition, it contained 293 poems.

One of the most famous poems was the lengthy "Song of Myself," which was split up into 52 sections and is considered Whitman's masterpiece. He also included two poems written to honor President Abraham Lincoln, "When Lilacs Last in the Door-yard Bloom'd" and "O Captain! My Captain!"

Whitman died in 1892; more than 115 years later, *Leaves of Grass* is still seen as a classic. His words honor the country—from its people and landscapes, to general topics such as war, death, love, and slavery. His poetry is still taught in literature classes, though some schools have banned the book for its sensuality.

> I hear America singing, the varied carols I hear;
> Those of mechanics—each one singing his, as it should be,
>   blithe and strong,
> The carpenter singing his, as he measures his plank or beam,
> The mason singing his, as he makes ready for work, or leaves off work.
>
> —*"I Hear America Singing"*

The Babylonian Talmud

SOMETIME BETWEEN A.D. 70 AND 200, Rabbi Judah the Prince decided to write down the Oral Law in what eventually became known as the Babylonian Talmud. Today, religious Jews regard Talmud scholars with the same reverence that secular society treats Nobel Prize laureates.

Previously, writing down the law had been resisted because leading rabbis felt that the law should be taught orally since people, rather than books, were considered the best teachers of the Jewish traditions. But more than one million Jews died in two failed uprisings, the Great Revolt in A.D. 66 and the Bar-Kokhba rebellion in A.D. 132–135, and with the loss of so many learned men in the uprisings, Rabbi Judah feared that the Oral Law would be forgotten if not recorded. His solution was to set down the Oral Law in 63 tracts called the Mishna. The rabbi arranged the Mishna topically so that all of the law on any one subject could be found in a single place.

The Mishna was studied by generations of rabbis in the centuries that followed. Eventually, some rabbis in Palestine around 400 recorded their discussions and comments about the Mishna in a series of books called the Talmud. In Hebrew, their books became known as the *Talmud Yerushalmi,* or the Palestinian Talmud. More than 100 years later, Babylonian rabbis did the same thing in a work called *Talmud Bavli,* or the Babylonian Talmud. Of the two, the Babylonian Talmud is more extensive, easier to use and read, and thus has became the more authoritative work. The *Babylonian Talmud* is almost invariably what people refer to and study today.

The book contains specific observations and information about a vast multitude of things, including tithes, the Sabbath, Passover, festival days, fasting days, marriage, animals killed for food, even sisters-in-law. For example, concerning marriage, the Talmud states that if a woman was married on the condition that she had no bodily defects, and she later was found to indeed have such defects, the marriage is invalid.

The Talmud also contains dietary information, such as the benefits of eating fish, stating: "He who makes it a habit to eat small fish will not suffer with indigestion; more than that, small fish make a man's whole body fruitful and strong." To this day, Jews use the Talmud in their religious observations.

The Spanish Inquisition

THE INQUISITION was as much political in nature as it was religious. The Crusades and Christianity's reconquest of Spain left a nation divided between Catholicism, Protestantism, Islam, and Judaism. King Ferdinand and Queen Isabella used Catholicism to unify the country and centralize their political authority. In 1478, they asked Pope Sixtus IV for authority to implement an inquisition. After Ferdinand threatened

to withdraw his troops that were helping protect Rome from Turkey, Sixtus agreed.

The primary target of the Spanish Inquisition was the *conversos,* those who had converted to Christianity from another religion. Faced with persecution, many Spanish Jews and Muslims had "converted" to Christianity, but they continued to practice their true religion in secret.

A pope-appointed inquisitor general oversaw the Inquisition. Denunciations were anonymous, and false accusations were common. Persons accused of heresy were presumed guilty, and acquittals were rare. The accused were given a chance to confess and to implicate others. Those who complied were generally fined or imprisoned. Despite the popular preconception of the Inquisition as a nonstop spree of medieval torture, torture was used in only about 2 percent of the cases.

Over the course of its existence, the Inquisition also prosecuted Protestants, alleged practitioners of witchcraft, moral degenerates, and heretics. The war against heresy also extended to books. Many of the prohibited books are now viewed as great works of Spanish literature.

Sixtus came to oppose the Inquisition's process, openly charging that its motivation was one of profit, since the system financed itself through the confiscation of property of wealthy victims. As an arm of the monarchy, the Inquisition also became a convenient way to dispose of political enemies.

Estimates vary as to the number of executions that took place over the course of the Inquisition—everything from about 3,000 to 5,000 to as many as 31,000 has been suggested. Thousands more were imprisoned or suffered lesser punishments before the Inquisition finally was abolished in 1834.

Konrad Adenauer and the Economic Miracle

AT THE CONCLUSION OF WORLD WAR II, Germany was in shambles. Twenty percent of Germany's housing was destroyed. Food production was half its 1938 prewar level, while industrial output was only one-third. A large percentage of working-age men were dead. Food shortages were severe; some people even traveled to the country on weekends to trade personal possessions such as furniture or clothes for potatoes.

Then Konrad Adenauer and Ludwig Erhard came into the picture. Born in 1876, Adenauer had a long career in German politics and government, particularly as the Mayor of Cologne, but he ran afoul of the Nazis and was interned in a prison camp. After the war, he formed the Christian Democratic Union political party. On September 15, 1949, he became chancellor of the new country of West Germany. Erhard, meanwhile, was part of a school of economic thought at the University of Freiburg known as "socially conscious free market." They advocated currency reform and the abolition of existing price controls.

On the other side were government officials, labor leaders, German manufacturing interests, and many Allied occupation officials who wanted to continue price controls. Erhard tested his ideas as director of the Office of Economic Opportunity under the occupation. In 1948, Erhard implemented (through U.S. General Lucius Clay) currency reform by replacing the existing reichs marks with a new currency of deutsche marks and eliminating price controls. These ideas began invigorating the economy. Adenauer saw this and selected Erhard as his minister of economic affairs.

The effect of Erhard's policies was immediate. The growth rate of industrial production was at 25 percent by 1950 and continued growing throughout the decade. By 1960, it was more than two times the level of 1950. During the same decade, the unemployment rate fell from 10.3 percent to 1.2 percent while the country's gross domestic product rose by two-thirds. Extra labor was supplied by thousands of *Gastarbeiter,* or guest workers. People began to talk about Germany's *Wirtschaftswunder,* or economic miracle.

Adenauer remained chancellor until 1963, when Erhard succeeded him. By then, however, Adenauer disliked Erhard personally and unsuccessfully tried to bar him from the post.

Jefferson Drafts the Declaration of Independence

D URING JUNE 1776, in his rented Philadelphia home, a red-haired Virginian named Thomas Jefferson hunched over a small desk, writing and rewriting. His document—the Declaration of Independence—would shape the emerging United States of America.

Jefferson had arrived in Philadelphia as a delegate to the Second Continental Congress. He was a tall gentleman farmer who detested public speaking but whose eloquent writing established him as a champion of the colonial cause. His 1774 work, *A Summary View of the Rights of British America,* forcefully argued that the British Parliament had no governing rights over the colonies.

On June 7, 1776, Congressional delegate Richard Henry Lee proposed that the 13 American colonies ought to be free and independent states. A committee of five was selected to prepare a document declaring independence: Benjamin Franklin, John Adams, Roger Sherman, Robert R. Livingston, and Jefferson. Jefferson proposed that Adams write it. Adams refused, saying that Jefferson should do it because he was a superior writer.

Jefferson returned to his rented house and began writing. Sipping tea brewed by his servant, and occasionally playing his violin, Jefferson wrote on a desk he had designed himself. His goal was to state the colonies' case "in terms... plain and firm" and to produce "an expression of the American mind."

The committee made a few minor changes to the document. The declaration later went before the Congress, where it was debated line by line. Whole sections were removed or weakened considerably, including Jefferson's attempt to condemn the slave trade, which was removed because of objections from South Carolina and Georgia. Other charges against the king were softened since some members still hoped to reconcile with England.

Jefferson said little during the debate, allowing Adams to speak in defense of the declaration. But Franklin noticed how dismayed Jefferson was as his document was radically altered and tried to ease his suffering by telling him a story about a hatmaker whose expressive store sign was ultimately edited down to a picture of a hat attached to the merchant's name. After Congress was through with it, enough of Jefferson's genius still remained that the declaration became one of history's greatest documents.

The Amritsar Massacre

I NDIAN NATIONALISTS supported the British government during World War I, expecting British victory to bring Indian independence. Instead, India's Imperial Legislative Council pushed through repressive legislation known as the Rowlatt Act in March 1919. The Rowlatt Act continued the special wartime powers of the 1915 Defense of India Act to deal with "revolutionary conspiracy"—in other words, nationalist activism. Indian members of the council resigned their seats in protest.

Brigadier General R.E.H. Dyer

Independence leader Mohandas Gandhi called on all Indians to "refuse civilly to obey" the so-called "Black Act." He declared a national work "suspension" day the first week of April as the first step to a full-scale campaign of *ahimsa,* or non-violent noncooperation.

On April 10, in the city of Amritsar, two Indian leaders who organized anti-Rowlatt meetings were arrested and deported without formal charge or trial. When their followers organized a protest march, troops fired on the marchers, causing a riot in which four Englishmen were killed. Brigadier General R.E.H. Dyer was called into Amritsar to restore order.

Dyer announced a ban on public gatherings of any kind. That afternoon, 10,000 Indians assembled in Jallianwala Bagh, an enclosed park, to celebrate a Hindu religious festival. Dyer arrived with troops and ordered them across the entrance to the walled park. Giving the unarmed crowd little warning and no way to escape, Dyer's soldiers fired 1,650 rounds in ten minutes, killing nearly 400 people and wounding more than 1,000.

A government commission severely censured Dyer and forced him to resign his commission. Even so, the British House of Lords passed a motion approving his action. The *Morning Post* newspaper collected money for his retirement and gave him a jeweled sword inscribed "Saviour of the Punjab."

Far from "saving India," Dyer's actions instead accelerated Indian nationalist activity. Many Indians who had been loyal supporters of the British Raj, or British India, joined the Indian National Congress, the largest of the nationalist organizations. Attempts to become equal partners within the Raj were over; the push for independence had begun.

Louis Riel and the Northwest Rebellion

Louis Riel was born into a devoutly Catholic family on October 22, 1844, in St. Boniface, Red River Settlement, in present-day Manitoba, Canada. Although his ancestry was primarily white, he always described himself as Métis, who were buffalo hunters and fur traders of mixed European and Canadian Indian ancestry. At age 14, he went to Montreal to study for the priesthood, but in 1868 he started back for the Northwest to join his widowed mother.

While on his journey, he heard of growing Métis unhappiness north of the Red River. The Hudson Bay Company wanted these lands to become part of Canada, without any input from the majority French-speaking Métis who inhabited them. Incensed, Riel took up their cause, raising an army and forming a provisional government for the region. On November 2, 1869, Riel's forces captured Fort Garry, the headquarters of the Hudson Bay Company. His movement had its resisters, including laborer Thomas Scott, who was ultimately caught, tried, and executed by Riel's group. Scott's death caused such outrage throughout Canada that Prime Minister John A. Macdonald finally sent an army to end the "Red River Resistance." Nevertheless, Riel is considered the father of Manitoba province.

As he fled to the United States, Riel had a vision on December 8, 1875, in which God appointed him "the prophet of the new world." Riel began behaving erratically, even after secretly returning to Quebec. In March 1876, he was placed in a mental institution under the name Louis R. David, where he stayed for more than a year. By 1883, Riel had married and was teaching in Montana's Sun River District. Manitoba, meanwhile, was rapidly becoming modernized and English speaking. The Métis moved further west to Saskatchewan, but the group had trouble adapting to the area.

In June 1884, the Métis asked Riel to return to Canada as their advocate. When his diplomatic efforts failed, Riel—perhaps guided by his visions—procured weapons, raised a ragtag Métis/Canadian Indian army, and launched the Northwest Rebellion. They won a small victory at Duck Lake on March 26, 1885, but were routed by Canadian regular troops two months later, when Riel was captured. At his trial, he was found guilty of treason with a recommendation of mercy, but the judge sentenced him to death. Riel was hanged on November 16, 1885. His death led to the beginnings of Quebec's nationalist movement.

England's Industrial Revolution

Prior to England's Industrial Revolution in the 18th century, weaving was largely a domestic industry. Children sorted, cleaned, and carded the raw fibers, women spun the yarn, and men wove the cloth. In rural areas, most weavers were also farmers; weaving was done in the seasons when the demand for agricultural labor was low.

The initial changes were small. The flying shuttle, widely adopted in the 1750s and '60s, allowed weavers to speed up their process. This created an acute yarn shortage. James Hargreave's spinning jenny, patented in 1770, solved the yarn supply problem: The largest jennies allowed a single person—helped by several children—to operate as many as 120 spindles at once.

The real change in the English textile industry began in 1769, when Richard Arkwright patented the water frame. Unlike the spinning jenny, Arkwright's water frame was designed as a factory machine. Originally horse-operated, it was eventually powered by water and then steam. Each technical improvement moved the textile industry further away from the domestic system. Spinning began to be concentrated in factories. By 1812, one spinner could produce as much yarn in a given time as 200 spinners could have produced using hand spindles.

The industrialization of the textile industry affected nearly everything, spurring the development of other industries, from forging steel to mining coal. The need for improved transportation led to the expansion of the canal system and the later development of roads and railways. Large industrial cities developed in the Midlands and the North.

Industrialization also created a new class of urban poor, as the population shifted from the countryside to the cities. New social and economic problems arose, including low wages, slum housing, and the use of child labor. Demobilized soldiers from the Napoleonic wars, unemployed farmworkers, and Irish immigrants swelled the workforce, driving wages further down.

The group that suffered most in the early years of industrialization was the weavers. Throughout 1811 and 1812, displaced textile workers, calling themselves Luddites after a possibly mythical leader named Ned Ludd, attacked the mills that were diminishing their livelihood. Within time, other calls for reform arose, including calls for minimum wage laws, apprenticeship regulations, child labor laws, and other protections for laborers.

Hellenistic Culture

THE HELLENISTIC AGE in the Middle East and Mediterranean is generally said to have begun with the conquests of Alexander the Great. In particular, his destruction of the Persian Empire in 330 B.C. helped spread Greek power and culture into non-Greek civilizations. What followed was a flowering of Greek-inspired culture; in fact, the word *Hellenistic* comes from the Greek word meaning "to imitate Greeks." The period saw major accomplishments in the arts, literature, philosophy, science, and religion.

One key diversion was a new emphasis in literature. Neo-Greek playwright Menander, for example, focused on comedy and often featured nonheroic characters such as prostitutes rather than the typical larger-than-life heroic figures of classical Greek drama. Sculptors also began to move toward a more realistic and less idealized vision of the human body, creating statues of everyday people.

Hellenistic philosophers challenged the dominance of Plato and Aristotle. Epicurus argued that mental happiness was the central goal of human life. Zeno of Citium, meanwhile, founded the philosophy of Stoicism, which argued that human virtue consisted in living uncomplainingly according to divine will as revealed in the laws of nature.

Scientific studies also flourished during this era. Scholars from Alexandria in Egypt developed the theory that Earth revolved around the Sun and was round, with a circumference that was actually within 200 miles of the correct figure. Both Euclid and Archimedes were giants in the world of geometry and mathematics, with Euclid creating the field of plane geometry and Archimedes establishing the value of pi.

In religion, a number of eastern mystery cults emerged, which later became a major influence on the way Westerners viewed their place in the universe. These cults, especially the Egyptian cult of Isis, became enormously popular because they offered a promise of eternal life through individual salvation.

The Hellenistic Age declined as Rome increased in power and conquered Egypt in 30 B.C.

POSTSCRIPT

▪ Perhaps the most important cultural monument in the Hellenistic world was the Great Library at Alexandria, Egypt, built around 300 B.C. It was the world's first research library and the largest library in the ancient world.

The Outbreak of the Iraq War

A T ONE POINT IN HISTORY, the United States was allied with Iraq. American and Western aid for its dictator, Saddam Hussein, is credited with helping Iraq fight Iran to a standstill during the Iran–Iraq War in the 1980s. But after the war, U.S.–Iraq relations rapidly deteriorated. In

1990, Iraq invaded the neighboring country of Kuwait, resulting in an American-led coalition of forces expelling the Iraqis from Kuwait during the Gulf War. After the war, the United States and Great Britain patrolled "no-fly" zones in Iraq. In addition, a United Nations resolution mandated ongoing inspections to prevent Iraq from developing chemical, biological, or nuclear weapons. Iraq chafed under these restrictions.

After the attacks on September 11, 2001, by Muslim extremist group al Qaeda, tensions between Iraq and the United States increased exponentially as President George W. Bush announced a "War on Terror."

In retaliation, Bush labeled Iraq as part of an "axis of evil" with Iran and North Korea and accused the Arab nation of manufacturing weapons of mass destruction (WMDs). In October 2002, Congress authorized the president to use any means necessary against Iraq. However, an appearance by American Secretary of State Colin Powell before the United Nations in February 2003, in which he presented claims that Iraq was allegedly producing WMDs, did not result in U.N. authorization to invade Iraq. Nevertheless, on March 20, 2003, the United States, supplying the majority of troops, led a coalition of forces into Iraq. Iraqi armed resistance was ineffectual, and on April 9, the capital of Baghdad fell. On May 1, Bush visited the aircraft carrier USS *Abraham Lincoln* and declared combat operations at an end. No WMDs were ever found.

But in the weeks and months following Bush's pronouncement, an anti-American insurgency grew in Iraq. Despite a new Iraqi government coming to power in May 2006 and the execution of Hussein in December, insurgent violence continued, threatening to tear the country apart. As of March 2008, 4,000 U.S. troops had been killed in Iraq.

The Hungarian Revolution

HUNGARY HAD NEVER BEEN a willing part of the Soviet sphere of influence. During World War II, approximately 200,000 Hungarian troops had fought on Nazi Germany's side against the Russians. But after the war, the country came under Communist control as one of the Eastern European satellites of the Soviet Empire. In 1949, the People's Republic of Hungary was declared, and the oppressive Mátyás Rákosi became its first prime minister.

The death of Stalin in 1953 ushered in a period of liberalization in the Soviet system. In Hungary, reformist Imre Nagy took over in 1955. A proreform victory in Poland gave Hungarians hope, even though Nagy was replaced by Rákosi in 1956. Rákosi's resignation in July further fueled reformist hopes. Students and journalists began holding meetings and demonstrations; official Communist Party organizations were ignored. Then, on October 23, after increasingly strident demonstrations by Hungarian writers and university students, a crowd of 200,000 tore down a statue of Joseph Stalin in Budapest. That night, Hungarian Communist Party Secretary Erno Gero called for Soviet military intervention, and the next day Russian tanks rumbled into Budapest.

Using Molotov cocktails, kitchen implements, and any other means, Budapest protesters fought Russian troops and the despised AVH (the secret police) to a standstill. When Nagy was brought back as prime minister and a cease-fire declared, it looked like the revolutionaries had won. On October 31, the Soviet Union issued a conciliatory statement. Combined with the recent Polish uprising, the Iron Curtain seemed to be falling.

However, a hard-line Kremlin element was afraid of having a hole punched in the ring of Eastern European defense states. They also feared how Soviet acquiescence would play to the rest of the Communist Bloc countries and decided to crush the rebellion. On November 4, the five previous Soviet divisions were strengthened to about 15, and air support was added. The tanks again rolled into Budapest and crushed the rebellion for good. An emergency appeal by Nagy for support fell on deaf ears in the West.

But the Soviet actions caused criticism and splintered Western Communist parties in Italy, Great Britain, France, and elsewhere. The "collective suicide of a whole people," as a United Nations representative called it, may have failed in Hungary, but it had worldwide repercussions for the Soviets.

The Rise of Artillery

MANY HISTORIANS DATE the invention of gunpowder to about A.D. 850, during China's Tang dynasty. From there, the technology traveled west along the trade route known as the Silk Road. By the 13th century, Islamic armies had begun to make effective use of artillery, which played an important role in the growth of the so-called "gunpowder empires" of the Ottomans, Mughals, and Safavids.

European use of cannons came about during the Hundred Years' War (1339–1453). Initially, these iron or cast-bronze cannons were rather small. Soldiers laid them on the ground with the muzzles elevated on a mound. The shot was a one- to two-pound iron ball. Cannons evolved by the end of the war into enormous bombards that shot iron or granite balls as large as 25 inches in diameter and weighing hundreds of pounds. Even a small cannon could destroy a stone castle at 3,400 yards.

Before 1500, artillery was limited to siege pieces that were not easily transportable. With the development of cast-iron balls and improvements in gunpowder and casting techniques, it became possible to produce lighter cannons that could be used in the field, as garrison defense, and on ships. The French invention of the limber, a two-wheeled wagon that carried ammunition and towed a field gun behind it, increased mobility.

In about 1525, pikemen and musketeers, in the formation known as the Spanish Square, began to show up on battlefields. They were able to move about with ease, and use of the heavier field artillery declined. The artillery was often so heavy as to be immobile, which left gunners stranded in the open—an easy mark for the enemy.

In the 17th century, Gustavus Adolphus of Sweden transformed the use of artillery. Recognizing the need for mobility, he used nothing heavier than a 12-pound gun in the field. He also increased the ratio of cannons to infantry from 1 per thousand men to 6 per thousand, and he attached a pair of light guns to every regiment. Adolphus used artillery to smash enemy infantry formations and cavalry charges to neutralize the still-immobile artillery of his opponents. His principles of artillery served as the standard for European armies from the 18th century until the development of trench warfare in World War I.

POSTSCRIPT

■ Early gunners weren't always soldiers. Usually, they were day-to-day civilians who were hired as needed.

McCarthyism

URING THE EARLY PART OF THE 1950s, many Americans worried that Communists were trying to subvert the American way of life. Wisconsin Senator Joseph McCarthy took advantage of these fears to make a name for himself.

McCarthy's first years as a senator were unremarkable. In fact, he was once labeled the "worst U.S. senator." On February 9, 1950, McCarthy spoke to a group of Republican women in Wheeling, West Virginia.

During the speech, he claimed that he had a list of 205 State Department employees who were members of the Communist Party. The press picked up McCarthy's speech, yet when pressed to release the names on his list, he refused.

As McCarthy's popularity continued to rise, he began using scare tactics to discredit his opponents. In this way, he heavily influenced the 1950 Senate

Senator Joseph McCarthy

elections, resulting in a Republican sweep. Now one of the most influential senators, McCarthy began holding hearings against individuals he accused of being Communists as well as the government agencies suspected of harboring them. During this time, *Washington Post* cartoonist Herbert Block coined the term "McCarthyism" to describe the senator's heavy-handed tactics.

McCarthy especially disliked President Harry Truman, a Democrat, and he attacked many in Truman's administration. When the Republican Dwight Eisenhower was elected president in 1952, McCarthy even attacked him for not being tough enough on Communism.

McCarthy began to overplay his hand when he attacked a celebrated World War II general and began to browbeat the secretary of the army. As a result, a series of televised hearings ran in which the army accused McCarthy of illegally pressuring them to gain favorable treatment for one of his friends. The American public saw McCarthy's bullying tactics firsthand, and the tide began to turn against him. Unfavorable publicity mounted, and the Senate censured McCarthy in late 1954. His power had been effectively broken.

Kenya Attains Independence

THE 1920s were marked by steady British immigration to Africa and the development of African political movements demanding a larger role in government. The Kikuyu Central Association (KCA) was formed in 1924 as an official native council to create the first widespread African nationalist movement.

Jomo Kenyatta (left) *with Mau Mau leader Field Marshal Mwariama*

Kenyan nationalism found a leader in Jomo Kenyatta. Kenyatta joined the KCA in 1925 and later led the Kenyan African Union (KAU), Kenya's first intertribal nationalist organization. He became the nationalist movement's most prominent spokesman, arguing for independence through peaceful means.

In 1952, the militant nationalist organization known as Mau Mau began a violent campaign to regain African lands. By 1956, Mau Mau insurgents killed approximately 2,000 African "loyalists" and 100 European settlers. The British declared a state of emergency, placing between 80,000 and 100,000 Kikuyu in detention camps. Using forged evidence to convict him as a Mau Mau leader, the British sentenced Kenyatta to seven years hard labor in 1953.

Informed that Britain would not provide a standing army to protect them from a Mau Mau revival, moderate white settlers took steps toward a system of shared power. Kenyan leaders insisted power be placed in the hands of the majority, campaigning for full democracy, full independence, and the release of Kenyatta.

Atrocities committed against black Africans by Kenyan police convinced British Prime Minister Harold Macmillan that Britain must grant Kenyan independence at once. The sticking point became Kenyatta, who was still in jail. African leaders campaigned for the first election with the caveat that they would not take office if Kenyatta were not freed.

Elected president of the newly formed Kenya African National Union in absentia, Kenyatta was released on August 21, 1961, and immediately reentered Kenyan politics. Kenya achieved full independence on December 12, 1963. Exactly one year later, Kenya became a republic, with Kenyatta as its first president.

Ancient Egypt

EGYPT, one of the world's great early civilizations, owes much of its success to its prime real estate. Egypt was centered on the Nile, the world's longest river. Every year between July and October, the Nile flooded, bringing precious water to the narrow valley that flowed through the desert into the Mediterranean. When the waters receded, lush new soil was left behind for planting crops.

Early artifacts show that civilization began in the Nile valley as long ago as 4500 B.C. The pharaoh Menes united Egypt into one kingdom by 3000 B.C. and established the capital at Memphis, just below the Nile Delta. Ancient Egyptians called their country *Kemet* (black soil), after their rich farmland.

Pharaohs, leaders who were the embodiment of harmony in the universe, ruled Egypt. According to Egyptian belief, without the pharaoh, the world would descend into chaos. It was believed the pharaoh was the living descendant of Ra, the sun god, who was one of more than 115 gods and goddesses the ancient Egyptians worshipped. Other Egyptian deities included the sky god Horus; Seth, god of disorder and violence; Osiris, god of the dead; and Isis, goddess of magic and life.

During the Old and Middle Kingdoms, from about 2675 to 1759 B.C., many of the pharaohs supervised massive building projects in an effort to immortalize their memory after their deaths. Many of these structures were pyramids, which also served as the pharaohs' tombs. Originally designed as *mastabas,* or step pyramids, the trend reached an apex with the Great Pyramid at Giza, built for Khufu, the second king of the fourth dynasty.

Egypt imported many items from Nubia to the south, including ivory, incense, cattle, grains, gold, and animal skins. As time went on, Egypt had to defend itself from other empires coming to power in the Middle East. Persia conquered Egypt in 525 B.C. and then again in 343 B.C. Egypt was under Greek rule when Alexander the Great occupied the country in 332 B.C. After Alexander's death, his general Ptolemy became pharaoh. Ptolemy's descendants lasted until 30 B.C., when the last Ptolemaic leader, Cleopatra, committed suicide after the Romans took control.

POSTSCRIPT

■ Egyptian priests mummified the bodies of the deceased so that they could travel to the afterworld and live forever.

The Republic

PLATO was a Classical Greek philosopher born in Athens around 428 B.C. He began to pursue a political career at a young age, but after the Peloponnesian War, he turned to philosophy. In 387, he founded the Academy, an Athenian school of philosophy and learning.

He studied under the great Greek philosopher Socrates, who said, "The unexamined life is not worth living." After Socrates's death in 400, many of his followers wanted to preserve his ideas and lessons by writing them down. Several of them did so, but it was Plato who did it with the most success. *The Republic* was his masterpiece, written when he was around 70 years old.

Based on what he had learned from his mentor, Plato wrote approximately 25 dialogues. *The Republic,* the most recognized of them all, is written as a Socratic dialogue; that is, the character of Socrates discusses philosophical problems with other characters.

The Republic explored some of humanity's most profound questions, which are as relevant today as they were when they were written around 360. In it, Socrates discussed various topics, such as the point of living honestly and ethically, what leads to happiness, and the definition of justice. While other characters in the dialogues such as Cephalus and Thrasymachus gave various answers to these questions, Socrates stated that morality was the key to justice, and it was worthwhile in itself.

Socrates, through Plato, went on to describe three different kinds of human souls. The *rational* soul is the mind or intelligence; it is the thinking portion within each person, in charge of discerning what is real and what is not, and what is true and what is false. The *spirited* soul is the will or volition; it is responsible for carrying out what the rational soul directs. Finally, the *appetitive* soul is emotion or desire; it is the portion that wants and feels things, calling for increased self-control. It was Socrates's—and thus Plato's—strong belief that a person can only be just when all three souls are in harmony and working together.

Much of *The Republic* still rings true today. In Book 4, Plato wrote that justice is "establishing the parts of the soul so that they dominate and are dominated by each other according to nature, injustice so that they rule and are ruled contrary to nature."

The Weimar Republic

THE WEIMAR REPUBLIC was Germany's attempt at democratic govern-ment after World War I. Unfortunately, it also hastened the rise of a dictator who plunged the world into yet another bloody war.

After Germany lost World War I in 1918, a key Allied point was that the country's government be switched from military to civil rule. With various political factions fighting in the streets of Berlin, the National Assembly, elected in January 1919, met in the city of Weimar, thus giv-ing the government its unofficial name. In August, a new constitution was adopted and signed by the new republic's first president, Friedrich Ebert. The constitution called for a bicameral assembly: The *Reichstag* represented the entire country, while the *Reichsrat* represented regional governments inside Germany, such as Saxony and Bavaria. Almost immediately the new republic was buffeted by armed conflict between left- and right-wing groups. The constitution's system of proportional representation meant that any party, no matter how small, could get seats in the Reichstag. It was a disruptive technique that the National Socialist German Worker's Party—the Nazis—effectively used in its early years.

Another problem for the republic was hyperinflation, caused by the overprinting of money so that there would be cash to pay war repara-tions. At one point, it took one million pieces of German paper money to buy a single U.S. dollar. Through the introduction of a new currency, and the efforts of statesman Gustav Stresemann, the republic seemed to be turning the corner. But Stresemann's death in early October 1929, followed quickly by the American stock market crash, dealt the republic a fatal blow. America had loaned the republic money twice before, but now America was broke and demanded repayment. German companies laid off workers by the hundreds of thousands as hyperinflation again wracked the country. Unemployment surged from 650,000 to more than five million from 1928 to 1932.

With no money and no jobs, workers were easily seduced by the siren song of the Nazis. The party gained 230 legislative seats in July 1932, making it the largest in the country. Ultimately, aging President Paul von Hindenburg made Nazi leader Adolf Hitler German chancellor in January 1933. Soon after, the Weimar Republic ceased to exist, as Hitler assumed dictatorial powers.

POSTSCRIPT

▓ Von Hindenburg contemptuously called Hitler "the little corporal."

Henry Ford Introduces the Model T

FOR YEARS, Henry Ford had toyed with the idea of a new type of internal combustion engine. In 1903, he got the chance to see it come to light when he, along with a group of investors, formed the Ford Motor Company in Detroit, Michigan. In 1908, he introduced the Model T, dubbed "America's Everyman Car." It was easy to operate, inexpensive to maintain, and reasonably priced. The car was an immediate success.

By 1912, there were 7,000 Ford dealers in the country. Ford built a new plant at Highland Park, Michigan, and began implementing new concepts, including precision manufacturing, interchangeable and standard parts, the division of labor, and a continuously moving assembly line. Not only did this lower cost and raise efficiency, it helped the company become the world's largest automotive manufacturer.

By 1918, half of all the cars in the United States were Model Ts. The company moved to a huge new plant in Dearborn, Michigan. It had almost seven million square feet of space, enough to hold 100,000 employees as well as a steel mill, a glass factory, and a huge assembly line capable of producing a complete car in 93 minutes.

Ford also instigated a policy eventually known as "welfare capitalism." The average amount paid to automotive workers at the time was $2.34 an hour for nine-hour days, but Ford proposed to pay his employees $5 an hour for an eight-hour day. It was considered a radical move, but the pay hike had a catch: Each employee had to agree to "live right," which to Ford meant no smoking or drinking, a strong marriage, and wise spending choices. To ensure that his workers followed these rules, his Sociological Department sent investigators into employee homes for inspections. If workers weren't fulfilling their obligations, they returned to $2.34 an hour, or worse, were fired. Two years later, this department was disbanded for being too expensive.

Ford revolutionized the automobile manufacturing business. Today, the Ford Motor Company is still a strong competitor in auto sales.

Mustafa Kemal Atatürk (1881–1938)

IF YOU TRAVEL ANYWHERE IN TURKEY, you'll see images of the great Atatürk on currency and in public buildings and private homes. Born in 1881 in Thessaloniki, Greece (then part of the Ottoman Empire), the man was first known as Mustafa Kemal; Kemal being a nickname given to him by a teacher at secondary school, meaning "perfect one." He attended military schools and eventually became an officer. During World War I, the Ottoman Empire was allied with Germany, and Kemal led troops during the Gallipoli landings in eastern Turkey against the Russians and later against the British advance from Palestine.

The war left the empire devastated and defeated. The 1920 Treaty of Sevres stripped away much of the Ottoman territory and allowed the Greeks to occupy eastern Anatolia. Ultimately, a group of Turkish nationalists gathered in Ankara; in 1920 they established the Grand National Assembly to fight all foreign invaders and protect Turkish territory. Kemal became commander of the army, and in 1921 they defeated the Greeks, who by that time had advanced to within 50 miles of Ankara. A year later, the Treaty of Lausanne replaced the 1920 treaty and freed Turkey from the burdens of Sevres. Turkey was the only defeated country to negotiate its own peace treaty. By that time, the old Ottoman Empire had been dissolved when the last sultan was exiled.

On October 29, 1923, the Republic of Turkey was proclaimed with Kemal as its president. With the cooperation of the Grand National Assembly, Kemal set about modernizing and westernizing Turkey. Kemal encouraged Western dress, abolishing the wearing of fezzes by men and discouraging veils on women. The Western calendar and clock were adopted, as was the metric system of measurement. Arabic script was discouraged in favor of a modified Western script for Turkish. People were required to take family names in the Western style. Mustafa Kemal became Kemal Atatürk, meaning the "Father of the Turks." In 1923, a vote passed to move the national capital from Istanbul to Ankara to symbolize the break with the antiquated past. Women received the right to vote in 1934, and female representatives were sent to the assembly.

Atatürk thus established a more modern, secular state. He summarized his programs in six words: republicanism, nationalism, populism, statism, secularism, and reformism. Ever since, Turkish leaders have tried to keep Atatürk's memory alive and maintain Turkey's secular government.

The Bolshevik Revolution

T HE RUSSIANS had tried revolution before. In 1905, they attempted to reform the repressive government under Czar Nicholas II, but he responded by restricting the press, calling out the army on demonstrators, and devising an elected assembly that he dissolved whenever he felt like it. By 1917, Russia had been fighting in World War I for three years and had sustained heavy losses. Food urgently needed by the populace had been diverted to the front for troops. Food riots broke out in Petrograd in February. As the resistance swelled, Nicholas abdicated on March 2. Revolution-

Vladimir Lenin in 1918

ary leaders who had once fled Russia now returned—including Vladimir Ilyich Ulyanov, also known as Lenin.

Born on April 22, 1870, Lenin studied law as an adult. In 1887, his brother Alexander Ulyanov was executed for terrorist activities. This sparked an interest in radical politics in Lenin, who began studying Karl Marx's theories.

Lenin later developed his own ideas on communism. It was up to the "bourgeois intelligentsia," as he called them, to lead the proletariat and for a rigidly hierarchical, strictly disciplined party to lead the intellectuals. His was the blueprint for totalitarian Communist regimes for decades to come.

Lenin, then living in Switzerland, wanted to return home but had difficulty traveling because of the war. He was helped in part by Germany, who hoped he would cause unrest in Russia and end the war on that front. After his 1917 return, Lenin immediately became a leading voice in the Bolshevik faction of the Social Democratic Labor Party. His "April Theses" speech directed the Bolsheviks to abandon the provisional government so that it would fall. By June, he and another returned exile—Leon Trotsky, leader of the Menshevik faction of the Social Democrats—had formed an alliance. Trotsky joined the Bolsheviks; by August, the group boasted more than 200,000 members. On October 24, the provisional government was ousted.

Despite promises of change, Lenin delivered the opposite: mindless killing during the "Red Terror"; autocratic rule instead of democracy; and large, collective farms run by absentee owners, rather than the redistribution of land to peasants.

Pierre Trudeau (1919–2000)

Part political rock star, part political fox, Pierre Elliott Trudeau became Canada's 15th prime minister in 1968. Smart, charismatic, and single, he drove a convertible and dated international celebrities. The nation was swept up in Trudeaumania.

As justice minister, Trudeau had shown his liberal stance by relaxing laws regarding abortion and homosexuality. "There's no place for the state in the bedrooms of the nation," he declared. But he was also a firm proponent of federalism. One of his first acts as prime minister was to promote bilingualism. He created the Official Languages Act, allowing civil servants a choice of speaking either French or English at work. His aim was to perpetuate one nation with "two official languages and a pluralist society."

In 1970, he demonstrated his toughness by invoking the War Measures Act after a group of Quebec separatists kidnapped a British diplomat. He went on to implement a number of popular social programs, pushing for universal health care and other liberal reforms.

As the '70s progressed, his popularity waned. The western provinces were alienated by Trudeau's seeming indifference to their concerns. Soaring inflation forced him to initiate wage and price controls. On a personal level, his 1971 marriage to flower child Margaret Sinclair, daughter of a former Liberal cabinet minister, ended in separation in 1977 after she culminated a series of embarrassments with a night of partying with the Rolling Stones. The couple divorced in 1984.

In 1979, after he and his Liberals suffered defeat at the polls, Trudeau announced his decision to retire. However, in 1980 he made an astonishing comeback, again assuming the mantle of prime minister. Some of his most important work followed. He was instrumental in persuading voters to turn down a referendum on a separate Quebec.

He then incorporated the British North American Act into the nation's law and implemented a new Canadian-controlled constitution, including a Charter of Canadian Rights and Freedoms to ensure protection of individual rights. Trudeau introduced a Constitutional Resolution, and after an 18-month political battle, all the provincial premiers except Quebec's signed it. On April 17, 1982, Queen Elizabeth II arrived in Canada to proclaim the new constitution. It was Trudeau's finest hour.

In February 1984, Trudeau announced his resignation from politics. He died of prostate cancer in 2000.

Lindbergh's Nonstop Flight

BORN IN DETROIT, MICHIGAN, on February 4, 1902, Charles Lindbergh was fascinated by aviation from an early age. He enrolled in a flying school in Lincoln, Nebraska, when he was 20 years old. Over the next two years, he juggled multiple aviation-related duties from mechanic and parachute jumper to wingwalker and barnstormer. In 1924, he enrolled in the U.S. Army's flying school, where he graduated top of his class. Several years later, he was an airmail pilot, although he had much higher ambitions.

In 1926, he convinced several businessmen to back him in a contest to make the world's first nonstop transatlantic flight for $25,000. Lindbergh's crew began work on his single-engine aircraft, the *Spirit of St. Louis.* On the morning of May 20, 1927, Lindbergh set off from New York with water, sandwiches, maps, charts, and 450 gallons of gasoline. He had no parachute and no radio. He gave those up in order to make room for extra gasoline. As the plane lifted off, people held their breath; it was so heavy that it only cleared the telephone lines and trees by 20 feet.

For the next 33½ hours and 3,610 miles, Lindbergh flew continuously. His biggest enemy was fatigue. He had been too excited to sleep the previous night and now, because of his flight, he couldn't. Though he fell asleep countless times, he was always pulled back to consciousness by the shudder of the control stick. By the time he landed in Paris before a thrilled crowd, he hadn't slept for 55 hours.

Lindbergh was immediately an international hero. The president congratulated him, and he was given the Medal of Honor and the first Distinguished Flying Cross. A ticker tape parade was held for him, and soon he was off on an 82-city tour of the United States. Elinor Smith Sullivan, winner of the 1930 Best Woman Aviator of the Year Award remarked, "It's hard to describe the impact Lindbergh had on people. Even the first walk on the moon doesn't come close. The '20s were such an innocent time and people were still so religious—I think they felt like this man was sent by God to do this."

Thomas Aquinas (1225–1274)

ARGUABLY THE MOST INFLUENTIAL Catholic theologian in the past 800 years, Thomas Aquinas was born in Italy, the son of an aristocratic family. When he was five, his family enrolled him in a Benedictine abbey near his home. When the area was ravaged by war, he was sent to study at the University of Naples. There he studied the teachings of Greek philosopher Aristotle, whose works had recently been reintroduced into the Western world by Muslim scholars. In spite of protests from his family, he joined the Dominican mendicant order.

He spent some time in Cologne studying with Albertus Magnus, a noted theologian who had also come under the influence of Aristotle. He completed his studies in Paris, where he held a chair in theology from 1256 to 1258. He then spent the rest of his life holding various teaching posts in Italy at the behest of the pope. He fell ill and died while on the way to defend papal positions at the Council of Lyon in 1274.

During his lifetime, Aquinas wrote a number of influential books in which he combined theology and philosophy in an attempt to help humans develop a fuller understanding of God and the church. His best-known works are *Summa contra Gentiles* (1258–1264) and *Summa Theologiae* (1266–1273), which he was unable to complete prior to his death.

In essence, his enormously complex ideas included several major points. First, he argued that faith and reason are not mutually exclusive; specifically, he believed that it was possible to reconcile Aristotle's scientific rationalism and the Catholic Church's doctrines of faith and divine revelation. Although he thought that such issues as the existence and nature of God could be captured through scriptural revelation, the use of reason could amplify, and in some cases help prove, propositions ordinarily based on faith. Perhaps most famously, in *Summa Theologiae*, he used rational methods, especially syllogistic reasoning, to propound five proofs for the existence of God.

While controversial at the time, Aquinas's ideas still remain a crucial component of official Catholic doctrine. In recognition of his contributions, he was canonized in 1323.

POSTSCRIPT

▓ Aquinas's family was so opposed to his joining the relatively obscure Dominican order that his brothers kidnapped him and kept him prisoner in the family castle for more than a year.

The World Wide Web

Isaac Asimov's story "Anniversary" describes how home computers called "multivac outlets" are connected by a "planetwide network of circuits" to a gigantic "super-computer." Although the story was written nearly 50 years ago, Asimov's vision is eerily close to reality.

Many people don't think about just how the entire world is connected by computers. The World Wide Web (the source of the *www* in Web site addresses) is a global information system that enables computer users to communicate with nearly anyone worldwide. Contrary to some beliefs, the Web is not a synonym for the Internet; the Web is simply a service that operates on the Internet, much the same way as e-mail.

The Web was originally developed at Switzerland's CERN (translated from French to the European Council for Nuclear Research), the world's largest particle physics center. Englishman Tim Berners-Lee came up with the idea in 1989, and he and colleague Robert Cailliau refined it a year later. In the beginning, the system was intended only for communication between physics laboratories around the world so they could share data. The two researchers quickly realized the system's potential and pitched their ideas at European Conference on Hypertext Technology in September 1990. Unfortunately, there were no takers.

By the end of 1990, the two had everything they needed to launch the Web. On August 6, 1991, Berners-Lee and Cailliau posted a summary of their invention on a newsgroup, officially announcing the Web as a public service on the Internet.

Since then, the World Wide Web has continued to evolve and grow. Currently, more than 237 million people in North America alone log on to the Web and use it for just about everything. Users can check the weather and current stock market figures. They can connect with long lost friends or make new ones through online dating sites. The World Wide Web opened the door to worldwide communication, and while some argue that it will end personal, face-to-face communication, others firmly believe that it has brought the world together in a way nothing else ever has.

POSTSCRIPT

■ Before the Web was named, other possibilities considered included The Information Mine (TIM, the creator's name) or Mine of Information (MOI, or "me" in French).

Leo Tolstoy (1828–1910)

TOLSTOY WAS BORN IN 1828 to an aristocratic, land-owning Russian family. He joined the army in 1851 and participated in the Crimean War. After the war, he returned home to start a school for local children.

In 1852, Tolstoy published his first writings, most of it autobiographical fiction. His first great novel, *War and Peace,* was published in serialized installments from 1865 to 1869. Tolstoy uses this panoramic account of Russia during the Napoleonic Wars to exemplify his belief that even though all human events are predestined, humankind must hold on to the illusion of free will in order to function in the world.

Four years after finishing *War and Peace,* he began another masterpiece, *Anna Karenina,* which he completed in 1877. Far more tightly focused than *War and Peace,* the novel centered on one family, particularly Anna and her fatal love affair. After finishing the novel, Tolstoy renounced his early

Leo Tolstoy on his deathbed

writing. Although he continued to publish fiction, Tolstoy began to see himself as a moral and religious philosopher rather than a novelist.

Indeed, it is in this philosophical role that Tolstoy may have had the greatest impact on world history. *A Confession,* written from 1882 to '84, outlines his religious struggle as he moved toward pacifism and asceticism. He also began writing religious and philosophical pamphlets and articles, of which more than 20 million were distributed worldwide.

Tolstoy attempted to practice what he preached. He lived a simple peasant life, extolling the virtues of hard work. He became a cobbler, immersed himself in Chinese philosophy, and gave up what he considered vices, ranging from white bread to hunting. He fervently believed in Jesus's Sermon on the Mount and argued that humans, above all, must learn to suppress anger and love their enemies. By 1901, the Russian Orthodox Church was so concerned by the impact of what it saw as Tolstoy's heresies that he was excommunicated. He died of pneumonia in 1910.

Tolstoy's reputation for leading a simple, moral life made him a hero to millions. His pacifism deeply influenced Mohandas Gandhi and Martin Luther King, Jr., while his communalism and simplicity helped inspire the kibbutz movement in Israel.

Clausewitz Publishes *On War*

GERMAN SOLDIER-PHILOSOPHER Carl von Clausewitz was one of the most influential military theorists in the 19th and early 20th centuries. He served in the Prussian army during the Napoleonic Wars. Later he served as chief of staff to a Prussian corps commander during the 1815 Waterloo Campaign. After the wars, Clausewitz worked as the director of a military school, an artillery inspector, and a major-general in the Prussian army.

In his great work *Vom Kriege* (*On War*), Clausewitz attempted to synthesize the changes in warfare brought about by the French Revolution. In prior wars, generals sought to avoid direct combat and instead concentrated on strategy. The French, however, changed all that with a national mobilization that resulted in larger armies fighting for a principle instead of for a king's desire to add territory. Napoleon took advantage of the situation and used his army to fight pitched battles, making the enemy army—and not the territory—the actual goal.

Clausewitz noted this change in how war was fought, and he tried to describe it to his readers. "War is thus an act of force to compel our enemy to do our will," he wrote. Clausewitz developed this idea to state that war was violence pushed to the utmost extreme. And, according to him, since war was entirely about violence, it was hard to call it scientific and thus rational. After studying the Napoleonic Wars, Clausewitz also concluded that war was simply an extension of politics; as a result, he theorized, war was a normal occurrence between nations. Everything done for the individual soldier, he wrote, such as supplying him with a uniform and a weapon, was all designed "merely to fight at the right time and place."

Clausewitz died in 1831 from cholera, leaving his book unfinished and riddled with inconsistencies. Ever since then, readers have argued about what he meant. Clausewitz himself realized that it was almost impossible to write an understandable theory of warfare. After all, he wrote, no matter how good a plan was concocted, the element of chance was always present to disrupt it. "Everything is very simple in war," wrote Clausewitz, "but the simplest thing is difficult."

POSTSCRIPT

■ Clausewitz directed that his writings were to be destroyed after he died. However, his wife still had his works published in 1832.

Iranian Revolution for Theocracy

BY 1925, Reza Khan had deposed the ruling Qajar dynasty of Persia and proclaimed himself Reza Shah Pahlavi. Increasingly dependent on German support, he began the program of Westernization that was a hallmark of the Pahlavi dynasty. In 1935, he renamed the country Iran.

Pahlavi also attacked the power of the Islamic clerics known as *ulama*. He created a secular school system as an alternative to ulama-controlled religious education. He also replaced the Islamic code of law, the *shari'ah*, with secular laws and reorganized the legal system based on the French model.

Demonstrators with posters of the Ayatollah

In 1941, British and Soviet forces invaded Iran and forced Pahlavi to abdicate in favor of his son, Muhammed Reza Shah Pahlavi. Although the country was technically a constitutional monarchy, the shah ruled with absolute power. In 1963, he initiated the program of Westernization known as the "White Revolution," including land reform and modest changes in the position of women. Rising oil revenues financed industrialization and military oppression—as well as a lavish lifestyle for the extensive Pahlavi family.

Popular discontent with the imposition of secular Western values and the authoritarian nature of the regime grew in the 1960s and '70s. Islamic religious leaders, including Shiite cleric Ayatollah Khomeini, were forced into exile for their opposition to the shah's regime.

In 1978, the revolution began when police shot into a group of religious demonstrators. Every 40 days protestors mourned the dead as martyrs. Protests grew in scale until the fall of 1978, when millions demonstrated against the regime. The shah fled the country the following year.

On February 1, 1979, Khomeini made a triumphant return to Iran, where he established the fundamentalist Islamic Republic and was given the title *rabhar* (leader). He appointed Dr. Mehdi Bazargan as prime minister, but the real power remained with Khomeini and the Islamic Revolutionary Council. The new republic replaced the shah's secular laws with a strict version of shari'ah, and fundamentalist Islamic traditions were enforced. Since then, Iran has become the world's largest theocracy.

Sergei Diaghilev
and the Ballets Russes

Russian impresario Sergei Diaghilev's career in the arts began in 1899 when he helped found and edit the Russian arts journal *Mir iskusstva* (*The World of Art*). The publication inspired an artistic movement in Russia. Diaghilev himself worked for several years arranging exhibitions of Russian art and music in his home country and abroad. In 1908, he produced Mussorgsky's opera *Boris Godunov* in Paris, starring renowned Russian opera singer Fyodor Chaliapin. The response was so great that the following year Diaghilev founded a permanent ballet company to stage performances in Paris, the Ballets Russes. His company staged seasons of opera and ballet, featuring the best young dancers from the prestigious Russian Imperial Ballet in St. Petersburg, including renowned ballerina Anna Pavlova.

The talent of the Ballets Russes went far beyond its dancers. The company's first choreographer was the influential Michel Fokine, who became frustrated with the constraints of the Imperial ballet system. In Diaghilev, he found a producer whose ideas of ballet matched his own, and together they worked to produce ballets that incorporated many art forms into a single performance. Diaghilev's collaborations made the Ballets Russes into an important force in the development of the Modernist movement. He commissioned music from now-famous composers such as Igor Stravinsky, Maurice Ravel, and Claude Debussy. The sets of Diaghilev's productions featured designs by visual artists including Alexandre Benois, Pablo Picasso, and Henri Matisse, and choreography by Vaslav Nijinsky, Bronislava Nijinska, and George Balanchine.

One notable example of Diaghilev's synthesis came in 1917's *Parade*. The production combined the talents of Jean Cocteau, Pablo Picasso, Erik Satie, and Léonide Massine. In addition to such challenging, modern offerings, under Diaghilev's leadership the Ballets Russes also staged revivals of great 19th-century ballets beginning with Tchaikovsky's *Sleeping Beauty* in 1921. However, sometimes he pushed the audience too far. During the first performance of *The Rite of Spring* in 1913, Stravinsky's "barbarous" score and Nijinsky's "savage" choreography caused the usually staid ballet audience to riot.

Unfortunately, despite its artistic successes, the Ballets Russes often operated on the verge of bankruptcy. The original company disbanded following Diaghilev's death in 1929. However, Diaghilev's influence on modern dance continues to this day.

The Fall of the Berlin Wall

ON NOVEMBER 9, 1989, the Berlin Wall—a structure with the sole purpose of keeping the people of East and West Berlin apart—came tumbling down, piece by piece. People from each side surged through gates while others mounted the wall and began hacking away large chunks of this 28-mile-long barrier.

In the summer of 1989, Hungary began allowing East Germans to pass through their country to reach Austria and West Germany. On November 9, East Germany announced that for the first time in almost 30 years, restrictions on traveling from one side to the other would be lifted. The announcement, which allowed some people to travel from one side of Germany to the other with visas, was a response to increased pressure to unite the two Germanys. The government hoped that the quick fix would be enough to appease the people until it devised other options. The response they got was not anticipated.

West Germans atop the Berlin Wall in 1989

When the government spokesperson announced the lifting of restrictions, he accidentally said it would be effective immediately, rather than the following day, as intended. Within minutes, people were jamming the gates between the sectors. Caught by surprise, East German border guards eventually gave up trying to see peoples' visas and just let them through. Germans rejoiced by tearing down the wall by any means possible. The following year, East Germany helped demolish the rest of the wall. East Germany was reunited with West Germany into one nation: the Federal Republic of Germany.

The week of the wall's destruction was a wild one in Berlin. Shops stayed open until whatever hours they wanted instead of closing at the previously mandatory 6:30 P.M. Public transportation was free, and people generally ignored the rules they were used to following just a few days earlier. Jubilation and exhilaration was on everyone's mind. "For anyone who didn't experience the Wall, it will be hard to imagine what an overwhelming feeling of relief, of joy, of unreality filled one that this monster was dead and people had conquered it," said an eyewitness.

The Stamp Act of 1765

AFTER HAVING FOUGHT in the Seven Years' War in Europe (and its corollary, the French and Indian War, in North America), Great Britain found itself with a large debt. But the British government also wanted to maintain a strong military presence on America's western frontier, to protect settlers from the threat of Native American attacks, such as from Ottowa Chief Pontiac, who rebelled in 1763.

Parliament believed the English colonists in America should help contribute the funds needed for these protections and imposed a direct tax on the colonists. The tax, called the Stamp Act of 1765, required all legal documents to carry a tax stamp. Other items such as newspapers, playing cards, and pamphlets were also subject to the tax.

The Stamp Act was not the first stamp tax Parliament had placed on items in the colonies—in fact, it was the fourth—but it was the first time they attempted to impose a direct tax. The British expected opposition to the act but hardly anticipated the extent. The colonists took the position they could not be taxed without representation and that any taxes could only be generated by their own colonial legislatures.

Colonial legislatures were unified in their response to the Stamp Act: They sent petitions of protest to the king and Parliament. The colonists also formed the Stamp Act Congress, which drafted and sent a letter of protest to the king and Parliament. Local resistance was also very strong against the tax; merchants and landowners throughout all the colonies corresponded with each other about the unfair tax. Communities held antitax demonstrations that sometimes became violent.

Back in England, British merchants and manufacturers also expressed their dissatisfaction with the act and tried to pressure Parliament into repealing it. The merchants knew that if the colonies had economic problems as a result of the newly imposed tax, they would face problems exporting goods to America.

In the end, the tax never amounted to much. The colonists continued to protest, and officials charged with collecting the tax were intimidated to the point of resigning, leaving England without a source for collection. Parliament decided to repeal the tax on March 18, 1766, but only because it was expedient. As Parliament repealed the Stamp Act, it reasserted its authority to tax the colonies in all cases and passed the Declaratory Act to support its authority. British domination in colonial America continued, ultimately leading to the American Revolution.

Galileo Forced to Recant

GALILEO GALILEI was born on February 15, 1564, in Pisa, Italy. He was a brilliant inventor and scientist whose contributions made an impact on how we see our place in the world. But in the end, the very thing that made him famous would prove to be his downfall.

Galileo entered the University of Pisa around 1581 to study medicine, but he became bored with what he considered old-fashioned teaching methods and shifted his focus to mathematics. In 1589, after numerous failed attempts to land a teaching job, Galileo gained the mathematics chair at the University of Pisa.

Perpetually short of money, Galileo sought to invent something that would bring him fame and riches. Then in 1609, at the age of 45, Galileo heard of an object invented in Holland called a spyglass that brought distant objects closer. Marshalling his formidable skills, he produced a similar but far superior device in only 24 hours. His spyglass was a sensation, and Galileo became rich as well as celebrated.

On January 7, 1610, Galileo first observed the moons of Jupiter through his telescope. After repeated observations, Galileo realized that their movements supported the heliocentric view of the solar system proposed by Polish astronomer Nicolaus Copernicus a half-century before, and not the geocentric view taught by Aristotle and the Catholic Church.

That year Galileo published the book *The Starry Messenger,* which detailed his astronomical findings. As years passed, his findings became more and more dangerous to the church, which had been grievously wounded by the Protestant Reformation. In 1616, he was called to Rome. There Cardinal Robert Bellarmine, the chief apostle of the infallibility of church dogma, ordered him not to "hold, teach, or defend" the heliocentric theory in any way.

Galileo held his tongue, but the spark of resentment against authoritarian decree smoldered inside him. Finally, in 1632 it burst forth with the publication of *Dialogue Concerning the Two Chief World Systems.* The book seemed to support the heliocentric view while ridiculing the geocentric view and, indirectly, Pope Urban VIII. In 1633, the 68-year-old scientist again was called to Rome, where he was relentlessly grilled and threatened with torture by inquisitors over his views. Broken and scared, Galileo finally recanted the heliocentric theory in a humiliating public apology. He spent the rest of his life under house arrest.

The Bastille

B<small>UILT IN</small> P<small>ARIS</small> as a fortress between 1370 and 1383, over the years the Bastille had also served as a castle, treasure house, and, more recently, a prison. Along the way, it had become a symbol of royal despotism and oppression.

France was in turmoil during the summer of 1789. Representatives from the Third Estate had met in June and had declared a "National Assembly."

Fall of the Bastille

Soon they set about creating a French Constitution. Paris was nearing rebellion—all that was needed was a spark. The catalyst came on July 11 when Louis XVI dismissed finance minister Jacques Necker, a supporter of reform.

Fearing a conservative coup, crowds began to gather. Skirmishes with government forces broke out. A mob seized approximately 40,000 muskets and 12 cannons but found no ammunition. Knowing there was powder and shot stored at the Bastille, they turned their attention to the old fortress.

Despite its grim history, the Bastille now housed only seven inmates, including four forgers, two "lunatics," and a "deviant" aristocrat. The garrison included 80 retired soldiers and 30 Swiss grenadiers, all under charge of Governor Bernard-René de Launay.

On the morning of July 14, about a thousand people gathered in front of the Bastille, demanding its surrender. At about 1:30 P.M., the mob surged over the drawbridge and into the inner courtyard. Gunfire broke out, and a battle ensued. The mob was soon joined by rebel soldiers and four cannons.

The fighting lasted until 5:00 P.M., when Governor de Launay ordered a cease-fire. Realizing he could not hold out indefinitely, he ordered the gates opened. Ninety-eight attackers had been killed in the fighting, along with one defender. Soon de Launay joined that list, as he was stabbed to death and decapitated by the angry mob. Six more members of the garrison were also murdered.

Crowds cheered as the symbol of royal tyranny was demolished. Soon the French monarchy itself would be consumed by the flames of revolution.

The Olympics in Modern Times

T HE MODERN OLYMPICS owe their existence not to a Greek, but to a Frenchman—Pierre de Coubertin.

De Coubertin came to believe in the importance of sports as key to the personal development of young people. He also saw that sports drew people together, and it occurred to him that sports could also bring nations together. An ideal mechanism for this, he thought, would be to revive the Olympic games of ancient Greece.

De Coubertin used his influence to organize an international congress, which was held June 16 to 23, 1894, in Paris. Delegates from the sports societies of 11 countries heard his proposal to reinstate the Olympics as an international event. The meeting led to the establishment of the International Olympic Committee (IOC) with de Coubertin as general secretary. After some discussion, it was decided that the first modern Olympics would be held in Athens in honor of the games' ancient Greek origin. The committee also agreed to hold the games every four years.

Greece's financial difficulties almost ended the modern Olympics before they could begin. The $448,000 cost was just too much for the small country. The games were salvaged through fund-raisers. Restoration of the Panathenaic Stadium, originally built in 4 B.C., was funded by wealthy Greek businessman Georgios Averoff.

The Olympics opened on April 6, 1896. Fourteen nations took part in events including cycling, fencing, gymnastics, shooting, swimming (in the sea), tennis, weight lifting, and wrestling. The highlight of the games was the foot race from Marathon to Athens, won by Greek runner Spiridon Louis.

The games were a great success, and within a few years de Coubertin's dream of an international sporting event was a well-established reality. He discouraged an early push to keep the games at Athens, as he saw the rotation of the games from country to country as key to international cooperation. The next Olympics were held in Paris in 1900.

De Coubertin remained honorary president of the IOC until his death in 1937. He is buried in Lausanne, but his heart was interred separately in a monument near the ruins of ancient Olympia.

POSTSCRIPT

■ De Coubertin designed the official Olympic flag in 1914.

INDEX

INDEX

INDEX

INDEX

INDEX

CONTRIBUTORS

Charles R. Branham, Ph.D., (writer) is a senior historian for the DuSable Museum of African American History. He was the writer, coproducer, and host of *The Black Experience* for Chicago's WTTW-TV. A recipient of the Silver Circle Excellence in Teaching Award from the University of Illinois, Branham was a consultant for *Profiles of Great African Americans* and *Great African Americans*.

Anthony O. Edmonds, Ph.D., (writer) is a professor of history at Ball State University in Muncie, Indiana. He teaches courses on the Vietnam War, recent U.S. history, American values, and the impact of popular culture on conceptions of history. He is the author of the book *The War in Vietnam* and has contributed to many other books, including *War and American Pop Culture* and *The Vietnam War on Campus: Other Voices, More Distant Drums*. Edmonds currently serves on the editorial board for the Popular Culture Association/American Culture Association Internet Network.

Daniel Gordon, Ph.D., (consultant/writer) is a professor of history at the University of Massachusetts Amherst. Initially educated in the field of European history, Gordon has translated Voltaire and written extensively about the Enlightenment. In 2002, he went back to school to earn a master's degree from the Yale Law School. He now teaches courses in comparative law and U.S. constitutional history, in addition to courses on European history. Gordon is also coeditor of the journal *Historical Reflections*.

James H. Hallas (writer) is a graduate of the Newhouse School of Communications at Syracuse University. A military historian, he has penned two World War II histories that focus on U.S. Marine Corps campaigns: *The Devil's Anvil: The Assault on Peleliu* and *Killing Ground on Okinawa: The Battle for Sugar Loaf Hill*. He also wrote *Doughboy War: The American Expeditionary Force in World War I* and contributed to the *World War II Chronicle*.

Nancy McCaslin (writer) freelances from her home in South Bend, Indiana. She has a master of arts degree in American history and has taught high school history and government. She is also an intrepid international traveler who has never visited a country she did not like.

Tamra B. Orr (writer) is the author of more than 30 nonfiction books, including *Ronald Reagan: Portrait of an American Hero* and *Sally Ride: The First American Woman in Space*. She has also contributed to *Armchair Reader™: Incredible Information* and *Great Hispanic Americans*. A professional journalist and former newspaper columnist, she has also contributed to more than 50 national magazines.

Russell Roberts (writer) is an award-winning freelance author. He has published more than three dozen books for both children and adults, including the best sellers *Down the Jersey Shore* and *10 Days to a Sharper Memory*. Among his children's books are examinations into the lives of Thomas Jefferson, Robert Goddard, Galileo, and Nostradamus. He also specializes in travel writing and public speaking.

Richard A. Sauers, Ph.D., (writer) is the author of more than two dozen books, including *America's Battlegrounds: Walk in the Footsteps of America's Bravest* and *Gettysburg: The Meade-Sickles Controversy*. Sauers was also a contributor to *American West Chronicle* and *The Civil War Chronicle*. Currently, he is the director of the Packwood House Museum in Lewisburg, Pennsylvania.

Roger K. Smith (writer) freelances from his home in Ithaca, New York. He also teaches writing and journalism at Ithaca College. Smith formerly worked at the United Nations, where he coordinated citizen networks in disarmament and international security.

Pamela D. Toler (writer) holds a Ph.D. in history from the University of Chicago. She currently is a freelance writer with a particular interest in the times and places where cultures touch and change each other. She may be reached at *pdtoler@sbcglobal.net*.